BASIMOV'S GUIDE TO THE BIBLE

THE NEW TESTAMENT

D0062465

Other Avon and Avon Discus Books by
Isaac Asimov

ASIMOV ON PHYSICS
ASIMOV'S GUIDE TO THE BIBLE: THE OLD TESTAMENT
COUNTING THE EONS
IN JOY STILL FELT: THE AUTOBIOGRAPHY OF ISAAC ASIMOV 1954-1978
IN MEMORY YET GREEN: THE AUTOBIOGRAPHY OF ISAAC ASIMOV 1920-1954
LIFE AND ENERGY
THE PLANET THAT WASN'T
THE SUN SHINES BRIGHT
THE UNIVERSE FROM FLAT EARTH TO QUASAR
'X' STANDS FOR UNKNOWN

BASIMOV'S GUIDE TO THE BIBLE

VOLUME TWO

THE NEW TESTAMENT

Maps by Rafael Palacios

◆ AVON
PUBLISHERS OF BARD, CAMELOT, DISCUS AND FLARE BOOKS

AVON BOOKS
A division of
The Hearst Corporation
105 Madison Avenue
New York, New York 10016

First Avon Printing, October 1971

AVON TRADEMARK REG. U.S. PAT. OFF. AND IN OTHER
COUNTRIES, MARCA REGISTRADA, HECHO EN U.S.A.

Printed in the U.S.A.

OP 20 19 17 16 15 14 13

To
Lawrence P. Ashmead
who still has faith

CONTENTS

INTRODUCTION

The most influential, the most published, the most widely read book in the history of the world is the Bible. No other book has been so studied and so analyzed and it is a tribute to the complexity of the Bible and the eagerness of its students that after thousands of years of study there are still endless books that can be written about it.

I have myself written two short books for young people on the earlier books of the Bible* but I have long wanted to take on a job of more ambitious scope; one that I can most briefly describe as a consideration of the secular aspects of the Bible.

Most people who read the Bible do so in order to get the benefit of its ethical and spiritual teachings, but the Bible has a secular side, too. It is a history book covering the first four thousand years of human civilization.

The Bible is not a history book in modern sense, of course, since its writers lacked the benefit of modern archaeological techniques, did not have our concept of dating and documentation, and had different standards of what was and was not significant in history. Furthermore, Biblical interest was centered primarily on developments that impinged upon those dwelling in Canaan, a small section of Asia bordering on the Mediterranean Sea. This area makes only a small mark on the history of early civilization (from the secular viewpoint) and modern histories, in contrast to the Bible, give it comparatively little space.

Nevertheless, for most of the last two thousand years, the Bible has been virtually the only history book used in Western civilization. Even today, it remains the most popular, and its view of ancient history is still more widely and commonly known than is that of any other.

So it happens, therefore, that millions of people today know of Nebuchadnezzar, and have never heard of Pericles, simply because

* *Words in Genesis and Words from the Exodus.*

Nebuchadnezzar is mentioned prominently in the Bible and Pericles is never mentioned at all.

Millions know of Ahasuerus as a Persian king who married Esther, even though there is no record of such an event outside the Bible. Most of those same millions never suspect that he is better known to modern historians as Xerxes and that the most important event in his reign was an invasion of Greece that ended in utter defeat. That invasion is not mentioned in the Bible.

Millions know certain minor Egyptian Pharaohs, such as Shishak and Necho, who are mentioned in the Bible, but have never heard of the great conquering Pharaoh, Thutmose III, who is not. People whose very existence is doubtful, such as Nimrod and the queen of Sheba, are household words because they are mentioned in the Bible, while figures who were colossal in their day are sunk in oblivion because they are not.

Again, small towns in Canaan, such as Shechem and Bethel, in which events of the Bible are described as taking place, are more familiar to us today than are large ancient metropolises such as Syracuse or Egyptian Thebes, which are mentioned only glancingly in the Bible, or not at all.

Moreover, usually only that is known about such places as happens to be mentioned in the Bible. Ecbatana, the capital of the Median Empire, is remembered in connection with the story of Tobit, but its earlier and later history are dim indeed to most people, who might be surprised to know that it still exists today as a large provincial capital in the modern nation of Iran.

In this book, then, I am assuming a reader who is familiar with the Bible, at least in its general aspects, but who knows little of ancient history outside the Bible. I assume a reader who would be interested in filling in the fringe, so to speak, and who would expect much of the Bible to become easier to understand if some of the places and people mentioned in it are made less mysterious. (After all, those places and people were well known to the original readers of the Bible, and it would be sad to allow so important a book to grow needlessly murky with the passing of the centuries because the periphery has grown dim and indistinct.)

I am attempting to correct this, in part at least. I will, for instance, speculate on who Nimrod might have been, try to define the time in which Abraham entered Canaan, place David's kingdom in its world setting, sort out the role played by the various monarchs who are only mentioned in the Bible when they fight against Israel and Judah, and work out the relationships among the Herods encountered by Jesus and the Apostles.

I am trying, in short, to bring in the outside world, illuminate it in terms of the Biblical story and, in return, illuminate the events of the Bible by adding to it the non-Biblical aspects of history, biography, and geography.

In doing so, there will be the constant temptation (born of the modern view of history) to bring in dates though few can be definitely assigned to individual events in the Bible. It will be convenient then to make use of a more or less arbitrary set of "periods" which will chop history into sections that will make for easy reference.

The period from the beginning of the earliest civilizations, say 4000 B.C. to A.D. 100, can be lumped together as "the Biblical period." Of this the period to 400 B.C. is "the Old Testament period," from 400 B.C. to 4 B.C. is the "inter-Testamental period," while the A.D. section is "the New Testament period."

The Biblical period can be broken down into smaller sections as follows:

4000 B.C. to 2000 B.C. — The Primeval period
2000 B.C. to 1700 B.C. — The Patriarchal period
1700 B.C. to 1200 B.C. — The Egyptian period
1200 B.C. to 1000 B.C. — The Tribal period
1000 B.C. to 900 B.C. — The Davidic kingdom

Thereafter, it is most convenient to name periods after the peoples who did, in fact, dominate western Asia. Thus:

900 B.C. to 600 B.C. — The Assyrian period
600 B.C. to 540 B.C. — The Babylonian period
540 B.C. to 330 B.C. — The Persian period
330 B.C. to 70 B.C. — The Greek period
 70 B.C. to A.D. 100 — The Roman period

During the last century of the Greek period, the Jews won a brief independence under the Maccabees, so that the century from 170 B.C. to 70 B.C. might be called "the Maccabean period."

I cannot pretend that in writing this book I am making any significant *original* contribution to Biblical scholarship; indeed, I am not competent to do so. All that I will have to say will consist of material well known to students of ancient history. (There will, however, be a few places where I will indulge in personal speculation, and label it as such.)

Nevertheless, it is my hope that this material, well known though it may be in separate bits, will now be presented in a newly useful way, since it will be collected and placed within the covers of a moderately sized book, presented in one uniform manner, and in a style and fashion which, it is hoped, will be interesting to the average reader of the Bible.

I intend to be completely informal in this book, and to adhere to no rigid rules. I won't invariably discuss a place or person at its first appearance in the Bible, if it seems to me I can make more sense out of it by bringing the matter up in a later connection. I will not hesitate to leave a discussion incomplete if I plan to take it up again later on. I will leave out items toward which I don't feel I can contribute anything either useful or interesting, and I will, without particular concern, allow myself to digress if I feel that the digression will be useful.

Again, since this book is not intended to be a scholarly compendium, I do not plan to burden its pages with such extraneous appurtenances as footnotes giving sources. The sources that I use are, after all, very general and ordinary ones.

First of all, of course, are various versions of the Bible:

a) The Authorized Version, originally published in 1611 and familiarly known as the "King James Bible." This is the Bible used in most Protestant churches. It is the version that is familiar to most Americans and it is from this version that I quote, except where otherwise indicated.

b) The Revised Standard Version, Thomas Nelson & Sons, 1946, 1952, and 1959.

c) Saint Joseph "New Catholic Edition," Catholic Book Publishing Co., 1962.

d) The Jerusalem Bible, Doubleday & Company, Inc., 1966.

e) The Holy Scriptures according to the Masoretic text, The Jewish Publication Society of America, 1955.

f) I have leaned particularly heavily on those volumes of the Anchor Bible (Doubleday) so far published, since these represent some of the latest and most profound thinking on the Bible.

Much of the Apocrypha is contained in the "New Catholic Edition" and, in addition, I have made use of the King James Version and the Revised Standard Version of these books.

I have also consulted, quite steadily, *A New Standard Bible Dictionary*, Third Revised Edition, Funk and Wagnalls Company, 1936, *The Abingdon Bible Commentary*, Abingdon Press, 1929, and *Dictionary of the Bible* by John L. McKenzie, S.J., Bruce Publishing Company, 1965.

In addition, I have turned to general encyclopedias, dictionaries, histories, geographies, and any other reference books available to me which could in any way be useful to me.

The result—well, the result can begin to be seen when you turn the page where I take up some of the apocryphal books and the New Testament—the Old Testament having been taken up in Volume One.

1. TOBIT

Tobit

Following the Book of Nehemiah in the Roman Catholic version of the Bible are two short historical books which are not found in either the Jewish or the Protestant canon. They are therefore part of the Apocrypha. First comes one that is set in the Assyrian period, roughly 700 B.C.; then one with a very confused chronology that speaks of Nebuchadnezzar, who was at the height of his power about 580 B.C.

These tales do not portray actual history, but seem to be what we would call today "historical romances." Their fictional nature does not prevent them from serving religious or ethical purposes, of course, but since in this book I am primarily interested in the secular aspects of the Bible, there will be a particular interest in trying to sort out the chronology.

The first of these tales is the Book of Tobit, which begins at once with the character for whom it is named:

Tobit 1:1. *The book of the words of Tobit . . .*

Tobit is a form of the Hebrew name Tobiah, which, in its Greek form, is Tobias. In the Catholic version, the Book of Tobit is termed the Book of Tobias.

The date at which the book was written is not known for certain, but it may be about 200 B.C. It is possible that the author lived in Alexandria, which at that time was the capital of Egypt. About 200 B.C., Judea passed from the friendly hands of the Macedonian rulers of Egypt (the Ptolemies) to the much harsher grip of the Macedonian rulers of Syria (the Seleucids). A new period of persecution of the

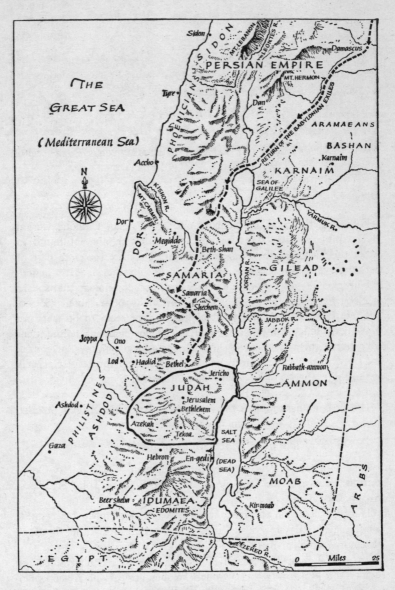

Jerusalem Restored

Jews began and the story of Tobit, dealing with the Assyrian persecution, five centuries before, reflects this.

The time in which the events described in Tobit are supposed to have happened are given:

Tobit 1:2. . . . [Tobit] *in the time of Enemessar* [Shalmaneser] *king of the Assyrians was led captive* . . .

This makes Tobit alive in 722 B.C. when the city of Samaria, having been besieged by Shalmaneser of Assyria, was taken by Shalmaneser's successor Sargon (see page I-377).* Numbers of the Israelites were taken off into exile and Tobit with them.

Tobit, speaking in the first person, describes himself as of the tribe of Naphtali.

Tobit 1:4. . . . *when I was* . . . *young, all the tribe of Nephthali* [Naphtali] . . . *fell from the house of Jerusalem* . . .

Apparently, Tobit is speaking here of the rebellion of Jeroboam which succeeded in founding an independent Israel in 933 B.C. Clearly, it is impossible for Tobit to have been alive both in the time of Jeroboam and in the time of Shalmaneser. Nor does the author intend to imply that Tobit was as long-lived as the antediluvian patriarchs, for at the time of a central event later in the book, Tobit is described as not too old a man.

Tobit 14:2. *And he* [Tobit] *was eight and fifty years old* . . .

Rather, it is merely the chronological confusion we would expect of an author writing some five centuries after the events related; an author who had only a hazy notion of the order of events and no records to use as a reliable source. In short, it is what one would expect if Tobit were originally written as a piece of edifying fiction, telling what might have happened, rather than what did happen.

Rages

Tobit, however, remained faithful to Jerusalem, even when carried off to exile in Nineveh. He managed to obtain a high position at the

* Where page references to Volume I are given they will be preceded by "I", otherwise not. Thus "page I-123" will refer to page 123 of Volume I while "page 123" will refer to page 123 of Volume II, the one you are now holding.

Assyrian court, being placed in charge of the purchasing of provisions with government money, and having freedom of movement about the dominion.

Tobit 1:14. *And I went into Media, and left in trust with Gabael . . . at Rages . . . ten talents of silver.*

This again is anachronistic, for though parts of Media were under the control of the Assyrian Empire, much of it (including the region about Rages) was not. It is very unlikely that Tobit could travel freely (as an official of the Assyrian court) outside the border, especially if he were carrying large quantities of government money. Nor is ten talents a mean sum of money. A talent would be equal to about $2000 in today's money.

In 200 B.C., however, the regions that had once been Assyria and Media were both under the domination of the Seleucid kings and formed part of a single realm. The writer of the Book of Tobit was thus reflecting the geography of his own time rather than that of the supposed time of the book.

Rages (also spelled Rhages) was an important city of Media, perhaps second only to Ecbatana (see page I-448). It was located about 150 miles northeast of Ecbatana, and its ruins are only five miles south of Teheran, the capital of modern Iran.

Rages' period of greatest glory came later, however, well after Biblical times. It was a capital of the Persian kingdoms that flourished in Roman times and before the coming of the Mohammedans it was the center of Zoroastrian religion. To the Persians, the city was known as Rai.

In Mohammedan times, it was the birthplace of Harun-al-Rashid, the Caliph of the Arabian Nights. It was also the birthplace of a great medieval physician who was known as "al-Razi" to the Persians, from his birthplace, and as Rhazes to Europeans.

Rages was devastated by the Mongol invaders in A.D. 1220 and never recovered.

Asmodeus

But misfortunes crowded upon Tobit. Once the Assyrian conqueror died, Sennacherib succeeded to the throne and he is pictured as a violent anti-Semite who ordered the killing of Jews and forbade their corpses to be buried.

It is considered a frightful thing in many cultures for a dead body to be left undisposed of, to be left deprived of appropriate religious rites. There are usually beliefs that the souls of such bodies must drift about aimlessly through shadows and cannot find rest until the bodies they once inhabited are appropriately cared for. The Greeks of Homer's time believed this, and so did the Jews.

In threatening a people with punishment, for instance, not only death is foretold but lack of burial. Thus, Jeremiah, quoting God's warning to Judea in the last years of the kingdom, says:

Jeremiah 16:4. *They shall die of grievous deaths . . . neither shall they be buried . . .*

Sennacherib, then, is pictured as deliberately punishing Jews after death, as well as in life. Tobit engages in an act of piety by burying such bodies and gets into trouble with the authorities in consequence. He is forced to leave the country, and his property is confiscated.

Esarhaddon succeeds to the throne and appoints a relative of Tobit to high office. The relative intercedes for Tobit, who returns to Nineveh. But then, after once again burying a corpse, he is stricken with cataracts of the eyes and goes blind. His faith remains strong and he continues to praise God, but he longs for death.

Meanwhile, in Ecbatana, a girl named Sara, a niece of Tobit, is also longing for death—

Tobit 3:8. *Because that she had been married to seven husbands, whom Asmodeus the evil spirit had killed, before they had lain with her . . .*

With seven husbands dead, each on the wedding night, she was being reproached as a husband-murderer.

Asmodeus, the real murderer, does not occur in any canonical book of the Bible. His name is a corruption of that of a demon in Persian mythology—"Aeshma deva," the demon Aeshma.

Partly because of this story in the Book of Tobit, Asmodeus was, in later centuries, taken to be the demon in charge of marital unhappiness. He played a role also in non-Biblical legends concerning Solomon and was sometimes held to be identical with Satan himself.

Raphael

But better days were coming for both Tobit and Sara, for their devoutness and prayers had their effect. God heard them—

Tobit 3:17. *And Raphael was sent to heal them both* . . .

Under the influence of Persian religious thought (which postulated vast armies of good and evil spirits), the Jews in the centuries after the restoration had worked out an increasingly complex structure for the celestial hierarchy. There were not merely angels, for instance, but archangels ("chief angels") as well. Tradition eventually listed seven such archangels, of whom only two, Gabriel and Michael, are to be found anywhere in the books included in the King James Version. In addition, Raphael is included here in the apocryphal Book of Tobit and Uriel in the apocryphal 2 Esdras. Others are mentioned in non-Biblical legends.

Mohammedan tradition lists four archangels. Mohammedans share Gabriel and Michael with the Jews and Christians and add Azrael and Israfel. Azrael is the angel of death, and Israfel sounds the trumpet on the day of judgment and resurrection (the task which falls to Gabriel in Christian tradition).

The choice of Raphael as the angel to heal Tobit and Sara is appropriate since Raphael means "God heals."

Azarias

Suddenly Tobit remembers the ten talents he had left in Rages and decides to send his son, Tobias, to Rages to collect it. To strengthen the son on his dangerous journey through heathen lands he gives him a code of behavior to follow (as, in *Hamlet*, Polonius lectures his son, Laertes, before the latter's trip to Paris). One of the maxims is:

Tobit 4:15. *Do that to no man which thou hatest* . . .

This is translated in the Revised Standard Version as "And what you hate, do not do to any one." This is the negative version of what is commonly called the Golden Rule—that of guiding your actions by empathy; that is, by putting yourself in the place of the other person.

The Golden Rule is more familiar to us in its positive form; a form which advises us not merely to refrain from doing what is hateful, but to proceed to do what is desirable. The positive form is given in the course of Jesus' Sermon on the Mount:

Matthew 7:12. *Therefore all things whatsoever ye would that men should do to you, do ye even so to them . . .*

or, as expressed in Luke:

Luke 6:31. *And as ye would that men should do to you, do ye also to them likewise.*

One often hears the Golden Rule expressed as follows: "Do unto others as you would have others do unto you." This is not the form, however, in which the saying occurs in the Bible, either in the King James Version or the Revised Standard Version.

Tobias, in preparing for the journey, comes across Raphael in human guise, and Raphael offers to guide the young man to Rages. Tobias' father, Tobit, inquires carefully as to the identity of the guide:

Tobit 5:12. *Then he* [Raphael] *said, I am Azarias . . . and of thy brethren.*

Azarias is the Greek form of the Hebrew Azariah, or Ezra, and the name is carefully chosen, for it means "Yahveh helps."

Tigris River

Tobias and the angel set out on their journey.

Tobit 6:1. . . . *they came in the evening to the river Tigris, and they lodged there.*

Here one can see that the writer may well be an Alexandrian for he shows himself deficient in knowledge of Asian geography. It would seem he believes Nineveh to be a day's journey from the Tigris (referred to elsewhere in the Bible as Hiddekel, see page I-27), when actually the Assyrian capital was situated right on that river.

What's more, Nineveh was on the eastern bank of the river and since Rages was some five hundred miles east of Nineveh, one does not have to reach or cross the Tigris at all in going from one city to the other.

While washing in the river, Tobias catches a large fish and Raphael instructs him to keep the heart, liver, and gall. The heart and liver, he explains, can be used in combating demons, while the gall is a cure for cataracts.

Edna

Eventually they reach Ecbatana, still 150 miles short of their goal. There, Raphael proposes they stay with Raguel, the father of Sara, and that a marriage be arranged between the two young people. When they arrived at Raguel's house, the host noted the family resemblance of Tobias at once:

> Tobit 7:2. *Then said Raguel to Edna his wife, How like is this young man to Tobit my cousin!*

It is a mark of the popularity of the books of the Apocrypha that so many proper names in them have come into common use. Tobias is itself an example, both in that form, and in its English abbreviation, Toby.

Edna is another case, perhaps a surprising one. It does not sound like a Biblical name and, in fact, it does not occur in the canonical books. At first thought, one might guess that it is an Anglo-Saxon name since the prefix "Ed-" (from "Aed-" meaning "property" and hence a natural component of the names of propertied people) was a common feature among the Anglo-Saxon gentry. Examples are Edward, Edwin, Edmund, Edgar among males and Edith and Edwina among females.

Edna, however, is a Hebrew word, meaning "rejuvenation."

After this, all goes well. Tobias obtains leave to marry Sara, although he is duly warned of the death of seven previous husbands. Tobias, however, burns the fish's liver in the wedding chamber and the charm drives Asmodeus away. The marriage is consummated happily and there is a long wedding feast.

Raphael travels onward to Rages and collects the ten talents due

Tobit. All return home after this and there Tobias uses the fish's gall to cure his father's cataracts.

Raphael then reveals himself and everything ends in total happiness. The family enjoys wealth, long life, and many descendants. In a veritable orgy of anachronisms and twisted chronologies, Tobit, on his deathbed, advises Tobias to leave Nineveh, which is soon to fall. Tobias retires to Ecbatana, his wife's city, and survives long enough to see the destruction of Nineveh:

> Tobit 14:15. . . . *before he* [Tobias] *died he heard of the destruction of Nineve* [Nineveh], *which was taken by Nabuchodonosor* [Nebuchadnezzar] *and Assuerus* [Ahasuerus] . . .

Actually, it was taken by Nabopolassar, the father of Nebuchadnezzar, and by the Median king, Cyaxares. Ahasuerus (that is, Xerxes) did not reign until a century and a quarter after the fall of Nineveh.

However, it may have been the author's intention to use the destruction of Nineveh as an indication to his readers that the Seleucid Empire would also be destroyed. If so, and if the book was indeed written in 200 B.C., then the writer was a fairly good prophet. The Seleucid Empire was not utterly destroyed, to be sure, but its power over Judea was broken and the Jews entered a period of prideful independence once more. And that time came but a generation after the Book of Tobit was written (if we accept 200 B.C. as the date of writing), so that its first readers may have lived to see the breaking of the Seleucid grip, as Tobias lived to see Nineveh fall.

2. JUDITH

NABUCHODONOSOR • ARPHAXAD • RAGAU • HYDASPES • HOLOFERNES • JOACIM •
BETHULIA • JUDITH • BAGOAS

Nabuchodonosor

The historical romance following the Book of Tobit is the Book
of Judith, named after the heroine of the tale. The best guess as to its
date of authorship is somewhere about 150 B.C., shortly after the tyranny
of the Seleucids had been overcome. It was a period of great nationalistic fervor and tales telling of great deeds against impossible
odds must have been much in favor. Judith is an example.

Despite the fact that the Book of Judith lacks the supernatural
elements found in Tobit, Judith is even more clearly fictional. It deals
with a victory that is mentioned nowhere outside this book, with places
and people not to be found elsewhere, and its chronology is hopelessly
twisted. It is not included in the Jewish canon or in the King James
Version. Nevertheless it has been immensely popular for the sake of
the story it told.

It begins by dating itself:

Judith 1:1. *In the twelfth year of the reign of Nabuchodonosor*
[Nebuchadnezzar], *who reigned in Nineve* [Nineveh] . . .

If this date is to be taken soberly, then the Book of Judith begins
in 594 B.C. when Zedekiah is on the throne in Jerusalem and the
kingdom of Judah is tottering toward its fall.

However, the confusion has already started, for Nebuchadnezzar
reigned in Babylon over a Chaldean Empire and not in Nineveh over
an Assyrian one. Indeed, Nebuchadnezzar came to the throne only
after Nineveh had completely been destroyed.

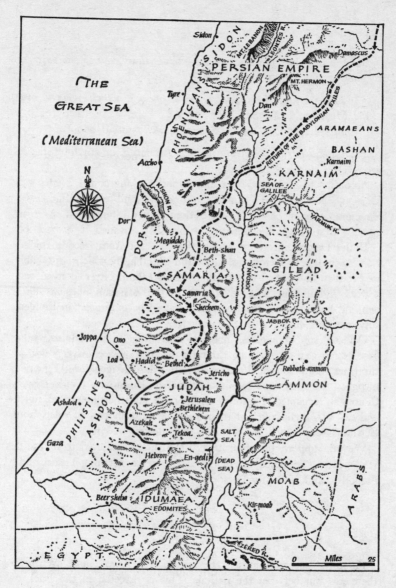

Jerusalem Restored

Arphaxad

But the tale does not begin with Nebuchadnezzar only; it switches to another monarch at once:

> Judith 1:1. . . . . *in the days of Arphaxad, which reigned over the Medes in Ecbatane,*
> Judith 1:2. *And built in Ecbatane walls round about . . .*

There is no record of anyone named Arphaxad, or anything like it, among the kings of the Medes.

According to Herodotus, the first important king of the Medes was Deioces, who came to the throne about 700 B.C. and reigned till 647 B.C. Southern sections of Media were then under intermittent Assyrian control after Sargon's conquering armies had invaded it in 710 B.C.

Under Deioces, however, Media regained a certain freedom of action. According to Herodotus, he built Ecbatana, by which is probably meant that he fortified it and made it his capital city and royal residence. Undoubtedly he paid tribute to the Assyrian kings at Nineveh, but he founded a royal line that was to become great in the century after his death.

Deioces' son, Phraortes, reigned, according to Herodotus, from 647 B.C. to 625 B.C. and he extended Median power. Assyria was at the time occupied with Elamite wars, Babylonian rebellions, Egyptian intrigue, and incursions by the Cimmerian barbarians. With Assyria thoroughly occupied, Phraortes could piece together the tribes north and east of Assyria and put them together into an empire ruled from Ecbatana—one which was soon to help destroy Assyria.

We can suppose, therefore, that the Arphaxad referred to in Judith 1:1 represents a telescoping of dim memories concerning Deioces and Phraortes, and is mostly Phraortes.

Ragau

Phraortes' successes roused the concern of Assyria and eventually there was war between the nations. This is reflected in the Book of Judith:

Judith 1:5. *Even in those days king Nabuchodonosor made war with king Arphaxad . . . in the borders of Ragau.*

Ragau is the city termed Rages in the Book of Tobit (see page 18). It is deep within Median territory, so one must envisage a slashing Assyrian offensive.

In real history, Phraortes ruled when Asshurbanipal (the Asnapper of the Book of Ezra, see page I-447) was on the Assyrian throne. Asshurbanipal did attack Phraortes and, according to Herodotus, Phraortes was defeated by the Assyrian armies, and killed, in 625 B.C. —the last year of Asshurbanipal's reign.

The dim memory of this war could have been converted into the battle of Ragau in which Nebuchadnezzar of Assyria defeats Arphaxad of Media.

Hydaspes

The army which had been gathered by Nebuchadnezzar is described:

Judith 1:6. *And there came unto him all they that . . . dwelt by Euphrates, and Tigris, and Hydaspes, and the plain . . . of the Elymeans, and very many nations of the sons of Chelod.*

By and large this isn't bad as a description of the eastern half of the territory ruled over by the Assyrians (or by the real Nebuchadnezzar, for that matter). The sons of Chelod are the Chaldeans, who were subject to Assyria in the time of Asshurbanipal and who ruled over the entire Fertile Crescent in the time of Nebuchadnezzar. The Elymeans are the Elamites, whom Asshurbanipal conquered (see page I-455).

The one serious flaw is the mention of the Hydaspes River. This is one of five rivers which flow through the Pakistani province of Punjab (the very name of which means "five rivers"). Its modern name is the Jhelum River.

The Hydaspes was at or near the easternmost boundary of the Persian Empire and of the short-lived dominion of Alexander the Great that followed. Indeed, Alexander fought the fourth of his four great battles in Asia on the Hydaspes River in 326 B.C.

In attempting to explain that Nebuchadnezzar was drawing his army from the most distant corners of his empire, the writer of Judith mentioned the Hydaspes almost automatically, for that was the limits of an empire with which he was far more familiar than with the Assyrian.

Nebuchadnezzar also demanded troops from the nations west and south of Assyria. These are listed in full but, in summary, consist of Asia Minor, Syria, Israel, Judah, and Egypt. The western lands refused help and Nebuchadnezzar swore vengeance, then went on to defeat Arphaxad with the army he had on hand.

Holofernes

With Media conquered, Nebuchadnezzar was ready to turn west.

Judith 2:4. . . . *Nabuchodonosor . . . called Holofernes the chief captain of his army . . . and said unto him,*

Judith 2:5. . . . *thou shalt go forth from my presence . . .*

Judith 2:6. *And thou shalt go against all the west country because they disobeyed my commandment.*

Asshurbanipal had, in the course of his reign, actually campaigned in the west. This was in Egypt, which was in revolt at the time of his accessions (see page I-390). There is no record, though, that in the process he inflicted any particular damage upon Judah. During his reign, indeed, Manasseh (see page I-425) was king of Judah, and he was loyally pro-Assyrian and had a peaceful reign.

To be sure, the tradition arose that in Manasseh's reign there had been some trouble with Assyria, for in 2 Chronicles there is mention made of Manasseh having been imprisoned and taken off to Babylon (see page I-425). The writer of Judith may have had some vague notion of Asshurbanipal's western campaign and Manasseh's reputed imprisonment.

But who, then, was Holofernes? There is no mention of any such general anywhere in the records of Assyria or Babylon.

As it happens, three centuries after the reign of Asshurbanipal, there arose a situation which involved events of a similar nature. It was the Persian Empire that now ruled western Asia with a mighty hand, and the monarch on the throne was Artaxerxes III, who reigned from 358 to 338 B.C. Just as Asshurbanipal was the last of the powerful Assyrian monarchs, so Artaxerxes III was the last of the powerful Persian monarchs.

Artaxerxes, like Asshurbanipal, had to conduct campaigns in Egypt, for Egypt rebelled periodically against Persian rule. In fact in 404 B.C., after the death of the Persian king, Darius II, Egyptian rebellions had succeeded to the extent where native kings held effective control of Egypt. The traditional histories list three dynasties, the 28th, 29th, and 30th, in this period of time. None of the native kings was particularly powerful and most ruled only briefly.

At the time Artaxerxes III came to the Persian throne, Nectanebo II, last king of the 30th dynasty and, indeed, the last native king ever to rule Egypt until medieval times, had just come to power. In 346 B.C., Artaxerxes III, after great preparations, sent an expedition westward into Egypt. There followed five years of hard campaigning which crushed Nectanebo II and re-established Persian rule.

And who was one of the generals who led the Persian host? Holofernes.

It seems reasonable, then, to suppose that the writer of Judith had telescoped the Egyptian campaign of Artaxerxes with that of Asshurbanipal and made Holofernes, the Persian general, the leader of the Assyrian hosts.

Joacim

The march of Holofernes is given in detail, with many geographical names apparently made up out of thin air, for they cannot be identified with anything on the surface of the Earth. One gathers, however, that Holofernes struck northwestward from Nineveh, conquered Asia Minor, then turned south to work his way down the coast, occupying or devastating Syria, Phoenicia, and Philistia.

It was next the turn of Judea:

Judith 4:1. *Now the children of Israel, that dwelt in Judea, heard all that Holofernes . . . had done . . .*

Judith 4:2. *Therefore they were exceedingly afraid . . . and were troubled for Jerusalem, and for the temple . . .*

Judith 4:3. *For they were newly returned from the captivity.*

This now adds an additional element of anachronism. We have the Assyria of the seventh century B.C. under the rule of Nebuchadnezzar of the sixth century B.C., which sends its army under a general of the fourth century B.C. to attack a re-established Judea of the fifth century B.C. Not a century is left out.

Nor is the period of re-established Judea left with a mere mention. Some circumstantial evidence is introduced in the form of the identity of the high priest.

Judith 4:6. *Also Joacim the high priest . . . was in those days in Jerusalem . . .*

Joacim would, in Hebrew form, be Joiakim, and he is mentioned in the Book of Nehemiah.

Nehemiah 12:10. *And Jeshua begat Joiakim, Joiakim also begat Eliashib . . .*

In other words Joiakim was the son of Jeshua who had rebuilt the Temple with Zerubbabel (see page I-440) and the father of Eliashib who had rebuilt the city walls with Nehemiah (see page I-457). By this it would seem that the events of the Book of Judith fall just between those chronicled in the Book of Ezra and those in the Book of Nehemiah.

Bethulia

Judea girds itself for a despairing defense and sends messages to strategic places:

Judith 4:6. *. . . Joacim . . . wrote to them that dwelt in Bethulia . . .*
Judith 4:7. *Charging them to keep the passages of the hill country . . . and it was easy to stop them that would come up, because the passage was strait, for two men at the most.*

Bethulia is a name that does not occur elsewhere in the Bible. Some suppose that it might be Shechem for that is located in a narrow pass between two mountains (see page I-99).

However, one can see that the writer of Judith owes a certain debt to Herodotus. The writer's mythical Nebuchadnezzar brings the huge power of his empire to bear upon a tiny Judea, as the real Xerxes bore down upon a tiny Greece. Holofernes moves westward then southward, as Xerxes' general Mardonius did. The inexorable progress is halted by the tiny Judean army as the other progress was halted by the tiny Greek army. And the crucial battle is to come at a narrow pass where a small force can hold off a vast army.

It is useless then to seek Bethulia on the map of Judea; it is sooner to be found on the map of Greece, for Bethulia is really Thermopylae. Indeed, as events prove, it is to be a combined Thermopylae and Marathon.

Judith

Holofernes lays siege to the city of Bethulia and captures its water supply so that the inhabitants, in the extremity of thirst, are ready to surrender, a course of action which now comes to the attention of the heroine of this book.

Judith 8:1. *Now at that time Judith heard thereof* . . .

Judith is the feminine form of "Judah" and means "Jewish woman." It is the popularity of this book and the excitement of the story it tells, and, consequently, the number of times its climax has been used as an inspiration in art, that has made the name Judith so common among us.

Judith is given a genealogy that is clearly nonhistorical. The names cannot be identified and some of them have no parallel elsewhere in the Bible. She is described as a beautiful and pious widow, her husband having died three years before.

Bagoas

Judith is indignant at hearing of the news of projected surrender. She exhorts the elders to hold firm while she puts her own plan into operation. She dresses herself in all her finery and leaves the city as a defector. Her beauty assures her respectful treatment and she is brought to Holofernes. She tells him that the Jews in Bethulia are sinning and are therefore sure to be beaten. She offers to help Holofernes win,

provided her own religious scruples are respected and she is allowed
to retire each night to pray in private.

For three days she keeps up a fixed pattern of behavior, getting the
sentries used to seeing her pass out of the camp late each night to
pray.

By the fourth day Holofernes thought he would improve the situation by having Judith join him at dinner:

> Judith 12:11. *Then said he to Bagoas the eunuch . . . Go now,
> and persuade this Hebrew woman . . . that she come unto us, and
> eat and drink with us.*

Bagoas is the Greek form of a Persian name meaning "given by
God" and was often used for eunuchs, so that the phrase "Bagoas
the eunuch" was almost a cliché.

The most famous "Bagoas the eunuch" was a renegade Egyptian
in the service of Artaxerxes III at the time of the latter's campaign
against Egypt, the very campaign in which the real Holofernes figured.
For a while, Bagoas was the power behind the throne and taxed and
plundered the subject peoples (including the Jews) remorselessly.

Eventually he aspired to full power. As a eunuch he could not
reign openly, but he might at least exert control over a thoroughgoing
puppet. In 338 B.C. he arranged for the murder of Artaxerxes III plus
all his children but the youngest. The youngest son, Arses, he placed
on the throne and when Arses showed signs of independence, Bagoas
had him and his children killed too, in 336 B.C.

A distant relative of the Persian royal line was then placed on the
throne by Bagoas. The new king called himself Darius III and would
have suffered the same fate as his two predecessors if he hadn't avoided
that by killing Bagoas. This, however, was the only forceful action of
Darius III. Soon he had to face Alexander the Great and the remainder
of his life was one long disaster. He died in 330 B.C. as Persia's last
king. With that, the Persian Empire that had been inaugurated by
Cyrus two and a quarter centuries before came to an end.

The writer of Judith must certainly have known of the wickedness
of the historical "Bagoas the eunuch" and it would be a natural name
for him to give Holofernes' minion.

Judith accepts the invitation, encourages Holofernes to drink to
excess. When the feast is over, all depart to allow Holofernes to have

Judith with him in private. By that time, however, Holofernes is in a drunken stupor and Judith cuts off his head with his own sword.

She wraps the head in the canopy of the bed and retires, apparently for private prayer, as she has done on previous nights. This time, however, she goes to Bethulia and displays the head. The Jews are heartened and the Assyrian army, on discovering the death of their commander, are driven into panic. They flee and are slaughtered by the pursuing Jews, who are thus (according to the tale) saved from Nebuchadnezzar forever.

3. 1 MACCABEES

1 Maccabees

With Malachi, the canonical books of the Old Testament (according
to the arrangement in the Christian versions of the Bible) come to an
end. The prophetic impulse, as the traditional Jewish view has it,
faded out after the return from the Babylonian Exile, and with the
rebuilding of the Temple and the walls of Jerusalem.

This does not seem actually to be so, since a number of the canonical
books were written well after 430 B.C., when Jerusalem's walls were
completed. In every such case, however, tradition insists on attributing
authorship to a period well before that critical date. Thus, the Book of
Jonah, written as a work of imagination in 300 B.C. or thereabouts,
was attributed back in time to some near contemporary of the historical
prophet, who was active about 780 B.C. Late psalms were attributed
to David; late compilations of proverbs to Solomon, while apocalyptic
writings composed in the Greek period were attributed to worthies
of the period of Exile and Return, such as Daniel and Zechariah.

This meant that historical events after 430 B.C. could never be dealt
with directly and inserted into the Bible. They had to be attributed
to ancients to comply with strict Jewish tradition and therefore had

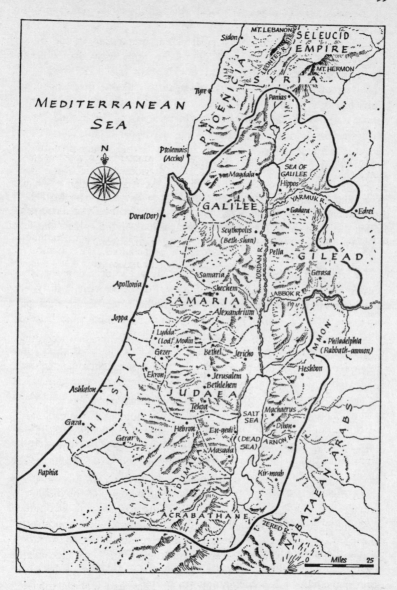

Palestine Under the Maccabees

to be presented in obscure, apocalyptic form, or else remain in the Apocrypha.

And yet Jewish history was eventful and interesting in the period between 200 B.C. and A.D. 100; more so in some ways than ever before. Once again an independent Jewish state was established as in the days of Saul and David. Once again a colossal catastrophe approached inexorably as in the days of Jeremiah. Once again prophets spoke out and changed the world as in the days of the Second Isaiah.

But in the Jewish canon, there is not a whisper of this. For knowledge concerning this period we must turn to the Apocrypha, to the New Testament, and to secular historians such as Josephus.

If we turn to the Apocrypha first, we encounter the books of the Maccabees (a name that will be explained later). There are five books grouped under this name, two of which are present in the Apocrypha since they were included in the Greek versions of the Bible. The first of these books, 1 Maccabees, is by far the better from the standpoint of historical value.

Its author is unknown but he was clearly a Jew of rationalist tendencies, for the book contains no miracles. It deals with a forty-year period, from 175 B.C. to 135 B.C., and (unless some of the final passages are later additions) must have been written some time between 135 B.C. and 100 B.C. by a Palestinian Jew.

It was originally written in Hebrew and a copy of that Hebrew version was seen as late as A.D. 400 by the Latin churchman, Jerome. The Hebrew version has not survived to our day, however. Our oldest versions are in Greek so that the King James Version of the translation (which I am using in my quotations) makes use of the Greek versions of the common names. The Revised Standard Version of the translation changes these, however, to conform with those used in translations from the Hebrew, as in the canonical books of the Old Testament.

Philip, the Macedonian

The Book of 1 Maccabees deals with the Jewish rebellion against overlords of Macedonian descent and the writer therefore begins with the foundation of Macedonian power over Asia.

The Macedonian conquest took place in the fourth century B.C., a

The Western Portion of the Empire of Alexander the Great

time when Judea was comparatively quiet. In fact, the history of the Jews under the Persians is virtually unknown to us—and this is probably a sign of the absence of disaster. (Thomas Carlyle said, "Happy the people whose annals are blank in history-books.")

Josephus mentions a Jewish rebellion against the Persians about 350 B.C. but Artaxerxes III, who was then the Persian king, quickly crushed it, and did so without much damage. Perhaps the Jews merely did not get out of the way fast enough when Artaxerxes III marched westward to put an end to an earlier Egyptian rebellion that had kept Egypt precariously independent for about fifty years. It is this event that may have inspired the Book of Esther and the Book of Judith. In this period, too, a final schism may have taken place between the Jews and the Samaritans, one that was never healed.

Yet while Jewish history was subsiding to a low murmur, great things were happening in Greece. After the Greeks had hurled back the attempt of Xerxes (Ahasuerus) to conquer their land, there followed a Golden Age that filled the fifth century B.C. Even while Jerusalem was painstakingly being rebuilt and while Nehemiah was struggling to give it walls again, the Greek city of Athens produced a culture that has been the pride of mankind ever since.

The culture went into decline by the end of the fifth century B.C., however, for a variety of reasons, among which the chief, perhaps, was the continuing and continual warfare between the Greek cities. By 350 B.C., when the Jews were rounding out a sleepy century after the time of Nehemiah and were stirring uneasily as Artaxerxes III marched past them toward Egypt, the Greek cities had ground themselves into virtual exhaustion. The time was ripe for some outside force to take over all of them and that force is named in the very first verse of 1 Maccabees:

1 Maccabees 1:1. . . . *Philip, the Macedonian* . . .

Macedon, or Macedonia, was a land just north of Greece, semi-barbarian at the time of Greece's golden age, but under strong Greek influence. Its people spoke a Greek dialect and its ruling classes were interested in Greek literature and culture. It remained without important influence in Greek history until the middle of the fourth century B.C. when two things happened at once. First, the Greek cities, as I said before, had exhausted themselves with warfare; and second, there came to rule over Macedon a most remarkable man, Philip II. It is he who is referred to in 1 Maccabees 1:1 as "Philip, the Macedonian" and who is often referred to in our own histories as "Philip of Macedon."

Philip seized power over Macedon in 359 B.C. at just about the time Artaxerxes III ascended the Persian throne. Philip at once began to reorganize his army, increase governmental efficiency, extend his power over surrounding barbarian powers, and engage in cautious warfare against the Greek cities.

In 338 B.C. Philip defeated the combined armies of the Greek cities of Athens and Thebes, and made himself the strongest power in Greece. At the battle, leading the charge which finally decided the outcome, was Philip's eighteen-year-old son, Alexander.

Once Philip had gained control of Greece, he forced the Greek cities to recognize him as the leader of a united force of Greeks and Macedonians which he intended to lead against Persia. In 336 B.C., however, almost at the very moment when he planned to cross the Aegean Sea, enter Asia Minor, and begin his Persian War, Philip was assassinated.

Alexander

Succeeding to the throne was Philip's son, now twenty years old, who ruled as Alexander III. In view of his amazing career, however, he is universally known as "Alexander the Great." Alexander began by re-establishing his father's power against revolts throughout his dominions, and once again defeated the Greeks. Then in 334 B.C. he left Greece for Asia.

1 Maccabees 1:1. *And it happened, after that Alexander son of Philip, the Macedonian, who came out of the land of Chettiim, had smitten Darius king of the Persians and Medes, that he reigned in his stead* . . .

Chettiim, or Kittim, is generally taken as being the island of Cyprus which contained the Greek city of Kition (see page I-47). Before the time of Alexander, Kition was the Greek city closest to Judea, and it was natural to broaden the name to include Greece generally.

Alexander found himself facing a weak adversary when he invaded the Persian Empire. Artaxerxes III, the last strong Persian monarch, had died in 338 B.C. and, after a couple of years of confusion, a gentle and unwarlike (even cowardly) individual succeeded to the throne under the title of Darius III. He did so just in time to receive the force of Alexander's invasion.

Alexander quickly won an initial victory over local Persian forces in northwestern Asia Minor. He then passed through the length of that peninsula before meeting the main Persian army in the southeast corner. There he won a great victory in 333 B.C., following which he marched southward through Syria and Judea (see page I-667).

He took Jerusalem without resistance. Josephus describes the high priest of Jerusalem emerging from the city in full priestly regalia to meet Alexander and protect the city. Alexander is then described as having said he had seen just such a man in a dream, so that he pro-

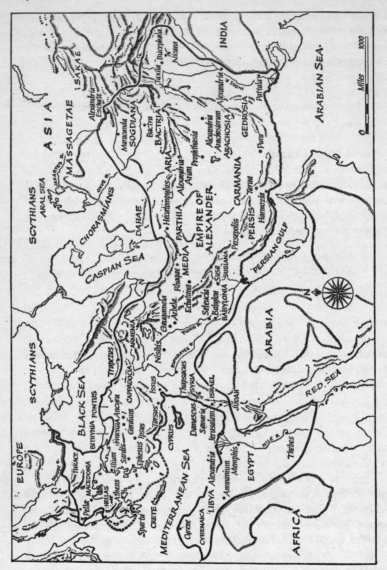

The Empire of Alexander the Great

ceeded to treat Jerusalem with respect. This may or may not be true; there is no evidence for it outside Josephus.

Alexander entered and took Egypt, also without resistance, and directed the establishment of the city of Alexandria (named for himself) in 332 B.C.

In 331 B.C. Alexander left Egypt and advanced eastward into Babylonia, where he defeated the Persians in a third great battle. That was the end of the Persian Empire. In 330 B.C., Darius III was assassinated by some of his own officials, exactly two centuries after the death of Cyrus (see page I-442) and Alexander ruled the vast land in his place.

The Macedonian conqueror spent seven more years marching and countermarching through the eastern stretches of what had been the Persian dominion, winning every battle he fought and eventually carrying his victorious troops into India.

Here they refused to go any farther and Alexander is supposed to have wept because there were no more worlds to conquer. In 324 B.C. he returned to Babylon.

Alexander's Servants

Alexander did not long survive his amazing victories. In 323 B.C., at the age of thirty-three, he died:

1 Maccabees 1:7. *So Alexander reigned twelve years, and then died.*

1 Maccabees 1:8. *And his servants bare rule every one in his place.*

1 Maccabees 1:9. *And after his death they all put crowns upon themselves; so did their sons after them . . .*

At Alexander's death, he left behind him a wife, an infant son, a shrewish mother, and a mentally retarded half brother. None of these could possibly withstand the ambitions of the powerful generals (Alexander's "servants" in the words of 1 Maccabees) who had been trained under Philip and Alexander.

The generals fought ceaselessly among themselves for mastery but none of them won a complete victory. By 301 B.C. it became obvious that Alexander's empire would never be reunited and that each general would have to be content with being king over but a portion of it.

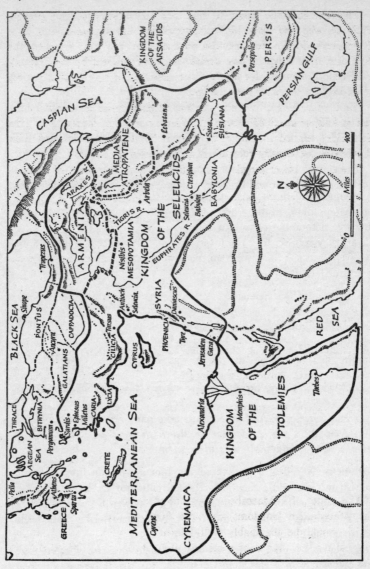

Ptolemaic Egypt and Seleucid Asia

The first to settle down to this new realization was the general, Ptolemy, who had made himself governor of Egypt immediately after Alexander's death. He kept this post and, in 306 B.C., assumed the title of king of Egypt, a title which was to be retained by his descendants (the Ptolemies) for nearly three centuries. Egypt, in this period, is referred to as "Ptolemaic Egypt."

Another of Alexander's generals was Seleucus, who established himself as king of much of western Asia in 306 B.C. His descendants (the Seleucids) reigned for almost as long as the Ptolemies did and their dominions are usually referred to as the Seleucid Empire.

There were other kingdoms established upon the ruins of Alexander's Empire, but it was those of the Ptolemies and the Seleucids that concerned the Jews. In the initial partition of the empire, the eastern shores of the Mediterranean were divided evenly between the two kingdoms. The southern half, including Judea, was part of the Ptolemaic dominion, and the Jews remained under the Ptolemies for a century.

Syria, to the north of Judea, was part of the Seleucid power from the beginning. The Seleucids, at the start, reigned also over Babylonia and the stretches to the east which came to be called Parthia.

It was the Syrian portion of the Seleucid Empire which was closest to Judea. In later centuries, when much of the eastern portion of that empire had been lost, its power was centered in Syria, where its western capital, Antioch, was located. For this reason the Seleucid Empire is frequently referred to as "Syria," though there is no connection except a geographic one, between Seleucid Syria and the Syria that fought against Israel in the days of Ahab (see page I-348).

Antiochus the King

The writer of 1 Maccabees does not pause to detail the history of the Macedonian kingdoms after the death of Alexander (a history which would be reasonably well known, in outline at least, to his original readers) but skips a century and a half to get immediately to the point:

> 1 Maccabees 1:10. *And there came out of them a wicked root . . . son of Antiochus the king . . .*

In most of the Hellenistic kingdoms of the time, successive rulers were known by some one of a very few names, so that there were many Ptolemies in Egypt and many Antiochuses among the Seleucids. The modern fashion of numbering kings of the same name was not in use in ancient times. Instead, each ruler took, or was given, some surname, usually some very flattering one.

Here, for instance, are the surnames of the first five Ptolemies, who ruled over Judea as well as over Egypt:

Ptolemy I Soter ("savior"), 306–285 B.C. He was given this surname in 304 B.C. when he came to the aid of the island of Rhodes at a time when it was being besieged by another Macedonian general. He was succeeded by his son.

Ptolemy II Philadelphus ("loving his sister"), 285–246 B.C. He was so called because late in life, in deference to Egyptian custom, he married his full sister. The name was applied to the two of them, really. Under the patronage of Ptolemy Philadelphus, the Museum and Library at Alexandria made that city the world center of science and learning. Also under his patronage, the Bible was first translated into some language other than Hebrew and the Septuagint came into being. He was succeeded by his son,

Ptolemy III Euergetes ("benefactor"), 246–221 B.C. Under him, Ptolemaic Egypt reached the peak of its power. He fought the Seleucids and defeated them, marching victoriously into Babylonia, annexing much of Syria and even parts of Asia Minor. He was succeeded by his son,

Ptolemy IV Philopater ("loving his father"), 221–203 B.C. This surname was perhaps a bit of propaganda, for this Ptolemy definitely ordered the execution of other close members of his family, including his mother. Some suspect he may have had a hand in the death of his father, too. Egypt began to decline in his reign. He was succeeded by an infant son,

Ptolemy V Epiphanes ("god manifest"), 203–181 B.C. The meaning of this name reflects the fact that in the ancient monarchies the king was considered the adopted son of the national god and therefore was himself a sort of god. Of course, the primitive notion of "god" was not as exalted or abstract as the notions developed by the Jews and Christians, and the Egyptian view toward a monarch as "god manifest" might be no stronger than a Jewish view concerning the high priest or a Christian view concerning the Pope.

As for the Seleucid Empire, the following are its early monarchs: Seleucus I Nicator ("conqueror"), 305–280 B.C., who was followed by his son,

Antiochus I Soter ("savior"), 280–261 B.C., who was in turn followed by his son,

Antiochus II Theos ("god"), 261–246 B.C. In his reign large stretches of the eastern portion of the Seleucid Empire gained their independence under native monarchs and the history of Parthia (a name that is actually a form of "Persia") begins. He was succeeded by his son,

Seleucus II Callinicus ("gloriously victorious"), 246–226 B.C. Despite his surname, he was deafeated by Ptolemy III Euergetes and the Seleucid Empire sank to a low ebb. Torn at by Parthians in the east and Egyptians in the west, his twenty-year disastrous reign closed with the succession of his son,

Seleucus III Ceraunus ("thunderbolt"), 226–223 B.C., who was assassinated in the course of a war with a small Macedonian kingdom in Asia Minor. His younger brother succeeded to the throne. This brother is Antiochus III and it is he who is referred to in 1 Maccabees 1:10 as "Antiochus the king."

Under Antiochus III, 223–187 B.C., the Seleucid Empire made a remarkable recovery. As a result of a series of wars, Antiochus III gradually extended Seleucid power over Asia Minor; he defeated the Parthian tribes and returned them to Seleucid control; and, finally, he tackled Egypt.

He fought two wars against Egypt. In the first of these, he was unsuccessful, losing an important battle at Egypt's borders. When the infant Ptolemy V Epiphanes came to the throne, Antiochus quickly tried again. With Egypt distracted by courtiers intriguing for control of the government, Antiochus was victorious by 198 B.C. As a result of this war, Judea was wrested from Egypt and passed under the domination of the Seleucids.

Rome

In a way, though, Antiochus III had been born too late. He gloried in his victories, which seemed, in his own eyes, to rival those of Alexander. He called himself therefore Antiochus III Magnus ("great") and is known in our own histories as Antiochus the Great.

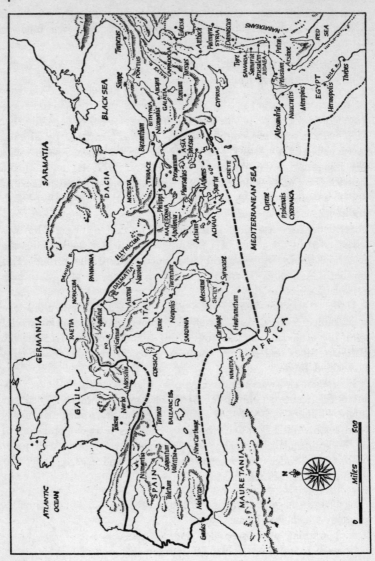

The Roman World in Maccabean Times

If he had died in 198 B.C. the name might have been deserved, but he lived on and found himself entangled with Rome, with results hinted at in the book of 1 Maccabees:

> 1 Maccabees 1:10. *And there came out of them a wicked root, Antiochus surnamed Epiphanes, son of Antiochus the king, who had been an hostage at Rome* . . .

The city of Rome, according to Roman legend, had been founded in 753 B.C. This was when Jeroboam II was king of Israel and Uzziah king of Judah, when Amos and Hosea were prophesying and when Isaiah was about to receive his call.

Rome was a kingdom at first but in 509 B.C., shortly after the Second Temple was dedicated in Jerusalem, it evicted its seventh king, Tarquinius Superbus, and established the Roman Republic. Little by little, over the centuries, it increased its power until, by 270 B.C. when the Jews were under the mild and beneficent rule of Ptolemy II Philadelphus, the Romans had gained control over the entire Italian peninsula.

From 264 B.C. to 202 B.C., while the Ptolemies and Seleucids were continuing their endless wars, Rome fought two gigantic wars of her own with the North African city of Carthage and eventually won a complete victory. Her power was established over the large islands near Italy (Sicily, Sardinia, and Corsica) and over the coasts of Spain. She was the greatest power of the western Mediterranean and her growing shadow began to darken the east.

Some of the smaller Macedonian kingdoms began to form alliances with Rome and to seek her protection against the Seleucid Empire, which, under Antiochus III, seemed invincible. Indeed, even Egypt had a treaty of friendship with Rome that dated back to Ptolemy II, and she too called on Rome for help.

Antiochus III, however, felt no need to be concerned about distant Rome. He considered himself unbeatable and had no hesitation in moving against the small kingdom of Pergamum in western Asia Minor, a kingdom which was Rome's ally.

Rome's warning was disregarded and, in 192 B.C., Rome and Antiochus were at war. Antiochus III invaded Greece but found that defeating the Roman army was by no means the same as defeating the poorly led Egyptian armies or smashing the disorganized Parthian hordes in the east. In 191 B.C. Antiochus III was badly defeated by the

Romans in Greece. When the disillusioned Seleucid monarch retreated hastily to Asia Minor, the Romans followed grimly (setting foot in Asia for the first time) and defeated him again in 190 B.C.

Antiochus III was forced to make a disastrous peace in 189 B.C. He had to pay a large indemnity, lose his fleet, and give up Asia Minor. One of his younger sons—the Antiochus referred to in 1 Maccabees 1:10—was handed over as hostage to the Romans, this serving as a guarantee that the terms of the treaty would be fulfilled. (The Parthian sections of the empire seized their chance to break away again, this time permanently, and the Seleucid Empire was confined to Syria and Babylonia. This was still a sizable dominion, for it was just about the empire ruled over by Nebuchadnezzar.)

In order to pay the indemnity to Rome, Antiochus attempted to force various temples to give up their store of gold. In one city, in 187 B.C., where he was supervising the looting of the temple, he was killed by the inhabitants.

Antiochus Epiphanes

Antiochus III was succeeded by his oldest son, Seleucus IV Philopater, under whom the Seleucid Empire began a slow recovery. The Romans, to make sure he would cause no trouble, forced him, on his accession, to send his son Demetrius as a hostage to Rome. Seleucus was assassinated in 175 B.C. by one of his own ministers, who then attempted to make himself king.

Meanwhile, Seleucus' younger brother Antiochus, who had been sent a hostage to Rome, had been well treated there and had grown to admire Roman institutions. Just about the time that Seleucus was assassinated, Antiochus had been released (or had slipped away) and was making his way back to Antioch. He hastened his steps and managed to seize the throne from the usurper and to take over the kingship. He became Antiochus IV Epiphanes.

1 Maccabees 1:10. *And there came out of them a wicked root, Antiochus surnamed Epiphanes . . . and he reigned in the hundred and thirty and seventh year of the kingdom of the Greeks.*

Seleucus I, the founder of the Seleucid Empire, had begun the practice of counting the years from a victory he gained in 312 B.C., a victory that had enabled him to establish himself firmly in Babylon. He considered his empire to have been founded at that time and 312 B.C. is therefore the first year "of the kingdom of the Greeks" or, as we would say today, the year 1 of the Seleucid era. Therefore, 176/175 B.C. would be the year 137 of the Seleucid era and it is in that year that Antiochus IV gained the throne.

In later years the Jews commonly used the Seleucid era in the course of their business and commercial transactions at a time when every kingdom and almost every city had its own methods for counting the years. As the Jews were scattered widely over the east, their use of the Seleucid era together with the local systems offered later historians a useful method of knitting together the various chronologies.

The Seleucid era remained the most important and widespread manner of counting the years in the Greek-speaking world until the establishment of the Roman era; that is, the system of counting from the year of the legendary founding of the city of Rome. (Later still, the now nearly universal system of counting the years from the birth of Jesus was adopted.)

The Place of Exercise

Alexander the Great, in conquering the Persian Empire, did more than merely make himself king over vast tracts of land. He introduced Greek culture to the east. This culture has always been a very attractive one and it was widely adopted. All of Asia Minor became Greek in culture if not in race, and throughout Egypt and Babylonia tendrils of Greek culture extended. Even in Bactria (the region we now call Afghanistan) a semi-Greek kingdom was set up which survived for over a century, from 250 B.C. to 135 B.C.

The Jews were not immune to the attractiveness of Greek culture, any more than they were immune to Canaanite culture in the days of the judges and the kings, or to American culture today. In the time of the Seleucids, there were many among them who wanted to "assimilate," and to establish gymnasia after the Greek fashion—something at which the writer of 1 Maccabees, strongly anti-Greek, stands aghast:

1 Maccabees 1:11. *In those days went there out of Israel wicked men, who persuaded many, saying, Let us go and make a covenant with the heathen that are round about us* . . .

. . . .

1 Maccabees 1:14. *Whereupon they built a place of exercise at Jerusalem according to the customs of the heathen:*
1 Maccabees 1:15. *And made themselves uncircumcised* . . .

At the gymnasia, the Greeks were accustomed to exercise and to engage in athletic contests in the nude. (The very word "gymnasium" is from a Greek word meaning "naked.") This in itself was horrifying to those Jews who clung to the old ways. Worse still, Jews who exercised in the nude could clearly be seen to be circumcised; to avoid this embarrassment, the custom arose of wearing false foreskins, thus making them "uncircumcised."

This development was, of course, welcomed by the Seleucid rulers. In the first place they, like all the Macedonian rulers, were seriously intent on spreading Greek culture, since they felt it to be far superior to all other cultures.

Then, too, people who clung to old non-Greek ways were more apt to revolt against the ruler in an effort to establish their independence so that they might then live their own way freely. This consideration might well apply particularly to the Jews, since they had only been under Seleucid domination for a quarter of a century and since many co-religionists remained under the Ptolemies, in Alexandria and elsewhere. It might well have seemed to Antiochus IV that the Jews would feel a natural bond to his traditional enemy, Egypt, unless they became Greek in culture and broke their ties with the well-treated Alexandrian Jews.

For this reason Antiochus IV did everything in his power to encourage the hellenization (the Greeks called themselves "Hellenes") of Judea. Nor must such behavior be considered as abnormal or unique to Antiochus. Rather it is common practice in most lands, then and now, to attempt to unify culture. Here in the United States, immigrants from lands of widely different language and culture have been encouraged to learn English and adopt American ways.

To be sure, such a program works best when it is conducted moderately, letting the dominant culture win its way by its own attractiveness and convenience, rather than attempting to impose it by naked force.

Ptolemy

Egypt had a new king too. When Ptolemy V died in 181 B.C., his son, Ptolemy VI Philometer ("loving his mother"), succeeded. He was a young man who was dominated by his mother, a fact that no doubt accounts for his nickname.

There remained bad blood between the Ptolemies and the Seleucids despite the overriding menace of Rome, for there was still the problem of Judea. Antiochus III had been defeated by Rome, but they had allowed him to retain Judea, which he had taken from the Ptolemies, and the Egyptians wanted it back.

Antiochus IV, however, felt no need to return territory that the Romans had let his father keep. He may even have felt that, in view of his own years of pleasant stay in Rome, the Romans would look upon him as one of their own, and favor his enterprises.

Ptolemy's mother remained a force for peace, but after she died, warfare broke out. It was Egypt, apparently, that struck the first blow, and in this she proved foolish, for Ptolemy VI was a weak and unwarlike king (though gentle and humane) while Antiochus IV was a capable general. Antiochus invaded Egypt in 170 B.C.

> 1 Maccabees 1:17. *Wherefore he* [Antiochus IV] *entered into Egypt with a great multitude* . . .
> 1 Maccabees 1:18. *And made war against Ptolemee king of Egypt: but Ptolemee was afraid of him, and fled* . . .

Antiochus pursued the retreating Egyptian king to the walls of Alexandria and actually captured him. The Egyptians, left without a king, promptly put Ptolemy's younger brother on the throne, as Ptolemy VII Euergetes II—note the repetition of the surname.

(Sometimes Ptolemy VII is reserved for the young son of Ptolemy VI, while the brother who now shared his throne is called Ptolemy VIII. However, there is no great chance of confusion here for the Ptolemy who was placed on the throne after the capture of Ptolemy VI is universally known in history not by number but as "Physcon" or "Pot-Belly" because he grew fat in the course of his long reign. It

was this Ptolemy VII, or Physcon, by the way, who was referred to
by the translator of Ecclesiasticus, see page I-517.)

Antiochus IV did not feel in a position actually to take Alexandria,
for he was uncertain as to Rome's attitude if he went that far. He
therefore released Ptolemy VI. He felt that with two Ptolemies quarrel-
ing over the throne, Egypt would fall into civil war and one side or
another would call on his help. He would then take over the country
under a show of legality.

The Egyptians, however, outmaneuvered him. The two Ptolemies
decided to rule jointly and did so in peace. The angered Antiochus
threw caution aside and invaded Egypt a second time in 168 B.C.

But now Rome had had enough. A Roman envoy from Alexandria
faced the Seleucid monarch in front of his troops and ordered him to
withdraw. Antiochus had to back down before this single representative
of the distant Roman power and, utterly humiliated, march back to
his own land.

Jerusalem

The Book of 1 Maccabees refers only to the first invasion of Egypt,
the one that was glorious from the standpoint of Antiochus IV. Of
course, even a victorious campaign consumes money and the Seleucids
had been dreadfully short of that commodity ever since Rome had
exacted its indemnity. One way out was to confiscate the hoarded
wealth of temples—something that had been the death of Antiochus
III—and Antiochus III's son, returning from Egypt, passed through
Jerusalem and looted its Temple as a matter of course:

> 1 Maccabees 1:20. *And after that Antiochus had smitten Egypt,*
> *he returned again in the hundred forty and third year* [169 B.C.] . . .
> 1 Maccabees 1:21. *And entered proudly into the sanctuary, and*
> *took away the golden altar* . . .
> . . . .
> 1 Maccabees 1:23. *He took also the silver and the gold, and the*
> *precious vessels: also he took the hidden treasures which he found.*

The writer does not go on to tell of the second invasion of Egypt
and of its humiliating end for Antiochus, but we needn't rely on

secular history only to know of it. The incident is mentioned in the Book of Daniel (see page I-619):

Daniel 11:30. *For the ships of Chittim* [Rome] *shall come against him* [Antiochus IV]: *therefore he shall be grieved, and return, and have indignation against the holy covenant* . . .

It seems reasonable enough to suppose that Antiochus IV, half-maddened with frustration, would be anxious to vent his anger on some victim. The Jews were weak enough for the purpose and were not protected by Rome and it is possible, besides, that they angered him further by being incautiously jubilant over this shameful defeat of the king who had looted their Temple only two years before.

Antiochus took action:

1 Maccabees 1:29. . . . *the king sent his chief collector of tribute* . . . *who came unto Jerusalem with a great multitude,*

1 Maccabees 1:30. *And* . . . *fell suddenly upon the city, and smote it very sore* . . .

With Jerusalem taken and sacked, Antiochus further decided that Hellenization was to proceed with all possible speed:

1 Maccabees 1:41. *Moreover king Antiochus wrote to his whole kingdom, that all should be one people,*

1 Maccabees 1:42. *And every one should leave his laws* . . .

As a climax of the new policy, the Temple was profaned. Antiochus decided that Judaism should be brought into line with Hellenism by identifying Zeus and Yahveh and erecting a statue to Zeus-Yahveh in the Temple itself, supplying it, very likely, with his own royal face. To the orthodox Jews this was the greatest imaginable blasphemy:

1 Maccabees 1:54. *Now* . . . *in the hundred forty and fifth year* [167 B.C.], *they set up the abomination of desolation upon the altar* . . .

To enforce the new policy, Antiochus ordered copies of the Jewish Scriptures to be destroyed, forbade circumcision and the Jewish dietary regulations, then executed those caught clinging to the old ways. For a time it looked as though Judaism would be destroyed and that those who held out uncompromisingly against Antiochus IV would die as martyrs.

Mattathias

But now a remarkable family appears on the scene:

1 Maccabees 2:1. *In those days arose Mattathias . . . a priest . . . from Jerusalem, and dwelt in Modin.*

Mattathias is the Greek form of the Hebrew Mattathiah ("gift of Yahveh"). This name is mentioned only once in the canonical books of the Bible and then only in a post-Exilic incident:

Nehemiah 8:4. *And Ezra the scribe stood upon a pulpit of wood, . . . and beside him stood Mattathiah . . .*

but it had grown popular in Seleucid times.

According to Josephus, the great-great-grandfather of Mattathias was named Hashmon (or Asmon, in the Greek form) so that the family may be called the Hasmonaeans or Asmoneans collectively. When Jerusalem had been taken by Antiochus' forces, Mattathias and his family moved to Modin (Modein in the Revised Standard Version), a town some seventeen miles to the northwest.

Judas Maccabeus

Mattathias had five stalwart sons:

1 Maccabees 2:2. *And he had five sons, Joannan* [Johanan], *called Caddis:*

1 Maccabees 2:3. *Simon, called, Thassi:*

1 Maccabees 2:4. *Judas, who was called Maccabeus:*

1 Maccabees 2:5. *Eleazar, called Avaran: and Jonathan, whose surname was Apphus.*

Even among the Jews it was becoming customary to adopt surnames to serve as identification. In this case, the surnames are of uncertain meaning, except, possibly, for that of Mattathias' third son: Judas Maccabeus.

This surname is often considered a Greek version of the Hebrew word "makkabi" ("the hammerer"). It is suggested that the third son is Judas the Hammerer, so called because of the hammer blows he was soon to inflict upon the Seleucid army. On the other hand, there is some indication that he had this name before the battles were joined, and an alternate suggestion is that it is from the Hebrew "makab" ("to appoint"). He would then be Judas the Appointed; appointed, that is, by God to lead his people against the Seleucids.

Judas itself is, of course, the Greek form of Judah. It is very likely that the heroism of Judas Maccabeus made the name Judas [Judah] so popular among the Jews in the centuries following.

Because Judas Maccabeus is the hero of what was to follow, the family has come to be called, in English, the Maccabees—a name that is more familiar now than the more accurate Hasmonaeans. Similarly, the Jewish kingdom that was eventually established under their rule is called the "Maccabean kingdom," and the times the "Maccabean era." Jewish writings dealing with this period of time are lumped together as the various books of the Maccabees even when they have nothing directly to do with the family, and the first of these, the one with which I am now dealing, is 1 Maccabees.

Assideans

The spark that initiated the Jewish rebellion against the Seleucids was set off by an officer of Antiochus who came to Modin to enforce the new laws. He asked Mattathias, as a prominent Jewish leader, to set a good example and to carry through a sacrifice in the manner required by law. To Mattathias, this was idolatry and he refused.

However, there were other Jews who were not so insistent on the old ways. The Seleucid officer, in asking Mattathias to perform the sacrifice, pointed out that it was being done by the Jews generally:

1 Maccabees 2:18. . . . *fulfil the king's commandment, like . . . the men of Juda . . . and such as remain at Jerusalem . . .*

In this, he was probably telling the truth. In aftertimes, a successful revolution is looked back upon as the rising of a united nation or group, but most of that is the patriotic gilding of memory, and it is not so. In all revolutions, those who ardently pursue the fight to the death are in the minority and there are usually at least as many who are ardently anti-revolutionary, plus an actual majority that is apathetic and will go where they are led (in either direction), if necessary, but who best prefer to be left alone.

Our own Revolutionary War was conducted by a minority of Rebels who faced not only the British, but Tories who were at least equal in numbers to themselves. And most colonists did not incline strongly to either side. And today the Civil Rights movement among Negroes has, as one of its problems, the apathy of most Negroes.

So it must have been that the Jews in the time of Antiochus were by no means all bitterly anti-Seleucid. Many were willing to conform; perhaps even eager, in their pro-Greek views, to do so. Thus, when Mattathias refused the sacrifice, someone else quickly stepped up to perform it, either out of conviction or, perhaps, out of the thought that unless someone did, the entire town would be massacred.

1 Maccabees 2:23. . . . *there came one of the Jews in the sight of all to sacrifice on the altar . . . according to the king's commandment.*

At seeing this, Mattathias flew into a rage, slew the Jew and the Seleucid officer. That was the Lexington-and-Concord of the Jewish rebellion. Mattathias and his sons had to flee to the hills, and around them they began to collect other rebels.

In particular, Mattathias was joined by a party of fervid men whose adherence to the traditional Mosaic Law was absolute:

1 Maccabees 2:42. *Then came there unto him a company of Assideans, who were mighty men of Israel, even all such as were voluntarily devoted unto the law.*

The word Assideans (or Hasideans in the Revised Standard Version) is the Greek form of the Hebrew "Hassidim," meaning "the pious ones." Their sole concern lay in religion. They were uninterested in politics and it was only when the practice of Judaism was outlawed that they were willing to resort to violence.

They were stalwart fighters, but in some ways they were an embarrassment, for a truly uncompromising adherence to the letter of the law can create problems. The many prohibitions that had grown up concerning the Sabbath day made many pious men feel that it was unlawful to take even such worldly action on the Sabbath as was required for self-defense. Thus, Josephus says that when Ptolemy I, in the first few years after Alexander's death, marched into Judea to establish his dominance over the region, he was able to seize Jerusalem without resistance by attacking on the Sabbath. The Jews would not defend the walls on that day.

Similarly, a party of the ultra-pious, tracked down by Seleucid forces on the Sabbath, decided to let themselves be killed without resisting. They said:

> 1 Maccabees 2:37. . . . *Let us die all in our innocency: heaven and earth shall testify for us, that ye put us to death wrongfully.*

There is something impressive about such faith, but it is no way to fight a war. Mattathias and his friends mourned the dead, but they insisted on a new policy:

> 1 Maccabees 2:41. . . . *Whosoever shall come to make battle with us on the sabbath day, we will fight against him . . .*

Here was an example of adjusting the Law to fit the serious needs of men, something that was to play a part in the later development of Judaism and in the teachings of Jesus, too.

Beth-horon

Mattathias did not live long. He was old, and the exertions of the field took its toll:

> 1 Maccabees 2:70. *And he died in the hundred forty and sixth year* [166 B.C.] *. . .*
> 1 Maccabees 3:1. *Then his son Judas, called Maccabeus, rose up in his stead.*

But now the forces of the Seleucid Empire were moving to put down the revolt and, as is often the case, the government began by underestimating the seriousness of the trouble. It was, to begin with, left to the governor of Samaria, Apollonius, the local official on the spot:

> 1 Maccabees 3:10. *Then Apollonius gathered the Gentiles together, and a great host out of Samaria, to fight against Israel.*

Judas Maccabeus came out to meet him. Apollonius was, in all likelihood, overconfident and marched forward carelessly, convinced he could easily handle a few rebels. That was his mistake. Judas' men swarmed down upon him, probably out of ambush, and his army was defeated. Apollonius himself was killed and Judas took his sword and used it in later battles.

The Seleucids had to do better than that, and the next step involved the army itself and a general, Seron. Now it was not the local levies from Samaria, but the army itself.

1 Maccabees 3:16. *And when he* [Seron] *came near to the going up of Bethhoron, Judas went forth to meet him with a small company* . . .

Beth-horon is about twelve miles northwest of Jerusalem, near Mattathias' adopted town of Modin. Here, Judas and his men lay in ambush in the surrounding hills and once again a lightning attack caught a Seleucid army by surprise and destroyed it.

Persia

The Jewish victory at Beth-horon was sufficiently spectacular to raise the rebellion from a local tumult to an internationally observed matter. Clearly, the prestige of the regime now required that a major effort be put into the suppression of the rebels.

Unfortunately for Antiochus it was easier to see the need than to do something about it. The same old problem arose—lack of money. Furthermore, the empire was fading at the other end, too. If Judas and his army of irregulars were shaking the west, in the east whole provinces were falling away.

The Parthian rulers, who had been subservient to the Seleucids even as late as the reign of Antiochus III, were little by little enlarging their independence. In 171 B.C., a vigorous king, Mithridates I, ascended the Parthian throne and the last vestige of dependence on the Seleucids disappeared. Indeed, Mithridates extended his power in all directions and was making himself a major factor in central Asia.

It may be that if Parthia had remained quiet, Antiochus could have handled the Jewish rebellion. As it was, he found himself pulled in both directions. His prestige abroad, already badly shaken by his humiliation in Egypt, demanded that he not allow the Jews to remain unpunished. On the other hand, if he could but bring the eastern provinces back into the fold, he could collect all the money he needed in the form of a punitive tribute.

With prestige pulling one way and money the other, he made the worst possible decision. He decided to divide his forces and embark on a two-front war:

> 1 Maccabees 3:31. *Wherefore, being greatly perplexed in his mind, he [Antiochus IV] determined to go into Persia [Parthia], there to take the tributes of the countries, and to gather much money.*
> 1 Maccabees 3:32. *So he left Lysias, a nobleman, . . . to oversee the affairs of the king from the river Euphrates unto the borders of Egypt . . .*

Antioch

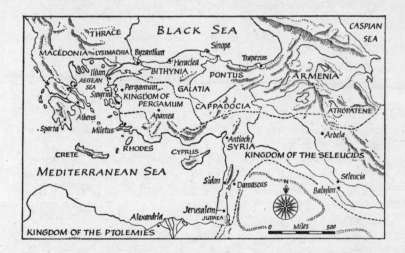

Antioch

Antiochus IV left his young son with Lysias, and half his army as well and his instructions were to wipe out the Jewish rebels.

> 1 Maccabees 3:37. *So the king took the half of the forces that remained, and departed from Antioch, his royal city, the hundred forty and seventh year* [165 B.C.]; *and . . . passed the river Euphrates . . .*

Antioch, the "royal city"—that is, the Seleucid capital—was, at this time, a comparatively young city.

When Alexander the Great died in 323 B.C., Babylon was still the gratest city of the east, and it was in Babylon that he died. Babylon remained a great prize for the generals who contended for the crown. It was captured by Seleucus I Nicator in 312 B.C. and that established him on the throne of Macedonian Asia and served to mark the date of the founding of the Seleucid Empire.

Yet the capture by Seleucus was the last important event in Babylonian history. Seleucus was a founder of cities and felt that his capital ought to be a new city, and not one as old and as hoary with non-Greek tradition as Babylon was. The year of his conquest of Babylon, Seleucus therefore began to build a new capital for himself on the Tigris River some twenty miles north of Babylon. He called the new city Seleucia, after himself.

As Seleucia grew, Babylon declined. The people left the old city for the new and the buildings of Babylon served as raw material for construction in Seleucia. By Maccabean times, the mighty Babylon of Hammurabi and Nebuchadnezzar was finished and sixteen centuries of histories closed with a whimper. The city that had carried off the Jews four centuries before was now a miserably dying village; and Jerusalem, which it had temporarily destroyed, was still alive after all and about to embark on a new period of independence.

However, Seleucia was not the only capital. To be sure, it was centrally located and it grew rich and prosperous. If the Seleucids had remained there and concentrated on the eastern portion of their empire they might have fused Greek and Persian into a combined society that would have lasted indefinitely.

Psychologically, though, the Seleucids were always drawn westward. The Greek core was to the west and the Seleucids were always aware of the enormous attraction of all things Greek. A few miles of Syria, or a stretch of the coast of Asia Minor, meant more to them than a thousand miles of central Asia. So they fought endless wars with Egypt while vast tracts of the east crumbled. And because of their concentration on the west, they needed a center there.

In 300 B.C., Seleucus had founded a city in northwest Syria near the Mediterranean. He named it Antiochea, in memory of his father, the Macedonian general, Antiochus, and we know it as Antioch. This city, near the Greek thick of things, was ideal as a western capital.

Through the succeeding reigns, each successive monarch enlarged and beautified Antioch. The center of gravity of the Seleucid Empire shifted westward and by the time of Antiochus IV, Antioch was the major city of the realm, and stood second only to Alexandria in the Greek world.

The Temple

While Antiochus IV, with half the army, had gone eastward to Parthia, Lysias was left with the other half to take care of the Jews. It was far easier for Lysias, however, to receive his instructions than to carry them out.

In the course of the next year, Lysias sent two armies into Judea and each was defeated. Judas Maccabeus had shown himself unbeatable and now he could count on a period of wary peace while the chastened Seleucids held back to recoup.

It was time, therefore, to rededicate the profaned Temple. Judas Maccabeus chose priests who had never compromised with the Seleucid authorities, tore down the profaned altar and buried the stones. A new altar was built and new vessels supplied, and finally:

1 Maccabees 4:52. . . . *in the one hundred forty and eighth year* [164 B.C.], *they rose up betimes in the morning,*

1 Maccabees 4:53. *And offered sacrifice according to the law upon the new altar* . . .

. . . .

1 Maccabees 4:56. *And so they kept the dedication of the altar eight days* . . .

. . . .

1 Maccabees 4:59. *Moreover Judas and his brethren* . . . *ordained, that the days of the dedication of the altar should be kept in their season from year to year by the space of eight days* . . .

The anniversary of the dedication of the Temple is celebrated to this day, by the Jews, as the eight-day feast of Hanukkah ("dedication").

Judas deliberately set the date of the dedication of the cleansed Temple, on the third anniversary of its profanation, and therefore three and a half years after the capture of Jerusalem by Antiochus IV.

This three-and-a-half-year interval is mentioned by the writer of Daniel, who was apparently at work on it at this time. Since he placed the book in the time of the Exile four centuries earlier and had Daniel relate it as a prophecy, he was forced to use apocalyptic language:

> Daniel 7:25. *And he* [Antiochus IV] *shall speak great words against the most High,* . . . *and think to change times and laws: and they* [the Temple and the pious Jews] *shall be given into his hand until a time* [one year] *and times* [plus two years] *and the dividing of time* [plus half a year].

Idumea

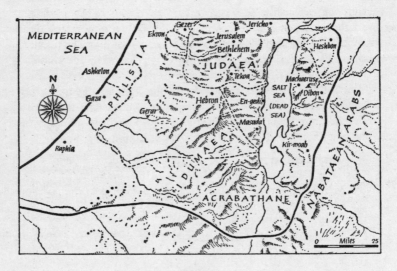

Idumea

The Temple was rededicated and Judas fortified Mount Zion, but there was no opportunity to rest. The enthusiasm of the victories would have declined and faded, if the Jews now remained on the defensive; the élan and esprit would vanish, the forces disperse, and the revolt would wither away. Judas apparently decided to pass over to the offensive, and attack the areas bordering on Judea:

> 1 Maccabees 5:3. *Then Judas fought against the children of Esau in Idumea . . . and he gave them a great overthrow . . .*

This was not the first example of the rapid about-face of the Jews from a persecuted minority to an imperial power. Eight and a half centuries before, David had taken a nation of Philistine vassals and, in the course of a few years, not only won Israelite independence but established Israelite hegemony over the Philistines and other surrounding nations.

Here the case was more limited, for the Maccabean state never approached the physical dimensions or the comparative power of David's kingdom. Nevertheless, the victory of Judas was the first step toward the conquest of Edom (or Idumea, which is the Greek version of the name).

Perhaps the nationalists of the time felt they could justify warfare against Idumea not only as a matter of traditional enmity, traced all the way back to the legends of Jacob and Esau (see page I-93), but also because during the period of the Babylonian Exile, the Idumeans, under the pressure of the Nabatean Arabs (see page I-457), had been forced northward. What was called Idumea in Maccabean times had been southern Judah in the time of the monarchy, and the Jews may well have felt they were but retaking what was their own. (Similar arguments have served as excuse for any number of wars since.)

But it was more than mere conquest. The Maccabeans eventually enforced Judaism on the conquered Idumeans; doing as they would not be done by. The case of a religious minority that becomes an oppressor as soon as it is in power has been seen numerous times in history. Consider, for instance, the Puritans who fled oppression in England and came to America for the sake of religious liberty and who then proved most keen in refusing it to others than themselves. The usual excuse, in all times, is that the victors are merely exalting Truth over Falsehood, and are selflessly saving the souls of the losers. The losers, however, generally have trouble recognizing the good intentions of those who are so thoughtfully converting them at the point of the sword.

Galilee

The forces of Judas struck outward in all directions, not only toward the south against Idumea, but eastward against the Ammonites. There was trouble in the north, too. The Greeks in Gilead (east of the Jordan and north of Ammonite territory) gathered against the Jews who

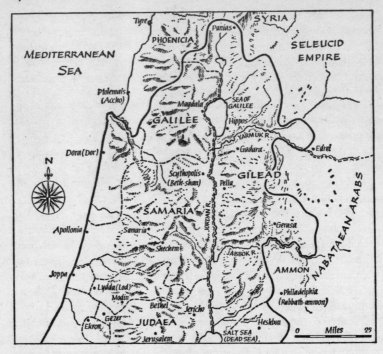

Galilee

lived there and laid siege to them in one of the Gileadite cities. The
besieged Jews sent letters to Judas and his brothers, pleading for help:

> 1 Maccabees 5:14. *While these letters were yet reading, behold,*
> *there came other messengers from Galilee . . . who reported on this*
> *wise,*
> 1 Maccabees 5:15. . . . *They of . . . all Galilee of the Gentiles,*
> *are assembled together against us . . .*

Galilee refers to the northernmost section of what had once been
Israel; the territory which, in the time of the judges, was settled by
the tribes of Naphtali and Zebulon.

This northern area was never firmly held by the Israelites. The
Canaanites remained strong in the north long after Joshua's conquest,
as is evidenced by the tales of the battle against Sisera (see page I-238).

Down to the time of David himself, the Phoenician coastal cities (inhabited by Canaanites, be it remembered) dominated the north.

To those at the center of Israelite power—farther south among the Rachel tribes of Ephraim, Manasseh, and Benjamin—the north could well be looked upon as *galil haggoyim*. This means, literally, "district of the nations" or "district of the [non-Israelite] tribes."

A Latin word for a tribe or clan was *gens* and members of the same tribe or clan were "gentiles." Therefore *galil haggoyim* could be translated as "district of the gentiles." *Galil* became *Galilaea* in Latin and "Galilee" in English, leaving us with "Galilee of the Gentiles."

The term Gentile, for non-Jew, is used steadily in 1 Maccabees, and has come down, in this sense, to modern times. Mormons, however, apply the word to non-Mormons, so that to a Mormon a Jew is a Gentile.

References to Galilee prior to the time of the Assyrian conquest and the destruction of the Northern Kingdom are not found in the Bible. Prior to that time, the lands of Naphtali and Zebulon are referred to instead. The turning point comes in Isaiah where the depredations of Assyria are described and both terms, pre-Assyrian and post-Assyrian, are used for the area:

Isaiah 9:1. . . . *at the first he lightly afflicted the land of Zebulun and the land of Naphtali, and afterward did more grievously afflict her . . . in Galilee of the nations.*

By Maccabean times, Jewish colonists had begun to penetrate Galilee once more, but its population was still largely Gentile.

Ptolemais

In the face of this double danger, Judas divided his forces. He and his younger brother Jonathan, with the smaller army, advanced into Gilead. His older brother, Simon (another version of the name Simeon, by the way), led the larger army into Galilee. The division of forces proved, for once, not to be fatal. Both were victorious and both were able to evacuate the besieged Jews back to the safety of Judea:

1 Maccabees 5:21. *Then went Simon into Galilee, where he fought many battles with the heathen, . . .*

1 Maccabees 5:22. *And he pursued them unto the gate of Ptolemais.*

Ptolemais was a city on the Phoenician coast some twenty-five miles south of Tyre—the southernmost of the Phoenician cities. Its older name had been Accho and it lay in the territory theoretically assigned to Asher. The northern tribes never did assert their theoretical supremacy over the Phoenician coast, of course; a fact recognized in the Bible:

Judges 1:31. *Neither did Asher drive out the inhabitants of Accho, nor the inhabitants of Zidon . . .*

The early Ptolemies controlled the area and in 260 B.C., Accho was renamed Ptolemais in their honor. It kept that name after the area had been wrested from Egyptian hands by Antiochus III, and indeed throughout the Roman period long after Ptolemies and Seleucids had alike vanished.

It resumed its original name after the Moslem conquest in A.D. 638. In the time of the Crusades, five centuries later, the city was known to the Christians as St.-Jean-d'Acre or, more simply, Acre. It is now a city of modern Israel, named Akko, and has a population of some thirty thousand.

Antiochus V Eupator

The Maccabean attacks were successful, in part, because the Seleucid Empire was more or less paralyzed by events in Parthia. Antiochus IV was having no success there. The writer of Maccabees tells of the failure of his attempt to loot a temple in Elymais and of his falling sick with grief in consequence; a grief further exacerbated by the news of Lysias' defeats in Judea.

The story of the temple-looting is undoubtedly a mistake. It is a tale transferred from Antiochus III (see page 48) to his son, perhaps through the writer's eagerness to have Antiochus IV sink into utter failure. His sickness, it would seem from secular sources, was not grief, but tuberculosis, something more likely to be fatal.

The despoiler of the Temple died in Gabae, a town now known as Isfahan, in central Iran, nine hundred miles east of Jerusalem.

1 Maccabees 6:16. *So king Antiochus died there in the hundred forty and ninth year* [163 B.C.].

1 Maccabees 6:17. *Now when Lysias knew that the king was dead, he set up Antiochus his son . . . to reign in his stead, and his name he called Eupator.*

Antiochus V Eupator ("of noble birth") was nine years old at the time of his accession. He was controlled by Lysias, who ruled the empire through him.

The accession of a young king was made to order for the Jewish rebels under Judas Maccabeus. There were bound to be dynastic squabbles and while the various candidates for the throne and for power behind it fought among themselves, the Jews could safely risk the offensive.

In 162 B.C., the year after the death of Antiochus IV, Judas even dared attack the citadel in Jerusalem; that is, the fortress within which the Seleucid garrison had retired at the time, over a year before, when the main city of Jerusalem had been taken and the Temple rededicated.

But that attack stirred Lysias, who decided to take a chance on dynastic troubles remaining in abeyance and mount a strong counterattack (something to which he was urged by parties of loyalist Jews —the "Tories" of the Maccabean rebellion).

A fresh Seleucid army advanced southward, stronger than any previous one, and armed with a new type of weapon not hitherto used against the rebels—elephants. Eleasar, one of the brothers of Judas, fought his way to one of the beasts, stabbed it in the abdomen, and killed it, but the elephant, in dying, fell upon Eleasar and killed him in turn. He was the first of the five sons of Mattathias to die.

Eleasar showed that elephants, too, were mortal, but the Jewish army was nevertheless facing odds that were too great for it. Fighting desperately, they were nevertheless slowly pushed toward the edge of exhaustion through famine.

But then Lysias' gamble failed. He was forced to face a dynastic problem. A nobleman who had been with Antiochus IV in the east had now made his way back with what was left of Antiochus' army and attempted to seize power. Lysias, faced with this threat to the very core of his policy, was forced to turn away from the trouble in the outskirts.

He therefore offered the Jews a compromise peace. Two points were involved, the religious liberty of the Jews and their political independence. Lysias felt that, under the circumstances, he could yield the first, if the Jews would yield the second. There were important elements in the rebel army, the Assideans, for instance, who were interested only in religious liberty, and Judas had to accept the compromise. At least, for the time.

Demetrius I Soter

Lysias returned to Antioch, now under the control of his competitor, defeated him and retook the city—but the situation remained unstable. There were other competitors in the field.

Seleucus IV Philopater, the predecessor and older brother of Antiochus IV, had sent a son, Demetrius, into Roman captivity (see page 48). That son of an older brother was, by modern standards, more deserving of the throne than the reigning monarch, Antiochus V, who was but the son of a younger brother. Demetrius, when he heard of the death of his uncle, Antiochus IV, at once petitioned the Roman Senate for permission to return to Antioch and assume the kingship. Rome, preferring a weak child on the Seleucid throne to a capable young man, refused permission and Demetrius promptly escaped and made his way to the Seleucid coast on his own.

> 1 Maccabees 7:1. *In the hundred and one and fiftieth year* [161 B.C.] *Demetrius the son of Seleucus departed from Rome, and came up with a few men unto a city of the sea coast, and reigned there.*

In the civil war that followed, Demetrius was a quick winner. Antiochus V and Lysias were captured and killed and the new king took the name of Demetrius I Soter. Rome accepted the reality of the situation and recognized Demetrius as king.

Demetrius attempted to retrieve the Seleucid position with respect to Judea, not so much by immediate military action as by first laying a careful foundation of support for himself among the Jewish "Tories" of whom there were many.

> 1 Maccabees 7:5. *There came unto him* [Demetrius] *all the wicked and ungodly men of Israel, having Alcimus, who was desirous to be high priest, for their captain:*
>
> 1 Maccabees 7:6. *And they accused the people* [the rebel forces] *to the king . . .*

With the Tories on the king's side and with the Assideans neutral, Demetrius felt it timely to send an army into Judea once more. At its head was Nicanor, a general who had been with the king in Rome and, according to Josephus, had escaped with him.

Judas, however, had not forgotten how to be a hammerer. Rallying his forces against a superior enemy yet once again, he met the Seleucid army at Beth-horon, some fourteen miles northwest of Jerusalem, and there he won the most remarkable victory of his career (and, as it turned out, the last). Nicanor himself was slain and once again the forces of the Seleucid Empire were forced to back off with burnt fingers.

The Romans

For five years now, Judas Maccabeus and his brothers had been facing superior forces and winning by rapid movement and surprise and by taking advantage of Seleucid preoccupation with other rebellions and with civil wars. But good luck, and even good management, cannot be expected to continue forever. What was needed was outside help, and at that time the smaller nations of the east found their friend in the new giant of the west, the giant who, in the end, would swallow them all:

1 Maccabees 8:1 *Now Judas had heard of the fame of the Romans . . .*

Even as late as the time of Alexander the Great, Rome had been merely another barbarian tribe of the hinterland as far as the Greeks were concerned. Possibly no Jew had as much as heard of the Roman name at the time.

It wasn't until 281 B.C., in fact, that Rome suddenly impinged upon the Greek world. At that time it was the Macedonian monarchs who seemed supreme. One of them, Ptolemy II Philadelphus, ruled over Egypt and under his mild sway Jews were translating the Bible into Greek. Another, Antiochus I Soter, ruled over the Seleucid kingdom. Other Macedonians ruled Greece itself and the districts to the north. In particular, a Macedonian named Pyrrhus ruled over Epirus, a region northwest of Greece. Of all the Macedonian rulers of his day, Pyrrhus was the most capable general.

The westernmost portion of the Greek world had, as its chief representatives, a number of wealthy cities on the coast of southern Italy. These cities had been settled five to six centuries before in the days

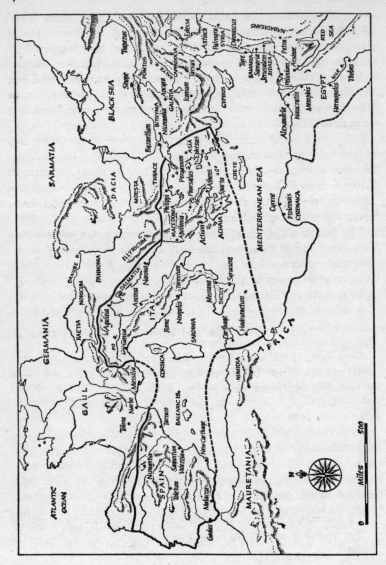

The Roman World

when Amos, Hosea, and Isaiah preached in Israel and Judah. These cities had always had their troubles with the poorly organized tribes of the interior and now the martial city of Rome had conquered all of Italy right down to the seacoast and the Greek cities were terrified.

They called in Pyrrhus to help. Pyrrhus eagerly responded and beat the Romans in two battles. The Romans persevered, however, and in the end beat Pyrrhus and by 270 B.C. had taken over every Greek city in southern Italy.

The Greek world ought to have grown alarmed at this point and united to defeat this strangely powerful newcomer. Unfortunately for themselves, they miscalculated. The western city Carthage measured its strength against Rome in two mighty wars, and the Macedonian kingdoms may have felt the two cities to be so evenly matched as to be certain to destroy each other.

The Macedonians relaxed therefore, let Rome and Carthage deal each other mighty blows, and amused themselves by interminable battling among themselves.

For a while it seemed that the Macedonians had calculated shrewdly indeed, for both Carthage and Rome came, each in its turn, to the very edge of disaster. In the end, however, it was not a stalemate but a complete and utter Roman victory and by 200 B.C. Rome was the strongest single power in the world.

Even then, the Macedonian kingdoms might have won out if they could have combined, but the rivalries that had grown up among them in a century of warfare were too powerful to bury.

The Galatians

Rome, therefore, continued to win victories, and these are summarized in this chapter of 1 Maccabees:

1 Maccabees 8:2. . . . *It was told him* [Judas Maccabeus] *also of their wars . . . among the Galatians, and how they had conquered them . . .*

The Galatians (or Gauls) had moved southward into Italy and taken Rome itself in 390 B.C. when that city was yet a small power, and when the Jews were vegetating peacefully under the Persians. Rome shook itself free, but the Gauls settled in the rich valley of the Po River. What is now northern Italy came to be called "Cisalpine Gaul" (Gaul on "this side of the Alps"—"this side" from the standpoint of the Romans).

As the Romans grew stronger, the Gauls grew weaker. In 295 B.C. the Romans inflicted a devastating defeat on the Gauls and by 222 B.C. they had annexed the whole region of Cisalpine Gaul and extended their power to the Alps.

This was the more remarkable to those easterners who had been watching the Roman advance, for even while the Romans were beating back the Gauls steadily, the Macedonian kingdoms were proving helpless against barbarians of the same kind.

In 280 B.C., even as Pyrrhus was fighting Rome in Italy, bands of Gauls raided southward into Macedon and for several years absolute terror and anarchy gripped that land, and Greece to the south as well.

In 278 B.C. the Gauls crossed over into Asia Minor and devastated that region. It wasn't until 235 B.C. that they were finally defeated and tamed. They were then forced to settle down in a region in central Asia Minor which came to be called Galatia. By that time they had become civilized and had adopted the Greek culture.

The ease with which the Romans had handled their Gauls could not but be noted and admired in the east.

Spain

The Romans had won victories outside Italy, too:

1 Maccabees 8:3. *And what they* [the Romans] *had done in the country of Spain . . .*

Even while the Romans had been defeating the Gauls, they had been fighting the first long war with Carthage to a successful conclusion. After that war, Carthage had tried to recoup by setting up a new empire in Spain, winning control of the Mediterranean region of that wild and, at that time, barbarous country.

In 219 B.C., then, shortly after the annexation of Cisalpine Gaul by Rome, Carthage was ready for a second war. This time the Carthaginian forces were led by Hannibal, one of the very greatest generals of all time. For sixteen years the Carthaginian managed to maintain himself in Italy, winning great victories and suffering not one real defeat.

Rome held on doggedly, however, sending its armies to fight outside Italy, even while Hannibal devastated their homeland. In particular, one of the Roman generals, Scipio, fought brilliantly in Spain, defeating the Carthaginians there and, in effect, annexing the land to Rome.

Scipio then went to Africa to attack Carthage itself. Hannibal returned to face him and in a final battle at the north African town of Zama in 202 B.C. Scipio and Rome won.

Philip and Perseus

The quick summary of Roman progress continues:

1 Maccabees 8:5. *Beside this, how they* [the Romans] *had discomfited in battle Philip, and Perseus, king of the Citims . . .*

This refers to happenings after the climactic battle of Zama. Of the Macedonian kingdoms, the one nearest to Rome was that of Macedon itself (referred to here as Citims, or more properly Kittim, see page I-47). Macedon was not the vigorous imperial power it had been under Philip II and Alexander the Great. The emigration of Macedonians to the conquered lands in the south and the east, the losses in war, and the havoc of the raids by the Gauls had reduced its power. Nevertheless, it was still strong enough to maintain control over Greece.

In 220 B.C., Philip V, an energetic and capable king, came to power over Macedon. He watched as Rome locked in deadly combat with Hannibal and attempted to give Hannibal support. For this, Rome never forgave him. Once Hannibal was defeated, Rome declared war upon Philip and, in 197 B.C., inflicted a decisive defeat upon him. Macedon lost its power over Greece and had to pay Rome a large indemnity. For the rest of his life, Philip kept cautiously out of trouble.

In 179 B.C., Philip died and was succeeded by his son, Perseus. Carefully Perseus prepared for revenge against Rome. His plans, however, miscarried. His allies betrayed him and he had to face the Roman army alone. He was beaten in battle in 168 B.C., the very year in which

Antiochus IV was profaning the Temple at Jerusalem. With that defeat the Macedonian monarchy was ended and Macedon was divided into four small republics.

Eumenes

If Rome could punish, it could also reward:

1 Maccabees 8:6. *How also Antiochus the great king of Asia . . . was discomfited by them* [the Romans];

. . . .

1 Maccabees 8:8. *And the country of India, and Media, and Lydia, . . . they took of him, and gave to king Eumenes.*

The Antiochus referred to here as the "great king of Asia" was, of course, Antiochus III, whose victories, and whose subsequent defeats by the Romans, were described earlier in this chapter (see page 47-48).

The Eumenes referred to is a king in western Asia Minor. At the time when the Jews were in Babylonian Exile, western Asia Minor made up a kingdom ruled by people known to the Greeks as Ludoi. These were the Ludim of the Bible (see page I-54) and the kingdom is known to us as Lydia. It reached a peak of prosperity and power under its king, Croesus, who reigned from 560 to 546 B.C. In 546 B.C. Lydia was conquered by Cyrus the Persian and its name disappeared from history. After the time of Alexander the Great, its people were rapidly hellenized. The Lydian language disappeared and was replaced by Greek.

In 283 B.C., when Asia Minor was loosely connected to the newly founded Seleucid Empire, a certain Macedonian viceroy named Philetaeros ruled over the city of Pergamum, in what had once been Lydia. He managed to make himself independent of the Seleucids after the death of Seleucus I Nicator and thus was founded the kingdom of Pergamum.

The nephew of Philetaeros succeeded to the throne as Eumenes I in 263 B.C. Soon after his accession he defeated Antiochus I, the second Seleucid monarch, and confirmed the independence of Pergamum. At this time the Gauls were creating havoc in Asia Minor, so that independence was a doubtful boon.

Eumenes I was succeeded by his nephew, Attalus I, however, in

241 B.C. and he managed to defeat the Gauls decisively in 235 B.C. That ended the Gallic menace and raised the prestige of Pergamum sky-high. It prospered under enlightened rule and learning was encouraged to the point where the library in Pergamum was second only to Alexandria in size and excellence. (Indeed, the jealous Ptolemies refused to export papyrus to Pergamum, thus depriving them of the material on which to copy books. The Pergamese invented a method of treating animal skins for the purpose—more permanent but also more expensive—and this gave us "parchment," a word derived from "Pergamum.")

In 197 B.C., Attalus I died and his son, Eumenes II, became king. This is the Eumenes of 1 Maccabees 8:8.

Eumenes II found himself facing Antiochus III at the height of that monarch's success, and for a while it looked as though Antiochus would retake all of Asia Minor. Eumenes II appealed to Rome, which had just beaten Philip V of Macedonia.

Rome responded and after defeating Antiochus III (with the army of Eumenes fighting alongside the Roman legions) his Asia Minor conquests were handed over to Pergamum, which now reached the peak of its power.

The writer of 1 Maccabees lists Lydia, Media, and India as being handed over to Pergamum. This is overenthusiastic of him. Lydia, representing the western half of Asia Minor, did, to be sure, make up the kingdom of Pergamum after the defeat of Antiochus. Indeed, Pergamum was almost Lydia come back to existence—but a Greek-speaking Lydia.

India and Media were, however, not given to Pergamum. They were far to the east and not even Rome could give them to anybody. Nevertheless, as the direct consequence of Antiochus' defeat, India, Media, and other eastern sections of the Seleucid Empire regained a permanent independence. If Pergamum did not gain them, the Seleucid Empire lost them.

The Grecians

And finally:

1 Maccabees 8:9. *Moreover how the Grecians had determined to come and destroy them* [the Romans];

1 Maccabees 8:10. *And that they* [the Romans] ... *fighting with them* [the Greeks] *slew many of them, and carried away captives* ...

To say that the Greeks had "determined to come and destroy" the Romans is to give entirely too much credit to the poor Greeks. They were in no position at the time to destroy anyone but themselves, but the writer of 1 Maccabees was living at a time when the Jews were intensely anti-Greek and this is reflected in the verses.

Actually, the crime of the Greeks was that some of their cities (united in what was called the "Achaean League") had, in the eyes of Rome, not been sufficiently active in supporting the Romans against Perseus of Macedon. The Greeks could not at that time possibly resist the power of Rome, and for Rome, attacking the Achaean League was like snatching a rattle from a baby. A thousand leading Greeks were carried away captive to Rome in 168 B.C.

Bacchides

Rome's conquests, its loyalty to its friends, its republican form of government, and its civic virtue are all described with a kind of lyrical exaggeration. Certainly there seemed some justification for the Jewish hope (at this time) in Rome.

Her defense of Pergamum against the Seleucids, and her strengthening of Pergamum at Seleucid expense, were very impressive. Surely, if Judea formed an alliance with Rome, similar benefits would befall her. (Of course, Rome supported her allies for her own reasons and, in the end, absorbed them all, enemies and allies alike, but the writer of 1 Maccabees did not have the advantage of our hindsight.)

The writer describes the emissary sent by Judas to Rome and the treaty of alliance formed with Rome, but one can only wonder if such an alliance were really formed. Perhaps it was merely reported by the forces of Judas as a kind of "war of nerves" against the Seleucids, who had ample reason to be in dread of the very name of Rome.

If the alliance was merely a propaganda weapon, it failed; and if it was real, it was a dead letter. Demetrius proceeded to move again against the rebels and Rome did nothing to help Judas.

1 Maccabees 9:1. . . . *when Demetrius heard that Nicanor and his host were slain in battle, he sent Bacchides and Alcimus into the land of Judea the second time, and with them the chief strength of his host:*

. . . .

1 Maccabees 9:3. . . . *the first month of the hundred fifty and second year* [160 B.C.] *they encamped before Jerusalem:*

The forces of Judas had themselves suffered numerous casualties in the fight against Nicanor, and in the face of a fresh army of Seleucids and Tories the spirits of many quailed. There were massive desertions and Judas found himself with only eight hundred men left.

The sensible thing to do was to retreat, but if he did that he would have been left without an army. A brave battle and an inspiring death might be better in the long run. That was the path he chose. In the battle that followed, the small band of rebels fought desperately, but the sheer weight of the enemy was insurmountable and they were virtually wiped out.

Judas Maccabeus died, with the rest, in 160 B.C., seven years after his father had sounded the trumpet call of revolt.

With the death of Judas, the Seleucids were, for the moment, triumphant, and Judea was now completely in the hands of the pro-Seleucid Jews:

1 Maccabees 9:23. *Now after the death of Judas the wicked began to put forth their heads in all the coasts of Israel, and there arose up all such as wrought iniquity.*

. . . .

1 Maccabees 9:25. *Then Bacchides chose the wicked men, and made them lords of the country.*

1 Maccabees 9:26. *And they made enquiry and search for Judas' friends, and brought them unto Bacchides, who took vengeance of them* . . .

Yet the defeat was not total. Demetrius had learned by the mistake of Antiochus and the laws against Judaism were not revived; the Temple was not profaned once more. The revolt had been a political failure, but it seemed to be a religious success.

Or was it? Could it not be that where force had failed, gradual assimilation under the guidance of a Tory high priest might succeed?

Jonathan

Judea was not to have a chance to find out, however. Two of the sons of Mattathias were dead, fallen in war against the Seleucids. Three remained, John the eldest, Simon the second, and Jonathan, the fifth and youngest.

It was Jonathan, who had already displayed talent as a leader of men, to whom the surviving rebels turned in the dark days after Judas' death, when the Seleucid general, Bacchides, controlled the country through his puppet high priest, Alcimus.

> 1 Maccabees 9:28. *For this cause all Judas' friends came together, and said unto Jonathan,*
>
> . . . .
>
> 1 Maccabees 9:30. . . . *we have chosen thee this day to be our prince and captain* . . .
>
> 1 Maccabees 9:31. *Upon this Jonathan took the governance upon him . . . and rose up instead of his brother Judas.*

The arms of the rebels were indeed feeble at this time, however. They could scarcely make head against the powerful Bacchides without help. John, the eldest brother, was sent to the Nabatean Arabs for such help and he was treacherously slain by them in 159 B.C. Only Jonathan and Simon were left now.

Fighting desperately, they led their rebel band to temporary safety across the Jordan River into the wilderness of the Transjordan:

> 1 Maccabees 9:48. *Then Jonathan and they that were with him leapt into Jordan, and swam over unto the farther bank* . . .
>
> . . . .
>
> 1 Maccabees 9:50. *Afterward returned Bacchides to Jerusalem, and repaired the strong cities in Judea* . . .

But Jonathan, safe in the Transjordan, mounted perpetual raids against Judea, and defeated or eluded all parties sent out after him. Eventually the Seleucids grew weary of endless petty fighting that drained their energies and weakened them in other more vital directions. They came to agreement with Jonathan; let him rule Judea as long as he maintained the peace of the kingdom and recognized Seleucid overlordship.

Alexander Epiphanes

This was, perhaps, an unstable situation, but it did not last long. After Demetrius I Soter had ruled, with comparative ability, for ten years, dynastic squabbles once again upset the Seleucid monarchy:

1 Maccabees 10:1. *In the hundred and sixtieth year* [152 B.C.] *Alexander, the son of Antiochus surnamed Epiphanes, went up and took Ptolemais* . . .

Actually, this Alexander was an impostor of obscure origin, whose real name was Balas. He pretended to be a son of Antiochus IV, and therefore a brother of the young Antiochus V Eupator whom Demetrius I had had killed.

Fortunately for himself, this Balas (known to us most commonly as Alexander Balas) had powerful support abroad. The Egyptian king, Ptolemy VI Philometer (see page 51), and the new king of Pergamum, Attalus II, who had succeeded his older brother Eumenes II in 160 B.C., both favored Alexander Balas. This was not because they believed Balas' claim to be the legitimate king, but because they were willing to do anything that would weaken their old enemy, the Seleucid Empire.

Both Pergamum and Egypt were allies of Rome, and Rome remembered now, perhaps, that Demetrius had become king without their permission (see page 68). At any rate, Rome, too, lent its support to Alexander Balas.

Demetrius was desperate. His troops might easily desert to the rising star of the impostor and he needed some reliable men to fight on his side. What about the Jews fighting under Jonathan? He had the best evidence that they were fierce fighting men and they might be bought. It was with that in mind, perhaps, that Demetrius named Jonathan to the post of governor of Judea.

With that appointment in his hand, Jonathan was able to take up residence in Jerusalem and suppress the pro-Seleucid faction which had been in power since the death of Judas eight years before.

To compete with this, Alexander Balas promptly offered Jonathan the post of high priest. This was a departure from custom. Till now the Seleucids had merely confirmed high priests who had been appointed by the Jews; this, however, was a direct Seleucid appointment. Nevertheless, Jonathan did not stand too firmly on the fine points but accepted:

> 1 Maccabees 10:21. *So in the seventh month of the hundred and sixtieth year, at the feast of the tabernacles, Jonathan put on the holy robe* . . .

Jonathan may have chosen this time of the year deliberately to take psychological advantage of a Messianic prophecy. A century before certain prophetic writings had appeared which were attributed to the earlier prophet Zechariah (see page I-664). These spoke of the ideal king receiving worship from all at the feast of the tabernacles:

> Zechariah 14:18. . . . *the Lord will smite the heathen that come not up to keep the feast of tabernacles.*

Jonathan might be well aware that the rigorously pious could not help but disapprove of a high priest who was not of the direct line of earlier high priests and who was but the appointee of a heathen king. By using Zechariah's words, he might have answered such objections in the eyes of the people generally, and he inaugurated a new high-priestly line that was to continue for over a century.

Demetrius again raised the stakes and finally granted Judea independence, adding to it Samaria and Galilee. Jonathan, however, remained with Alexander Balas. Either his resentment against Demetrius as the conqueror of Judas and the oppressor of the Jews was too great or, as is more likely, his cool estimate of the situation was that Demetrius was going to lose and his promises would not be kept.

In 150 B.C., Demetrius and Alexander Balas finally met in battle. Alexander was completely victorious and Demetrius was slain on the field of battle after a twelve-year reign. Alexander Balas ascended the throne in Antioch as Alexander Epiphanes.

Alexander Balas remembered his allies, forming a marital alliance with Egypt by marrying Cleopatra, daughter of Ptolemy VI. The two kings met with much ceremony, in Ptolemais, and Jonathan was called to the city to meet with them, too. There he was confirmed in his rule over Judea.

Demetrius II Nicator

This interval of happy-ending-for-everyone was not to continue. The only thing, it seemed, that ever continued was dynastic rivalry. The dead king, Demetrius I, had a son, another Demetrius, who was abroad in exile. He now returned, and with him was a band of Cretan mercenaries:

1 Maccabees 10:67. . . . *in the hundred threescore and fifth year* [147 B.C.] *came Demetrius son of Demetrius out of Crete into the land of his fathers* . . .

The civil war was renewed and the Jews were deeply involved, for the new Demetrius was completely hostile to Jonathan, who, after all, had turned against his father and had supported the usurping Alexander. The Jews, however, as in the days of Judas, withstood Demetrius' general, Apollonius, and won a resounding victory.

Ptolemy VI of Egypt, observing the new civil war, could not resist interfering. To be sure, he had placed Alexander Balas on the throne and had given him his daughter in marriage, but why be satisfied with an ally when you can have the kingdom itself?

The Egyptian monarch therefore invaded the Seleucid dominions, taking advantage of the confusion of the renewed civil wars. He passed by Judea without incident and took Antioch, making himself, for the moment, ruler of the Seleucid realm as well as of Egypt.

Alexander Balas, who was in the northern provinces at the time, dealing with a local rebellion, hastened to Antioch and the two armies met and fought in 145 B.C. Alexander Balas was defeated and his five-year reign was ended. He fled to Arabia, where he was murdered. The victor, Ptolemy VI, had been wounded in battle, however, and died soon after.

This left Demetrius the only contender remaining in the field and by default he became king as Demetrius II Nicator ("conqueror").

1 Maccabees 11:19. *By this means Demetrius reigned in the hundred threescore and seventh year.*

Antiochus VI

By now, however, the everlasting dynastic minuet had had deadly results. Mithridates I (see page 58) was still king of Parthia, and all the while that the Seleucid kings had been fighting useless battles in the west and growing steadily weaker, he had been expanding his own power constantly. In 147 B.C., just when Demetrius II had landed on the Seleucid shores, the Parthians took Babylonia, driving the Seleucids from an area that had been theirs for a hundred and fifty years.

The great empire which had been two thousand miles wide even as late as the time of Antiochus III had, in a mere half century, shrunk to almost nothing. It had come to include little more than the province of Syria.

Demetrius at the head of a mere nubbin of what had once been the Seleucid Empire—a nubbin, moreover, bled white by continuing warfare—found himself short on funds. Desperately he tried to economize at the expense of his army. This is certainly the most effective means of economizing from a sheer dollars-and-cents point of view since the army is almost always the greatest swallower of funds, but as many rulers both before and after the time of Demetrius II have found out, such economy is virtually suicide when the army controls the government.

A discontented army is bound to be a tempting tool in the hands of any ambitious general; especially since the old king, Alexander Balas, still had a young son in exile, one who might serve as a useful rallying device:

1 Maccabees 11:39. . . . *there was one Tryphon, that had been of Alexander's part afore, who, seeing that all the host murmured against Demetrius, went to Simalcue the Arabian, that brought up Antiochus the young son of Alexander,*

1 Maccabees 11:40. *And lay sore upon him to deliver him this young Antiochus, that he might reign in his father's stead . . .*

Meanwhile Jonathan was trying to profit once again through Seleucid troubles and offered to strike a bargain with Demetrius. Jonathan had been besieging the citadel in Jerusalem, which was still, after all this time, in Seleucid hands, and was not succeeding. He offered therefore to help Demetrius against his disaffected army, in return for Seleucid evacuation of the citadel.

Demetrius gladly accepted a contingent of three thousand tough Jewish fighters and used them to put down disorders in Antioch. He would not, however, abandon the citadel, and the outmaneuvered Jonathan waited angrily for the chance to strike back.

The chance came soon enough. Tryphon had managed to talk Simalcue into releasing his ward and, returning with him, raised the standard of revolt:

1 Maccabees 11:54. *After this returned Tryphon, and with him the young child Antiochus, who reigned, and was crowned.*

This was in 143 B.C. and the new boy king reigned as Antiochus VI Epiphanes Dionysus. He was merely a puppet, of course. The real ruler was Tryphon.

This was Jonathan's chance. He promptly transferred his support to the young Antiochus.

Lacedemonians

Apparently Jonathan during this period strove further to strengthen his appearance by judicious alliances abroad. The writer of 1 Maccabees chooses to describe two such alliances in detail, but out of considerations of prestige only, for neither alliance ever helped Jonathan. The first was a renewal of the alliance with Rome, which (if it existed at all) had been ineffective so far and continued ineffective.

The other was still more useless:

1 Maccabees 12:2. *He [Jonathan] sent letters also to the Lacedemonians . . .*

The Lacedemonians are the people living in Lacedemon, a region more commonly known to us as Sparta. They are therefore the Spartans.

Sparta, a city in southern Greece, had had a great history. In the time of Nebuchadnezzar and the Jewish Exile in Babylon, Sparta had been the most powerful of the Greek cities and it maintained this position for two additional centuries. Together with Athens, Sparta had defeated the Persian invasion under Xerxes (Ahasuerus) in 479 B.C.

Sparta

Then, after a long war with Athens, Sparta emerged victorious in 404 B.C. and for thirty years controlled Greece.

In 371 B.C., however, the Spartans had been defeated by the army of the Greek city of Thebes and, at one blow, fell from power and never regained it.

Sparta retired into sulky isolation. They refused to join the armies of Alexander the Great in his conquest of Persia (the only mainland Greeks to refuse) for they insisted that only Spartans could lead such an army. They were defeated on several occasions by Macedonian armies thereafter and, by the time of the Maccabees, Sparta had been reduced to a complete nonentity. Her alliance was worth nothing except, perhaps, for the glow cast about her by the glamour of her name and past history.

The basis of this alliance between Jews and Spartans was made a matter of family relationship. The writer of 1 Maccabees quotes letters that were supposed to have passed between the two peoples a century and a half before. These were quoted as saying:

1 Maccabees 12:21. *It is found in writing, that the Lacedemonians and Jews are brethren, and that they are of the stock of Abraham* . . .

This is an odd tradition that could only have been inspired to encourage a political marriage of convenience. No one takes it seriously, even though some scholars now maintain that Hebrew and Greek civilizations may have had some strands of origin in common.

Tryphon

But Tryphon wearied of the indirection of possessing power under the cover of the boy Antiochus VI and decided he would prefer the role of king, undisguised:

1 Maccabees 12:39. *Now Tryphon went about to get the kingdom of Asia, and to kill Antiochus the king, that he might set the crown upon his own head.*

This, he feared, might alienate his strongest ally, Jonathan. In order to prevent that, he maneuvered the Jewish leader into a trap, inviting him to come to Ptolemais with a small escort. For once, Jonathan's shrewdness deserted him and he accepted the invitation.

1 Maccabees 12:48. *Now as soon as Jonathan entered into Ptolemais, they of Ptolemais shut the gates, and took him* . . .

With that done, Tryphon felt that there would be sufficient confusion and uncertainty in Judea to make invasion of the land easy. In the course of this invasion, he rid himself finally of his two encumbrances:

1 Maccabees 13:23. *And when he came near to Bascama, he slew Jonathan, who was buried there.*

. . . .

1 Maccabees 13:31. *Now Tryphon dealt deceitfully with the young king Antiochus, and slew him.*

1 Maccabees 13:32. *And he reigned in his stead, and crowned himself king of Asia* . . .

This was in 142 B.C. Jonathan had led the Jewish forces for eighteen years with skill and ability and would be better known today if his career had not been overshadowed by the shorter but more glamorous one of his older brother, Judas.

Simon

But even now, one son of Mattathias was left alive; Simon, the second oldest. He was quickly elected the new leader:

> 1 Maccabees 13:8. *And they* [the people] *answered with a loud voice, saying, Thou* [Simon] *shalt be our leader instead of Judas and Jonathan thy brother.*

Simon attempted to ransom Jonathan but failed and when it was certain that Jonathan had been killed, he obtained the buried body and reburied him in Modein, the city where the Jewish revolt had broken out a quarter century before.

Simon prepared himself for renewed war:

> 1 Maccabees 13:33. *Then Simon built up the strong holds in Judea, and fenced them about . . . and laid up victuals therein.*

Furthermore, Simon now approached Demetrius II Nicator, who, all during the period of time when first Antiochus VI and then Tryphon had called themselves kings, had maintained an army and had insistently held on to his own claim. In return for Simon's offer of help, Demetrius now finally granted Judea formal independence:

> 1 Maccabees 13:41. *Thus the yoke of the heathen was taken away from Israel in the hundred and seventieth year* [142 B.C.].
> 1 Maccabees 13:42. *Then the people of Israel began to write in their instruments and contracts, In the first year of Simon the high priest, the governor and leader of the Jews.*

Independence was thus won a quarter century after the beginning of the revolt. The independence was symbolized by altering the system of dates. The year 142 B.C., which was Year 170 of the Seleucid era, became Year 1 of the "Era of the Maccabees."

Simon was religious and military leader of the Jews, having succeeded his brother as high priest and general. He did not call himself king, however. Perhaps he felt that, not being of the Davidic line, he could not be a true king of the Jews.

Soon after the gaining of their independence, the Jews successfully completed their long siege of the citadel in Jerusalem with its Seleucid garrison. The garrison, facing starvation, surrendered:

1 Maccabees 13:50. . . . *and when he* [Simon] *had put them* [the garrison] *out from thence, he cleansed the tower from pollutions:*

1 Maccabees 13:51. *And entered into it the three and twentieth day of the second month, in the hundred seventy and first year* [141 B.C.] . . .

And for the first time since Nebuchadnezzar's destruction of Jerusalem 445 years before, the land of Judah was completely free and the foot of no foreign soldier was to be found in Jerusalem. That freedom, alas, was to last no more than eighty years and was not to remain unbroken even in that short period.

Arsaces

Demetrius, having secured Jewish aid against Tryphon, attempted to strengthen himself in the east as well in preparation for the final showdown with the usurping general:

1 Maccabees 14:2. *But when Arsaces, the king of Persia and Media, heard that Demetrius was entered within his borders, he sent one of his princes* . . .

1 Maccabees 14:3. *Who went and smote the host of Demetrius, and took him, and brought him to Arsaces* . . .

Almost all the kings of Parthia (referred to here as Persia and Media) bore the throne-name of Arsaces, so that the entire dynasty is referred to as the Arsacids. The king who fought against Demetrius was the same Mithridates I who had come to the throne in the time of Antiochus IV and who was now approaching the end of his long reign of more than thirty years. His throne name was Arsaces V Epiphanes.

In 147 B.C., Mithridates I had taken Babylonia from the Seleucids and now, in 139 B.C., he capped his career by taking prisoner the

Seleucid monarch himself, the great-grandson of Antiochus the Great. Mithridates treated Demetrius kindly, however, and even gave him his sister's hand in marriage.

And meanwhile Simon ruled in peace over Judea and the power was made hereditary in his descendants.

Antiochus VII Sidetes

The imprisoned Demetrius had, abroad, a younger brother, Antiochus, who was now to make the attempt to seize the kingdom. He confirmed the independence of the Jewish state to avoid trouble in that direction, and then invaded the land:

1 Maccabees 15:10. *In the hundred threescore and fourteenth year* [138 B.C.] *went Antiochus into the land of his fathers: at which time all the forces came together unto him, so that few were left with Tryphon.*

Tryphon was eventually forced to flee the land and Antiochus was accepted as monarch, ruling as Antiochus VII Euergetes, although he is far better known as Antiochus VII Sidetes. The surname "Sidetes" is derived from the fact that he was brought up in the town of Side in southern Asia Minor.

Antiochus VII was the last vigorous monarch of the Seleucid line. Having gained the throne, he visualized the restoration of his kingdom to its former glories and broke with Simon. Once again (and for the last time) Judea found itself facing the threat of Seleucid invasion.

John Hyrcanus I

But Simon was growing old and was eager to transfer the responsibilities of government to younger men. He had three stalwart sons: Judas, John, and Mattathias:

1 Maccabees 16:2. *Wherefore Simon called his two eldest sons, Judas and John, and said unto them . . .*

1 Maccabees 16:3. . . . *I am old . . . be ye instead of me . . . and go and fight for our nation . . .*

Unfortunately, Simon had also a son-in-law, Ptolemy, who coveted power for himself. He therefore invited his father-in-law and brothers-in-law to a banquet.

1 Maccabees 16:14. . . . *in the hundred threescore and seventeenth year* [134 B.C.] . . .

Simon, Judas, and Mattathias came and, after they had drunk enough to be harmless, Ptolemy had them disarmed and murdered. Thus died Simon, the last of the five sons of Mattathias the priest, eight years after he had assumed the rule and thirty-three years after the beginning of the Jewish rebellion.

With the death of Simon, the Book of 1 Maccabees comes to an end. It is worth while, however, to add a short epilogue.

For a time it seemed that the early years of the rebellion had returned. Simon's remaining son, John (better known as John Hyrcanus), took to the hills with a guerrilla band to fight Ptolemy, who played the role of the Jewish Tories of the previous generation and called in Antiochus VII.

In 133 B.C. Antiochus invaded Judea and, after a prolonged siege, took Jerusalem. He accepted a large tribute, however, and left the land.

Then in 130 B.C., Antiochus VII, elated by his successes, turned to the east. Perhaps he could still win back the eastern provinces. The formidable Parthian king, Mithradates I, had died in 138 B.C. and had been succeeded by Phraates II (also called Arsaces VI Euergetes) and it may be that Antiochus felt the new king would be less vigorous than the old.

If so, he miscalculated. In 129 B.C. the Parthians won a great victory over Antiochus, who was killed. His brother, Demetrius II, was then released from Parthian imprisonment (that had endured ten years) and became the Seleucid king again. He remained so until 125 B.C., when he died and was succeeded by his son, Antiochus VIII.

However, with Antiochus VII had died every spark of Seleucid vigor. The kingdom was just a shadow now, destined to drag on in inglorious existence for another half century, but of no account whatever in international affairs.

Judea could ignore it and, under the rule of John Hyrcanus, it expanded its territories and entered into a half-century period of prosperity and glory. It was John Hyrcanus who felt himself strong enough to force the Idumeans to accept Judaism. He reigned till 104 B.C. and his son succeeded and, finally, found the dynasty to be well enough established to deserve the title of king.

For the first time since the destruction of the First Temple nearly five centuries before, the Jews had a king—but not, of course, of the line of David.

4. 2 MACCABEES

Jason of Cyrene

The second Book of Maccabees, written perhaps a century later
than the first, is not a continuation of the first, but is rather a parallel
history covering only the period to the death of Judas Maccabeus.
Whereas 1 Maccabees is primarily secular in character, 2 Maccabees
centers to a much greater extent on the story of the high-priestly factions and is primarily interested in religion.

It declares itself to be the abridgement of a much larger work:

> 2 Maccabees 2:23. *All these things, I say, being declared by Jason
> of Cyrene in five books, we will assay to abridge in one volume.*

Cyrene was a city on the north African coast about five hundred
miles west of the Nile. It was founded by Greek colonists in 631 B.C.
when Josiah ruled in Judah. It was at Cyrene that Pharaoh-hophra's
soldiers rebelled and declared Aahmes to be their king (see page I-580).
It was taken by Alexander the Great in 331 B.C. and it became part of
Ptolemaic Egypt. Cyrene was second only to Alexandria as a Jewish
center in Egypt.

Jason is, of course, a Greek name, but in the Greek period it was not
unusual for Jews to adopt Greek names that were close to the Hebrew
originals. Many a Joshua called himself Jason.

The original history of Jason of Cyrene is, unfortunately, lost. It
was written in Greek and so was the abridgement we call 2 Maccabees.

The abridger begins by quoting a pair of letters that have nothing

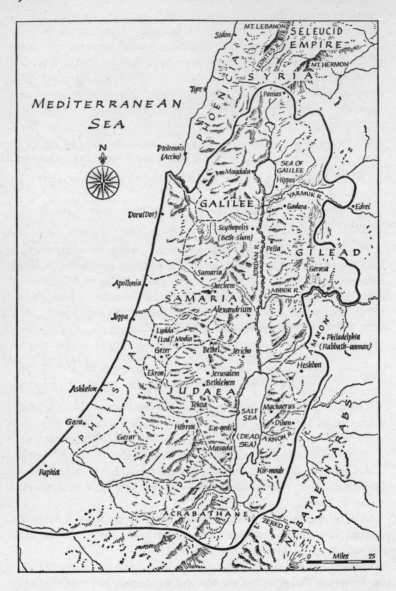

Palestine Under the Maccabees

really to do with the subject matter of the book, but urge the Jews in Egypt to keep the new feast of Hanukkah, even though it was not part of the Mosaic commandments. Since the feast commemorated events in Judea that may have seemed beyond the horizon to the Egyptian Jews, there might well have been a lack of motivation among the latter to celebrate. There would, instead, have been the usual religious conservatism against all innovations.

The two letters are dated:

2 Maccabees 1:7. *What time as Demetrius reigned, in the hundred threescore and ninth year* [143 B.C.], *we the Jews wrote unto you in the extremity of trouble that came upon us in those years* . . .

. . . .

2 Maccabees 1:10. *In the hundred fourscore and eighth year* [124 B.C.], *the people that were at Jerusalem . . . sent greeting and health unto Aristobulus, king Ptolemeus' master* . . .

The earlier letter was sent in the time of Demetrius II, just about the time that Jonathan was captured and killed by the usurper Tryphon (see page 85), one of the dark moments of the Jewish rebellion.

By the time the second letter was sent, Demetrius had just died and his young son, Antiochus VIII, was on a powerless throne. John Hyrcanus I was ruling in peace in Jerusalem.

On the Egyptian throne was Ptolemy VII "Physcon" (see page 51). He had reigned first with his older brother, Ptolemy VI, and then alone, from 170 B.C. to 116 B.C., the longest reign in Ptolemaic history. Aristobulus is apparently a learned Jew who was one of the scholars patronized by Ptolemy and therefore considered Ptolemy's teacher (or "master").

Naphthar

The writer of 2 Maccabees, in quoting the letter to Aristobulus, stresses the continuity of Jewish ritual. The letter seeks to prove that it was unbroken by the Exile into Babylonia. (The letter speaks of Babylonia, erroneously, as Persia.)

Thus, the letter states that at the time of the Exile, some of the priests preserved the fire of the altar in the hollow of a dry cistern. A

century and a half later, when Nehemiah was in Jerusalem, the fire was
recovered:

> 2 Maccabees 1:20. . . . *Neemias* [Nehemiah] . . . *did send of
> the posterity of those priests that had hid* . . . *the fire: but* . . .
> *they found no fire, but thick water* . . .

The "thick water" (that is, a viscous fluid) was brought up, and
used to help light a strong fire.

> 2 Maccabees 1:36. *And Neemias called this thing Nephthar, which
> is as much as to say, a cleansing* . . .

Naphthar or, as we would say, naphtha is a word that can be traced
back to the Persian "naft" and further back still to the Babylonian
"naptu." It is not surprising that Nehemiah, who had lived at the
Persian court, should use a Persian word for a substance that was un-
familiar to the Jews.

Naphtha is a viscous organic fluid which is inflammable. It is an
oil that issues forth from the rocks and its modern name is "petroleum"
(from Latin words meaning "rock oil"). The Middle East is one of the
great reservoirs of petroleum and even in ancient times there were
places where petroleum seeped out to the surface. Such seepages,
if set on fire, could give rise to "eternal flames," which would be of
important religious significance to many of the ancients. This was
particularly true in Persia, where such seepages were known and where
fire was, in any case, worshipped as a manifestation of Ahura Mazda,
lord of light (see page I-409).

Thus, when Nehemiah reported the find to the Persian monarch:

> 2 Maccabees 1:34. . . . *the king, inclosing the place, made it
> holy* . . .

It is doubtful that any historical value at all can be placed on this
legend, but it does seem that the writer must be at least aware of the
uses of natural naphtha seepage. And the passage is interesting as an
early reference to petroleum.

Judaism

Having completed his letter-quoting, the writer then goes on to
introduce his history concerning:

2 Maccabees 2:21. . . . *those that behaved themselves manfully to their honour for Judaism* . . .

This is the first known use of the term Judaism.

Onias

The historical section of 2 Maccabees begins with the picture of peace and quiet before the coming of Antiochus IV:

2 Maccabees 3:1. . . . *the holy city [Jerusalem] was inhabited with all peace, and the laws were kept very well, because of the godliness of Onias the high priest* . . .

Here is a reference to the last of the legitimate high priests, stretching in an unbroken line from Zadok, who served under Solomon when the First Temple was built (see page I-322). The continuity had been maintained even during the Babylonian Exile, and Zadokite high priests were in charge when the Second Temple was constructed.

In the Book of Nehemiah, the line of high priests is carried down to Jaddua:

Nehemiah 12:11. *And Joiada begat Jonathan, and Jonathan begat Jaddua.*

From passages in the histories of Josephus, the first-century Jewish historian, it is thought that this Jaddua was high priest at the time that Alexander the Great passed through Judea. It was Jaddua who, according to legend, confronted Alexander in his high-priestly regalia (see page 39).

Jaddua was high priest from about 350 B.C. to 300 B.C. Following him, according to the information given by Josephus, was Onias I, who held the office from 300 B.C. to 280 B.C. It was in his time that Ptolemy I took Jerusalem and began the century-long domination of Ptolemaic Egypt over Judea. He is also the Onias who, according to the dubious story in 1 Maccabees, first formed an alliance with Sparta (see page 83).

In the letter quoted there as having been written to Sparta in Maccabean times, it is stated:

1 Maccabees 12:7. *There were letters sent in times past unto Onias the high priest from Darius, who reigned then among you* . . .

(Of course, no Darius ever reigned over the Spartans. Elsewhere in the chapter the Spartan king is referred to as Areus. He reigned from 309 to 265 B.C.)

Onias I was succeeded by a son, Simon I, by another son, Eleazar, and about 276 B.C. by a brother, Manasseh. Then Onias II, a son of Simon I, became high priest in 250 B.C. It may have been under Onias II that the Greek translation of the Bible, the Septuagint, was produced in Egypt.

Onias II was eventually succeeded by his son, Simon II, who was mentioned by Jesus, son of Sirach (see page I-516), with great approval:

> Ecclesiasticus 50:1. *Simon the high priest, the son of Onias, who in his life repaired the house again, and in his days fortified the temple . . .*

Simon II, also called "Simon the Just," was high priest from about 219 B.C. to 196 B.C. It was in his time that Antiochus III the Great wrested Judea from the Ptolemies. The Jews did not participate in this war and Antiochus III left them in peace.

In 196 B.C. the son of Simon the Just, Onias III, succeeded to the office of high priest. He too is depicted as pious and holy, wedded to the conservative doctrines of Judaism. It is Onias III who is referred to in 2 Maccabees 3:1.

Seleucus

The felicity of the period is perhaps exaggerated by the historian in order to make a dramatic contrast with the horrors to follow. Even the Seleucid monarch himself is depicted as patronizing the Jewish rites:

> 2 Maccabees 3:3. . . . *Seleucus king of Asia of his own revenues bare all the costs belonging to the service of the sacrifices.*

The Seleucus here referred to is Seleucus IV Philopater, elder son of Antiochus the Great, who succeeded to the throne in 187 B.C. His generosity to the Temple seems most strange, for the Seleucid monarchy was virtually bankrupt at this time. The defeat of Antiochus III by Rome, just a few years before, had placed the load of a back-breaking indemnity upon the land. It could be paid only by rifling the various temples of their hoarded wealth. Antiochus III had died in a popular uprising when he attempted such rifling and his son was in no position to pay to a Temple when circumstances were much more likely to force him to steal from one.

Indeed, the book goes on at once to point out that this was actually the case.

Simon

As often happens, external trouble comes upon a land because internal trouble invites it:

2 Maccabees 3:4. . . . *one Simon . . . , who was made governor of the temple, fell out with the high priest about disorder in the city.*

During post-Exilic days, the high priest had been both the religious and the civil head of Judea, but this sound policy came to an end during the time of Onias II. This was when Judea was still under the control of Egypt and the strong king, Ptolemy III Euergetes, was on the throne.

For some reason Onias II refused to pay the annual tax laid upon the Temple. This was unwise and would have led to serious troubles had not Onias' nephew, Joseph, taken action. He persuaded Onias II to let him go to Egypt and there he managed to placate Ptolemy III. He also managed to win for himself the post of "governor of the temple." In other words, the prerogatives of Onias II were henceforth restricted to matters of religion and his civil powers were given to Joseph.

Now there were two lines of Zadokite officials in Jerusalem—a religious line and a civil line. Onias III was of the religious line and Simon (the son of Joseph) was of the civil line.

Naturally, when powers formally confined to one official come to be shared by two there are constant quarrels over jurisdiction. The fact that Onias III and Simon were second cousins did not make the quarrels less bitter.

In such quarrels, one or the other of the disputants is bound to appeal to some outside power. This Simon did. He reported to the Seleucid governor of the district that the Temple was filled with wealth that was being withheld from the king.

Seleucus IV, who needed money badly, sent an official named Heliodorus to investigate the matter.

The attempt of Heliodorus to investigate the Temple is described in the book as having been thwarted by supernatural means. Afterward, Heliodorus grew friendly with Onias. It is possible, however, if history is viewed cynically, to suppose that Onias bribed Heliodorus to "lay off" and that Heliodorus conceived the idea of gaining power for himself with, perhaps, the financial help of the Temple at Jerusalem.

In 175 B.C., Heliodorus assassinated Seleucus IV. He then made some sort of attempt to make himself king but Seleucus' younger brother, Antiochus, was returning from Roman captivity (see page 48) and he seized the throne as Antiochus IV Epiphanes.

Jason the brother of Onias

If Antiochus IV knew of (or suspected) any intrigue between the high priest and his brother's assassin, he would naturally have harsh feelings toward the former. As for Onias III, fearing reprisal, he would be bound to cast about for help to Egypt, a land with which Antiochus IV intended to go to war.

Antiochus IV could scarcely be expected to march against Egypt, leaving an enemy such as Onias III in his rear to rouse, perhaps, a Jewish rebellion that would negate any Egyptian victories he might gain.

Again, rivalries within the family of the high priest paved the way for infringing upon Jewish prerogatives. Onias had a brother, Joshua, who coveted the office of high priest. Joshua was a Hellenizer rather than a conservative and showed it by adopting the Greek name of Jason.

> 2 Maccabees 4:7. . . . *when Antiochus . . . took the kingdom, Jason the brother of Onias laboured underhand to be high priest,*
> 2 Maccabees 4:8. *Promising unto the king . . . three hundred and threescore talents of silver, and of another revenue eighty talents:*
> 2 Maccabees 4:9. *Beside this, he promised to assign an hundred and fifty more, if he might have licence to set him up a place for exercise . . .*

The desire to be high priest was not only a matter of honor and prestige. Whoever was high priest controlled the revenues of the Temple, which were considerable, and was therefore (if he were not scrupulously honest) on the highroad to wealth. Jason obviously planned to enrich himself through graft, particularly since he maneuvered to maintain what we would today call the "gymnasium concession" for himself as well. The aristocratic youth of Judea, eager to participate in the Greek way of life, would pay for the privilege and a good part of the money would stick to Jason's hands.

For all this, Jason was willing to share some of the loot with Antiochus IV for he needed the king's word to be made high priest. Since Antiochus IV needed money badly for his projected Egyptian war, the arrangement with Jason was made.

Now Antiochus could march off into Egypt.

Menelaus

When it came time to remit an installment of the promised payment to Antiochus IV, Jason sent an emissary:

> 2 Maccabees 4:23. . . . *Jason sent Menelaus, the aforesaid Simon's brother, to bear the money unto the king . . .*

It was a case of brothers all around. A few years before, Simon had coveted the post held by Onais III and had therefore intrigued with Seleucus IV. Now the brother of Simon coveted the post held by Jason, the brother of Onias III, and intrigued with Antiochus IV, the brother of Seleucus IV.

Simon's brother was named Onias but he took the Greek name of Menelaus, and once Jason was so incautious as to give him entry to Antiochus, Menelaus seized the chance at once. He offered Antiochus three hundred talents more than Jason had agreed to pay. This was fine as far as Antiochus IV was concerned. He was willing to sell the high priesthood to the highest bidder at any time. Jason was forced to flee across the Jordan and Menelaus became high priest.

Daphne

Meanwhile, Onias III, who was looked upon by all conservative Jews as the only legitimate high priest, was living in semi-imprisonment in Antioch. When the news of Menelaus' open-faced thievery reached Onias (Menelaus was reported to have used certain gold vessels of the Temple as bribes to Seleucid officials), the old high priest denounced the usurper:

> 2 Maccabees 4:33. . . . Onias . . . reproved him [Menelaus], and withdrew himself into a sanctuary at Daphne, that lieth by Antiochia.

Daphne was a suburb of Antioch, about five miles away, and undoubtedly Onias made use of a Greek temple, from which it would have been sacrilege, in Greek eyes, to remove him.

Menelaus, however, persuaded the Seleucid commander in the district (with bribes perhaps) to induce Onias to leave the sanctuary, by giving oath for his safety. Once Onias was out of the Temple, he was promptly murdered. This was in 170 B.C.

The murder at once became a cause célèbre. The Jews were on the verge of rebellion at this slaughter of the last legitimate high priest. Even many Greeks were horrified at the sacrilege committed against their own temple. Antiochus IV, returning from the suppression of a rebellion in part of his dominion in Asia Minor, was forced to quiet the populace by executing the officer who had committed the deed.

Scholars are quite certain that it is Onias III to whom the writer of the Book of Daniel refers in his passage about a Messiah, or "anointed one" (see page I-613); that is, a high priest:

> Daniel 9:26. And after threescore and two weeks shall Messiah be cut off . . .

After that, Antiochus IV made a second foray into Egypt, achieved complete success but was driven out by a Roman ultimatum (see page 52). He then turned against Jerusalem, which had been the scene of disorders between the factions of Jason and Menelaus, took the city, pillaged the Temple, and killed many Jews who resisted, all with the help and the official backing of Menelaus.

Eleazar

The Temple was then profaned and rededicated to Zeus, and Judaism was outlawed. The writer of 2 Maccabees gives details lacking in

1 Maccabees concerning the martyrdom of conservative Jews who would not give up their religious customs even under torture.

Since such stories are not told in the more reliable 1 Maccabees, one might wonder if they are not merely atrocity stories made up after the fact. However, the history of Nazi Germany has proved to all of us that atrocity stories are sometimes simple truth, and understatements at that.

In any case, the stories, whether strictly true or propaganda inventions, are told in grisly detail as edifying examples of loyalty to the death. These are the first martyr-tales in the Judeo-Christian tradition and formed a precedent for the many later such tales that formed so large a part of early Christian literature.

An example is that of Eleazar:

2 Maccabees 6:18. *Eleazar, one of the principal scribes, an aged man, . . . was constrained to . . . eat swine's flesh.*

2 Maccabees 6:19. *But he, choosing rather to die gloriously, . . . spit it forth, and came of his own accord to the torment.*

2 Maccabees 6:20. *As it behoved them to come, that are resolute to stand out against such things . . .*

Eleazar is described as dying on the rack, even though every attempt was made to persuade him to go through a nominal acquiescence to paganism. An even more gruesome tale is told of the torture and death of a woman and her seven sons.

Alcimus

Thereafter the tale passes on to the rebellion of the Jews under the leadership of Judas Maccabeus. The same story told in 1 Maccabees is repeated, though, it is generally thought, less reliably.

The deaths of the villains of the piece are given in considerable (but implausible) detail. Thus, Antiochus IV is described as dying in lingering torments from a loathsome disease, and as attempting to make up for his evils in order to recover—even vowing to become a Jew.

Menelaus was executed by the Seleucids themselves in the reign of Antiochus V Eupator. He was left to rot unburied (a supremely terrible fate in the eyes of the Jews of the time).

When Demetrius I Soter became king he was approached by still another representative of the Zadokite line:

2 Maccabees 14:3. *Now one Alcimus, who had been high priest, and had defiled himself wilfully in the times of their mingling with the Gentiles, . . .*

2 Maccabees 14:4. *Came to king Demetrius in the hundred and one and fiftieth year* [161 B.C.] . . .

Alcimus was accepted as high priest by Demetrius and led invasions into Judea, in the course of one of which there took place the battle in which Judas Maccabeus was killed.

For a while Alcimus ruled over Jerusalem as a Seleucid puppet. His end is not told in 2 Maccabees, which ends with Judas' last victory over Nicanor. It is, however, described in 1 Maccabees:

1 Maccabees 9:54. . . . *in the hundred fifty and third year* [159 B.C.], . . . *Alcimus commanded that the wall of the inner court of the sanctuary should be pulled down . . .*

1 Maccabees 9:55. *And as he began to pull down, even at that time was Alcimus plagued . . .*

1 Maccabees 9:56. *So Alcimus died at that time with great torment.*

That was the end of the Zadokites, if Alcimus was indeed one. Seven years later, Jonathan, brother of Judas Maccabeus, was made high priest (see page 80) and a new line, non-Zadokite in origin, was initiated.

3 Maccabees

There are other books dealing with the general period of the Maccabees that have never been considered canonical by any important group and are therefore not included even in the Apocrypha.

The Book of 3 Maccabees, the best known of these, is a work of fiction written probably by an Alexandrian Jew toward the end of the first century B.C., or even later, when Roman rule was becoming increasingly oppressive.

Just as the Book of Esther was written in Seleucid times to encourage Jews of that period with tales of miraculous rescues under a previous oppressor, so 3 Maccabees was written in Roman times for the same purpose through use of the same literary device.

The time of the incidents told in the book actually falls a generation before the Maccabean revolt and the Maccabees themselves play no part in it.

The book opens in the last decades of Ptolemaic control of Judea. Ptolemy IV Philometer of Egypt and Antiochus III of the Seleucid Empire are at war. Eventually Antiochus is to be the victor, but the book opens at a stage where Ptolemy has just won a victory in southern Judea (at Raphia, near Gaza), in 217 B.C.

Flushed with victory, Ptolemy enters Jerusalem and conceives a desire to enter the sanctuary of the Temple, where only the high priest might enter. (In later years, the Roman general, Pompey, entered the sanctuary and that incident might have helped inspire this story.) Ptolemy IV, unlike Pompey, is thwarted by the opposition of the high priest and the people and, according to the story, by divine intervention as well.

Ptolemy IV decides to seek revenge by having all the Jews of Alexandria killed. He plans to shut them into the hippodrome and have them trampled by five hundred elephants who are first maddened with wine. On three successive days, this plan is prevented by divine intervention and, eventually, angels turn the elephants back on the Egyptian army.

At once Ptolemy IV turns from persecuting the Jews to befriending them (as Ahasuerus does in the Book of Esther) and all ends in happiness and triumph.

As for 4 Maccabees, written about the same time as 3 Maccabees, that is essentially a sermon on the value of martyrdom. The martyr atones for the sins of others and achieves eternal blessedness in heaven. The author uses as his examples the cases of Eleazar and of the woman and her seven sons, which were described in 2 Maccabees.

Finally, 5 Maccabees is a sober history of the Maccabean period from beginning to end. However, its first part is based on 1 and 2 Maccabees and its remainder is based on Josephus, so it adds nothing to what is known from other sources.

5. MATTHEW

The New Testament

The books considered part of the Biblical canon by the Jews are
thirty-nine in number, and all have been considered in the first volume
of this book.

The central theme of the Bible, in Jewish eyes, is the contract or
covenant entered into between God and the Jewish people. The first
mention of this covenant is God's promise to give Canaan to the
descendants of Abraham.

Genesis 15:18. *In the same day the Lord made a covenant with
Abram [Abraham], saying, Unto thy seed have I given this land,
from the river of Egypt unto the great river, the river Euphrates . . .*

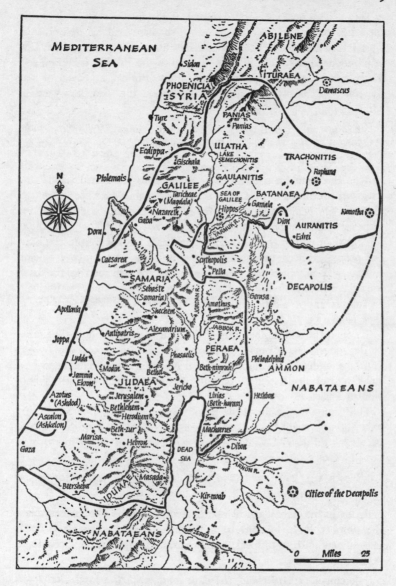

The Dominions of Herod the Great

This promise was repeated several times in Genesis, and clearly there had to be some return made by Abraham and his descendants. This return was made through the Israelites' acceptance of the Law as pronounced at Mount Sinai, according to the Biblical tradition, and incorporated into the first five books of the Bible. The covenant was therefore specifically mentioned again when the Israelites were at Mount Sinai.

Exodus 34:27. *And the Lord said unto Moses, Write thou these words: for after the tenor of these words I have made a covenant with thee and with Israel.*

After the Israelites entered and occupied the "Promised Land," the covenant continued to hold. They were to remain God's special charge, a people "peculiar" to Him, and their stay in the land was to continue in peace and security, as long as they adhered to the Law and, therefore, to their end of the bargain. When Israel fell away from the Law, the people received the punishment due those who broke a solemn contract. Then, when the people repented and returned to the Law, they were always forgiven. This cycle of apostasy and punishment, repentance and forgiveness, is the constant theme of the Book of Judges (see page I-232).

Through the Biblical account of the centuries that follow the period of the judges, the covenant is broken on numerous occasions by the Israelites. Indeed, it would seem to have been adhered to by only a small, and often persecuted, minority until after the return from Babylonian Exile.

Thus, some of the pre-Exilic prophets conceived of God as growing weary of a covenant that seemed never to be kept. The prophet Hosea names his third son Lo-ammi ("not my people"), stating this to have been at God's direction:

Hosea 1:9. *Then said God, Call his name Lo-ammi: for ye are not my people, and I will not be your God.*

Again, in the eschatological visions recorded in the Book of Jeremiah, the prophet looks forward to a triumphant day when God would make a new start, so to speak, with his people; wipe the slate clean and begin again:

Jeremiah 31:31. *Behold, the days come, saith the Lord, that I will make a new covenant with the house of Israel, and with the house of Judah . . .*

The followers of Jesus came early to believe that in the teachings of Jesus was to be found exactly this new covenant; a new contract between God and man, replacing the old one with Israel that dated back to Sinai and even beyond that to Abraham.

Thus, in the Epistle to the Hebrews (traditionally written by the Apostle Paul), this is specifically stated.

Hebrews 8:6. . . . he [Jesus] *is the mediator of a better covenant, which was established upon better promises.*

The writer then goes on to quote from Jeremiah to show that the coming of such a new and better covenant was predicted.

The word "testament" is used in the Bible as a synonym for "covenant." Thus Jesus himself, shortly before his trial and conviction, is quoted as referring to a new covenant to which his death is to bear witness:

Matthew 26:27. *And he took the cup, and gave thanks, and gave it to them, saying, Drink ye all of it;*
Matthew 26:28. *For this is my blood of the new testament . . .*

(The adjective "new" was not present in the earliest versions but seems to have been added later to emphasize the fresh turn taken in the scheme of things with the advent of Jesus. The Revised Standard Version keeps the older word for testament and omits the adjective, making the passage read, "For this is my blood of the covenant," a reading with which the Jerusalem Bible agrees.)

The Jewish Scriptures, dealing with the older covenant, can therefore be referred to as the "Old Testament." The books written about Jesus and his earliest disciples are called the "New Testament."

The Christian versions of the Bible include both Old and New Testaments. Christians consider them equally inspired, but with the New Testament representing the fulfillment and climactic completion of the Old. The Jews, on the other hand, adhere to the original covenant only and to them the Old Testament is the whole of the Bible.

The Gospel According to St. Matthew

The New Testament opens with four different biographies of Jesus by, according to tradition, Matthew, Mark, Luke, and John, in that

order. Each of these biographies is called a "gospel" and the second
is specifically so named:

> Mark 1:1. *The beginning of the gospel of Jesus Christ, the Son
> of God . . .*

The word gospel is from the Anglo-Saxon "god spell" meaning "good
news." In other words, the term refers not so much to the biography
of Jesus as to the higher meaning of his life. The story of Jesus is
the story of the coming of the Messiah, the initiation of the new
covenant between God and man, the arrival of salvation—and this
certainly must be considered good news.

The Greek form of the word is "evangelos" ("bringing good news")
and the four biographers of Jesus are therefore called "the four evangelists."

Each of the evangelists is given the title "saint." This is from the
Latin "sanctus" meaning "holy." In the Old Testament the term is used
in the Book of Daniel to represent those Jews who are faithful to the
Law despite the pressure of Seleucid persecution.

> Daniel 7:21. . . . *the same horn* [Antiochus IV] *made war with
> the saints, and prevailed against them . . .*

Among Christians, it means, in part, those pious and godly people
who keep themselves from all corruption, are devoted to the teachings
of Jesus, and are the object of God's particular love.

The first three gospels, those of Matthew, Mark, and Luke, are very
similar (although they are by no means identical). They are therefore
called the "synoptic gospels." The word "synoptic" is from Greek
terms meaning "with one eye." The three gospels can be placed side
by side, in other words, and viewed simultaneously with a single glance
without the contents going badly out of focus.

Matthew is the first of the gospels in the New Testament because,
according to early tradition, it was the first to be written. This, however, is now doubted by nearly everyone. The honor of primacy is
generally granted to Mark, which is the second gospel in the Bible as
it stands.

Matthew incorporates almost all of Mark and, in addition, includes
material which is thought by some to belong to a still earlier collection
of sayings of Jesus. This collection is now lost and its existence can be

deduced only indirectly. It is usually termed Q for *Quelle*, the German word for "source."

There is some possibility that Matthew was written originally in Aramaic. At least a Christian writer of the second century, Papias, is quoted by a somewhat later writer as having referred to Matthew composing his work "in the Hebrew language." One would suppose Aramaic to have been meant by that since that was the common speech in the Judea of New Testament times (see page I-446). There is no certainty that Papias in referring to Matthew's gospel is referring to the one we now have and call by Matthew's name.

In any case, if Matthew was originally written in Aramaic, it was quickly translated into Greek and the Aramaic original (if it existed at all) was lost. The Jerusalem Bible speculates that the Aramaic version of Matthew was indeed the oldest of the gospels (could it have been Q?) and was the source used by Mark. Matthew was then translated into Greek (our present version) and Mark was used as an additional source.

Certainly Matthew is the only book of the New Testament that can possibly have been first written in Aramaic. It seems quite certain that all the other books of the New Testament were first written in Greek.

Little can be said as to the time when Matthew was written. From the references to the destruction of the Temple, which are found in various places in the gospel, it is often suggested that the book reached its present form shortly after the fateful year of A.D. 70.

Matthew

But who was Matthew? The name is associated with the first gospel by a tradition which seems to trace back to the reference by Papias, mentioned earlier, to a gospel written by Matthew.

Matthew is the English form of the Greek "Mattathias" or, in Hebrew Mattathiah ("the gift of God"). It is a name that grew common by New Testament times, partly because of the great pride of the Jews in the achievements of the Maccabean period. Mattathias is, of course, the name of the father of Judas Maccabeus and the heroic initiator of the revolt against the Seleucids (see page 54).

Matthew is also the name of one of the disciples chosen by Jesus, according to this gospel.

Matthew 9:9. *And . . . Jesus . . . saw a man, named Matthew, sitting at the receipt of custom: and he saith unto him, Follow me. And he [Matthew] arose, and followed him.*

Christian tradition points to this particular Matthew as the author of this gospel, but there is no evidence beyond that tradition.

It is annoying that the gospels do not carry a clear statement of authorship in the modern fashion, but there are several possible reasons for anonymity. Holy books, in the Jewish tradition, rarely carried any notice of real authorship but were assigned to some ancient worthy. Indeed, there might be considered the very real force of the feeling that a truly holy book was inspired by God and that the worldly author acted only as a mouthpiece and deserved no credit.

On a more mundane level, the time of the writing of the gospels was a hard one for Christians. Jewish hostility was pronounced and so was Roman hostility. The sharp persecution by the Emperor, Nero, was not long in the past and, in the aftermath of the Jewish rebellion, the Jews that survived were resentful, indeed, of Christian failure to join the rebellion. It might well be that a gospel writer preferred to remain anonymous out of considerations of personal safety.

Jesus Christ

The notion of the coming of the Messiah must have had hard sledding in the Maccabean era. Judas Maccabeus had about him a heroism that might easily have been equated with the vision of the Messiah as a conquering king. And when he died, that vision might easily have been transferred to the first few of his successors, since under them the Jewish state briefly returned to a period of glory such as it had not known since the days of Solomon.

Certainly, if a comparatively feeble individual such as Zerubbabel could be greeted as the Messiah by Haggai (see page I-662), one of the heroic Maccabees might have been.

But it had been stressed over and over again in the prophetic books of the Old Testament that the Messiah would have to be an offspring of the line of David. Zerubbabel had indeed been such an offspring, but the Maccabees had not, and the Maccabees therefore could not include the Messiah among their number, in the view of pious Jews, no matter what other arguments there might be in favor of it.

The Messiah still belonged to the future, therefore, in the time of the Maccabees. While the Maccabean kingdom was prosperous, Messianic longings could be muted, but when the kingdom fell and Judea came under the domination of Rome, those longings sharpened again. Matthew begins his good news, or gospel, with the announcement of the coming of the Messiah:

Matthew 1:1. *The book of . . . Jesus Christ . . .*

The Hebrew word Messiah means "the anointed one." The Greek word "khrisma" is the oil used for anointing (our word "cream" traces back to "khrisma"). The Messiah, to whom such oil is applied would be "Khristos" in Greek, "Christus" in Latin, "Christ" in English. Since Jesus is the Greek form of the Hebrew name Joshua, the first verse of Matthew is equivalent to "The book of . . . Joshua the Messiah . . ."

David

To someone as steeped in the Jewish tradition as Matthew, it is obvious that the first task to be undertaken if the story of the Messiah is to be told is to demonstrate that he *is* the Messiah. And to do that, it must be shown, first of all, that the Messiah is a member of the line of David. Matthew therefore begins with a genealogy.

Matthew 1:1. *The book of the generation of Jesus Christ, the son of David, the son of Abraham.*

The genealogy begins with Abraham, who is by no means the first man, but is the one with whom God first made a covenant relating to the Jewish people who were to descend from him. From the Jewish interpretation of history as the tale of a covenant between man and God, a covenant to be fulfilled by the Messiah, one would naturally begin with Abraham, and Matthew with his deep-ingrained Jewishness does just this.

Matthew follows a highly artificial scheme in presenting this genealogy:

Matthew 1:17. . . . *all the generations from Abraham to David are fourteen generations; and from David until the carrying away into Babylon are fourteen generations; and from the carrying away into Babylon unto Christ are fourteen generations.*

Why Matthew should feel it necessary to establish such symmetry is not certain. Perhaps he felt that by pointing out the great events that took place after two sets of fourteen generations, he made it reasonable that one ought to expect the Messiah after a third set of fourteen generations.

Or it may be that there is numerological significance now lost or that Matthew was trying to set up some acrostic device that can no longer be followed. In any case, in order to obtain his sets of fourteen, Matthew was forced to distort the genealogy, and this can scarcely be considered as adding to the plausibility of whatever argument he might have had in mind.

Rachab

The first set of fourteen are: (1) Abraham, (2) Isaac, (3) Jacob, (4) Judas [Judah], (5) Phares [Perez], (6) Esrom [Hezron], (7) Aram [Ram], (8) Aminadab, (9) Naasson [Nahshon], (10) Salmon, (11) Booz [Boaz], (12) Obed, (13) Jesse, and (14) David.

The names down to Perez are given in Genesis and the remainder are given in Ruth.

Included in the list are three women, and, oddly enough, each of the three is, in one way or another, tainted. The first appears as follows:

Matthew 1:3. *And Judas* [Judah] *begat Phares* [Perez] *and Zara* [Zerah] *of Thamar* [Tamar] . . .

Zerah is mentioned because he was a twin brother of Perez and both were born at the same time. However, it was through Perez that David and, therefore, Jesus traced their descent. Tamar begot them of Judah by a kind of deceit that was justified according to patriarchal custom, but in doing so, she played the part of a harlot:

Genesis 38:15. *When Judah saw her, he thought her to be an harlot; because she had covered her face.*

The other two women are mentioned shortly after:

Matthew 1:5. *And Salmon begat Booz* [Boaz] *of Rachab* [Rahab]; *and Booz* [Boaz] *begat Obed of Ruth* . . .

Ruth was, of course, a Moabite woman, something which would make a strict Jew of New Testament times uneasy, even if she were an ancestress of David.

The real curiosity, however, is Rahab. The tale of both Tamar and Ruth are given in some detail in the Old Testament, but nothing at all is mentioned, at least in the canonical books, of any marriage between Salmon and Rahab.

Salmon is mentioned at the end of the Book of Ruth as part of the line of descent going from Perez to David, a passage which Matthew uses as reference. In Ruth, however, no wife is mentioned for Salmon.

In the Book of 1 Chronicles, a person with a name similar to Salmon is mentioned in the genealogical tables:

1 Chronicles 2:51. *Salma the father of Beth-lehem* . . .

If this Salma is the same as the Salmon who is David's great-great-grandfather, then the verse might signify that Salmon was the first of the family to settle in Bethlehem. He may even have led the contingent that took it from the Canaanities. But here too no wife is mentioned.

Who, then, is Rahab? There is a Rahab in the Old Testament, and she is the woman who sheltered Joshua's spies when they entered Jericho (see page I-211). This woman, however, did not merely play the part of a harlot, as Tamar did. According to the Biblical statement, she *was* a harlot.

Joshua 2:1. *And Joshua . . . sent out . . . two men to spy . . . And they went, and came into an harlot's house, named Rahab, and lodged there.*

Can this be the Rahab referred to as Salmon's wife? Chronologically it is possible. If David was born in 1050 B.C. as the youngest son of Jesse, who might therefore himself have been born about 1100 B.C., it is quite possible that Jesse's grandfather might have been a warrior between 1200 B.C. and 1170 B.C., when Joshua's conquest might have taken place.

It is very likely that, in later Jewish tradition, Rahab was viewed as a convert to Judaism after the fall of Jericho, and as meriting a reward for her protection of the spies. If she were a convert, like Ruth, she might very well merit a part of the ancestry of David, as Ruth did.

Of course, one wonders how much significance to give to the term "harlot." She might, conceivably, have been the priestess of a Canaanite goddess and as such may have engaged in fertility rites. This would make her a harlot in the puritanical eyes of the Jewish Yahvists, but surely not an ordinary harlot in the modern sense.

Matthew may have mentioned these because each was involved in a colorful event taken note of in the Old Testament and probably popular among its Jewish readers and easily coated with legend. For this reason he may have fallen prey to the temptation of pedantry, and displayed his knowledge of and interest in the Scriptures. On the other hand, one might also reason that if Moabites and harlots are in the line of Jesus' ancestry, it might signify that Jesus arose from all kinds of people and therefore came to suffer for all kinds of people, the sinful as well as the saint, the Gentile as well as the Jew.

The Wife of Urias

The list of fourteen names following David, down to the Babylonian captivity, are: (1) Solomon, (2) Roboam [Rehoboam], (3) Abia [Abijam], (4) Asa, (5) Josaphat [Jehoshaphat], (6) Joram, (7) Ozias [Uzziah or Azariah], (8) Joatham [Jotham], (9) Achaz [Ahaz], (10) Ezekias [Hezekiah], (11) Manasses [Manasseh], (12) Amon, (13) Josias [Josiah], and (14) Jechonias [Jehoiachin].

A fourth woman is mentioned among this group:

> Matthew 1:6. . . . David the king begat Solomon of her that had been the wife of Urias [Uriah] . . .

This, of course, was Bathsheba, with whom David committed adultery (see page I-310). Again a woman is mentioned who is the subject of a dramatic story that involves a taint.

Matthew here lists fourteen kings who reigned after David, but in achieving what is to him a magic number of fourteen, he omits several. Thus, he states:

> Matthew 1:8. . . . and Joram begat Ozias [Uzziah] . . .

Bur Joram died in 844 B.C. and Uzziah began to reign in 780 B.C., leaving a sixty-four-year gap. This gap contained three kings of Judah, as well as a usurping queen. Joram was succeeded by his son, Ahaziah, who (after an interregnum in which Queen Athaliah reigned) was succeeded by his son, Joash, who was succeeded by his son, Amaziah. Uzziah then followed as Amaziah's son.

Ahaziah, the first of the omitted kings, was the son of Athaliah and therefore the grandson of Ahab of Israel and of his wife, Jezebel (see page I-362). One might almost suspect that Ahaziah and his immediate descendants were omitted in order to avoid mentioning this fact. Nevertheless, mentioned or not, it must follow from Matthew's genealogy that the wicked queens Jezebel and Athaliah are to be included among the ancestors of Jesus.

Still a fourth king is omitted from the line of succession:

Matthew 1:11. And Josias [Josiah] begat Jechonias [Jehoiachin] . . .

But Josiah was the father of Jehoiakim, who was, in turn, the father of Jehoiachin.

Zorobabel

The final portion of Matthew's genealogy includes the descendants of Jehoiachin after the Exile. The first two generations follow the genealogy given in the Book of 1 Chronicles (see page I-405):

Matthew 1:12. And after they were brought to Babylon, Jechonias [Jehoiachin] begat [1] Salathiel [Shealtiel]; and Salathiel [Shealtiel] begat [2] Zorobabel [Zerubbabel] . . .

After Zerubbabel, a list of names is given that is not found anywhere else in the Bible and which, if valid, we must assume to have been taken from genealogical listings no longer available to us. They are: (3) Abiud, (4) Eliakim, (5) Azor, (6) Sadoc, (7) Achim, (8) Eliud, (9) Eleazar, (10) Matthan, (11) Jacob, and (12) Joseph.

The climax of the genealogy is reached:

Matthew 1:16. And Jacob begat Joseph the husband of Mary, of whom was born [13] Jesus, who is called Christ.

The names in this third group are only thirteen in number, despite Matthew's statement there are fourteen. Since it is quite certain that Matthew could count we can only assume that somewhere in the early copyings of this list, a name in the third group dropped out and has been lost forever.

Attempts have been made to twist matters so that the magic number fourteen is reached with the list before us. Some have counted Jehoiachin in this list despite the fact that he is also counted in the middle third. Others have attempted to count Mary as a separate generation, since she is mentioned, but in that case one ought also to count Tamar, Rahab, Ruth, and Bathsheba.

No, the best that can be done is to state that, on the face of it, there are fourteen generations from Abraham to David, eighteen from David to the Exile, and thirteen from the Exile to Jesus. Fortunately, though, Matthew's little game with numbers is not really of importance and it isn't paid much mind, except as an interesting quirk in Matthew's system of thought.

The Holy Ghost

In chapter 1:16, Matthew clearly avoids concluding the list of "begats" by saying that Joseph begat Jesus. Rather he carefully identifies Joseph as merely the husband of Mary "of whom was born Jesus."

This paves the way for Matthew's account of Jesus having been born of a virgin:

> Matthew 1:18. *Now the birth of Jesus Christ was on this wise: When as his mother Mary was espoused to Joseph, before they came together, she was found with child of the Holy Ghost.*

The word "ghost" is of Anglo-Saxon origin and means "spirit" or "soul." Ghost, spirit, or soul—whatever it be called—represents something intangible which can be regarded as the essence of life, apart from the material body. It can be the essence of life within a body (a man's soul) or the essence of life in the absence of a body altogether (a supernatural being).

Primitive peoples, generally, consider the universe to be populated by myriads of spirits of all sorts; spirits capable of interfering with human activity and, in some cases, capable of taking possession of a human body in successful competition with its own proper spirit.

The monotheistic Jews also had their popular tales of evil spirits capable of taking possession of human bodies (as in the Book of Tobit, see page 19). Even at its most lofty, Judaism speaks of angels, though viewing them always as messengers of God, who are incapable of independent action. (The case of Satan and his rebellion against God is a rather late development in Jewish thought, adopted only after exposure to Persian dualism, see page I-409.)

Angels might be viewed as merely an extension of God; as representing the spirit of God manifesting itself on Earth in order to guide human action.

It was felt that whenever a man took decisive action and exhibited unusual traits of leadership, it was not so much the action of his own feeble spirit but that of the Spirit of God which entered into him and guided him. Thus:

> Judges 3:10. *And the Spirit of the Lord came upon him [Othniel], and he judged Israel, and went out to war . . .*

Or:

> Judges 6:34. *But the Spirit of the Lord came upon Gideon, and he blew a trumpet . . .*

Again, when Samson is described as performing a feat of more-than-human strength:

> Judges 14:6. *And the Spirit of the Lord came mightily upon him, and he rent him* [a lion] *as he would have rent a kid . . .*

The Spirit of God might well be called the Holy Spirit, to avoid using the term "God" (something the Jews of the New Testament period did avoid whenever possible—Matthew especially so). In the King James Version it is called the Holy Ghost, which is synonymous. However, the popular usage of "ghost," as signifying the spirits of the dead, has so robbed the word of its dignity that "Holy Ghost" seems odd to modern ears and Holy Spirit is preferable. The Revised Standard Version uses Holy Spirit throughout.

To say, then, that Mary "was found with child of the Holy Ghost" is to say that her pregnancy was the direct result of the working of the divine influence within her and had nothing to do with the usual manner of achieving pregnancy.

Mary

Joseph, finding that his betrothed is pregnant, assumes she has behaved improperly and feels that he cannot go through with the marriage. He is warned against this by an angel:

> Matthew 1:20. . . . *the angel of the Lord appeared unto him in a dream, saying, Joseph, thou son of David, fear not to take unto thee Mary thy wife: for that which is conceived in her is of the Holy Ghost.*

The name of Jesus' mother is, in Hebrew, Miriam (the name of Moses' sister). In Aramaic, the name became Mariam, and in Roman times it was easy to change this, by dropping the final letter, to Maria, the feminine version of the good Roman name, Marius. Maria is still the version of the name used in most European languages, though it becomes Marion or Marie in French, and Mary in English.

Because of the emphasis here on the fact that her pregnancy was the result of the action of the Holy Spirit and not of man, she is considered by Christians to have been a virgin even while pregnant and is therefore commonly called the "Virgin Mary" or just "the Virgin."

Matthew's emphasis on the virgin birth would seem to negate his earlier emphasis on the Davidic genealogy of Jesus. He shows that Joseph, the husband of Mary, was a descendant of David, but then goes on to show that this same Joseph was not the father of Jesus.

One might account for this by saying that Joseph was considered by the people of his time to be the father of Jesus, so that in the course of *ordinary* human affairs Jesus was of Davidic descent, thus fulfilling that qualification for Messiah-hood. Then, the line of argument might go, Jesus came to be recognized as the divine Son of God and this was so much greater a qualification for Messiah-hood that Davidic descent could be dismissed as an Earthly detail of only Earthly importance.

Another explanation is to suppose that while Matthew gives the genealogy of Joseph, Mary herself is of Davidic descent also, and Jesus is of that descent through his undoubted mother as well as through his merely reputed father. The gospels do not say this directly but the belief of the Davidic descent of Mary, as well as of Joseph, is firmly ensconced in Christian tradition.

And yet virgin birth is completely outside the Jewish tradition and is not demanded by any of the Old Testament prophecies concerning the Messiah. How, then, does Matthew come upon it? Being Matthew, he is bound to support the virgin birth by citing an Old Testament prophecy and he can find only one:

> Matthew 1:22. *Now all this was done, that it might be fulfilled which was spoken of the Lord by the prophet, saying,*
> Matthew 1:23. *Behold, a virgin shall be with child, and shall bring forth a son . . .*

This refers to a passage in Isaiah:

> Isaiah 7:14. . . . *Behold, a virgin shall conceive, and bear a son . . .*

but it is not a very useful passage in this connection. Matthew's use of the word "virgin" in his quotation is mistaken, though it has led early translations of the Bible, including the King James Version, to make use of the word "virgin" in the Isaiah passage as well. In fact, the Hebrew word used by Isaiah means "young woman" and can apply equally well to one who is not a virgin. And, in any case, whether "virgin" or "young woman," the passage from Isaiah is unlikely to have Messianic significance (see page I-532) and, but for these verses in Matthew quoting it, would never be taken to have it.

But then, why the tale of the virgin birth, told with such urgency, that a marginal Old Testament verse has to be searched for and found by Matthew to account for it?

Perhaps we can indulge in a little speculation here. That which was first known about Jesus must have been the tale of his ministry when disciples flocked about him. Presumably he was an obscure Galilean, until his preaching made him famous, and the details of his birth and childhood were not known. Mark, the oldest of the gospels, has nothing to say about his birth and childhood. Rather, Mark starts his tale of Jesus with Jesus as an adult, beginning his ministry.

After Jesus' death, tales of his birth and childhood arose. It is quite possible that many were legitimate reminiscences of those who had known him as a youngster or of members of his family. On the other hand, people being what they are, embroidery may have entered into the legends concerning so remarkable a person as the Messiah and the Son of God.

The sort of detail which individuals of completely Jewish background would expect of the Messiah would be a detailed genealogy that would connect him with David. Such a genealogy is given by Matthew and we have no reason to say that it is inaccurate (aside from the small discrepancies we have pointed out that arise out of Matthew's eagerness to attain the magic number of fourteen).

But the Jews were, in those days, surrounded by a vast world of Gentiles who had traditions of their own. It was quite customary and usual in Gentile legend (almost necessary, in fact) that any great hero, any wonder-worker be the son of a god. A virgin could be impregnated by a god in magical fashion—this would not be impossible in the Greek tradition.

And, as it happened, there were Jews not only in Judea, where Jewish thought was provincial and conservative, but in Alexandria and other places where the Greek influence was strong. Greek versions of the Bible used the Greek word for "virgin" in the Isaiah quotation, and it is quite possible that Matthew followed the Greek version rather than the Hebrew version in supporting the virgin birth, and that he did not deliberately misquote.

In Jesus' time, the possibility of virgin birth may have taken on added force. The Roman historian Livy, who died just a few years before the start of Jesus' ministry, had written a history of Rome that proved enormously popular. In it he retells the tale of the founding of Rome by the twin brothers Romulus and Remus. The interesting part of that legend is that Romulus and Remus are described by him as being of virgin birth. Their mother, Silvia, was a Vestal Virgin whose children were fathered by Mars.

Greek-speaking Jews would surely place no credence in that, and yet there might have been the impulse to feel that if a virgin birth could be used to exalt the founders of the pagan city of Rome, how much more could one rightly be used to exalt the founding of the kingdom of God.

One might wonder, then, if Matthew might not have been faced with two traditions concerning Jesus' birth, the strictly Jewish genealogy of Davidic descent, and the Greek-Jewish story of the virgin birth. And, although mutually exclusive, Matthew accepted both.

It is interesting that the tradition of the virgin birth is firmly and clearly stated only in this first chapter of Matthew. There are verses in Luke that can be made to support it, but not indisputably, and there are no other references to it at all anywhere else in the New Testament.

Herod

The general period of Jesus' birth is given:

Matthew 2:1. . . . *Jesus was born . . . in the days of Herod the king . . .*

The mention of Herod at once tells us that the day of the Maccabean kingdom is over. Much has happened in the century that passed between the ending of 1 Maccabees and the opening of Matthew.

1 Maccabees had ended with the assassination of Simon in 135 B.C. His second and sole surviving son established himself as John Hyrcanus I in 134 B.C., coming to a peaceful arrangement with Antiochus VII Sidetes (see page 88), the last Seleucid monarch of any consequence.

John Hyrcanus extended the boundaries of Judea by conquest. He established his rule over Samaria and Galilee to the north and he brought Idumea, to his south, under complete domination. The Samaritans retained their heretical religion, but orthodox Judaism was established in Galilee and in Idumea.

The Idumeans accepted Judaism (in some cases at the point of the sword) but the converts were not wholeheartedly accepted by the Jewish nationalists. Despite their observance of the proper religion, Idumeans were still viewed as Edomites, descendants of Esau, and therefore the hereditary enemies of the Jewish descendants of Jacob.

John Hyrcanus I died in 104 B.C. and was succeeded by an elder son, Aristobulus, who assumed the title of king, something the Seleucid kingdom, now under Antiochus VIII Grypus ("hook-nosed"), was powerless to prevent.

Aristobulus reigned only a year and, in 103 B.C., his younger brother, Alexander Jannaeus, succeeded. In the course of a twenty-seven-year-reign, Alexander raised Judea to the peak of its power. By the time he died, in 79 B.C., Judea was very much in the position of Israel in the time of Jeroboam II, six and a half centuries before (see page I-369).

Under Jeroboam II, Israel seemed great and prosperous, but its greatness was overshadowed by Assyria, a fact which became evident immediately after Jeroboam's death. In the case of Alexander Jannaeus, Judea's greatness was darkened by the even greater shadow of Rome.

The substance of that shadow was making its way onto the Judean stage after the death of Alexander Jannaeus, and its coming was hastened by dynastic squabbles that set various Maccabees at each other's throats.

Since the time of Jonathan, brother of Judas Maccabeus, the high priesthood had remained in the family of the Maccabees and Alexander Jannaeus was, for instance, at once king and high priest.

After Alexander's death, however, this combination of offices fell apart. The high priesthood went to Alexander's elder son, John Hyrcanus II, but the civil rule remained with Alexander's widow, Alexandra.

Alexandra died in 67 B.C. and one might have expected John Hyrcanus II to serve now as real king as well as high priest, but in this he was disputed by his younger brother, Aristobulus II. In the civil war that followed, John Hyrcanus II had the support of a very able man, Antipater, who had been governor of Idumea under Alexander Jannaeus. Antipater was an Idumean by birth, although Jewish by religion.

The civil war could not have come at a worse time, for Roman armies under General Gnaeus Pompeius (called Pompey in English) were cleaning up the east. The last of the various small powers that, a century before, had been brawling and squabbling on the international stage were now being swallowed, one by one.

In 64 B.C., Pompey entered Antioch and put an end to the Seleucid monarchy. A little over a century before, that monarchy had tyrannized over Judea, but now, under its last kings, it was a feeble patch of territory absorbed by Rome as the province of Syria.

Independent Judea survived the great Seleucid Empire as she had once survived the great Assyrian Empire—but not for long. Both sides in the Jewish civil war were appealing to Pompey for help, of course, and the Roman general, as was to be expected, agreed at once to move in. In 63 B.C. he invaded Judea and took Jerusalem after a three-month siege. Out of curiosity he invaded the Holy of Holies in the Temple but did it no harm otherwise.

Pompey ended by deciding in favor of John Hyrcanus II. He left him as high priest and carried off Aristobulus II and his two sons to Rome.

The Roman did not allow Hyrcanus any secular power, however. He gave that over to Antipater the Idumean in return for Antipater's services to the Roman cause. (It was good policy to do so. Antipater, an Idumean, could never be accepted wholeheartedly by the narrowly nationalistic Jews, and he would therefore always require Roman support to keep his position safe against his subjects. While he needed the Roman soldiers, he would naturally be loyal to the Roman cause.)

Thus, in 63 B.C., a little more than a century after the revolt of Mattathias and his sons, the Maccabean monarchy came to an end.

The fate of the last Maccabees was generally sad. Aristobulus II and his elder son, Alexander, escaped from Rome and made an attempt to regain the kingdom, but they were captured and both were killed in 49 B.C. The younger son, Antigonus Mattathias, survived. Before he died the elder son had married Alexandra, daughter of John Hyrcanus II, and by her had had a son, Aristobulus III.

There were thus, in 49 B.C., three male Maccabees left: (1) John Hyrcanus II, the high priest; (2) his nephew, Antigonus Mattathias; and (3) his grandson, Aristobulus III. The real ruler remained Antipater the Idumean.

But now it was Rome itself that was involved in a civil war. The general, Pompey, had gone to war with another and greater Roman general, Julius Caesar; and Pompey died in the course of the struggle. Antipater had made his way carefully among the contending factions and when Caesar emerged as victor, Antipater found himself still in favor, even though he had been Pompey's man to begin with.

But Caesar was assassinated in 44 B.C. and a new civil war erupted. Antipater the Idumean was assassinated in 43 B.C. and his sure ability to maneuver safely over slippery footing was removed.

Furthermore, Parthia, which ruled Babylonia and vast regions to the east, took advantage of the Roman civil wars to strike westward. For a while it was as though the times of Nebuchadnezzar were reborn, as conquering horsemen rode out of the east to take over Syria and Judea in 40 B.C.

The Jews welcomed the Parthians, though, as they had never welcomed the Chaldeans, for they saw the Parthians as rescuers from the Romans. Antipater's older son, Phasael, was killed in war against the invaders, and the high priest, John Hyrcanus II, was carried off into captivity. What's more, his ears were cut off so that, as a physically mutilated person, he could never serve as high priest again.

In place of the mutilated Hyrcanus, Antigonus Mattathias was made king and high priest. One might almost imagine the Maccabean kingdom to have been restored but, of course, the new king served merely as a Parthian puppet.

But Antipater the Idumean had a second son, Herodes (called Herod in English). He was, like his father, Jewish in religion, though an Idumean by descent. Under his father, he had served as governor of Galilee. When the Parthians took Judea, Herod managed to escape and made his way to Rome.

In Rome he persuaded the Roman general, Marcus Antonius (Mark Antony), who was then in power, to declare him king of Judea and to outlaw Antigonus Mattathias. Herod then returned to Judea and found the Parthians already on the run before a Roman counterattack. With the help of Roman arms, Herod invaded Judea and, after three years, took Jerusalem itself in 37 B.C. Antigonus Mattathias was executed.

Now two Maccabees were left. John Hyrcanus II returned from captivity in 36 B.C., but his cropped ears kept him permanently retired, so his grandson, Aristobulus III, served as high priest.

Herod, although king now with the full support of the Romans, could never feel secure while there were Maccabees alive about whom a nationalist revolt might center.

He tried to neutralize the Maccabean attraction by entering into a marriage alliance with the family. Aristobulus III had a sister, Mariamne (still another version of the Hebrew name, Miriam), and Herod took her as his second wife.

Even that did not erase his insecurity. He had Aristobulus III executed in 35 B.C. and the crop-eared Hyrcanus in 30 B.C. In a fit of jealousy he killed his wife, Mariamne, in 29 B.C. and that was the end of the Maccabees, except for Herod's own children by Mariamne. (Herod, the Henry VIII of his time, married eight times after Mariamne's death, so that he had ten wives altogether, although only one at a time.)

The birth of Jesus during the reign of Herod raises an interesting point in chronology. The Romans dated events from the year in which, according to legend, the city of Rome had been founded. That year was 1 A.U.C., where the initials stand for *ab urbe condita* ("from the founding of the city"). According to this scheme, Pompey took Jerusalem in the year 690 A.U.C.

Unfortunately, however, none of the gospels date the birth of Jesus according to this scheme or, for that matter, according to one of the other schemes used in the Bible. The evangelists might have used the Seleucid era that was used in the books of the Maccabees, for instance. Or they might have named the number of the year of Herod's reign after the fashion of the dating in 1 and 2 Kings.

But no scheme was used. Matthew simply says "in the days of Herod the king" and anything closer than that must be worked out by deduction.

Some five hundred years after the time of Jesus, such deductions were made by a scholarly theologian and astronomer named Dionysius Exiguus, who lived in Rome. He maintained that Jesus had been born in 753 A.U.C., and this date for Jesus' birth was widely accepted.

Gradually, as the centuries passed, the old Roman system of counting the years was dropped. Instead, it became customary to count the years from the birth of Jesus. That year was A.D. 1, or "Anno Domini" ("the year of our Lord").

The years prior to the birth of Jesus were labeled B.C. ("before Christ"). Thus, if Jesus was born in 753 A.U.C., then Rome was founded 753 years before his birth, or 753 B.C. The entire system of dating used in this book (and, indeed, in any modern history book) follows this "Christian Era" or "Dionysian Era" in which A.D. 1 is equated with 753 A.U.C.

And yet scholarship in the centuries since Dionysius Exiguus has made a revision necessary. For instance, from sources outside the Bible it is quite clear that Herod ascended the throne in 716 A.U.C., that is, 37 B.C. He reigned for thirty-three years, dying in 749 A.U.C. or 4 B.C.

But if that is so, it is impossible for Jesus to have been born in 753 A.U.C. and still have been born "in the days of Herod the king," since Herod had died four years before. If Jesus were born in the time of Herod then he must have been born no later than 4 B.C. (four years "before Christ," which certainly seems paradoxical).

And even this is merely the latest he could have been born by that verse in Matthew. He could well have been born earlier, and some have suggested dates even as early as 17 B.C.

Wise Men from the East

The birth of Jesus was accompanied by remarkable circumstances, according to Matthew, who tells first of a pilgrimage to the place of Jesus' birth:

Matthew 2:1. *Now when Jesus was born in Bethlehem of Judaea in the days of Herod the king, behold, there came wise men from the east to Jerusalem . . .*

"Wise men" is a translation of the Greek "magoi," which has entered our language by way of the Latin as "magi." The word is derived from "magu," the name given to their priests by the Persian Zoroastrians.

Throughout ancient history, the priests were considered the repositories of important knowledge. Not only did they know the techniques for the propitiation of the gods, but—in Babylonia particularly—they studied the heavenly bodies and their influences upon the course of human affairs. The priests were therefore learned astrologers (who, in the course of their studies, picked up considerable legitimate astronomy as well).

The Jews had learned of the Babylonian priesthood in the time of the Exile, and in the Book of Daniel the word "Chaldean" is used as synonymous with "wise man." If the Jews had forgotten this, there was occasion to refurbish that knowledge during the brief Parthian supremacy over Judea. (The arcane powers of the "magi" are memorialized in our language, by the way, with the word "magic," which is derived from "magi.")

The tale of the wise men is short. They come to see the infant Jesus, they leave presents, and depart; their impact on legend is great, however. In the popular imagination, the wise men have been taken to be three in number and have become three kings and have even been given names: Melchior, Gasper, and Balthazar.

According to medieval legend, their bodies were taken by Helena (the mother of Constantine I, the first emperor to become Christian) to Constantinople. From there, they were eventually removed to Milan, Italy, and still later to Cologne, Germany. There, in Cologne Cathedral, they are supposed to be buried, so that they are sometimes referred to as the "Three Kings of Cologne."

King of the Jews

The wise men, having arrived in Jerusalem, had a simple question:

Matthew 2:2. . . . *Where is he that is born King of the Jews? . . .*

They were searching, in other words, for the Messiah.

There had been a decline in the passionate intensity of longing for a Messiah during the palmy days of the Maccabees, but the longing had not disappeared altogether. After all, the Maccabees did not set up a completely ideal state that ruled over all the world and, in any case, they were not of the Davidic line.

To be sure, the Maccabees realized that dreams of a Messiah would have to be directed against their own Levite dynasty, unless properly deflected, and they must have encouraged writings that would tend to do this.

During the Maccabean period, for instance, the apocryphal work "The Testaments of the Twelve Patriarchs" appeared. This purported to be a transcript of the last words of the twelve sons of Jacob as they lay on their deathbeds. Passages in it pointed clearly to a Levite Messiah. Psalm 110, with its mention of Melchizedek as both king and high priest (see page I-504) although not of Davidic lineage—having lived, in fact, nearly a thousand years before David—may have been used to support the Maccabees, too. (Indeed, some suspect the psalm may have been written in early Maccabean times and slipped into the canon at the last minute.)

All attempts, however, to set up a Levite Messiah must have failed to win any enthusiasm at all among the Jews generally. The prophetic writings were too clear on the point of the Davidic descent of the Messiah and the hallowed memory of David himself and of the empire he founded remained too sharp and clear. Messianic hopes may have ebbed under the Maccabees but what hope remained was for a Messiah of the line of David.

And then the Maccabees were gone. Despite the heroism of Judas Maccabeus and his brothers, despite the conquests of John Hyrcanus I and Alexander Jannaeus, the line had been a brief and, in the end, unsuccessful interlude in Jewish history. And those who piously awaited the Messiah might well have been pleased, rather than otherwise, at the Maccabean failure. After all, the Maccabees were not of the stock of David; how could they possibly have succeeded?

Now under the heavy hand of Herod, the alien from Idumea, and under the still heavier weight of the Roman arms that supported him, the Jews were growing increasingly restive. Surely it was time for the Messiah to come, establish himself as the ideal King of the Jews, bring the heathen oppressors to justice, and place all the world under his mild rule so that all peoples everywhere might finally come to Jerusalem to worship.

There is no reason to be surprised that the Messianic fervor in Judea made itself felt far outside the borders of the land. There were large colonies of Jews outside Judea, notably in Alexandria and in Babylonia. The three wise men from the east could, conceivably, have heard of such matters from the Jews in their land and been impressed by the tale.

The Star

But even if the wise men had heard of Jewish speculations as to the Messiah, what made them choose that moment to head for Jerusalem? It would have to be divine inspiration and Matthew casts that inspiration, quite fittingly, into the form of an astrological manifestation—something that would professionally interest the Babylonian priesthood:

Matthew 2:2 . . . *Where is he that is born King of the Jews? for we have seen his star in the east, and are come to worship him.*

There is nothing in Old Testament prophecy to make a star the specific manifestation of the Messiah. To be sure, one of Balaam's oracles states:

Numbers 24:17. . . . *there shall come a Star out of Jacob . . . and shall smite the corners of Moab . . .*

and this has been taken as a Messianic utterance by many. Nevertheless, modern scholars accept this as a reference to David, written into the oracle in the time of the kingdom and attributed to the legendary sage Balaam.

Then, too, there is a passage in Isaiah which goes:

Isaiah 60:3. *And the Gentiles shall come to thy light, and kings to the brightness of thy rising.*

This refers to Isaiah's vision of an ideal Jerusalem, to arise after the return from exile, but it is easy to interpret it as referring also to the Messianic period and, specifically, to the manner in which the wise men of the east followed the light of the star to the birth of Jesus.

If, however, Matthew has this in mind, he does not quote the verse from Isaiah.

If Matthew had quoted that verse, it might be easier to accept the star as a miraculous manifestation of divine guidance visible only to the wise men and to no one else. But Matthew calmly refers to the star without reference to prophecy, as though it were a perfectly natural phenomenon (bent to the divine purpose, of course) and much effort and imagination has been expended to determine what that natural phenomenon might have been.

The most obvious solution would be that the star was a "nova"— a new star appearing suddenly in the heavens, possibly attaining startling brightness, and then fading out to invisibility after some months.

Such events have indeed been known to happen. Astronomers know that stars can sometimes explode and increase in brightness a millionfold or more for a short period of time. In the case of particularly tremendous explosions ("supernovae") among stars reasonably close to ourselves, the result may be the sudden appearance of a star that will grow as bright as the planet Venus in a spot where previously no star bright enough to be seen by the naked eye had been visible.

Three such supernovae have been known to have appeared in the last thousand years—one in 1054, one in 1572, and one in 1604. Could one also have appeared in Herod's time?

It seems doubtful. Surely such a supernova would have been noticed. Of course, the supernova of 1054 was not noticed by European astronomers, but this was during the Dark Ages, when astronomy in Europe was virtually nonexistent. It *was* observed by astronomers in China and Japan, and we have their records. (We know they were correct because in the spot where they located their "guest-star" there is now a cloudy ball of gas that is the clear remnant of an explosion.)

In Herod's time, Greek astronomy was still alive, however, even though past its greatest day, and a supernova would most certainly have been noted and referred to. It seems quite unlikely that such a reference would not have existed and survived to our time and so the chance of a supernova is generally dismissed.

Another possibility is that the star might have been the result of a close approach of two or more of the heavenly bodies, so that they would shine together with abnormal brightness for a short period of time. The only bodies in the skies that move independently against the starry background are the planets, and occasionally two or more approach fairly close to each other.

Astronomers understand these movements quite well now and can trace them back with considerable accuracy for thousands of years. They can tell, for instance, that in 7 B.C., Jupiter and Saturn approached each other quite closely.

The approach was not so close as to make it in the least possible that observers would mistake the two for a single unusually bright star. Still, there is no reason to suppose this would be necessary. The close approach of the two planets is a rare event (although a still closer approach of Jupiter and Saturn than that in 7 B.C. took place in 1941) and to astrologers there might have been significance in it. It is not inconceivable that the approach might in the minds of some have been associated with the coming of a Messiah.

And, finally, there is the possibility of a bright comet. Comets come and go erratically and, until a little over two centuries ago, there was no known method to predict those comings and goings. Comets were generally considered to presage disasters—plagues, wars, deaths of notable men—but to the wise men of the east perhaps a particular comet might have been associated with the coming of the Messiah.

Nowadays we can calculate the paths of a number of comets and can trace them backward in time. We can know of one comet that did appear in the reign of Herod. This was Halley's Comet, which made one of its returns of every seventy-six years to the inner Solar System in the year 11 B.C.

One might suppose then that in the decades following Jesus' death, when his disciples piously scraped together whatever records they could find of his life, some might remember the appearance of an unusual phenomenon in the heavens at about the time of his birth—either Halley's Comet or the close approach of Jupiter and Saturn. The Jews were not themselves astronomers (indeed, they eschewed astronomy, because the study of the stars in those days was invariably and notoriously associated with heathen idolatry) and would describe any such manifestation as simply "a star."

Matthew may well have picked up the story, with the miraculous associations that gathered about it, and included it in his gospel.

Bethlehem

The question of the wise men was a disturbing one:

Matthew 2:3. *When Herod the king had heard these things, he was troubled, and all Jerusalem with him.*

Herod and "all Jerusalem" (that is, the ruling groups of the city, whose welfare was tied to the king and his court) might well be troubled by any rumor that a possible Messiah had arisen. For one thing, such a Messiah would be considered the rightful king of Judea, and Herod would suddenly be a usurper in the eyes of all pious Jews. It is a rare king who would willingly face the possibility of being removed from the kingship, without some attempt to protect himself. In fact, in all kingdoms, ancient and modern, any attempt by someone other than the king to declare himself the rightful king, or to be declared so by others, is considered treason and treated as such.

It might be argued that the concern of Herod and the aristocracy was not only for themselves, but for the nation as a whole, too. Herod is usually pictured as a bloody, cruel tyrant, but this is largely through the picture drawn of him by the Jews who opposed him and by this chapter of the New Testament. If this is disregarded, and if the excesses of his private life (which were horrible but not noticeably more so than those of other rulers of his time) are also discounted, then Herod seems to have been a capable ruler who made a considerable (though futile) effort to win the regard of the people he governed. Reports of Messiahs were indeed dangerous to everyone in Judea, from Herod's standpoint, more so to the people, in fact, than to Herod himself (who was old and was soon to be removed from his throne in the ordinary course of nature anyway).

The trouble was that to the more militant Jewish nationalists, there seemed no question but that the Messiah would prove a warrior-king, a super-David who would settle matters with the Romans, and make Judea what it should rightly be—the master of the world. This would happen because the Messiah would be filled with the Spirit of the Lord and God himself would fight on behalf of the nation as he had done so many times in the past.

Indeed, there was the example of the Maccabean revolt, of the courage and devotion of Judas Maccabeus and his brothers in turning back and defeating the powerful Seleucid kingdom.

It is not difficult to see that the glorious victories of Judas must have had, in the end, a disastrous influence on Jewish history, for it filled Judea with enthusiastic nationalists who discounted mere disparities of number and power. The Romans, to them, seemed as capable of being beaten by sheer determination, patriotic fervor, and trust in God, as the Seleucids had been.

Those Jews who were less blind to Earthly realities and less confident of divine support, understood the great strength of Rome and must have viewed nationalist agitation with absolute terror. They must have realized that there was the constant danger of a suicidal uprising; one that would be followed by the full exertion of Roman power, which would descend like a sledge hammer, crushing the state into extinction, nationalists and moderates alike. This was no idle fear, either, for at the time of Jesus' birth exactly such a tragic denouement was just seventy years in the future.

Herod might therefore be viewed as clearly feeling it to be his duty to nip all Messianic hopes in the bud—for the good of all. He therefore inquired of the chief priests and scribes (those best acquainted, that is, with Biblical lore) as to where the Messiah might be found.

> Matthew 2:5. *And they said unto him, In Bethlehem of Judea: for thus it is written by the prophet,*
> Matthew 2:6. *And thou Bethlehem, in the land of Juda* [Judah] *. . . out of thee shall come a Governor, that shall rule my people Israel.*

The reference is to a quotation from Micah (see page I-653). Thus, the "little town of Bethlehem," locally famous till then as the birthplace of David, entered a new career of world-wide fame as the reputed birthplace of Jesus.

Herod next instructed the wise men to go to Bethlehem and to bring him back news of the child that he might worship him too. There is no question, though, that his real intention was to do away with the supposed Messiah. This is so certain that Matthew doesn't even bother to specify it at that moment.

The wise men depart and:

> Matthew 2:9. *. . . the star, which they saw in the east, went before them, till it came and stood over where the young child was.*

Because of the association of the star with the place of birth of Jesus at Bethlehem, it is commonly called "the star of Bethlehem."

The Children . . . in Bethlehem

The wise men worshipped the child, left their gifts, and then— warned in a dream (a favorite device of Matthew's)—left without reporting back to Herod. Herod, lacking the knowledge he needed, desperately ordered a general killing of all the infants in Bethlehem, hoping to include among them the reputed Messiah:

Matthew 2:16. *Then Herod . . . sent forth, and slew all the children that were in Bethlehem . . . from two years old and under . . .*

Matthew 2:17. *Then was fulfilled that which was spoken by Jeremy [Jeremiah] the prophet, saying,*

Matthew 2:18. *In Rama [Ramah] was there a voice heard, lamentation, and weeping, and great mourning, Rachel weeping for her children, and would not be comforted, because they are not.*

The reference is to a passage in Jeremiah (see page I-560) which refers to the carrying off of Israel into exile by Sargon. Rachel was the ancestress of the chief tribes of Israel, Ephraim, and Manasseh, and her weeping over "her children" is therefore metaphorically apt. The tribe of Benjamin was also descended from Rachel, and Jeremiah, brought up in Benjamite territory, would be sensitive to the thought of Rachel's weeping; Ramah being a town in Benjamin that was a traditional site of Rachel's grave.

The application of the verse from Jeremiah to the "slaughter of the innocents" by Herod is far less apt. To be sure, such a slaughter would be well worth bewailing, but the fact remains that Leah, not Rachel, was the ancestress of the Judeans, and the children of Bethlehem were Judeans. Perhaps the use of the quotation was suggested to Matthew by the fact that there was a tradition that placed Rachel's grave close to Bethlehem:

Genesis 35:19. *And Rachel died, and was buried in the way to . . . Beth-lehem.*

And yet this dreadful deed of Herod's seems very likely to be apocryphal. It is hard to believe that it ever happened. Not only is the slaughter not mentioned anywhere else in the New Testament, but it is not mentioned in any of the secular histories of the time, either. It is rather remarkable that such a deed would be overlooked when many more far less wicked deeds of Herod were carefully described.

Surely Matthew would not have accepted this tale of the killing of the infants merely because of his eagerness to introduce a not-very-apt quotation.

Perhaps something more is involved. Many heroes of pagan legend survived infancy only after a narrow escape from some king who tried to kill him. This is true of legends concerning Cyrus, who founded the Persian Empire, and Romulus, who founded Rome. Cyrus had a grandfather and Romulus a great-uncle who, in each case, were kings and had divine foreknowledge that the just-born child would someday depose them. Both children were exposed and left to die; both survived. In Jewish legend, Abraham, as an infant, miraculously survived the attempts of evil King Nimrod upon his life. It is not surprising that similar tales might arise concerning Jesus after his death.

Out of perhaps many such tales that were spread about, Matthew chose one he felt best suited the situation. The Biblical tale of Moses' infancy involves the child's suspense-filled escape after Pharaoh had ordered the indiscriminate slaughter of the Israelite children . . .

> Exodus 1:15. *And the king of Egypt spake to the Hebrew midwives . . .*
> Exodus 1:16. *. . . When ye do the office of a midwife to the Hebrew women . . . if it be a son, then ye shall kill him . . .*

Moses escaped Pharaoh's slaughter and Jesus escaped Herod's slaughter. It may have been this parallel that was in Matthew's mind. He seized upon this particular tale and buttressed it with the quotation from Jeremiah in order to present Jesus as a new and greater Moses.

Egypt

The infant Jesus escaped the slaughter because Joseph, like the wise men, was warned in a dream:

Matthew 2:13. . . . *Arise, and take the young child and his mother, and flee into Egypt . . .*

Matthew 2:14. *When he arose, he took the young child and his mother by night, and departed into Egypt:*

Matthew 2:15. *And was there until the death of Herod: that it might be fulfilled which was spoken . . . by the prophet, saying, Out of Egypt have I called my son.*

The reference is to the prophet, Hosea:

Hosea 11:1. *When Israel was a child, then I loved him, and called my son out of Egypt.*

On the face of it that verse in Hosea is a clear reference to the Exodus and it is only Matthew's quotation of it that would make anyone give it Messianic significance. Indeed, it might seem natural to wonder if the flight into Egypt was introduced only so that Matthew could indulge in his favorite exercise of quoting an Old Testament verse, for Jesus' stay in Egypt is not referred to in any other place in the New Testament.

One might speculate that here too, perhaps, Matthew adopted a tradition for inclusion in his gospel in order to make even clearer the parallel he was drawing between Moses and Jesus. Moses came out of Egypt—and so did Jesus.

Archelaus

Eventually Herod died (in 4 B.C., as stated earlier), perhaps not long after Jesus' birth:

Matthew 2:22. . . . *Archelaus did reign in Judaea in the room of his father Herod . . .*

Herod, with his many wives, had many children (fourteen all told) but few survived him. This was not only the results of the natural hazards of infancy, but because of Herod's own pathologically suspicious nature, particularly in later life. He was easily moved to anger by hints of possible conspiracies against him. It was this which led him to kill his beloved wife, Mariamne (the Maccabean), and to follow that, eventually, by the execution of the two sons she bore him. He had other sons also executed, including his oldest, Antipater.

Upon his death, however, he still had several sons surviving; including Archelaus, Antipas, and Philip. He divided his kingdom among them. (The family name, Herod, is often added to the names of these sons, so that we may speak of Herod Archelaus, Herod Antipas, and Herod Philip. The name Herod was almost a throne name for those descendants of Antipater the Idumean who ruled over parts of the land.)

Archelaus, the eldest survivor, was given control of the core of the realm: Judea, with Samaria, to the north and Idumea to the south. Herod tried to give him the title of king, too, but the Roman Emperor, who had to approve Herod's will, refused to allow it. Archelaus was given the lesser title of "ethnarch" (equivalent to "provincial governor") as though deliberately to lessen his prestige and power.

Antipas received Galilee for his share, as well as Perea, the district east of the Jordan River (which had once been called Gilead, (see page I-191). Philip received Iturea, the district east and north of the Sea of Galilee.

Antipas and Philip were both called "tetrarchs" ("ruler of a fourth part of a province"), which would have made literal sense if Herod's kingdom had been divided among four sons rather than three. However, it might be reasoned that Archelaus, as the eldest, received a double share and ruled two fourths of the kingdom while Antipas and Philip ruled one fourth each.

Nazareth

Once Herod died, it was safe for Joseph and his family to return, and he is so informed by an angel in terms which again reinforce the parallel between Moses and Jesus:

> Matthew 2:19. *But when Herod was dead, behold, an angel of the Lord appeareth in a dream to Joseph in Egypt,*
> Matthew 2:20. *Saying, Arise, and take the young child and his mother, and go into the land of Israel: for they are dead which sought the young child's life.*

The parallel is to the period when Moses fled into Midian after he had killed the Egyptian overseer (see page I-129). There he remained till Pharaoh's death, upon which he is told by God:

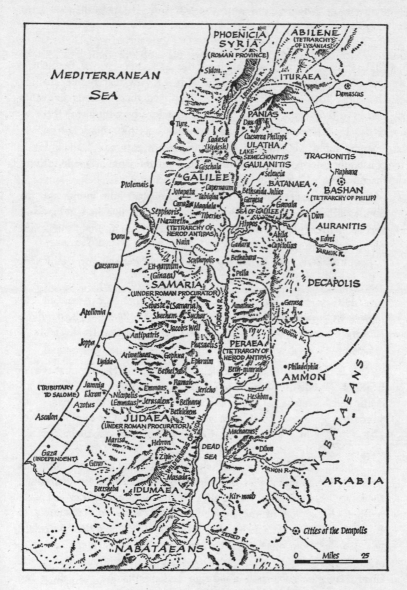

The Divisions of Herod's Kingdom

Exodus 4:19. . . . *Go, return into Egypt: for all the men are dead which sought thy life.*

But Matthew now faces a problem. He has reported the traditions that clustered about Jesus' birth at the Messianic city of Bethlehem and everything he says is consistent with the view that Bethlehem was the native town of the family; that they lived there as their ancestors had lived there before them. It would therefore be natural for them to return to Bethlehem after Herod's death, but this would not do.

Jesus, during his ministry, was considered a native of Galilee. He is constantly referred to as a Galilean and no reference is made, during his ministry, of his birth in Bethlehem.

It is therefore necessary for Matthew to explain how Joseph and his family, although natives of Bethlehem, came to live in Galilee—and very soon after Jesus' birth, too, so that his Bethlehem origin might not play much role in his adulthood.

Joseph is described, therefore, as indeed setting out for Bethlehem after Herod's death:

Matthew 2:22. *But when he* [Joseph] *heard that Archelaus did reign in Judaea . . . he was afraid to go thither: notwithstanding, being warned of God in a dream, he turned aside into the parts of Galilee . . .*

This is not unreasonable. Archelaus, the son of Herod, might have heard of the tale of the birth of the Messiah shortly before his father's death and he might be just as anxious to do away with the dangerous youngster. To be sure, Galilee was under the control of another son of Herod, but it may well be that Joseph judged Antipas to be the less dangerous of the two.

Certainly Archelaus, by his behavior, soon antagonized both the Jews and Samaritans under his rule to such an extent that, although they were bitter enemies who could virtually never agree, they did agree in their detestation of the new ruler. Both appealed desperately to Rome for relief, and such was the justice of their case that Archelaus was removed from office after he had ruled ten years. Herod Antipas, on the other hand, ruled for over forty years without too greatly antagonizing his subjects, a good sign perhaps that he was milder and more reasonable than his brother.

Matthew goes on to specify the town in Galilee to which Joseph brought his family:

Matthew 2:23. *And he [Joseph] came and dwelt in a city called Nazareth . . .*

Nazareth, a town in southern Galilee, is not mentioned in the Old Testament. The modern city usually identified as Nazareth lies just halfway between the Mediterranean Sea and the southern edge of the Sea of Galilee, about twenty miles from each. It is some seventy miles due north of Bethlehem. Its population today is about twenty-six thousand. It is part of the modern nation of Israel, but most of its inhabitants are Christians.

Matthew goes on to explain the coming of Joseph and his family to Nazareth in terms of Old Testament prophecy:

Matthew 2:23. *. . . that it might be fulfilled which was spoken by the prophets, He shall be called a Nazarene.*

What quotation Matthew might have in mind here is uncertain. Certainly at no point in the Old Testament is the Messiah referred to as a Nazarene in the sense that he was to be living in Nazareth.

It could be that Matthew stumbles into a confusion with Nazarite here (see page I-248) and that the reference is to the passage where Samson's mother is warned by an angel of a forthcoming son who is to fulfull God's purpose. The angel says:

Judges 13:5. *. . . the child shall be a Nazarite unto God from the womb: and he shall begin to deliver Israel out of the hand of the Philistines.*

Another possibility is that what Matthew is referring to is the habit of calling the Messiah the "Branch"—that is, the new, flourishing growth from the decaying stump of the Davidic line. This first appeared in Isaiah:

Isaiah 11:1. *And there shall come forth a rod out of the stem of Jesse, and a Branch shall grow out of his roots . . .*

As a result, prophets began to speak of the "Branch" as a covert way of referring to the Messiah, when an open mention might have been interpreted as treason. When Zechariah speaks of the Messiah, he says:

Zechariah 6:12. . . . *Behold the man whose name is The Branch* . . .

The Hebrew word for "Branch" in this case is "netzer," and Matthew may see a similarity here to "Nazarene."

In either case, whether Matthew is matching Nazarene and Nazarite, or Nazarene and Netzer, he is indulging in, at best, a play on words, and is not referring to any actual prophecy of the Messiah being an inhabitant of Nazareth.

John the Baptist

Matthew now passes from the tales of Jesus' birth and childhood and comes immediately to his adult work and what seems to be, in this and the other synoptic gospels, the final year of his life. No date is given in Matthew for this final year. It is merely stated:

Matthew 3:1. *In those days came John the Baptist, preaching in the wilderness of Judaea* . . .

A more careful chronological note in the Gospel of St. Luke, which will be discussed in time (see page 275), suggests the date is A.D. 29, at which time Jesus must have been at least thirty-three years old, very likely thirty-five, and just possibly even older.

John the Baptist is the first of several important individuals named John in the New Testament. The Hebrew version of the name is more closely represented as Johanan and it is in this form that it appears in the Old Testament. The eldest son of Josiah was Johanan, as was the eldest of the five Maccabean brothers.

The Greek version of Johanan is Ioannes and this eventually reached English as John.

John the Baptist could be considered the last of the Hebrew prophets of the old school. Like the prophets of the Old Testament, he maintained that the day of the Lord was at hand and the final establishment of the ideal world was imminent. The burden of his preaching was:

Matthew 3:2. . . . *Repent ye: for the kingdom of heaven is at hand.*

By "kingdom of Heaven" is meant "kingdom of God," with heaven substituted because Matthew shares the increasing reluctance of the Jews of the time to use any divine name. The expression "kingdom of God" is freely used in the New Testament outside Matthew.

What's more the establishment of the kingdom of God is to be preceded by a thorough winnowing of good from evil, saints from sinners, as had been promised by the earlier prophets too:

Matthew 3:11. . . . *he that cometh after me is mightier than I . . .*

Matthew 3:12. . . . *he will throughly purge his floor, and gather his wheat into the garner; but he will burn up the chaff with unquenchable fire.*

Those who came to John in repentance were baptized; that is, dipped in water ("baptize" is from a Greek word meaning "dip in water") in a symbolic washing away of sin and preparation for the new state of affairs.

Baptism was not a rite prominent in Jewish practice. Ezekiel speaks of the symbolic use of water to cleanse Jews after the profanation of their exile among the heathen and their exposure to heathen practices:

Ezekiel 36:24. *For I will take you from among the heathen, . . . and will bring you into your own land . . .*

Ezekiel 36:25. *Then will I sprinkle clean water upon you, and ye shall be clean . . .*

Ezekiel 36:26. *A new heart also will I give you, and a new spirit will I put within you . . .*

And this was what John the Baptist claimed to be doing by means of the baptismal rite. He used the water of the Jordan River and we might wonder whether he was not influenced here by Elisha's words to the Syrian leper Naaman (see page I-360):

2 Kings 5:10. . . . *Go and wash in Jordan . . . and thou shalt be clean.*

Whatever use Jews may have put baptism to, however, circumcision remained the rite marking the true entry of the Gentile into the brotherhood of Judaism. In Christian practice, partly as a result of the work of John the Baptist, baptism replaced circumcision as the initiatory rite.

Elijah

One might assume from the words quoted by Matthew of the Baptist's teachings, that John was awaiting the imminent arrival of the divine fury of a warlike king of heaven and that the last chapter of Earthly history was at hand. In Christian tradition, however, he is the forerunner of Jesus, a Messiah who did not at all fit the imaginings of the Jewish nationalists.

Matthew characteristically interprets the Baptist's role in terms of an Old Testament verse:

> Matthew 3:3. *For this* [John] *is he that was spoken of by the prophet Esaias* [Isaiah], *saying, The voice of one crying in the wilderness, Prepare ye the way of the Lord, make his paths straight.*

This verse comes from the very beginning of the utterances of the Second Isaiah (see page I-547):

> Isaiah 40:3. *The voice of him that crieth in the wilderness, Prepare ye the way of the Lord, make straight in the desert a highway for our God.*

It is possible to interpret this verse, in view of its position, as a reference by the Second Isaiah to himself, almost as a title to his writings. In this view, the verse might represent something like "Utterances, by a Prophet that Crieth in the Wilderness." And yet, to be sure, even if this were the primary meaning of the verse, it might well seem applicable to some future precursor of the Messiah.

Certainly John the Baptist viewed himself as the precursor of the Messiah and even saw the precise role he was playing, for he seemed to model himself deliberately on Elijah:

> Matthew 3:4. *And the same John had his raiment of camel's hair, and a leathern girdle about his loins; and his meat was locusts and wild honey.*

Compare this with a description of Elijah in the Old Testament:

> 2 Kings 1:8. . . . *He was an hairy man, and girt with a girdle of leather about his loins . . .*

John's ascetic diet of food which one might gather in the desert (and the ascetic diet, with much fasting, that he imposed upon his disciples) called to mind the time that Elijah remained in the wilderness, eating nothing more than was brought to him, miraculously, by ravens:

1 Kings 17:6. *And the ravens brought him* [Elijah] *bread and flesh in the morning, and . . . in the evening; and he drank of the brook.*

The re-enactment of Elijah was not without its point. A late development in Jewish Messianic thinking had been that Elijah would return to Earth as a precursor of the Messiah. Indeed, the last passage of the last prophetic book of the Bible makes this statement:

Malachi 4:5. *Behold, I will send you Elijah the prophet before the coming of the great and dreadful day of the Lord . . .*

In the Christian versions of the Bible, Malachi is the last book of the Old Testament and there is a kind of neatness about the fact that the last book of the Old Testament ends with the promise of Elijah, and the first book of the New Testament opens with a prophet modeling himself on Elijah.

Matthew later quotes Jesus as confirming this identification of John the Baptist and Elijah:

Matthew 17:12. *But I say unto you, That Elias* [Elijah] *is come already, and they knew him not . . .*
Matthew 17:13. *Then the disciples understood that he spake unto them of John the Baptist.*

Pharisees and Sadducees

John's preaching was popular—he was what we would today call a successful revivalist. The fact of his popularity rests not only on Biblical evidence, but on that of Josephus, who mentions John the Baptist with approval.

Nor was it the nameless common herd alone that flocked to be baptized. Some of the leaders of the religious thought of the time came as well; perhaps sincerely, perhaps out of curiosity, perhaps a little of both.

Matthew 3:7. . . . *he* [John the Baptist] *saw many of the Pharisees and Sadducees come to his baptism* . . .

The Pharisees and Sadducees are two of the Jewish religious sects of the period; sects that had their origin in the travail of the Seleucid persecution and the Maccabean rebellion.

There were Jews who were sympathetic to Hellenism and who did not take part in the rebellion; who even fought on the side of the Seleucids against the Maccabees (see page 67).

Even after the success of the rebellion, there were many Jews who felt some sympathy with Hellenism and were loath to expand Jewish ritual and make Jewish life more and more different from that of the rest of the world.

Naturally, these tended to be drawn from among the upper classes. These were more apt to have a knowledge of Greek and to have studied Hellenic culture. In particular (and almost paradoxically) they included the high priests and their circles. Indeed, the party called itself the "Zadokim," presumably from Zadok, the first of the high priests of the Temple of Solomon. The word Zadokim became Saddoukaioi in Greek and Sadducees in English.

The Sadducees accepted only the written law (there was no avoiding that) and refused all the embroidery that tradition and custom had added to it in the centuries since the Exile. They refused to accept the beliefs and legends of angels, spirits, and demons which had expanded in the Persian and Greek periods; nor did they accept the doctrines of resurrection and an afterlife of reward and punishment.

It seems odd to moderns to read of an important Jewish sect in Roman times denying the resurrection, but actually that doctrine did arise late. References to it appear in the Old Testament only in very late passages. The clearest reference is at the end of Daniel, just about the last book to be added to the canon:

Daniel 12:2. *And many of them that sleep in the dust of the earth shall awake, some to everlasting life, and some to shame and everlasting contempt.*

Opposed to the Hellenizers during the Maccabean revolt were the Assideans or, in Hebrew, Hasidim (see page 56), a word meaning "the pious ones." They were laymen and country folk who utterly rejected Hellenism and who held to a colorful variety of Judaism about which all sorts of traditions had grown. (This is not an unusual phenomenon. Compare today the subtle Christianity of the ministers of important urban congregations and the manner in which it accepts modern science and contemporary thought, with the fervor and traditionalism of those who accept the "old-time religion" in what is called the Bible Belt.)

After the revolt had succeeded, the Assideans developed into two groups. The smaller of the two were the Essenes, who never numbered more than a few thousand. The name is of unknown derivation but is sometimes traced back to a Hebrew word meaning "healers." They lived in isolated communities, practicing celibacy and asceticism, rather like Christian monks. They are not mentioned in the New Testament, but scholars speculate on the possibility that John the Baptist may have been influenced by Essene thought. The main groups of Essenes were concentrated on the northwestern shores of the Dead Sea, and the "Dead Sea scrolls," recently discovered, seem to have been the relics of an Essene-like community.

The greater portion of the Assideans developed into a more worldly group of pietists, ones less removed from society and taking an active part in the political developments of the time. They called themselves, in Aramaic, "Perishaiya," meaning apparently "the separated ones." Since the word "holy" carries the notion of being separated from worldly things and consecrated to God, to call one's self "separated" is not very far removed from calling one's self "holy." This carries a note of smug self-approval which was, perhaps, the least attractive facet of this party. The word "Perishaiya" became "Pharisaios" in Greek and "Pharisees" in English.

The Pharisees accepted not only the written Law itself but also the oral traditions that had grown up about it. They tended to be milder in practice than the Sadducees because oral tradition often softened the harsh letter of the Mosaic Law.

Indeed, Pharisaic teaching at its best very much resembles that of the New Testament. The Jewish teacher Hillel, who died about A.D. 10, taught a kindly religion of love and represents a kind of Jewish parallel to the doctrines of Jesus. Hillel was even, purportedly, of the line of David. However, no miracles are associated with Hillel's name nor did he (or anyone else on his behalf) ever claim Messiah-hood.

At its worst, though, the Pharisees evolved so many trivial rites as an adjunct to religion that no one without great study could be sure of mastering them all. The Pharisees tended to look down upon those who, for lack of leisure time or for lack of learning, did not or could not obey all the ritual, and this did not particularly endear them to the common people. The people in turn tended to adhere to more popular and dramatic teachers who gave them the consolation they needed and demanded a proper inner attitude rather than the mechanical adherence to a complicated set of rites. They turned to men like John the Baptist, and Jesus. In fact, Jesus' teaching might almost be considered as Pharisaic ethics without Pharisaic ritual.

The Sadducees and Pharisees took turns at being politically dominant in the Judea of Maccabean times. Immediately after the rebellion, the Pharisees were in control, for the Sadducees were tarred with the disgrace of having been what we would call, today, "Quislings."

However, although the Seleucid monarchy had been defeated, Hellenic culture remained as attractive as ever, and the Maccabean kings began to Hellenize and to take on the role against which their fathers had fought and died.

The Sadducees therefore regained control of the Temple under John Hyrcanus I and the Pharisees entered the opposition. (It was at this time they adopted their name. Perhaps a little self-praise helped ease the pain of having lost power.)

They were in open revolt under Alexander Jannaeus—a kind of Maccabean revolt against the Maccabees which was repressed bloodily. Later, Alexander's widow, Alexandra, made peace with the Pharisees and for a while things were quiet.

After her death, however, the civil war between her two sons, John Hyrcanus II and Aristobulus II broke out. The Pharisees supported the former and for a while were in control again. During the reign of Herod, and afterward, it was again the turn of the Sadducees to be in power and the Pharisees to be in the opposition.

When representatives of these two parties came to John for baptism he reviled them both, taking up the stand of the common man, so to speak, against those who, like the Sadducees, emptied Judaism of its content and those who, like the Pharisees, filled it too full.

Indeed, he took up a Jeremiah-like attitude. Jeremiah, in his Temple sermon (see page I-562), had warned that the mere existence of the Temple would not protect an ethically evil people. John warned that the mere fact of being Jewish would not serve as protection, either:

Matthew 3:9. And think not to say within yourselves, We have Abraham to our father: for I say unto you, that God is able of these stones to raise up children unto Abraham.

The Son

Now, finally, Jesus appears as an adult coming to John the Baptist in order to be baptized.

As it happens, Josephus, who mentions John the Baptist, does not mention Jesus. There is, to be sure, a paragraph in his history of the Jews which is devoted to Jesus but it interrupts the flow of the discourse and seems suspiciously like an afterthought. Scholars generally believe this to have been an insertion by some early Christian editor who, scandalized that Josephus should talk of the period without mentioning the Messiah, felt the insertion to be a pious act.

Nor, in fact, is there mention of Jesus in any contemporary or nearly contemporary record we have, outside the New Testament.

There have been those who have maintained, because of this, that Jesus never existed, but this seems going too far. The synoptic gospels do not bear the marks of outright fiction as do the books of Tobit, Judith, and Esther, for instance. The synoptic gospels are not filled with anachronisms but prove accurate when they discuss the background of their times. What they say of John the Baptist, for instance, jibes with what Josephus says. Moreover, they contain no incidents which seem flatly to contradict known historical facts.

To be sure, the synoptic gospels are full of miracles and wonder tales which are accepted, *in toto*, by many pious Christians. Still, if some of us, in this rationalist age of ours, wish to discount the miracles and the element of the divine, there still remains a connected, non-miraculous, and completely credible and sensible story of the fate of a Galilean preacher. We can try to trace this story as it is told in Matthew.

For instance, suppose we discount Matthew's tales of Jesus' birth and childhood, as after-the-fact traditions designed to accomplish two things: (1) show him to be a Bethlehem-born scion of the line of David, and therefore qualified to be the Messiah, and (2) demonstrate a similarity between his early career and that of Moses.

If we do this, then what we might call the "historic Jesus" enters the scene first as an adult Galilean, who has heard of the preaching of John the Baptist and has traveled to Judea to be baptized.

As a matter of fact, the gospel of St. Mark, the oldest of the four, starts exactly in this fashion. There is no mention in Mark of a virgin birth at Bethlehem, or of any of the tales of the first two chapters of Matthew. Mark starts with John the Baptist and the baptism of Jesus.

With his baptism the "historic Jesus" feels the impulse to become, himself, a preacher and prophet. In modern terms, he feels the "call to the ministry," but Matthew expresses it in a fashion appropriate to his own time.

> Matthew 3:16. *And Jesus, when he was baptized, went up straight-way out of the water: and, lo, the heavens were opened unto him, and he saw the Spirit of God descending like a dove, and lighting upon him . . .*

This, as described here, seems to be a vision which only Jesus experienced; the heavens were opened "unto *him,* and *he* saw." Undoubtedly, there was a large crowd being baptized at this time, and there is no indication, in the synoptic gospels, at least, that this was an open manifestation visible to all.

The passage goes further than that, however. Jesus is portrayed as becoming conscious at this time of more than a mere call to preach:

> Matthew 3:17. *And lo a voice from heaven, saying, This is my beloved Son, in whom I am well pleased.*

The statement "This is my beloved Son" would seem to mean that at this moment Jesus knew himself to be the destined King; that is, the Messiah. Even non-Messianic kings of Judah were considered to be the adopted sons of Yahveh (see page I-489); how much more so the Messiah.

This, however, may be a matter of the gospel writer's pious interpretation of matters after the fact. If we try to follow the "historic Jesus" it would seem that the realization of Messiah-hood came considerably later.

(The phrase "the Son of God" is considered, in Christian thought, to signify something far more transcendental and subtle than the role assigned to the Messiah in Jewish thought. The later Christian view does not, however, appear clearly in the synoptic gospels. It does do so in the gospel of St. John.)

To Mark, the Spirit of God enters Jesus at the time of the baptism, and it is then and only then, apparently, that he enters his role as Messiah. In Matthew, however, things can't be that simple. The Spirit of God, according to him, entered Jesus at the moment of conception (see page 116), so that he was born the Messiah and could scarcely have need of baptism. Matthew, therefore, must have John the Baptist recognizing this fact. When Jesus came to be baptized:

Matthew 3:14. . . . *John forbad him, saying, I have need to be baptized of thee, and comest thou to me?*

Matthew 3:15. *And Jesus answering said unto him, Suffer it to be so now: for thus it becometh us to fulfil all righteousness . . .*

And yet this realization, on the part of John, of Jesus' role as Messiah, does not fit the tale of the "historic Jesus" as told in Matthew; for at a later period John is clearly revealed as quite uncertain as to the nature of Jesus' mission.

Satan

Once Jesus felt the desire and impelling drive to become a preacher, it is reasonable to suppose that he might have retired for a period of contemplation and decision. What kind of preacher was he to be? What would be his general approach? What would he try to accomplish?

Matthew, expanding on a verse in Mark, puts this into the vocabulary of the time by recounting how, after the baptism, Jesus retired to the wilderness, fasted, and was tempted by Satan to adopt the wrong approach in his ministry. It is characteristic of Matthew that he recounts the struggle between Jesus and Satan as a battle of Old Testament quotations.

Satan urged Jesus, in the first temptation, to satisfy his hunger after fasting by turning stones to bread, something God ought to be glad to do at the request of a devout and pious man. Jesus answers that with a quotation:

Matthew 4:4. *But he* [Jesus] *answered and said, It is written, Man shall not live by bread alone, but by every word that proceedeth out of the mouth of God.*

The quotation is from Deuteronomy:

Deuteronomy 8:3. . . . *man doth not live by bread only, but by every word that proceedeth out of the mouth of the Lord doth man live.*

This might be interpreted as representing Jesus' decision that his role was not to aim merely at an improved economy or a betterment of man's material lot, but to induce moral and ethical regeneration.

Satan next urges Jesus to demonstrate his powers by flinging himself from the top of the Temple and allowing angels to rescue him.

Matthew 4:6. *And* [Satan] *saith unto him, If thou be the Son of God, cast thyself down: for it is written, He shall give his angels charge concerning thee: and in their hands they shall bear thee up, lest at any time thou dash thy foot against a stone.*

Here Satan is described as lending a metaphorical statement in the Psalms a literal interpretation:

Psalm 91:11. . . . *he shall give his angels charge over thee . . .*
Psalm 91:12. *They shall bear thee up in their hands, lest thou dash thy foot against a stone.*

But Jesus retorted with another quotation:

Matthew 4:7. *Jesus said unto him, It is written again, Thou shalt not tempt the Lord thy God.*

(Deuteronomy 6:16. *Ye shall not tempt the Lord your God . . .*)

That is, God is not to be put to the test and made to perform tricks to satisfy the vanity or uncertainty of man. This answer might be interpreted as a decision by Jesus to reject spectacular methods in his mission; to win hearts, that is, by an exhibition of his goodness and not of his power. (Actually, the accounts of the evangelists combine the two aspects and have Jesus demonstrate God's power by miracles of kindliness—the healing of the sick, for the most part.)

In the final temptation, Satan offers him all the kingdoms of the world:

Matthew 4:9. . . . *All these things will I give thee, if thou wilt fall down and worship me.*

To which Jesus responds with a third quotation:

Matthew 4:10. . . . *Get thee hence, Satan: for it is written, Thou shalt worship the Lord thy God, and him only shalt thou serve.*

(Deuteronomy 6:13. *Thou shalt fear the Lord thy God, and serve him . . .*)

(Deuteronomy 6:14. *Ye shall not go after other gods . . .*)

Thus, apparently, Jesus rejects the traditional interpretation of the Messiah as a powerful and ideal king who overthrows the enemies of Israel by force and establishes his rule over all the world in the fashion of a super-Alexander.

This decision to be a Messiah of peace rather than one of war is crucial, apparently, to the tale of the "historic Jesus."

Herodias

Jesus' decision to devote his life to the ministry of God must have been sharpened by the news of the arrest of John the Baptist, since that increased the need for someone to take John's place and continue to spread his message:

Matthew 4:12. *Now when Jesus had heard that John was cast into prison, he departed into Galilee; . . .*

. . .

Matthew 4:17. *From that time Jesus began to preach, and to say, Repent: for the kingdom of heaven is at hand.*

Matthew does not, at this point, give the reason for the arrest of the Baptist, but he returns to the subject later.

Matthew 14:3. *For Herod had laid hold on John, and bound him, and put him in prison for Herodias' sake, his brother Philip's wife.*

Matthew 14:4. *For John said unto him, It is not lawful for thee to have her.*

The story behind this is a complicated one. To begin with we must consider the sons of Herod "the Great" (the king reigning at the time of Jesus' birth; see page 124). Three have been mentioned already as sharing Herod's dominion after his death. One of these, however,

Herod Archelaus, is now out of the picture, having been deposed in A.D. 6, a quarter century before the beginning of Jesus' ministry.

Of the other two, we have first, Herod Antipas, the tetrarch of Galilee and Perea. He was the son of Herod the Great by Malthace, Herod's sixth wife, who had been a Samaritan. Herod Antipas was, therefore, half Idumean and half Samaritan by birth and, consequently, doubly obnoxious to Jewish nationalists. He had been tetrarch ever since his father's death in 4 B.C. and, indeed, ruled altogether for forty-three years, a period which was for the most part one of peace and prosperity for the land.

Second, there is Herod Philip, a son of Herod the Great by his seventh wife, Cleopatra, a Judean woman (despite her name). Herod Philip was made tetrarch of Iturea on Herod's death and he may therefore be called "Philip the Tetrarch." He, too, was still ruling at the time of Jesus' ministry and seems to have been a model ruler.

But there appears to be still another son of Herod the Great, one who does not rule over any section of the kingdom and who, to the confusion of the narration, is also called Philip. We will call him simply "Philip" to distinguish him from Philip the tetrarch. He was Herod's son by Herod's fifth wife, Mariamne II. (She must be distinguished from Mariamne I, who was Herod's second wife.) Mariamne II was not of Maccabean descent and so Philip was in no way a Maccabean.

Finally, we have Herodias, who was the daughter of Aristobulus, who was in turn the son of Herod the Great by Mariamne I. Since it was Mariamne I who was a Maccabean, we can consider Herodias, the granddaughter of Herod the Great, a Maccabean through her grandmother. (Herodias' father, Aristobulus, had been excuted by *his* father, Herod, in 6 B.C., when the old king, sick and soon to die, had grown paranoid and was seeing conspiracies everywhere in his complicated family life.)

Herodias married Philip, her half uncle, while Herod Antipas married the daughter of Aretas, a king of the Nabatean Arabs.

Early in his reign, Herod Antipas tired of his wife and divorced her, taking, as his second wife, Herodias, who divorced Philip. Herodias had thus left one half uncle to become the wife of another half uncle.

As a result, Aretas, feeling the rejection of his daughter to be an insult, declared war on Herod Antipas and defeated him. He achieved nothing by this, however, except perhaps the soothing of his pride. The

Romans could not allow local wars to get too out-of-hand and they interfered, allowing Herod Antipas to keep both his tetrarchy and his new wife.

John the Baptist violently denounced this new marriage as incestuous, not so much because Herodias was Herod Antipas' half niece, but because she was his ex-sister-in-law.

Herod Antipas did not allow himself to be driven by this denunciation into giving up Herodias. Rather, he grew impatient with John the Baptist. He didn't mind John's theological doctrines—Judea was a land of constant and complicated theological dispute in those days—but he did object to any interference with his private life. Besides, he may well have suspected a political motivation behind the denunciation, and felt that John was in the pay of the Nabateans, and was attempting to stir up an internal revolt that would suit the purposes of the still-angry Aretas.

John was therefore imprisoned by Herod at Machaerus (according to Josephus), a fortified village on the southern border of Perea, east of the Dead Sea. Herod did not, however, dare take the logical step of executing John and closing his mouth once and for all, for he feared the unrest that might follow from John's numerous disciples. John therefore remained imprisoned for a period of time.

Zabulon and Nephthalim

Matthew sees Jesus' return to Galilee to begin his ministry as the fulfillment of a prophecy:

Matthew 4:14. *That it might be fulfilled which was spoken by Esaias [Isaiah] the prophet, saying,*

Matthew 4:15. *The land of Zabulon [Zebulon], and the land of Nephthalim [Naphtali], by the way of the sea, beyond Jordan, Galilee of the Gentiles;*

Matthew 4:16. *The people which sat in darkness saw great light; and to them which sat in the region and shadow of death light is sprung up.*

The quotation appears in the Old Testament as:

Isaiah 9:1. *Nevertheless the dimness shall not be such as was in her vexation, when at the first he lightly afflicted the land of*

Zebulun and the land of Naphtali, and afterward did more grievously afflict her by the way of the sea, beyond Jordan, in Galilee of the nations.

Isaiah 9:2. *The people that walked in darkness have seen a great light: they that dwell in the land of the shadow of death, upon them hath the light shined.*

The two verses in Isaiah do not, however, belong together. The first verse (9:1) belongs to the material in the eighth chapter, in which Isaiah is talking about the destruction, not long before, of Israel by the Assyrian forces under Sargon. The second verse (9:2) represents a complete change of subject and even a shift from prose to poetry. It starts a coronation hymn which might have been written, originally, to celebrate the anointing of a new king, possibly Hezekiah (see page I-423).

In the Hebrew Bible (and in the new Jerusalem Bible as well), Isaiah 9:1, with its reference to Naphtali and Zebulon, is to be found as the last verse of the eighth chapter (Isaiah 8:23), while what is Isaiah 9:2 in the King James Version begins the ninth chapter as Isaiah 9:1.

This is by far the more logical separation of the two chapters, and the combination of the two verses in the same chapter was undoubtedly influenced by their quotation together by Matthew, who was anxious to make it seem that the reference to the light in darkness referred particularly to Zebulon and Naphtali so that he might indulge in his hobby of making as much of Jesus' career as possible seem to have been predicted by the Old Testament.

The Carpenter's Son

It might be supposed that in returning to Galilee, Jesus would first of all go back to his own town. If he did, however, he remained there only a short while, something that Matthew skips over hurriedly:

Matthew 4:12. . . . *he* [Jesus] *departed into Galilee;*
Matthew 4:13. *And leaving Nazareth . . .*

What happened in Nazareth at this time, if anything, Matthew does not say, but later in the gospel, Matthew does recount the events that took place during a (presumably) later visit to Nazareth. These same events are recounted by Luke as having taken place during a visit to Nazareth near the start of his ministry, and it is tempting to wonder if perhaps it did not happen at the *very* start of that period of his life.

We could suppose, in tracing the "historic Jesus," that, filled with his new sense of mission, he returned to Nazareth and began to preach there first of all:

> Matthew 13:54. *And when he was come into his own country, he taught them in their synagogue, insomuch that they were astonished* . . .

But in doing so, he did not please his audience. They remembered him as a youngster who had grown to manhood in their town, and now he had the nerve, apparently, to set himself up as a preacher over them. Matthew quotes the audience as asking, resentfully:

> Matthew 13:54. . . . *Whence hath this man this wisdom* . . .
> Matthew 13:55. *Is not this the carpenter's son? is not his mother called Mary?* . . .
> Matthew 13:56. . . . *Whence then hath this man all these things?*

Both Jesus' father and mother are here mentioned, but his father, Joseph, never appears as a living person anywhere in the New Testament except in connection with the tales of Jesus' birth. It is usually assumed, therefore, that he died some time during Jesus' youth.

It would appear from these verses that Joseph was a carpenter, but what about Jesus? Luke, in telling the same incident, has the audience ask:

> Luke 4:22. . . . *Is not this Joseph's son?*

and there is no mention of carpentering.

Mark, on the other hand—author of the oldest of the gospels—records the incident and has the audience ask:

> Mark 6:3. *Is not this the carpenter, the son of Mary* . . .

Is it possible, then, that the "historic Jesus," before his baptism by John and his call to the ministry, was a carpenter in Nazareth and that his townspeople were highly offended that a common laborer with no theological education (the common people were notoriously unlearned in the Pharisaic complications of the Law in those days) should presume to set himself up as a preacher? And if he displayed knowledge of the Law, having learned it through intelligence and industry, that would not alter the fact that as a common laborer he ought to sit in the audience and listen to his "betters."

Both Luke and Matthew, writing later, when Jesus had grown mightier in the memory of his disciples, might indeed have felt reluctant to emphasize Jesus' position as a laborer. Matthew made Joseph the carpenter (though it is quite possible that father and son were both carpenters; that Jesus was brought up in his father's trade) while Luke drops the embarrassing word altogether.

In any case, Jesus assuages his disappointment by a thought similar to our own "Familiarity breeds contempt."

Matthew 13:57. . . . *Jesus said unto them, A prophet is not without honour, save in his own country, and in his own house.*

The experience seems to have shown Jesus that if his mission were to be successful, it would have to be some place where he wasn't known so well that people would let themselves be influenced by the nature of his earlier trade or the state of his formal education.

Jesus' Brethren

The incident at Nazareth reveals something else about Jesus' family. The audience ironically recites the names of Jesus' relatives to show that they are not mistaken, that this upstart preacher is indeed the lowly carpenter they know and not some visiting dignitary. They mention not only his mother and father, but his brothers and sisters as well.

Matthew 13:55. *Is not this the carpenter's son? is not his mother called Mary? and his brethren, James, and Joses, and Simon, and Judas?*
Matthew 13:56. *And his sisters, are they not all with us?*

If one interpreted these verses in the simplest possible manner, one would come to the conclusion that the "historic Jesus" was the member of a large family, and that Joseph and Mary had five sons and several daughters.

Even if one were to accept Matthew's tale of the virgin birth of Jesus, this possibility is not eliminated. He says:

> Matthew 1:25. *And [Joseph]* knew her *[Mary]* not till she had brought forth her firstborn son: *and he called his name Jesus.*

Even if Mary remained a virgin till Jesus' birth, there is nothing in this verse which would force us to believe that Joseph had no relations with Mary *after* the birth of Jesus, and that Mary might not have borne a number of children in the normal manner who would then have been younger brothers and sisters to Jesus. One might even argue that a "firstborn" son implies at least a secondborn son and possibly others. It would have been easy to say "only son" or even "only child" if Mary had had no more children.

This picture of a normal home life, of Mary as a multiple mother, of Jesus with four younger brothers and several younger sisters, is, however, unacceptable to many Christians who believe firmly in the tradition of the perpetual virginity of Mary, and reasons have been advanced to make the apparently clear words of the verse mean other than they seem to mean.

One theory is that the individuals referred to as the brothers and sisters of Jesus were actually Joseph's children by a previous marriage and not the sons of Mary at all. They would then be Jesus' older half brothers and half sisters. Against that, is the fact that no such earlier marriage of Joseph is mentioned anywhere in the Bible.

A more tenable theory is that the men were not his brothers but relatives of another kind—say, cousins. The word "brother" is indeed used in the Bible to mean, on occasion, "kinsman." Thus Lot is Abraham's nephew, but:

> Genesis 13:8. *And Abram* [Abraham] *said unto Lot, Let there be no strife, I pray thee, between me and thee, . . . for we be brethren.*

Again Jacob is Laban's nephew, but:

> Genesis 29:15. *And Laban said unto Jacob, Because thou art my brother, shouldest thou therefore serve me for nought? . . .*

However, in such cases enough genealogical material is usually given to enable the exact relations of the individuals involved to be worked out. This is not so in the case of Jesus' brethren, and those who argue for a more distant relationship must seek indirect evidence.

Thus, Matthew speaks of several women witnessing the crucifixion:

> Matthew 27:56. *Among which was . . . Mary the mother of James and Joses . . .*

Names are frequently repeated from family to family, but here we have a James and Joses who are the sons of Mary. Could these be the James and Joses mentioned as Jesus' brothers, along with Simon and Judas, here unmentioned? If so, they must be the sons of another Mary, for if this Mary were Jesus' mother as well, surely Matthew would have said so. In that case, who was this other Mary?

In an analogous verse in the gospel of St. John, we have:

> John 19:25. *Now there stood by the cross of Jesus his mother, and his mother's sister, Mary the wife of Cleophas . . .*

Could it be that the brothers mentioned in Matthew 13:55 are the sons of Jesus' aunt Mary, rather than of his mother Mary, and are therefore actually his first cousins?

However, many modern scholars do not seek roundabout explanations but accept Mary, the mother of Jesus, as being the mother of others as well. Certainly, if we try to trace a "historic Jesus" in whom the tale of the virgin birth is not involved, there is no reason to question the fact that he had true brothers and sisters.

Capernaum

Leaving Nazareth, Jesus went to a larger city in Galilee, where he might expect more success than in his small home town:

> Matthew 4:13. *And leaving Nazareth, he [Jesus] came and dwelt in Capernaum, which is upon the sea coast . . .*

Capernaum is about twenty miles northeast of Nazareth and, in the time of Jesus, was an important town with a Roman garrison, a tax-collection office, and a sizable synagogue. Its Hebrew name was "Kapharnahum" ("village of Nahum"), which became "Kapharnaoum" in Greek and "Capernaum" in English.

Despite the fame of Capernaum as the site of Jesus' preaching, it

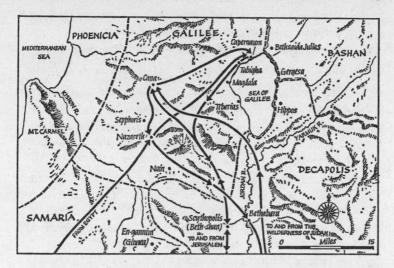

Early Journeys of Christ

eventually faded away until, in modern times, there was even a dispute as to its location.

It was located "upon the sea coast" but that does not mean the Mediterranean Sea, as one might think, but upon the inland lake of fresh water that is found to the east of Galilee along the upper courses of the Jordan River.

The lake is pear-shaped with the broad end at the north. It is not large, only thirteen miles long and seven and a half miles wide at its broadest point. It has a surface area of only sixty-five square miles (three times the size of Manhattan Island).

The lake has had a variety of names, all taken from cities or districts along its western shores. For instance, a very early town near its southern end was named Chinnereth. It is mentioned in the records of the conquering Thutmose III of Egypt (see page I-122) long before the Exodus. It gave its name to the lake and to the western shores of that lake.

The lake is barely mentioned in the Old Testament, for the centers of population and power in Israel and Judah lay well to the south. When it is mentioned at all, it is usually brought in as part of a boundary delineation:

Numbers 34:11. . . . *and the border shall descend, and shall reach unto the side of the sea of Chinnereth eastward* . . .

The western shores of the lake are mentioned in connection with a Syrian invasion of about 900 B.C.

1 Kings 15:20. *So Ben-hadad* [of Syria] . . . *smote* . . . *Cinneroth* [Chinnereth], *with all the land of Naphtali.*

Modern Israel still uses the Old Testament name for the lake, calling it "Yam Kinneret," and on its shores is a town called Kinneret, with a population of about a thousand.

On the northwestern shores of the lake is a small plain, not more than two miles each way, where two small rivulets enter it. It was called Gennosar or Gennesarat, a name of uncertain origin. Perhaps it means "garden of Hazor," Hazor being the Canaanite ruler of the region in the time of the judges (see page I-235).

At any rate, that district gave its name to the lake also, and the names are used in the Bible, the Apocrypha, and in Josephus. Thus:

1 Maccabees 11:67. *As for Jonathan and his host, they pitched at the water of Gennesar* . . .

and, in the New Testament:

Luke 5:1. . . . *he* [Jesus] *stood by the lake of Gennesaret,*

In modern Israel a village stands on the northwest shore of the lake. It has a population of perhaps five hundred and its name is Ginnosar.

After the exodus when the northern reaches that had once made up the tribal territory of Naphtali and Zebulon became known as Galilee (see page 64), the lake became known as the Sea of Galilee:

Matthew 4:18. *And Jesus, walking by the sea of Galilee* . . .

That is perhaps the name by which it is best known to Christians ever since, but it is not the latest of its names. In Jesus' own time, still a newer name arose.

The largest and most modern city on the shores of the lake in Jesus' time was one that was built in A.D. 20 (less than a decade before Jesus began his ministry) by Herod Antipas. It was named Tiberias after the Roman Emperor then reigning and Antipas made it his capital. It was primarily a Gentile city and was looked upon by the Jews with horror, partly for that reason and partly out of superstition, for it was built on the site of an ancient cemetery.

The city is mentioned only once in the New Testament, and then only in the gospel of St. John, the latest and most Greek-oriented of the gospels:

> John 6:23. (*Howbeit there came other boats from Tiberias . . .*)

That city, too, gave its name to the sea, a name also found in John:

> John 6:1. *After these things Jesus went over the sea of Galilee, which is the sea of Tiberias.*

Tiberias still exists and is still the largest city on the shores of the lake. It has a population of about twenty-two thousand, and its name is still affixed to the lake, which is known in Arabic as "Bahr Tabariya" and in American geographies as "Lake Tiberias."

Simon

In Capernaum, Jesus rapidly attained the success and got the hearing that he was denied in Nazareth. He even began to collect disciples:

> Matthew 4:18. *And Jesus, walking by the sea of Galilee, saw two brethren, Simon called Peter, and Andrew his brother, casting a net into the sea: for they were fishers.*
> Matthew 4:19. *And he saith unto them, Follow me, and I will make you fishers of men.*
> Matthew 4:20. *And they straightway left their nets, and followed him.*

Simeon is the form of the name used in the Old Testament, and in one place that form is used for Simon Peter:

> Acts 15:14. *Simeon hath declared how God at the first did visit the Gentiles . . .*

There was a strong tendency, however, to shorten it to Simon, since that happened to be a perfectly good Greek name and there was a continuing tendency among even conservative Jews in this period to adopt or be given Greek names.

The Jews did not have our system of surnames and it was customary to distinguish an individual from others of the same name by the use of his father's name. Thus, at one point, Jesus says:

Matthew 16:17. . . . *Blessed art thou, Simon Bar-jona* . . .

By Simon Bar-jona is meant, "Simon, son of Jona."

But this too might be insufficient, and it was common to add to a man's name some nickname drawn from his personal appearance or character, something that would be highly individual. This was noted in the case of the sons of Mattathias, the priest who sparked the Maccabean rebellion (see page 54).

Simon, perhaps because of his size and strength, or because of his firmness of will, or both, was called, in Aramaic, Simon Cephas (Simon, the Rock). In Greek, "rock" is "petros" and in Latin it is "petrus." This becomes "peter" in English and so Simon is frequently referred to as Simon Peter.

The nickname can be used by itself if it is sufficiently distinctive and becomes sufficiently well known. Thus, Paul, in his First Epistle to the Corinthians, denounces the factionalism of the early Church, saying:

1 Corinthians 1:12. . . . *every one of you saith, I am of Paul; and I of Apollos; and I of Cephas* . . .

where Cephas is Simon. And we, of course, know him best simply as Peter.

Andrew is not a name that occurs in the Old Testament. It is the English version of the Greek "Andreas" meaning "manly." The final "-ew" in the English version may have been influenced by the form of Matthew.

Matthew's story makes it seem that Peter and Andrew were simply called and they followed, unable to help themselves, attracted and mesmerized by the divine in Jesus. And yet, if we are tracing the "historic Jesus," it isn't at all unreasonable to assume that Peter and Andrew first heard him preach, were attracted to his doctrines, and then joined him.

James

Nor were the brothers, Peter and Andrew, the only disciples gained in Capernaum. Another pair of brothers were quickly collected:

Matthew 4:21. *And going on from thence, he saw other two brethren, James the son of Zebedee, and John his brother, in a ship with Zebedee their father, mending their nets; and he called them.*

Matthew 4:22. *And they immediately left the ship and their father, and followed him.*

Zebedee, the name of the father of James and John, is the English version of the Greek "Zebedaios" which is, in turn, derived from the Hebrew Zebediah. A number of men of that name are mentioned in the Old Testament but none of importance.

John, son of Zebedee, is the second of the important Johns in the New Testament, the first being John the Baptist, of course.

James would seem, at first, to be a name distinct from any in the Old Testament, but that appears so only if we look upon the English version of the name. It comes from the Greek "Iakhobos" and the Latin "Jacobus," so that James is clearly equivalent to Jacob.

Decapolis

The fame of Jesus' preaching began to spread widely. In the Jewish kingdoms of that time, a skillful preacher, learned in the Law and ready to illustrate his points with interesting tales that pointed an analogy or a moral ("parables"), was bound to attract attention. Word concerning him would travel quickly, as one person excitedly told another, and many would come to see and hear the new attraction. The effect would be the same as that of a new philosopher in Athens, a new gladiator in Rome, or a new popular play in New York.

Concerning holy men of all ages, reports of miraculous cures have always been circulated. This has been true not only of the times before Jesus, but of the times since. The kings of England, few of whom were particularly holy, and some of whom were particularly unholy, were considered capable of curing a disease called scrofula simply by touching the sick individual; and the monarch touched for the "king's evil" into the eighteenth century. Even today there are any number of faith-healers who cure people by the "laying on of hands." Such is the complicated nature of disease and the important influence of mental attitude upon it that a patient who thoroughly believes a certain course of treatment will help him (even if it is only the casual touch of an indifferent king or of a backwoods healer) is indeed often helped.

Many tales of cures brought about by Jesus are recorded by the enthusiastic evangelists, and it is useless to try to suggest naturalistic explanations for each one. To the believing Christian, all the cures described are completely possible, having been brought about not by faith-healing or by a kind of primitive psychiatry, but by the direct intervention of divine power.

In the search for the "historic Jesus," however, it may be sufficient to say that many who accepted Jesus as a holy man believed he could help their illnesses and were indeed helped by him. The tales of his cures were spread abroad (and were exaggerated in the telling and retelling, as is invariably and inevitably the case in such situations). Such tales helped increase his fame further:

> Matthew 4:24. *And his fame went throughout all Syria . . .*
> Matthew 4:25. *And there followed him great multitudes of people from Galilee, and from Decapolis, and from Jerusalem . . .*

The mention of Decapolis ("ten cities") is particularly interesting. At the time of the conquests of Alexander the Great, Greek cities were planted everywhere that his armies trod; and this tendency continued under the Macedonian kings who fell heir to his dominions. Under the Seleucids, the region east of the Jordan River and the Sea of Galilee came to be studded with Greek towns.

At the height of the Maccabean monarchy, the area was conquered by Alexander Jannaeus, but when Pompey marched into Judea and reorganized the area, the Greek cities were freed. They formed a league among themselves and in the time of Jesus enjoyed considerable self-government. The ten cities that formed part of the league are given differently by different authorities, but apparently the northernmost was Damascus itself, sixty miles northeast of Capernaum. This is the same Damascus that had been the capital of the Syrian kingdom against which Ahab had fought.

If people came from the Decapolis to hear Jesus, they may have included some Gentiles. This is not specifically stated, but there is nothing impossible about it. Just as some Jews were strongly attracted to Greek culture, some Greeks would be strongly attracted to Judaism. Even if such Greeks stopped short of conversion, they might yet be sufficiently interested to go hear some outstanding preacher.

In view of the later history of Christianity, the fact that Jesus' preaching may early have spread among Greeks, and Gentiles generally, is of extreme importance.

The Law

At this point Matthew feels it appropriate to give a sampling of the doctrines that Jesus was preaching, and that attracted such wide attention. He does so in a sermon covering three chapters. Probably the passage as given by Matthew is not actually a single sermon spoken at one time, but is a collection of representative "sayings." The sermon is introduced thus:

Matthew 5:1. *And seeing the multitudes, he [Jesus] went up into a mountain: and when he was set, his disciples came unto him:*
Matthew 5:2. *And he opened his mouth, and taught them . . .*

In A.D. 394 the Christian bishop St. Augustine wrote a commentary on this sermon which he entitled "Concerning the Lord's sermon in the mountain" and since then these chapters of Matthew have been referred to as "The Sermon on the Mount."

There have been attempts to pick out some particular hill near Capernaum on which the sermon might have been delivered, but there seems no way of reaching a decision.

The Sermon on the Mount, as given in Matthew, is, as is to be expected, closely tied in with Old Testament teachings. Many phrases which we associate very strongly with the Sermon and with Jesus' teachings have close parallels in the Old Testament. Thus an often quoted passage appears in the early verses of the Sermon, verses that give blessings to various groups of individuals and are therefore called the "Beatitudes" from the Latin word for "happiness" or "blessedness." It goes:

Matthew 5:5. *Blessed are the meek: for they shall inherit the earth.*

Compare this with:

Psalm 37:11. *But the meek shall inherit the earth . . .*

Indeed, it might be supposed that one of the purposes of Matthew in recording the Sermon on the Mount is to support a particular point of view which he represents among the early Christians.

After Jesus had passed from the scene, his sayings survived only because they were remembered and repeated by word of mouth. There is no evidence that Jesus ever put his teachings into permanent written form.

Oral teaching that must be carried on by word of mouth can give rise to disputes. There were naturally many sayings quoted by one listener or another and in some cases a saying might be reported in one form by one person and in another form by someone else. The sayings might even be quoted in self-contradictory forms and could be used to support widely divergent theological points.

Perhaps the most basic of the early splits among Christians was between those who held the teachings of Jesus to be merely a refinement of Judaism, and those who held them to be a radical change from Judaism. The former would maintain the supremacy of the Mosaic Law even for Christians; the latter would deny it.

Matthew, the most Jewish of the evangelists, apparently believed in the supremacy of the Law, and in the Sermon on the Mount he quoted Jesus as being strenuously and unequivocally of that belief:

Matthew 5:17. *Think not that I am come to destroy the law, or the prophets: I am not come to destroy, but to fulfil.*

Matthew 5:18. *For verily I say unto you, Till heaven and earth pass, one jot or one tittle shall in no wise pass from the law, till all be fulfilled.*

Matthew follows that with another verse which seems aimed by him directly at the heads of those among the early Christians who took up the other point of view:

Matthew 5:19. *Whosoever therefore shall break one of these least commandments, and shall teach men so, he shall be called the least in the kingdom of heaven . . .*

This extreme view, as quoted, is strengthened by a consideration of the meaning of "jot" and "tittle." Jot is the Hebrew letter "yodh," the smallest (little more than a fat dot) letter in the Hebrew alphabet. In Greek the letter is named "iota," and is the smallest in the Greek alphabet (so that one says "not an iota" meaning "not a bit"). In English the letter is "i" and it is the smallest in our alphabet.

A tittle is a translation of a Greek word meaning "little horn." It would be a small mark that would distinguish one Hebrew letter from another. The equivalent in English would be the small line that distinguishes a Q from an O.

The Revised Standard Version translates the verse: "For truly, I say to you, till heaven and earth pass away, not an iota, not a dot, will pass from the law until all is accomplished." Nothing, in other words, would change in the Law as a result of Jesus' coming, not even the smallest particle.

The interpretation of this passage depends on the phrase "till all be fulfilled." Matthew seems to imply that this is synonymous with "till heaven and earth pass." Other views are possible, however, and are stated in the Bible, as we shall see, and it was these other views that eventually won out.

It may very well be that the "historic Jesus" did indeed hold the view given here in Matthew, for in the synoptic gospels he is always pictured—despite his disputes with the Pharisees—as an orthodox Jew, adhering to all the tenets of Judaism.

Publicans

If anything, Jesus (as represented by Matthew) would strengthen the Law, rather than weaken it. Thus, in the Sermon on the Mount, Jesus is quoted as preaching the necessity for exceeding the letter of the Law in matters of morals and ethics. It is not sufficient to refrain from killing one's fellow man; one must refrain from even being angry with him, or expressing contempt for him. It is insufficient to refrain from committing adultery; one must not even allow one's self to entertain lustful feelings. It is insufficient to refrain from swearing false oaths; one should not swear at all, but simply tell the truth.

Although the Mosaic Law permitted retaliation in kind to personal injuries, Jesus held it better that there were no retaliation at all. One should return good for evil. After all, he points out, to return good for good is easy; that is a natural tendency that affects even the irreligious. Those who wish ethical perfection must do more than that:

Matthew 5:46. *For if ye love them which love you, what reward have ye? do not even the publicans the same?*

The publicans are held up here as an extreme. If even the publicans can do this, anyone can. The Greek word used here is "telonai" which is translated into the Latin "publicani" and which becomes, in English, "publicans."

In Rome the publicani were originally the contractors who agreed, for appropriate payment, to perform public works and services. One of the most important of these public works and services was to collect taxes.

It was difficult to collect taxes in a realm the size of the Roman Empire in a day when modern means of transportation and communication did not exist, and when modern business procedures were unheard of. The mere fact that Arabic numerals did not exist, enormously multiplied the difficulties of regulating the Roman economy.

Roman financial procedures were always inefficient and wasteful and the burden of this was laid upon the people of the empire, particularly, in New Testament times, upon the people of the provinces.

The Roman government did not have the organization required to collect taxes, so what they did was to farm out permission to make such collections to rich men who had considerable cash available. These could, for a large sum, buy the right to collect the taxes of a certain province. The sum they paid would represent the tax collection as far as the government was concerned. The government would have the taxes it needed on the spot. It need take no further trouble for it.

The publicani, however, would now have to recoup their payment out of the taxes they collected, which they could then keep. It was as "tax collectors" that the people of the provinces best knew the publicani, and the word is translated as "tax collector" in the Revised Standard Version.

The trouble with this system was that if the publicani, or tax collectors, gathered less than they had paid out, they would suffer a loss, whereas if they could gouge out more than they had paid, they would make a profit. The more merciless the gouging, the higher the profit, so it was to the interest of the publicani to force payment of every cent they could get by the harshest application of the letter of the Law as interpreted most favorably to themselves.

No tax collector, however lenient and merciful, is actually going to be loved, but a "publican" of the Roman sort was sure to be hated above all men as a merciless leech who would take the shirt off a dying child. It is not to be wondered at, then, that the word "publican" is used as representing an extreme of wickedness in the Sermon on the Mount.

Of course, the men to whom Jesus referred were not the publicani themselves, not the wealthy businessmen in Rome who waxed fat on the misery of millions. They were merely the army of small employees who owned the actual outstretched hands and who then passed the money on to their superiors.

But in a way, these were even worse, for they were usually Jews who took the job as a means of making a living and, in this fashion, earned the hatred and contempt of their fellow Jews. There were numerous Jewish nationalists at this time who felt the Romans to be oppressors who must be fought against and overthrown in Maccabean fashion. To endure the presence of the Romans was bad enough, to pay taxes to them was worse, but to collect taxes for them was the limit and beyond the limit.

Paternoster

Jesus continues the Sermon on the Mount, denouncing ostentation in piety. He decries giving alms openly, praying in public, or deliberately exaggerating one's appearance of suffering while fasting, all in order to receive admiration and gain a reputation for piety. Jesus points out that if it is human acclaim that is wanted, then it is received and that is all the reward that is likely to come.

He also counsels against uselessly long or ritualistic prayers:

Matthew 6:7. . . . *when ye pray, use not vain repetitions, as the heathen do: for they think that they shall be heard for their much speaking.*

. . . .

Matthew 6:9. *After this manner therefore pray ye: Our Father which art in heaven, Hallowed be thy name.*

and there follows the well-known "Lord's Prayer," so-called because it is the prayer recited by Jesus himself. In Latin the first words "Our Father" are "Pater noster," so that the prayer is sometimes called "the Paternoster."

Ironically enough, in view of Jesus' admonition in Matthew 6:7, it is often customary to repeat the Paternoster a number of times in a fast, mumbling sort of way—so that the word "patter" for such fast, mumbling speech is derived from "Paternoster."

Mammon

As is not unusual for preachers who gather their disciples from among the poor, Jesus had harsh words to say about wealth and the wealthy. The "historic Jesus" was himself a carpenter, his first four disciples were fishermen. Undoubtedly it was the poor and unlearned who followed him, while the aristocracy (the Sadducees) and the intelligentsia (the Pharisees) opposed him.

It is not surprising, then, that the gospels, and early Christian teaching in general, had a strong note of the social revolutionary about it. It may even have been this note that contributed greatly to the gathering of converts in the first couple of centuries after Jesus' death.

In the Sermon on the Mount, Jesus urged less care for gathering the material riches valued on Earth and more care for the gathering of the ethical riches valued in heaven. Indeed, to care too much for Earthly things meant, inevitably, that one would withdraw one's attention from the subtler values of heaven:

> Matthew 6:24. *No man can serve two masters: . . . Ye cannot serve God and mammon.*

Mammon is, here, an untranslated Aramaic word meaning "wealth." Because of its use in this manner in this verse, it is very commonly supposed that mammon is an antithesis of God; that it is the name of some demon or heathen idol that serves as a god of wealth. Thus, John Milton, in his *Paradise Lost*, makes Mammon one of the fallen angels who followed Satan. In fact, he makes him the most despicable of the lot, for even in Heaven, before his fall, Milton pictures him as exclusively concerned with admiring the gold of Heaven's pavement.

It would get the meaning across more efficiently if the phrase were translated (as in the Jerusalem Bible) as "God and money."

In a way, this represented a shift from early Jewish thought. In the absence of a hereafter of reward and punishment, it was felt that the pious were rewarded on earth with wealth, health, and happiness, while the sinful were punished with impoverishment, sickness, and misery. It was this thought which sparked the intricate discussion concerning the attitude of God toward good and evil which is found in the Book of Job (see page I-479).

With reward and punishment-reserved for the next life, the thought might naturally arise that people who had it "too good" on Earth would have to suffer for it in the hereafter just to even the score. There could well be some comfort in this view to those who were poor and oppressed and the evangelists sometimes quote Jesus in such a way as to make him appear to support this view.

Placing God and mammon in opposition, as in Matthew 6:24, is an example. An even more extreme example, which virtually damns rich men merely for being rich, is the familiar verse in which Jesus says:

Matthew 19:24. . . . *It is easier for a camel to go through the eye of a needle, than for a rich man to enter into the kingdom of God.*

Once Christianity became widespread and popular enough to attract the rich and powerful, much effort had to be expended to explain away this verse. Thus, for example, it was sometimes pretended that "Needle's Eye" was the name of a narrow gate through the Jerusalem walls and that a full laden camel could not pass through until some of the load was removed. Therefore, the verse could be taken as meaning that a rich man could get into Heaven only after a suitable portion of his wealth had been given to charity—or the Church. However, it makes more sense to accept the verse as meaning just what it seems to mean —an expression of a savage feeling against the rich on the part of the poor who made up the early Christian congregations.

The Dogs

Toward the end of the Sermon on the Mount, a verse occurs that is not connected with what precedes or succeeds, but stands by itself:

Matthew 7:6. *Give not that which is holy unto the dogs, neither cast ye your pearls before swine, lest they trample them under their feet, and turn again and rend you.*

Both dogs and swine were ritually unclean animals which were scavengers and therefore literally unclean as well. To apply either term to someone was a matter of high insult—and still is in many cultures. (Consider the German expletive "Schweinhund" or "pig-dog.")

The question is: What or whom are the dogs and swine being referred to in this verse? The verse might simply mean that one ought not to try to teach religious truths to inveterate scoffers or those utterly lost in sin, and yet that scarcely seems to be right. To whom ought one to teach the truth? To those who already believe?

Jesus himself refutes this, for when he is accused of associating with sinners, he is quoted as saying:

Matthew 9:12. . . . *They that be whole need not a physician, but they that are sick.*

On the other hand, the reference to dogs and pigs may be a quotation selected by Matthew to support his own view of a Jewish-oriented Christianity. In other words, he might be saying that one ought not to make a great effort to spread the teachings of Jesus among the Gentiles. Perhaps it was Matthew's view that there was too great a danger of the Gentiles being offended by efforts at proselytization and indulging in forceful persecution of the Christians; they would "turn again and rend you" as, in fact, they actually did on occasion. He might also feel that those Gentiles who accepted Christianity without knowledge of the Mosaic Law would pervert the teachings of Jesus; they would "trample them under their feet."

That all this might indeed be so is supported by another passage in Matthew where the matter is stated quite plainly and where the meaning of the word "dog" is unmistakable.

During a stay north of Galilee, Jesus is accosted by a Canaanite woman who requests him to heal her sick daughter.

At first, Jesus does not answer her at all, but when she persists:

Matthew 15:24. . . . *he answered and said, I am not sent but unto the lost sheep of the house of Israel.*

. . . .

Matthew 15:26. . . . *It is not meet to take the children's bread, and to cast it to dogs.*

Here Matthew clearly presents his version of a Jesus whose business lies entirely within the boundaries of Jewish nationalism. (To be sure, these verses are not the end of this particular passage; more of that shortly.) Furthermore the antithesis of "children" and "dogs" is

clearly meant to represent that of "Jews" and "Gentiles." This shows
a strong anti-Gentile bias on the part of some of the early Jewish
Christians; a bias which, as we shall see in later gospels, was amply
returned by some of the early Gentile Christians.

This view of Jesus' teachings—as pictured by Matthew—is also
shown when Jesus' disciples are sent out to spread those teachings. They
receive clear instructions:

Matthew 10:5. . . . *Jesus . . . commanded them, saying, Go not
into the way of the Gentiles, and into any city of the Samaritans
enter ye not:*

Matthew 10:6. *But go rather to the lost sheep of the house of
Israel.*

The Centurion

And yet Matthew could not possibly present the situation too narrowly. At the time that the gospel was written, it was quite clear that
most Jews were resolutely rejecting the Messiah-hood of Jesus and would
never accept it, whereas a surprising number of Gentiles were asking
admittance. Christianity could not close the door upon the Gentile or
it would die. Even Matthew saw that.

He therefore pictures the Gentile as allowed to enter but, it must
be said, sometimes does so rather grudgingly. Thus, consider again the
case of the Canaanite woman who accosts Jesus with a request to heal
her daughter and is told that the children's food is not to be cast to
dogs. She accepts the analogy submissively:

Matthew 15:27. *And she said, Truth, Lord: yet the dogs eat of
the crumbs which fall from their masters' table.*

Whereupon Jesus accepts the justice of the remark (one might almost consider it a gentle reproof) and heals the woman's daughter.
According to Matthew's view here, it would seem, the Gentile is
accepted, if he enters humbly, with full knowledge of his inferior status.

A less grudging attitude is evidenced by an incident related of
Jesus immediately after the Sermon on the Mount, one that not only
welcomes Gentiles, but warns obdurate Jews.

Matthew 8:5. . . . *when Jesus was entered into Capernaum, there
came unto him a centurion, beseeching him,*

Matthew 8:6. *And saying, Lord, my servant lieth at home sick of the palsy . . .*

A centurion was an officer who commanded a hundred men, and the word is derived from the Latin "centum" meaning "a hundred men." He would be equivalent to a noncommissioned officer in our army. It is uncertain in this case whether the centurion was actually a member of the occupying Roman army or in the forces of Herod Antipas. In either case, he was not Jewish.

The centurion begs Jesus not to bother coming personally, but to say the healing word from a distance. Jesus does as the centurion asks, saying:

Matthew 8:10. . . . *I have not found so great faith, no, not in Israel.*

Matthew 8:11. *And I say unto you, That many shall come from the east and west, and shall sit down with Abraham, and Isaac, and Jacob, in the kingdom of heaven.*

Matthew 8:12. *But the children of the kingdom shall be cast out into outer darkness . . .*

Matthew considers Jesus' miracles of healing to bear out an Old Testament prophecy:

Matthew 8:17. *That it might be fulfilled which was spoken by Esaias* [Isaiah] *the prophet, saying, Himself took our infirmities, and bare our sicknesses.*

This is from a verse in Second Isaiah in which the prophet describes the suffering servant (see page I-550):

Isaiah 53:4. *Surely he hath borne our griefs, and carried our sorrows . . .*

The Son of Man

Jesus is pictured in the synoptic gospels as careful, during this early part of his ministry, to avoid arousing the suspicion of the authorities with respect to his Messianic status. Both the religious and secular leaders would strike quickly at those they considered were falsely claiming to be the Messiah, since such false Messiahs would stir up revolts and do much damage.

Even if Jesus himself were discreet, his growing popularity might cause those who followed him to proclaim him the Messiah in too incautious a fashion, and this, apparently, he wished to avoid. He is therefore described as preferring that his miraculous cures not be too widely publicized. Thus, after curing a leper:

Matthew 8:4. . . . *Jesus saith unto him, See thou tell no man; but go thy way, shew thyself to the priest, and offer the gift that Moses commanded . . .*

In other words, the cured leper is to have himself declared ritually clean according to the Mosaic system, but he is not to say how it came about. Jesus showed the same discretion in references to himself. Thus, when a scribe offered to become his disciple, Jesus points out the hardships involved:

Matthew 8:20. *And Jesus saith unto him, The foxes have holes, and the birds of the air have nests; but the Son of man hath not where to lay his head.*

The phrase "Son of man" is a common way of saying simply "man." It is frequently used in the Book of Ezekiel, when God is quoted as addressing the prophet:

Ezekiel 2:1. *And he [God] said unto me, Son of man, stand upon thy feet, and I will speak unto thee.*

The phrase seems to emphasize the lowliness of man as compared to God; the infinite inferiority of the former to the latter. It is as though God addressed a man as "Mortal!"

Outside of Ezekiel, the phrase does not appear in the Old Testament except in the very late Book of Daniel. There it is used in one case precisely as in Ezekiel, when the angel Gabriel speaks to Daniel:

Daniel 8:17. . . . *he [Gabriel] said unto me, Understand, O son of man . . .*

But in the second place, Daniel is describing an apocalyptic vision (see page I-610):

Daniel 7:13. *I saw in the night visions, and, behold, one like the Son of man came with the clouds of heaven, . . .*

Daniel 7:14. *And there was given him . . . an everlasting domin-*
ion . . . and his kingdom . . . shall not be destroyed.

Daniel had previously symbolized a variety of heathen nations op-
pressing Israel in the form of wild beasts; now he symbolized the ideal
kingdom of a Messianic Israel in the form of a man, to show its
greater worth. "One like the Son of man" can be paraphrased, "a
figure in the shape of a man."

Because of this one passage, however, the phrase "son of man"
came to be used as a metaphoric way of speaking of the Messiah.
Perhaps this was useful at times when it was dangerous to be too openly
Messianic in one's hopes. By speaking of the "son of man" one could indicate the Messiah to those who were in sympathy; but before a judge
one might maintain that the phrase meant simply "man."

Jesus is quoted as referring to himself in this fashion on a number
of occasions. It is, indeed, the most frequent title he gives himself. We
might picture the "historic Jesus" as pleased by his own success and
beginning to think that his mission might be a great one indeed.
Cautiously he could begin to refer to himself as "son of man," a Messianic title which could always be defended as a form of humility
used after the fashion of Ezekiel.

Gergesenes

Jesus' successes at Capernaum encouraged him, apparently, to try
to extend his work beyond Galilee:

Matthew 8:18. *Now when Jesus saw great multitudes about him,*
he gave commandment to depart unto the other side.

By "the other side" is meant, of course, the eastern shore of the
Sea of Galilee. This eastern shore was outside the tetrarchy of Galilee
and was, rather, part of the Decapolis.

Matthew 8:28. *And when he was come to the other side into the*
country of the Gergesenes, there met him two possessed with
devils . . .

"Gergesenes" is apparently a copyist's error, as is the version
"Gadarenes" which appears elsewhere in the gospels. The best version

would be "Gerasenes," for the reference seems to be to a Greek town named Gerasa, a place which has been identified with the present village of Kersa on the east shore of Lake Tiberias, five miles across the water from Capernaum.

Jesus is described as casting out the demons who, at their own request, are transferred into a herd of swine who then dash into the Sea of Galilee and are drowned.

The Greek inhabitants of the place seemed unappreciative of this invasion of a prophet from Galilee and of the disturbances his revivalist preaching seemed to bring.

> Matthew 8:34. . . . *the whole city came out to meet Jesus: and . . . besought him that he would depart out of their coasts.*

The Twelve Apostles

The increasing numbers of those who flocked to him seem to have convinced Jesus that he would have to place more of the responsibility upon those among his disciples whom he considered most trustworthy and capable. (Perhaps he attributed the failure of his mission to Gerasa to the fact that the work he was attempting was too great for him to attend to properly, preventing him from achieving completely satisfactory results.) He therefore appointed deputies:

> Matthew 10:1. . . . *he . . . called unto him his twelve disciples* [and] . . . *gave them power against unclean spirits . . .*
> Matthew 10:2. *Now the names of the twelve apostles are these; the first, Simon, who is called Peter, and Andrew his brother; James the son of Zebedee, and John his brother;*
> Matthew 10:3. *Philip, and Bartholomew; Thomas, and Matthew the publican; James the son of Alphaeus, and Lebbaeus, whose surname was Thaddaeus . . .*

Of these ten, the calls of five—Peter, Andrew, James, John, and Matthew—were mentioned specifically. The others are here named for the first time.

The word "apostle" is from the Greek "apostolos" meaning "one who is sent away." In the New Testament it means, specifically, one who is sent away to preach, as now Jesus is sending away his disciples to do. The word "missionary" (one who is sent forth on a mission) is exactly synonymous.

The word is most frequently applied to the twelve men appointed by Jesus, but it can be used for any missionary. In fact, the most famous apostle is none of these twelve, but Paul who did not take up his mission till after Jesus' death, and who never saw Jesus during the latter's lifetime.

Simon the Canaanite

The eleventh name to be included is a rather startling one:

Matthew 10:4. *Simon the Canaanite* . . .

Can there be a Canaanite among the apostles?

Actually, the word is a mistranslation of the Greek "Kananaios." It should be "Simon the Cananaean" and is so given in the Revised Standard Version. A Cananaean has nothing to do with Canaan but comes from an Aramaic word "kannai" meaning "a zealous one."

In Luke this is made clearer, for in his list of apostles we have:

Luke 6:15. *Matthew and Thomas, James the son of Alphaeus, and Simon called Zelotes* . . .

In the Revised Standard Version, this phrase is given as "Simon who was called the Zealot."

The Zealots, mentioned in the Bible only on this occasion, made up an important and even fateful party among the Jews of Roman times. They were that branch of the Pharisees who demanded action against the Romans. Where the Pharisees, generally, were inclined to suffer foreign domination patiently as long as their religious views were respected, the Zealots were not.

They slowly gained power in Judea and Galilee and eventually their belligerency and intransigence, combined with Roman rapacity, forced the Jewish revolt in 66 B.C. The Zealots held out with a kind of superhuman obstinacy that forced the war to drag on for three years and killed off those same Zealots virtually to the last man.

Judas Iscariot

Just as Simon Peter is invariably placed first in all the lists of the apostles, Judas Iscariot is always placed last since it is he who, in the end, betrays Jesus:

> Matthew 10:4. . . . *Judas Iscariot, who also betrayed him.*

Usually the word "Iscariot" is taken to mean "man of Kerioth." Kerioth, a city in Judea proper, is listed in the Book of Joshua among the cities in the territory assigned to Judah:

> Joshua 15:25. *And Hazor, Hadattah, and Kerioth* . . .

It is often stated, then, that Judas was the only Judean in an assemblage of Galileans. One would then be entitled to wonder whether the feeling of being an "outsider" did not play a part in the eventual betrayal.

Actually, though, there is no indication anywhere in the gospels that Judas was a Judean rather than a Galilean—except for this very doubtful interpretation of the word "Iscariot." Actually, a more recent and much more interesting interpretation is that the word "Iscariot" arose out of a copyist's transposition of two letters and that it should more accurately be "Sicariot." If so, Judas would be a Galilean like all the other apostles, chosen by Jesus from the local citizens of Capernaum and environs.

But then, what is "Sicariot"? This can be someone who is a member of the party of the "Sicarii." These were so called from a Greek word meaning "assassins" because it refers to men carrying little knives, "sicae," under their robes. This was the name given to the most extreme Zealots who believed in outright assassination of Romans and pro-Romans as the most direct and effective means of fighting foreign domination.

Judas Iscariot might be called "Judas the Terrorist," and if we accept this version of the meaning of the name it helps give a useful interpretation to events in the career of the "historic Jesus."

Samaritans

Jesus sends the apostles to the Israelites only (see page 172):

> Matthew 10:5. . . . *Go not into the way of the Gentiles, and into any city of the Samaritans enter ye not* . . .

The Samaritans, who had established themselves as a distinct sect at the time the returning Jews had refused to allow them a share in the Second Temple (see page I-441), still survived. (In fact, a small number of them survive down to this very day.)

For a while, after the return from exile, the Jews and Samaritans progressed in parallel fashion. Under the Persians, both lived in peace and were protected from each other. To match the Jewish temple in Jerusalem, the Samaritans built one on their sacred Mount Gerizim (see page I-203) in 332 B.C. Both were persecuted by Antiochus IV and both the Jewish and the Samaritan temples were profaned.

After the Maccabean revolt, however, matters changed. Now the Jews were dominant. The Maccabeans conquered Samaria and, in 129 B.C., John Hyrcanus I destroyed the Samaritan temple.

The Samaritans survived the destruction of their temple and clung stubbornly to their beliefs (just as the Jews had). When the Romans established control over Judea, the Samaritans were liberated and allowed the free exercise of their religion. This was good policy for the Romans, who weakened the Jews by establishing an enemy in their midst and these made both of them easier to rule.

In New Testament times the hatred between Jew and Samaritan was particularly intense, as hatred often is between peoples with similar but not identical views, with histories of having inflicted wrongs upon each other. This hatred plays an important role in a number of gospel passages, as, for instance, in the one quoted above in which Samaritans are classed with Gentiles.

The Disciples of John

But Jesus' successes were attracting the attention not only of the plain people who came to hear him or to follow him, but also of many religious leaders.

For one thing, he attracted the attention of John the Baptist. John was in prison, of course, but his disciples were active. His disciples may even have looked with impatience and disapproval upon this new leader who, it might have seemed to them, was merely trying to strut in the borrowed feathers of their imprisoned leader.

They were ready to find faults and shortcomings in Jesus and his teachings and they picked on his greatest weakness (at least in the eyes of the orthodox of the times). That was his failure to adhere to the letter of the Law and the tradition, let alone go beyond it as a sign of particularly exemplary piety.

Matthew 9:14. *Then came to him the disciples of John, saying, Why do we and the Pharisees fast oft, but thy disciples fast not.*

Jesus answered by pointing out that while he was present with his disciples they had cause for rejoicing and therefore did not fast (fasting being a sign of mourning).

Perhaps this explanation was brought to John the Baptist, who pondered on the possible Messianic significance of such a reply. John had declared himself to be the immediate forerunner of the Messiah and, now that he was imprisoned, he must have been certain that the Messiah would momentarily appear. One could imagine him respond-ing eagerly to any news that might be interpreted as Messianic and Jesus' suggestion that his very presence was cause for rejoicing might be significant. Could he be the Messiah?

Matthew 11:2. . . . *John . . . sent two of his disciples,*
Matthew 11:3. *And said unto him* [Jesus], *Art thou he that should come, or do we look for another?*

Jesus asked that the tales of his achievement be brought back to John, but he does not directly and specifically claim to be the Mes-siah.

The Pharisees

But John was in prison and even if he and his disciples refused to accept Jesus or were actively displeased with him, the harm they could do was small. Much more dangerous were the Pharisees, especially those among them who were entirely given over to the belief that salvation lay in the meticulous observation of all the precepts of the Law as interpreted in the most stringent manner. (The scribes, too, as students of the Law—see page I-450—tended to be wedded rather inflexibly to ritual. For this reason, the scribes and the Pharisees are often coupled in the gospels, as groups who separately and together opposed Jesus.)

Not all the Pharisees were like this, by any means, and at their best (see page 145) Pharisaic teachings were very like those in the New Testament. However, there were Pharisees whose regard for the minutiae of ritual was superstitious in intensity, or who actually welcomed the fact that so few people had the time, inclination, or learning to uphold the ritual to the last degree. When this was so, the few who could (these Pharisees themselves) might feel smugly superior to all the rest.

In a parable quoted in Luke, Jesus himself describes such a Pharisee, as praying after that fashion:

Luke 18:11. . . . *God, I thank thee, that I am not as other men are . . .*

Of course, it sometimes happens that people who behave with great affectation of sanctity don't always live up to the ideals they profess. And it also happens that those who smart under the snubs of another's self-consciously superior sanctity rejoice in any shortcomings they discover in that sanctity. There is a tendency, therefore, to find some scribes and Pharisees to be hypocrites as well, and all three words are found together in various places in the gospels.

Indeed, in our own language, the word "pharisaical" is applied to a self-conscious and hypocritical sanctimoniousness.

While all this was undoubtedly true of some Pharisees, it was certainly not true of all. But it was the more narrow Pharisees who particularly opposed Jesus that were identified as *the* Pharisees—with no indication that there was any other kind—by the naturally hostile evangelists.

As Jesus' fame grew, then, the attention of the scribes and Pharisees was attracted, and they disapproved. Social prejudice may well have been involved. After all, Jesus was merely an unlearned carpenter from some small town.

This could not very well be used as an open argument against him, but it would predispose the scribes and Pharisees (proud of their learning) against him. They would then be all the readier to find fault with his laxity in observing ritual.

Thus, in treating a sick man, Jesus said:

> Matthew 9:2. . . . *Son, be of good cheer; thy sins be forgiven thee.*
>
> Matthew 9:3. *And, behold, certain of the scribes said within themselves, This man blasphemeth.*

After all, only God could forgive sins, so that Jesus seemed to be arrogating to himself Messianic, if not actually divine, powers.

Jesus also seemed to have no hesitation about subjecting himself to the social stigma of associating with disreputable people, including even publicans (see page 167). He actually accepted a publican as a disciple:

> Matthew 9:9. . . . *Jesus . . . saw a man, named Matthew, sitting at the receipt of custom: and he saith unto him, Follow me. And he arose, and followed him.*

The Pharisees, conscious of their own strict rectitude, questioned this disapprovingly.

> Matthew 9:11. *And when the Pharisees saw it, they said unto his [Jesus'] disciples, Why eateth your Master with publicans and sinners?*

Jesus pointed out in response that it was not the letter of the Law that was demanded by God and not correct ritual. What was demanded was ethical behavior.

> Matthew 9:12. . . . *Jesus . . . said unto them, . . .*
>
> Matthew 9:13. . . . *go ye and learn what that meaneth, I will have mercy, and not sacrifice . . .*

The quotation is from the prophet Hosea, who quotes God as making the same point:

> Hosea 6:6. *For I desired mercy, and not sacrifice; and the knowledge of God more than burnt offerings.*

The Pharisees could not very well deny the quotation or disown Hosea, but their disposition could scarcely be improved at having a "backwoods preacher" reading them lessons from the Scriptures. Antagonism continued to grow.

The Sabbath

What seems to have been the final break with the Pharisees arose over the question of Jesus' attitude toward the Sabbath:

> Matthew 12:1. *At that time Jesus went on the sabbath day through the corn; and his disciples were an hungred, and began to pluck the ears of corn, and to eat.*
> Matthew 12:2. *But when the Pharisees saw it, they said unto him, Behold, thy disciples do that which is not lawful to do upon the sabbath day.*

The origin of the Sabbath, the seventh day of the week, as a holy day to be devoted to God, is, according to Hebrew legend, placed in the epoch of the creation. God is described as creating the heaven and the earth in six days:

> Genesis 2:2. *And on the seventh day God ended his work . . . and he rested . . .*
> Genesis 2:3. *And God blessed the seventh day, and sanctified it . . .*

The name "Sabbath" is derived from a Hebrew word meaning "to break off" or "to desist." The worldly purpose of the Sabbath was to desist from work one day a week, to rest; as God had rested from His work.

Observance of the Sabbath was made one of the Ten Commandments received by Moses at Mount Sinai:

> Exodus 20:8. *Remember the sabbath day, to keep it holy.*
> Exodus 20:9. *Six days shalt thou labour, and do all thy work:*
> Exodus 20:10. *But the seventh day is the sabbath of the Lord thy God: in it thou shalt not do any work . . .*

But the Pentateuch, the first five books of the Bible, reached its final written form only during the Babylonian Exile, and it was not till then, perhaps, that the Sabbath received its present significance. There are, after all, but few and inconsiderable mentions of the Sabbath in the historical books dealing with the period before the Exile. It is not mentioned in the Psalms, in the Proverbs, or in the Book of Job. It is not mentioned in Deuteronomy, except for its listing in the Ten Commandments.

There is speculation that the Sabbath originated among the Babylonians as a full moon festival. The Babylonians called the fifteenth day of the month "sappatu," and in a lunar month that begins with the new moon the fifteenth day is the full moon.

The possibility that the Sabbath was a full moon festival complementary to the well-known new moon festival might be argued from various Biblical verses dated from before the Exile, verses in which the new moon and the Sabbath are mentioned together in complementary fashion.

Thus, when a woman wished to go to the wonder-working prophet Elisha after her son had died of sunstroke, her husband said to her:

2 Kings 4:23. . . . *Wherefore wilt thou go to him to day? it is neither new moon, nor sabbath.*

The prophet Hosea quotes God as threatening Israel:

Hosea 2:11. *I will also cause all her mirth to cease, her feast days, her new moons, and her sabbaths . . .*

And Amos, characterizing the greediness of the merchants, eager to make unfair profits with false weights, pictures them sarcastically, with the parallelism characteristic of Hebrew poetry:

Amos 8:5. . . . *When will the new moon be gone, that we may sell corn? and the sabbath, that we may set forth wheat . . .*

It may be that the Sabbath became more than just another lunar festival during the Exile, when the priests and scribes sought for ways to mark off Jewish thinking and keep Judaism alive. They would want to prevent the assimilation that had caused the men of the Northern Kingdom of Israel to disappear in the course of their Assyrian exile.

Ezekiel ("the father of Judaism") may have made the significant contribution of making observance of the Sabbath part of the fundamental contract between God and Israel, for Ezekiel quotes God as saying:

Ezekiel 20:12. *Moreover also I gave them my sabbaths, to be a sign between me and them . . .*

By the time of the return from Exile, the Sabbath had definitely taken on the connotation it has borne among Jews ever since. Nehemiah, visiting the restored Jerusalem, is horrified at seeing work done on the Sabbath:

Nehemiah 13:15. *In those days saw I in Judah some treading wine presses on the sabbath . . .*

Nehemiah 13:16. *There dwelt men of Tyre also therein, which brought fish, . . . and sold on the sabbath unto the children of Judah . . .*

Nehemiah 13:17. *Then I contended with the nobles of Judah, and said unto them, What evil thing is this that ye do, and profane the sabbath day?*

Increasing numbers of restrictions hedged about the Sabbath until, by the time of the Seleucid persecution, the observation of the Sabbath had become, among the conservative faction, the very touchstone separating the orthodox Jews from the Hellenizers. Indeed, the orthodox Assideans would not violate the Sabbath even to save their lives (see page 57). The Maccabees had to arrange a general understanding to allow at least self-defense on the Sabbath. Nevertheless, the more ritualistic factions among the Jews, and that included certain groups of Pharisees in particular, were particularly rigid about Sabbath behavior.

Jesus' disciples, by plucking ears of grain, removing the hulls, and eating the kernels, were involved in a form of harvesting and that was expressly forbidden on a Sabbath:

Exodus 34:21. *Six days thou shalt work, but on the seventh day thou shalt rest: in earing time and in harvest thou shalt rest.*

Jesus' attitude, however, was one of scorn for legalistic positions that exalted the Sabbath at the expense of humanitarian considerations, a view expressed most succinctly in the Gospel of St. Mark:

Mark 2:27. *And he [Jesus] said unto them [the Pharisees], The Sabbath was made for man, and not man for the sabbath . . .*

Jesus' Mother and Brethren

To the Pharisees, it must have seemed that Jesus was aiming to break down the very core of Judaism; the careful ritual that preserved it (as though in amber) from the overwhelming numbers of the hostile outside world. Jesus had to be stopped.

Matthew 12:14. *Then the Pharisees . . . held a council against him* [Jesus], *how they might destroy him.*

Presumably what the Pharisees wish to do is destroy his influence; matters have not yet reached the stage where it would seem necessary to bring about his death. Apparently, the strategy decided upon by the Pharisees is to accuse him of black magic:

Matthew 12:24. *. . . they* [the Pharisees] *said, This fellow doth not cast out devils, but by Beelzebub the prince of the devils.*

Jesus countered that by demanding to know how one devil could be made to cast out another, since such a civil war in the ranks of devildom would destroy them all:

Matthew 12:25. *. . . Every kingdom divided against itself is brought to desolation; and every city or house divided against itself shall not stand . . .*

Nevertheless, there may well have been a falling away of his followers. Many must have felt that if the learned Pharisees tabbed a man as a demon-worshipper, they must know what they were talking about.

Indeed, it could well be argued that his family, too, was disturbed at this. Undoubtedly, word of Jesus' successes must have been coming back to Nazareth and the family would naturally be pleased. Once evil reports started reaching them, however, they would be quite justified in fearing for his safety—and they went in search of him.

At least it is at just about this point that Matthew mentions their coming:

Matthew 12:46. *While he* [Jesus] *yet talked to the people, behold, his mother and his brethren stood without, desiring to speak with him.*

Were they come to urge him to return home with them? Were they hoping to persuade him to abandon his mission before incalculable harm came to him?

Matthew doesn't say, but Mark's version of this same incident is preceded (over not too great a distance) by what might well be considered a most significant passage:

> Mark 3:21. . . . *his friends . . . went out to lay hold on him:*
> *for they said, He is beside himself.*

The word here translated as "friends" could mean "kinsfolk," and, indeed, the Jerusalem Bible says "his relatives" rather than "his friends."

This verse in Mark is not embarrassing for that evangelist. He makes no mention of Jesus' virgin birth or of the miracles attendant thereon, so he has no reason to suppose that Jesus' mother and brethren should more readily have faith in him than anyone else.

Matthew's account of the virgin birth, however, and of the unusual events accompanying it—the worship of the kings, Herod's search for the baby, the warning dream—present a situation in which Jesus' mother and, probably, other kinsmen as well couldn't help but have at least a strong suspicion of Jesus' Messianic mission. Matthew, therefore, couldn't very well include the verse about Jesus' relatives thinking he was out of his mind, without being inconsistent, so he omits it.

Nevertheless, if we are following the "historic Jesus" we are strongly tempted to believe that Jesus' family did fear for him and did come to take him home where they might keep him safe and sane. Matthew's account of Jesus' reaction to the coming of his relatives could, it might be argued, lend this view credence. If his mother and brothers had come for an ordinary friendly visit, surely Jesus would gladly have seen them and spoken to them. If, however, Jesus suspected they were coming to dissuade him from his mission, and if he placed his mission even above family ties, he would naturally react just as Matthew describes:

> Matthew 12:49. . . . *he [Jesus] stretched forth his hand toward*
> *his disciples, and said, Behold my mother and my brethren!*

Apparently, he refuses to see his family and, as a matter of fact, his family does not appear again in the remainder of Matthew. (They are mentioned a chapter later in the account of Jesus' failure to impress the people of Nazareth—but they do not appear.)

Parables

In the gospels, Jesus is often described as making his points by means of parables (from a Greek word meaning "comparison"). These are short tales which could be taken literally at face value, or could be compared point by point with an analogous message concerning the relationship of God and man.

And it is immediately after the account of the visit of Jesus' mother and brothers that Matthew chooses to present a collection of such parables:

Matthew 13:3. *And he* [Jesus] *spake many things unto them* [his audience] *in parables* . . .

It is possible, of course, to miss the point of a parable and the disciples of Jesus are pictured as puzzled when their master seemed deliberately to remain parabolic and to refrain from plain speaking:

Matthew 13:10. *And the disciples came, and said unto him, Why speakest thou unto them in parables?*

The explanation given is that the very murkiness of the parables acts to sift the hearts of men. Those who honestly want to enter the kingdom will make the effort to understand, while those who are insufficiently eager will not do so.

It is possible to interpret this, however, as a rational response to the gathering force of Jesus' enemies. For Jesus to speak directly concerning his unorthodox religious views might further enrage the Pharisees and perhaps even bring down upon his head political dangers. By speaking in parables, those unsympathetic to him could be fobbed off with the literal tale (it's just a story about a man planting wheat) while those who sympathized with Jesus would have no trouble seeing the point.

The Daughter of Herodias

And there was good reason for Jesus to speak cautiously and in parables, for dangers even beyond the Pharisees were lowering upon him. John the Baptist was dead!

Herod Antipas had hesitated to execute John, for fear of the political complications that might follow as a result of the anger and resentment of those who followed him. The vindictive Herodias, however, on whom the weight of John's denunciation had rested (see page 152), maneuvered Herod into a rash vow.

Matthew 14:6. . . . *When Herod's birthday was kept, the daughter of Herodias danced before them, and pleased Herod.*

Matthew 14:7. *Whereupon he promised with an oath to give her whatsoever she would ask.*

Matthew 14:8. *And she, being before instructed of her mother, said, Give me here John Baptist's head in a charger.*

Matthew 14:9. *And the king was sorry: nevertheless for the oath's sake . . . he commanded it to be given her.*

Matthew 14:10. *And he sent, and beheaded John in the prison.*

The girl who danced was Herodias' daughter by Philip, her first husband. She is not named in the Bible, but her name is given in the writings of Josephus as Salome (a feminine version of Solomon).

To complete the complexities of the Herodian family arrangement, this Salome later married her half great-uncle, Philip the tetrarch, so that she was at one and the same time the half great-niece, the step-daughter, and the half sister-in-law of Herod Antipas—and, through her mother, a descendant of the Maccabees as well.

Bethsaida

The death of John the Baptist did not result in serious trouble, after all, for Herod Antipas. Probably he gained courage from this fact and grew the more ready to take a stern stand against troublesome reformers. To him, Jesus seemed merely another John the Baptist.

Matthew 14:1. . . . *Herod the tetrarch heard of the fame of Jesus,*
Matthew 14:2. *And said unto his servants, This is John the Baptist; he is risen from the dead . . .*

Presumably, since Herod Antipas had had no repercussions from his execution of John, he would not hesitate to imprison and execute the new prophet who had stepped into John's shoes. Jesus decided not to give Herod Antipas the chance to do this.

Matthew 14:13. *When Jesus heard of it, he departed thence by ship into a desert place apart . . .*

Luke, in telling this incident, is more specific:

Luke 9:10. . . . *And he . . . went aside privately into a desert place belonging to the city called Bethsaida.*

By a desert place is meant a lonely place, an unfrequented one.

Bethsaida ("house of the fishers") is located just north of the Sea of Galilee, to the east of the place where the Jordan River enters. Since the Jordan River is the eastern boundary of Galilee, Bethsaida is not in Galilee but in Iturea. Thus, Jesus places himself outside the jurisdiction

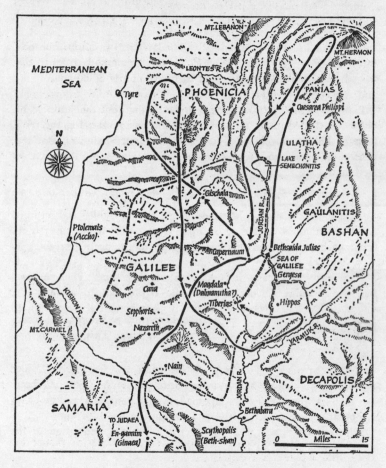

The Galilee Mission

of Herod Antipas, and within that of the mild Philip the tetrarch from whom no violence was to be feared.

Bethsaida had been rebuilt by Philip the tetrarch about a quarter century before Jesus had begun his ministry and it had been renamed Julias, in honor of Julia, daughter of the then-reigning Roman Emperor.

Matthew tells of crowds following Jesus to his place of retreat and of numerous miracles which he performed. In particular, he tells of Jesus feeding five thousand men plus an indefinite number of women and children on five loaves and two fish, miraculously multiplied.

This miracle of feeding the multitude is quite unique for it is the only miracle that is described in similar terms in all four gospels. But even if we discount miracles, we can suppose that Jesus continued to preach in Bethsaida and gathered crowds of both the pious and the curiosity-seekers.

Perhaps Herod Antipas, chagrined at having Jesus slip out of his grasp, demanded that his brother Philip return the fugitive. And perhaps Philip, unwilling to do so, merely sent word to Jesus, suggesting he move on. Whatever the reason, Jesus did not stay in Bethsaida long.

> Matthew 15:39. *And he sent away the multitude, and took ship . . .*

That sounds as though he recrossed the Sea of Galilee and returned to the dominions of Herod Antipas. If he did, it was merely to accomplish some purpose before moving onward again, for soon he is to be back in Iturea.

Jesus may well have felt defeated at this time. The populace had not risen in defense of John the Baptist, or to avenge him, either. They had flocked to Jesus in numbers, but when things grew hard they fell away. They did not gather about him to protect him from the Pharisees and from Herod. Instead, he had to go into flight.

It may have seemed to him at this point that his entire Galilee mission was a failure as his initial attempt in Nazareth had been. He had lasted longer in Capernaum and had had enormous, if temporary, success—but in the end he had been driven out.

Possibly, it was now that he uttered a bitter denunciation of the cities in which he had been preaching:

> Matthew 11:20. *Then began he to upbraid the cities wherein most of his mighty works were done, because they repented not:*

Matthew 11:21. . . . *woe unto thee, Bethsaida!* . . .

Matthew 11:22. . . . *It shall be more tolerable for Tyre and Sidon at the day of judgment, than for you.*

Matthew 11:23. *And thou, Capernaum, which art exalted unto heaven, shalt be brought down to hell* . . .

Caesarea Philippi

Jesus, on leaving Bethsaida, must have felt himself abandoned. Only a group of his most faithful disciples were with him and he had left the scene of his Galilean triumphs far behind.

Matthew 16:13. . . . *Jesus came into the coasts of Caesarea Philippi* . . .

Caesarea Philippi was an Iturean city some thirty miles north of the Sea of Galilee. The town had grown in importance in Herodian times. Herod the Great had built a temple there and his son, Philip the tetrarch, had enlarged the city and renamed it Caesarea in honor of the family name of the Roman Emperor.

Since there were many Caesareas in the empire, this one was called Caesarea Philippi ("Philip's Caesarea") by way of identification.

Peter

Perhaps Jesus was seriously questioning the nature of his mission now that he found himself driven far from home. Was it a failure? Had the call he had felt on the day of his baptism by John been an illusion? He turns to his disciples:

Matthew 16:13. . . . *Whom do men say that I the Son of man am?*

In response to Jesus' question, the disciples told him that various people thought he was John the Baptist risen from the dead, or that he was Elijah or Jeremiah or some other prophet of the past. But Jesus pressed on. That was the opinion of those who had been casually exposed to him. What about the disciples themselves, who by now knew him very well?

Matthew 16:15. . . . *But whom say ye that I am?*

Matthew 16:16. *And Simon Peter answered and said, Thou art the Christ, the Son of the living God.*

This is the turning point of the gospel. Jesus greeted the assurance joyfully. After all, Peter's confidence in his Messiah-hood could not come from his mission's worldly success, which was, at the moment, nonexistent. It could only be inspired by heaven.

Matthew 16:17. *And Jesus answered . . . Blessed art thou, Simon Bar-jona: for flesh and blood hath not revealed it unto thee, but my Father which is in heaven.*

It was on this assurance of faith and confidence on the part of his disciples that Jesus felt he could continue and carry on to final success. In return for Peter's avowal, Jesus could appoint him "second in command," so to speak, and his successor:

Matthew 16:18. *And I say also unto thee, That thou art Peter, and upon this rock I will build my church; and the gates of hell shall not prevail against it.*

Matthew 16:19. *And I will give unto thee the keys of the kingdom of heaven . . .*

Jesus was punning here. Since "Peter" means "rock," he was saying: "You are Rock and on this rock . . ."

It was the most influential pun in all history. Peter, according to tradition, went to Rome in later life and became the first Bishop of Rome. It was believed that succeeding Bishops of Rome inherited this role as the rock upon which the Church was built and each continued to hold the keys of the kingdom of heaven.

It was the Bishop of Rome who came to be called the Pope (from the word "papa," a general term for priests) and thus began the doctrine of papal supremacy over the Church, and through the Church over all Christians. Not all Christians accepted this doctrine and there are still hundreds of millions who don't today—but there are also hundreds of millions who do.

Nevertheless, although Jesus now accepted the role of Messiah-hood, he did not lose all sense of caution:

Matthew 16:20. *Then charged he his disciples that they should tell no man that he was Jesus the Christ.*

Moses and Elias

The acceptance of Messiah-hood by Jesus and, on his behalf, by the disciples is then placed in miraculous terms. Jesus is described as taking his chief disciples, Peter, James, and John, to a high mountain—

Matthew 17:2 *And was transfigured before them: and his face did shine as the sun, and his raiment was white as the light.* Matthew 17:3. *And, behold, there appeared unto them* [the disciples] *Moses and Elias* [Elijah] *talking with him* [Jesus].

Then, too, it was unthinkable to the evangelists that Jesus could be the Messiah and yet not be able to foretell his own fate; or that this fate could come to him against his will and not have an important Messianic purpose. Jesus is therefore described not only as foreseeing his death and its purpose but as explaining it not once but several times to his disciples:

Matthew 16:21. *From that time forth began Jesus to shew unto his disciples, how that he must go unto Jerusalem, and suffer many things . . . and be killed, and be raised again the third day.*

In the search for the "historic Jesus" this pious view of the Evangelists must, however, be discounted. Despite their report of Jesus' plain speaking and of the overwhelming evidence of the "Transfiguration," there are various points later in the gospels where the disciples (Peter most of all) behave as though they had no premonition of disaster; and as though disaster, when it came, left them in despair and the abandonment of their belief in Jesus' Messiah-hood.

We can continue the story, therefore, on the assumption that Jesus and his disciples, now that they were secure in their feeling that they were carrying through the mission of the Messiah, were counting on a straightforward Messianic triumph.

James and John

Indeed, now that the disciples accepted the belief that Jesus was the Messiah, so far were they from understanding what the consequences were fated to be that two of them asked for positions of honor. Mark tells the incident most baldly:

> Mark 10:35. *And James and John, the sons of Zebedee, come unto him* [Jesus], *saying . . .*
> . . . .
> Mark 10:37. . . . *Grant unto us that we may sit, one on thy right hand, and the other on thy left hand, in thy glory.*

They were asking for high office in the Messianic kingdom, which, they felt, was about to be established; and doing so, moreover, behind the backs of the rest.

> Mark 10:41. *And when the* [other] *ten heard it, they began to be much displeased with James and John.*

and Jesus had to work hard to restore amity among his followers.

Matthew, in his version, softens it considerably by absolving James and John of sole responsibility for this exercise in intrigue, and placing at least part of the blame on the easy-to-forgive partiality of a mother:

> Matthew 20:20. *Then came to him* [Jesus] *the mother of Zebedee's children with her sons . . .*

According to Matthew, it was the mother who actually asked the favor of Jesus. But perhaps one might prefer Mark's version of the two apostles boldly asking for preference on their own responsibility, rather than hiding behind their mother's skirts to do so.

The restoration of peace among the disciples may well have come about through the promise of equal rank for all:

> Matthew 19:28. *And Jesus said unto them, . . . ye which have followed me, in the regeneration when the Son of man shall sit in the throne of his glory, ye also shall sit upon twelve thrones, judging the twelve tribes of Israel.*

Once again, Matthew interprets Jesus' Messianic mission in a strictly Jewish sense.

The Mount of Olives

Now that Jesus was determined to carry through his role as Messiah, he had to go to Jerusalem, for it was there that, according to all the prophecies, the Messianic kingdom would be established.

Matthew 19:1. . . . *Jesus . . . departed from Galilee, and came into . . . Judaea beyond Jordan . . .*

Jesus crossed the Jordan to Jericho and then traveled westward toward Jerusalem, deliberately following the activities predicted of the Messiah's coming:

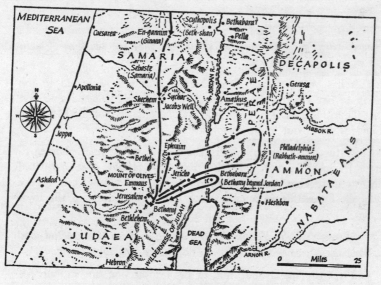

The Journey of Jesus to Jerusalem

Matthew 20:29. *And as they departed from Jericho, a great multitude followed him.*

. . . .

Matthew 21:1. *And . . . they drew nigh unto Jerusalem, and were come to Bethpage, unto the mount of Olives . . .*

The Mount of Olives, a hill about half a mile high, is less than half a mile east of Jerusalem. Jesus did not select that route by accident. It was from the Mount of Olives, according to prophecy, that the Messiah would appear. Thus, Zechariah, in predicting the divine coming on the day of the Lord says:

Zechariah 14:4. *And his feet shall stand in that day upon the mount of Olives, which is before Jerusalem on the east . . .*

At Bethpage, a village on the mount, Jesus made his final preparations. The excitement among his disciples must have been extreme, for it is reasonable to suppose that they expected Messianic success to follow at once. At least, Jesus is quoted as having predicted this to his disciples shortly after he had undertaken his Messianic role in Caesarea Philippi.

Matthew 16:28. *Verily I say unto you, There be some standing here, which shall not taste of death, till they see the Son of man coming in his kingdom.*

This has been variously interpreted, but if this were said to the disciples, one could assume that it was accepted at face value and that the trip to Jerusalem was made in the assurance that the Messianic kingdom was about to be established.

With the establishment of the kingdom in mind, Jesus planned to enter Jerusalem mounted, in the traditional fashion of a king, and not on foot. Thus, when Solomon was acclaimed king, one of the symbolic forms this acclamation took was his mounting of the royal mule:

1 Kings 1:38. *So Zadok the priest, and Nathan the prophet, and Benaiah . . . caused Solomon to ride upon king David's mule . . .*

And yet the mount was not to be a royal one, for in one important prophesy the Messiah is recorded as destined to come into Jerusalem in humble fashion, riding upon an ass.

Zechariah 9:9. *Rejoice greatly, O daughter of Zion; . . . behold, thy King cometh unto thee: . . . riding upon an ass, and upon a colt the foal of an ass.*

In order to fulfill the prophecy, Jesus sent two disciples to get a young ass for him so that he might make his entry upon it. This is done, and he is described as entering Jerusalem upon an ass in all the gospels but that of Matthew.

Matthew, in his eagerness to quote the passage from Zechariah (which is not quoted in the other gospels) and to demonstrate its fulfillment to the letter, misses the point of Hebrew poetic parallelism. The phrase "riding upon an ass, and upon a colt the foal of an ass" describes the *same* act in two slightly different phrases.

Matthew assumes, instead, that two different animals are involved and has the disciples bring two, an ass and its colt:

Matthew 21:7. And [the disciples] *brought the ass, and the colt, and put on them their clothes, and they set him* [Jesus] *thereon.*

This gives us a rather odd picture of Jesus riding two animals at once.

Hosanna

As described by Matthew, Jesus had an important and large party enthusiastically on his side. Part may have come with him, drawn by his teachings; others may have been in Jerusalem but had heard tales of a wonder-working prophet coming to Jerusalem. In any case, his passage toward Jerusalem from the Mount of Olives is pictured as a triumph:

Matthew 21:8. *And a very great multitude spread their garments in the way; others cut down branches from the trees, and strawed them in the way.*

Matthew 21:9. *And the multitudes that went before, and that followed, cried, saying, Hosanna to the Son of David: Blessed is he that cometh in the name of the Lord; Hosanna in the highest.*

The word "hosanna" is a Greek version of a Hebrew phrase meaning "Save! We pray!" or, in ordinary language, "Please help us." The acclamation is a paraphrase from the Book of Psalms.

Psalm 118:25. *Save now, I beseech thee, O Lord: O Lord, I beseech thee, send now prosperity.*

Psalm 118:26. *Blessed be he that cometh in the name of the Lord . . .*

The twenty-fifth verse has "Hosanna" translated into "Save now, I beseech thee." Left untranslated, the verse would read, "Hosanna, O Lord: O Lord, hosanna . . ."

It was clear that Jesus was being acclaimed with a passage that was applied to God in the Psalms, and that he was therefore being called the Messiah. Indeed, the use of the term "Son of David" made that explicit.

The disciples led and guided the cheering, and there were those in the crowd who were horrified at the blasphemy involved in acclaiming a Galilean preacher as the Messiah. This is brought out in Luke:

Luke 19:39. *And some of the Pharisees from among the multitude said unto him, Master, rebuke thy disciples.*

Luke 19:40. *And he [Jesus] answered . . . I tell you that, if these should hold their peace, the stones would immediately cry out.*

It was no longer a matter of overenthusiastic disciples. Jesus himself was, if not actually proclaiming Messiah-hood in the full view of the people of Jerusalem, accepting such a claim by others.

The Temple

In his new role as ultimate authority, Jesus took drastic action in the very Temple itself:

Matthew 21:12. *And Jesus went into the temple of God, and cast out all them that sold and bought in the temple, and overthrew the tables of the moneychangers, and the seats of them that sold doves,*

Matthew 21:13. *And said unto them, It is written, My house shall be called the house of prayer; but ye have made it a den of thieves.*

Actually, the moneychangers and merchants performed an essential service for those who wished to perform those rites that required the donation of small sums and the sacrifice of small birds. Through laxness, however, commercialism seems to have been allowed to invade

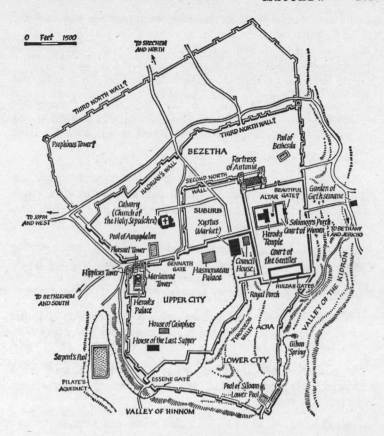

Jerusalem

the sacred precincts of the Temple instead of being kept well outside. Perhaps, too, some of the merchants were not above sharp practice at the expense of ignorant and naïve pilgrims from the country districts. (It is quite possible that Jesus, in Galilee, heard indignant tales concerning the manner in which his neighbors were cheated on their visits to the Temple.)

Jesus' exercise of power within the Temple and his preachings there bitterly offended the Sadducees. They might have ignored fine doctrinal points and questions of ritual since they themselves rejected all the Pharisaic traditions that had grown up about the written

Law. The Temple, however, was their own preserve and they did not take lightly the forceful actions of outsiders within it. Furthermore, Jesus' quotation was an offensive one, for in referring to the Temple as "a den of thieves" he was making use of Jeremiah's Temple Sermon, which, of all passages in the Old Testament, must have been least pleasing to the priests of the Temple (see page I-561).

Jeremiah 7:11. *Is this house* [the Temple] . . . *become a den of robbers in your eyes? Behold, even I have seen it, saith the Lord.*

The reaction of the Temple priesthood is described:

Matthew 21:15. *And when the chief priests and scribes saw the wonderful things that he* [Jesus] *did, and the children crying in the temple, and saying, Hosanna to the Son of David; they were sore displeased* . . .

Nevertheless, Jesus' preaching, as well as his deeds, was gathering enthusiastic crowds about him and the Temple priests could hardly claim to be popular among the unlettered and impoverished multitude. They were at a loss for proper action:

Matthew 21:46. . . . *when they sought to lay hands on him, they feared the multitude, because they* [the multitude] *took him* [Jesus] *for a prophet.*

Nor could they take the opportunity to seize him at night when he was relatively alone, for Jesus was cautious enough not to remain in Jerusalem overnight.

Matthew 21:17. . . . *he* [Jesus] *left them, and went out of the city into Bethany; and he lodged there.*

Bethany was a suburb of Jerusalem, about a mile to the east and just on the other side of the Mount of Olives.

The Son of David

Jesus was greeted as the Son of David on his entrance into Jerusalem and is so addressed at various times in the gospel. The phrase is synonymous with "Messiah," since the Messiah was generally expected (on the basis of numerous Old Testament prophecies) to be of the line of David and therefore to be a son (that is, a descendant) of David.

In the first couple of chapters of Matthew (and of Luke as well), Jesus is considered to be literally a descendant of David and his line of descent is given, as well as the tale of his birth in Bethlehem. Nowhere else, however, is this taken into account. Jesus is always identified as being of Nazareth and nowhere is he reported as correcting the impression by declaring himself to be of Bethlehem.

Even when he was entering Jerusalem and being acclaimed as Messiah, he was identified as a Galilean:

> Matthew 21:10. And when he [Jesus] was come into Jerusalem, all the city was moved, saying, Who is this?
> Matthew 21:11. And the multitude said, This is Jesus the prophet of Nazareth of Galilee.

This was a serious bar to Jesus' claim to be the Messiah. Matthew cannot say so since he maintains that Jesus was indeed of the Davidic line. In the gospel of St. John, however, where the birth at Bethlehem and the Davidic descent play no part, the objection is stated:

> John 7:41. Others said [of Jesus], This is the Christ. But some said, Shall Christ come out of Galilee?

We could imagine, then, that the Pharisees of Jerusalem must have been outraged at this sight of a Galilean nobody coming into town and claiming to be the Messiah. The claim could easily have been scotched. They had only to face him and say, in effect, "You say you are the Messiah, and if so of whose descent must the Messiah be?" Jesus would have had to answer, "He is a descendant of David," and the Pharisees could then say, "Well, then, since you are not a descendant of David, how can you be the Messiah?"

If Matthew's tale of Jesus' Davidic descent is true, we might then expect that Jesus would win the argument by a shattering display of evidence as to his birth at Bethlehem and his descent from David.

Suppose, though, that Jesus were not born in Bethlehem and were not of Davidic descent—that these elements in Matthew are legends of comparatively late origin. In that case, Jesus would have had to counter the argument by demonstrating, somehow, that the Messiah did not have to be of Davidic descent; that it was impossible, in fact, that he be of Davidic descent.

In Matthew's account, Jesus does precisely this, disproving the Davidic descent of the Messiah, even though it goes squarely against Matthew's tale of Jesus' descent from the line of David.

In Matthew's account, however, it is Jesus who raises the point, for no clear reason:

> Matthew 22:41. *While the Pharisees were gathered together, Jesus asked them,*
>
> Matthew 22:42. *Saying, What think ye of Christ? whose son is he? They say unto him, The Son of David.*

Jesus then demonstrates that they are wrong by the clever use of an Old Testament verse. It is perhaps the neatness of his argument that made the tale so popular that it could not be left out of the gospel even though it was an embarrassing contradiction to Matthew's tale of Jesus' birth:

> Matthew 22:43. *He [Jesus] saith unto them, How then doth David in spirit call him Lord, saying,*
>
> Matthew 22:44. *The Lord said unto my Lord, Sit thou on my right hand, till I make thine enemies thy footstool?*
>
> Matthew 22:45. *If David then call him Lord, how is he his son?*

The reference here is to one of the Psalms:

> Psalm 110:1. *The Lord said unto my Lord, Sit thou at my right hand, until I make thine enemies thy footstool.*

Jesus is quoted as interpreting the second "Lord" as signifying the Messiah, something which, indeed, was a common interpretation among the Jews in Roman times and among Christians now. Therefore the writer of the Psalm (presumably David) speaks of the Messiah as "my Lord" and David, Jesus argues, would scarcely address his own descendant as a superior—so that the Messiah must be more than merely a descendant of David.

(Of course, the Psalm could be interpreted non-Messianically. It is thought to be a coronation psalm in which God is described as addressing the new king of Judah. The second "my Lord" is the common address of respect for the king and the verse could be translated as beginning "God said to the king . . .")

By having Jesus ask the original question, one might speculate that Matthew was trying to present the passage as a battle of wits between

Jesus and the Pharisees, in which Jesus by a clever bit of what we would today call "Talmudic" reasoning presents a thesis to the Pharisees and dares them to refute it. The thesis need not be true—that is not the issue—but the failure of the Pharisees to answer establishes Jesus' superiority over them. And they failed:

Matthew 22:46. *And no man was able to answer him a word . . .*

Nevertheless, it is tempting to suggest that the Pharisees proposed the original question and that Jesus calmly denied the necessity of Davidic descent, saving himself—to the Pharisees' surprise—from what they believed to be a crushing gambit, and that only Matthew's commitment to the Davidic descent prevented him from presenting it as such. The passage could then be considered as a glance at the "historic Jesus" who was a Galilean carpenter but insisted on being regarded as the Messiah despite that.

The Herodians

It grew increasingly clear to the Temple authorities that Jesus' claims would not easily be quashed. Galilean backwoodsman or not, he had a quick wit and a fund of ready quotations. Yet he had to be stopped just the same before Messianic fervor produced dangerous unrest all across the city. If Jesus' doctrinal views could not be used against him, what about his political views?

If Jesus could be forced to say something politically subversive, instead of merely doctrinally heretical, the Romans could be called in. Roman soldiers could act at once without having to stop to exchange Old Testament quotations:

Matthew 22:16. *And they* [the Pharisees] *sent out unto him their disciples with the Herodians, saying, Master, we know that thou art true . . . neither carest thou for any man . . .*

By this flattery, they hoped they would trick him into making some uncompromising statement regardless of whom it would offend. And just in case he did, they had the Herodians with them. These were civil officials who supported the Herodian dynasty. Presumably they worked constantly with the Romans, had entry to the Roman governor, and could report to him quickly of any subversive remark made by Jesus.

It seemed certain to those now questioning Jesus that anyone claiming to be the Messiah would have to hold out hopes for the overthrow of the Roman Empire and for the establishment of the ideal Jewish state. It was exactly this that the populace expected of a Messiah. A question that was bound, it seemed, to force Jesus either to advocate rebellion or to give up all Messianic pretenses was now fired at him:

> Matthew 22:17. *Tell us therefore, What thinkest thou? Is it lawful to give tribute unto Caesar, or not?*

("Caesar," of course, was the title given to the Roman Emperor. It harked back to Julius Caesar, who had been assassinated in 44 B.C., but whose grandnephew became Rome's first Emperor, fifteen years later.)

If, now, Jesus refused to answer, surely he would be despised as a coward by those in the audience who advocated resistance to Rome, and they must have represented the majority of those who eagerly acclaimed Jesus as the Messiah. If he advocated payment of tribute, that would be even worse. If, on the other hand, he advocated non-payment of tribute, that would give the Romans instant reason to intervene.

Jesus sought a way out. The coins used in paying tribute had the figure of Caesar on them. That made those coins unfit to be handled by Jews anyway, strictly speaking. The first of the Ten Commandments forbade the making of any representations of any living thing and Jewish monarchs, such as the various Herods, were usually careful to avoid stirring up the orthodox by putting their own portraits upon their coins. The idolatrous coin, which it was sinful for Jews to handle, might just as well be given to the man whose portrait was there. Jesus said:

> Matthew 22:21. . . . . *Render therefore unto Caesar the things which are Caesar's; and unto God the things that are God's.*

Jesus had thus found a safe path between the horns of what had seemed an insoluble dilemma. He had advocated tribute payment, which kept the Romans from interfering; but had done so for a thoroughly religious reason which was consistent with his role as Messiah.

And yet Jesus' enemies may have won a point here, too. One can easily picture the Zealots among Jesus' audience as waiting impatiently for his answer. They were fiercely anti-Roman and they wanted a Messiah who would lead them with divine force against the hated Romans.

Here, then, was the question. Shall we pay tribute?

The proper Messianic answer, in the Zealot view, was a thunderous "No!"

That would begin the rebellion at once; just as at one time, the refusal of Mattathias to participate in a heathen sacrifice had begun the rebellion of the Maccabees.

And instead, Jesus found refuge in an evasion. If the crowd in general applauded Jesus' clever retort, might it not be that some of the more extreme Zealots now fell away in contempt. This was not their man. This was not the Messiah they were waiting for.

And how must Judas Iscariot have felt? If it were indeed true that he was an extreme Zealot (see page 179) he may well have been filled with a wild anger at the failure of this man he had believed to be the Messiah. If this is so, it explains what was to follow.

Zacharias son of Barachias

But if Jesus was careful to avoid offending the Romans, he did not hesitate to strike back at the religious leadership. He is pictured by Matthew as preaching to the multitude, at this time, and in the course of his talk, denouncing the scribes and Pharisees unsparingly, as individuals whose piety was concerned entirely with ritual and not with substance, and who were therefore hypocrites.

He spoke ominously, furthermore, of the manner in which truly pious men in the past had been killed by an unappreciative people, and he warns of retribution:

> Matthew 23:35. . . . *upon you may come all the righteous blood shed upon the earth, from the blood of righteous Abel unto the blood of Zacharias son of Barachias, whom ye slew between the temple and the altar.*

This is generally believed to be a reference to the fate of Zechariah, the high priest in the time of Joash of Judah (see page I-422). Zechariah had berated the court for tolerating idolatry and had won the enmity of the king and his courtiers:

> 2 Chronicles 24:21. *And they conspired against him* [Zechariah], *and stoned him with stones at the commandment of the king in the court of the house of the Lord.*

This identification is the more convincing since it would make it seem that Jesus was deliberately including all the unjust murders of just men that had been mentioned from one end of the Bible to the other. In the Hebrew Bible, the books of Chronicles are placed at the end, and all the Old Testament books are divided (by modern usage) into a total of 929 chapters. The murder of Cain is the first to be mentioned and is found in the fourth chapter; that of Zechariah is the last and is in the 917th chapter.

It must be admitted, however, that the Zechariah spoken of in 2 Chronicles is differently identified as to his father's name:

> 2 Chronicles 24:20. *And the Spirit of God came upon Zechariah the son of Jehoiada . . .*

Why, then, Jesus should identify him as the "son of Barachias" is uncertain. Is a different individual being referred to after all? Or is the mention of Barachias a copyist's (mistaken) added identification, based on confusion with another Zechariah casually mentioned in Isaiah?

> Isaiah 8:2. *And I took unto me faithful witnesses to record, Uriah the priest, and Zechariah the son of Jeberechiah.*

The Abomination of Desolation

There follows, then, an apocalyptic passage in which Jesus describes the future. Some of it seems to deal quite specifically with the destruction of Jerusalem by the Romans that was to take place forty years after the gospel period.

> Matthew 24:15. *When ye therefore shall see the abomination of desolation, spoken of by Daniel the prophet, stand in the holy place . . .*

Matthew 24:16. *Then let them which be in Judaea flee into the mountains . . .*

The abomination of desolation was the statue of Zeus erected in the Temple by Antiochus IV, and could mean, more generally, the triumph of pagan forces over Jerusalem, something which happened in A.D. 70.

In the course of the Jewish rebellion against Rome, the followers of Jesus took the pacifist view and did not participate in the defense of Jerusalem, but fled into the hills. It may be, therefore, that these verses were added to the traditional apocalyptic discourse of Jesus, after the fact, and that this gospel (and the other synoptic gospels, as well) did not reach their completed present form till after A.D. 70.

After the reference to the fall of Jerusalem, there follows a general description of the future beyond, given in typical Old Testament terms of total destruction:

Matthew 24:29. *Immediately after the tribulation of those days shall the sun be darkened, and the moon shall not give her light, and the stars shall fall from heaven . . .*

Following that will be the appearance of the Messiah and the establishment of the ideal kingdom.

Matthew 24:30. *. . . and they shall see the Son of man coming in the clouds of heaven with power and great glory.*

This, however, raises a problem. To those who believed that Jesus was the Messiah, the Messiah had already come. Apparently there would have to be a "second coming." This second coming was not to be long delayed:

Matthew 24:34. *Verily I say unto you, This generation shall not pass, till all these things be fulfilled.*

To be sure, it is usually now maintained that this verse refers to the fall of Jerusalem and not to the second coming, which is described immediately before. Nevertheless, this was not the view of the early Christians, who, in line with this verse, expected the second coming daily.

Still, Jesus refused to specify an exact time for the second coming.

Matthew 24:36. *. . . of that day and hour knoweth no man, no, not the angels of heaven, but my Father only.*

Talent

One of Jesus' parables, quoted in connection with the suddenness
and unexpectedness of the second coming, deals with a man who
gives money into the care of servants, then returns suddenly and de-
mands an accounting.

> Matthew 25:15. *And unto one he gave five talents, to another*
> *two, and to another one; to every man according to his several*
> *ability* . . .

The "talent" was originally a Greek unit of measure, from a word
meaning "a balance." This is a reference to the time when gold and
silver were carefully weighed out on a balance before being used for
payment—before the time (in the sixth century B.C.) when coins of
standard weight, stamped with the portrait of the monarch as a guarantee of honest measure, came into use.

The talent was a large unit of money, especially for ancient times.
The talent used in Judea in New Testament times was equal to six
thousand shekels and that was undoubtedly the equivalent of several
thousand dollars in modern money.

The use of the word in the verses above, in which each man receives
a number of talents according to his abilities, has given rise to the use
of the word as an expression of a particular ability possessed by an
individual. In fact, in modern English, the use of the word as a unit
of money has completely died out and the only meaning of "talent"
of which most people are aware is that of a superior ability of some
sort.

Caiaphas

To the Pharisees and to the Temple authorities, Jesus' final speeches
must have seemed to represent an intolerable danger. The ignorant
populace was being aroused into fury by Jesus' accusations against
them. Anything might follow and the case was taken to the very
highest religious authority among the Jews, the high priest himself:

Matthew 26:3. *Then assembled together the chief priests, and the scribes, and the elders of the people, unto the palace of the high priest, who was called Caiaphas* . . .

The office of the high priest was not what it once was. The true Zadokites had passed in the time of Antiochus IV. The Maccabean high priests had passed with the coming of Herod. The last of the Maccabean high priests, Aristobulus III, had been executed in 35 B.C. at the order of Herod. In the century that followed (the last century of the existence of the Temple) there had been numerous high priests set up by Herod or by the Roman authorities and these were chosen out of one or another of a few of the aristocratic Judean families.

The hold of these last high priests, without either Zadokite or Maccabean prestige, on the allegiance of the common people must have been slight indeed, but they controlled the Temple and grew rich and powerful because of that.

In A.D. 6, Annas ("Hanan" in Hebrew) was appointed high priest and remained in office until A.D. 15. He was then deposed by an incoming Roman official who, undoubtedly, felt he could use the bribes that would come his way if he were in a position to appoint a new high priest. For a while Simon, the son of Annas served and then, in A.D. 18, Caiaphas (his given name was Joseph, according to Josephus), the son-in-law of Annas, succeeded to the post. At the time of Jesus' stay in Jerusalem, Caiaphas had already been high priest for eleven years and was to remain high priest for seven more.

Caiaphas could see the seriousness of the situation for, in his position, he was bound to know the Romans well. He had to deal with them frequently and he undoubtedly obtained his office in the first place only through financial dickering with them.

The Judean of the countryside, or of the Jerusalem slums, or (even more so) the Galilean of the provinces could have little knowledge of the true strength of Rome. He could see only the few Roman soldiers who might have been present in a nearby garrison. The common people might believe the Romans could be beaten, especially if they felt that a miraculous Messiah was on their side.

However, Caiaphas knew that the Romans could *not* be beaten— not at this stage in their history—and forty years later this was proved tragically correct to the Jews.

To be sure, Jewish rebels of this period usually believed the Messiah

ASIMOV'S GUIDE TO THE BIBLE

to be with them, and at this particular moment the Jerusalem populace was hailing Jesus as the Messiah. Caiaphas, however, did not believe this. It is important to remember that, in the century after the fall of the Maccabees, many men with Messianic pretensions arose and that every one of them had some following. Concerning every one of them, there rose wonder tales of miraculous feats and cures, tales that grew in the telling.

Matthew quotes Jesus himself as witness to this in the apocalyptic discourse:

> Matthew 24:24. *For there shall arise false Christs, and false prophets, and shall shew great signs and wonders; insomuch that, if it were possible, they shall deceive the very elect.*

To Caiaphas, Jesus could only be one of these "false Christs." From his point of view Jerusalem was rumbling with excitement over a provincial preacher, who was rabble-rousing the populace to a dangerous pitch. In just a couple of days, the Passover was to be celebrated and pilgrims would be flocking into the city from all directions to worship at the Temple. Excitement would reach the fever point and, fortified by the certainty of Messianic help, someone would kill a Temple official or, worse still, attack a Roman soldier. Then all would be lost.

There would be a rebellion and Judea would be crushed and wiped out. What Antiochus IV had failed to do, the Romans would succeed in doing.

Indeed, this point of view is made explicit in John where at this point of the story the following views of the priestly officials are quoted:

> John 11:48. *If we let him thus alone, all men will believe on him: and the Romans shall come and take away both our place and our nation.*
>
> John 11:49. *And one of them, named Caiaphas, being the high priest that same year, said unto them . . .*
>
> John 11:50. . . . *it is expedient for us, that one man should die for the people, and that the whole nation perish not.*

This last remark is often quoted as an example of appalling cynicism, but of course it is a principle that is used constantly by all nations both before and after the time of Caiaphas.

Nor can the high-priestly view be considered as overly pessimistic, since forty years later it all turned out as they had feared. The Romans did come and take away their place and their nation. It might even be argued that only because the authorities took action against Jesus were forty years of additional life given the nation.

Judas Iscariot

Not only did the authorities decide that Jesus must be apprehended and removed as a great danger to the nation, they felt also that it had to be done at once. In two more days it would be Passover and it might then be too late. The very act of trying to make the arrest on that most nationalistic of all Jewish holidays (when God had smitten the Egyptians) might stir passions to the point of revolt, even if revolt had not already broken out spontaneously:

Matthew 26:4. *And* [the chief priests] *consulted that they might take Jesus by subtilty, and kill him.*

Matthew 26:5. *But they said, Not on the feast day, lest there be an uproar among the people.*

It was clear, moreover, that the arrest had best be carried through at night, when the city was sleeping, so that there be no uproar at the very moment of arrest, and so that the city might be presented with a completed deed in the morning. Indeed, if the deed could be carried through without an immediate revolt, the mere success of it would prevent a revolt, since what kind of Messiah could be arrested by a few soldiers? To many, Jesus would then seem a false Messiah and there would be a vast falling-away from him.

But—and here was the problem—where was Jesus staying at night? The authorities would find him, but would they find him in time?

As it happened, Caiaphas found an unexpected ally. One of Jesus' chief disciples, Judas Iscariot, defected:

Matthew 26:14. *Then one of the twelve, called Judas Iscariot, went unto the chief priests,*

Matthew 26:15. *And said unto them, What will ye give me, and I will deliver him unto you? . . .*

In other words, he would point Jesus out to them in the quiet of night and make it possible for them to arrest him without fuss.

Judas' action here has made his name a byword for villainy through all ages since. To call someone "a judas" is to call him a traitor in the extreme.

But what was Judas' motive? Matthew implies that it was greed since he asked for money, "What will ye give me . . ."

In John, this view is sharpened, and it is implied that as treasurer of the group Judas was in charge of funds and helped himself to them:

John 12:6. . . he [Judas] was a thief, and had the bag, and bare what was put therein.

Could it be that his defalcations had been detected and that he was forced into betrayal in a wild attempt to avoid disgrace?

But if it were greed that motivated Judas, it would seem that he profited very little. The priestly officials were in a position where they would have been willing to pay handsomely indeed for the service Judas was offering and yet Matthew reports:

Matthew 26:15. . . . And they covenanted with him for thirty pieces of silver.

One can't help but wonder if Matthew's penchant for Old Testament prophecies hadn't gripped him here. This was the price mentioned by Zechariah in connection with his mysterious shepherd (see page I-669):

Zechariah 11:12. And I said unto them . . . give me my price; . . . So they weighed for my price thirty pieces of silver.

Matthew must have had this verse in mind. Only Matthew of all the Evangelists mentions the specific sum paid for the betrayal, for only he feels it necessary to match Old Testament prophecy.

Could it be that the betrayal was only secondarily for money (if at all) and that the real motive was something else?

It is frequently mentioned (see page 179) that Judas was the only Judean among the apostles and that he was therefore less loyal to a Galilean preacher than were the other apostles, all of whom were Galileans.

Indeed, there have been strongly anti-Semitic individuals who have argued that only the Judeans were the true Jews in the modern sense and that Galileans were only converted Jews who were not really of Jewish descent. It follows, in their line of reasoning, that Galileans are virtuous and that Jews are wicked and that no further reason is needed to explain Judas' betrayal.

Such arguments are, of course, beneath contempt, even if Judas were indeed the only Judean. But was he? That view depends entirely on the thought that Iscariot means "man of Kerioth," a theory which has been accepted very widely for centuries but is doubtful nevertheless. If, indeed, Judas Iscariot is a misreading for Judas Sicariot ("Judas the Terrorist") then it is possible to view the betrayal in an entirely different light.

Suppose Judas was heart and soul one of those extremists who desired and demanded instant war against Rome. He may have attached himself to Jesus in the hope that this man might indeed be the Messiah whose coming would put an end to the hated Roman dominion at once. It may have been with a gathering excitement that he traveled with Jesus to Jerusalem, that he witnessed Jesus' triumphant entry, his cleansing of the Temple and his gathering popularity.

Judas may have felt sure that Passover would be the signal for the divine battle, so often foretold in detail by the prophets, in which all the forces of heathendom would be destroyed and the Son of David would be seated on the throne of the kingdom.

What changed things? It may well have been the matter of the Roman tribute and Jesus' retort that what was Caesar's would have to be given to Caesar (see page 206). To Judas, this may have seemed a disclaimer of any intention to oppose Rome politically and a declaration on Jesus' part that he was concerned with religious and ethical matters only. If so, that would have been a crushing blow to him.

Then, too, if Jesus did in fact preach the second coming, and if that passage (see page 209) is not an insertion by later hands after Jesus' death, then that could well have completed Judas' disillusionment. It was now that Judas wanted action—not having it postponed after the Messianic coming to a second coming.

What happened next might be explained in one of two ways. Judas might have been so sick with disillusionment as to have yearned for revenge. Feeling he had been made a fool of, he might have hastened, in a fit of rage, to get back at what he considered a deceiver by arranging to have him arrested and executed.

Or, it might be that Judas still felt Jesus to be the Messiah, but one who was, unaccountably, backing away from the final showdown. Perhaps by placing him in danger of arrest, he could *force* Jesus to take what Judas would have considered appropriate Messianic action.

All this, of course, is guesswork—nothing more than supposition. Still, there is one more item that may be added.

While the priests were conferring, and while Judas was arranging his betrayal, Jesus was spending his last night in Bethany. There a woman pours a jar of expensive ointment over his head.

The disciples are pictured as annoyed at the waste, feeling that the ointment might have been sold and the proceeds donated to the poor, but Jesus consoles them with the observation that he was being anointed for his forthcoming burial.

In John, however, it is only Judas who is recorded as complaining:

John 12:4. *Then saith . . . Judas Iscariot . . .*

John 12:5. *Why was not this ointment sold for three hundred pence, and given to the poor?*

(It is at this point that John states that Judas said this not out of regard for the poor but because he was a thief who was in charge of the treasury.)

In John, it was after this event that Judas carried through his betrayal. If we consider John's account, might this not fit in with the theory of Judas' disillusionment. Might he not have been irritated at the act of anointment—the traditional rite of establishing the kingship? The physical action emphasized Jesus to be the Messiah, the "Anointed One," and that must have sharpened Judas' sick feeling that Jesus was betraying the Messiah-hood by refusing to lead a revolt against Rome.

Gethsemane

On Passover Eve, Jesus and his disciples dined within Jerusalem. This is the "last supper." Judas Iscariot was at this meal, but immediately afterward must have slipped away to consult with the priestly officials.

Jesus and the remaining disciples then left but did not go far:

Matthew 26:36. *Then cometh Jesus with them unto a place called Gethsemane . . .*

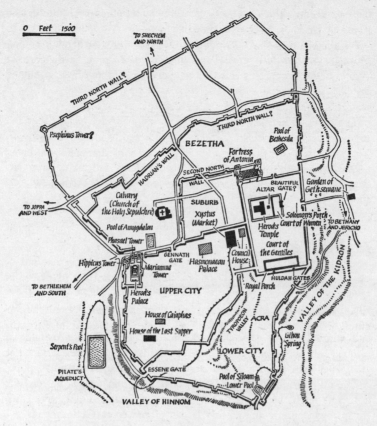

Jerusalem

Gethsemane was just outside Jerusalem on the western slopes of the Mount of Olives and, presumably, in an olive grove where once an oil press had stood. (The name "Gethsemane" means "oil press.") Judas knew Jesus would be there, something that is made specifically clear in John:

John 18:2. And Judas . . . knew the place: for Jesus ofttimes resorted thither with his disciples.

Interpreted from a rationalistic standpoint, the "historic Jesus" possibly expected the next day to be crucial and to be the day on which the city would rise in his favor so that, under the circumstances, he stayed as close to the city as possible.

Presumably, now that the moment of decision was at hand, a feeling of uncertainty gripped him. Was what he was doing really correct? Would he succeed? He is recorded as spending the time in an agony of prayer.

Matthew 26:39. *And he . . . fell on his face, and prayed, saying, O my Father, if it be possible, let this cup pass from me: nevertheless not as I will, but as thou wilt.*

One can, in this verse, see the "historic Jesus" shrinking from attempting the final test, uncertain of success, fearing the consequences, and yet feeling that there was no way out.

The Judas Kiss

The suspense was suddenly ended, however, with the arrival of the armed men sent by the priests. Judas had guided them to the place where Jesus was to be found—a place known to Judas but not to the authorities. It was now, in the quiet of night, that Jesus could be taken, and when Passover Day dawned the potential rebellion would be stymied because of the sudden lack of a leader—and the revelation that Jesus had been nothing but a deceiving and false Messiah.

The only possibility of failure now lay in the fact that, by mistake, a disciple might be arrested and Jesus might escape. There were three disciples with Jesus at this final scene of prayer at Gethsemane:

Matthew 26:37. *And he [Jesus] took with him Peter and the two sons of Zebedee . . .*

and any one of the three might be mistaken for Jesus. It was, after all, dark, and the armed men did not, presumably, know Jesus by sight.

Judas therefore had to identify Jesus unmistakably and he offered to do so:

Matthew 26:48. *. . . he [Judas] . . . gave them a sign, saying, Whomsoever I shall kiss, that same is he: hold him fast.*

To modern Americans, this seems to aggravate the treason; to betray with a kiss is peculiarly villainous. That is, in part, a reflection of our own social customs, in which kissing has been made a sign of particular intimacy and affection. In other cultures, however, a kiss between men on meeting can be quite common. It would be the normal greeting and of no greater significance than a handshake in our culture. The treason is, of course, bad enough even so.

Jesus is pictured by Matthew as surprised at Judas' coming and as unaware of the traitor's purpose:

> Matthew 26:49. . . . he [Judas] *came to Jesus, and said, Hail, master; and kissed him.*
>
> Matthew 26:50. *And Jesus said unto him, Friend, wherefore art thou come? Then came they* [the armed men], *and laid hands on Jesus, and took him.*

To be sure, this section of the gospel is full of indications that Jesus knew beforehand of Judas' treasons and the results thereof, as would be expected of the divine foreknowledge of a Messiah. And it is some-times suggested that Jesus' question of Judas, "Wherefore art thou come?" is a metaphoric way of saying, "Do what you have come to do." That is, "Let's get this over with."

Nevertheless, if we consider the "historic Jesus" we might well con-sider him to have been surprised at Judas' sudden appearance and unaware, for just a moment, as to the significance of it. The question then makes sense at face value.

One of the disciples present offered a token resistance. He is un-named here, but John states it to have been Peter:

> Matthew 26:51. . . . *one of them which were with Jesus stretched out his hand, and drew his sword, and struck a servant of the high priest's, and smote off his ear.*
>
> Matthew 26:52. *Then said Jesus unto him, Put up again thy sword . . .*

We might picture the "historic Jesus" as seeing that resistance was useless and unwilling to have his disciples killed for nothing. Perhaps he felt a sense of relief that the crisis of the revolt would not come. Or perhaps he still considered himself the Messiah and was certain that there would yet be a divine intervention on his behalf.

(The traditional Jesus, as accepted by virtually all Christians since then, knew what was to come, and that the trial, crucifixion, and resurrection were part of the divine scheme.)

The disciples at that point reacted, however, as though they were facing the arrest of the "historic Jesus" rather than that of a divine Messiah:

Matthew 26:56. . . . *Then all the disciples forsook him, and fled.*

Christ

It now became necessary for the priestly authorities to find some sort of crime for which Jesus could be convicted; one, if possible, that would carry the death penalty. If he were merely punished and released, or worse yet, acquitted, after all this trouble they had taken, the result would surely be told throughout Judea as an example of the divine protection of the Messiah and revolt would be a certainty.

And yet to convict Jesus on a matter of purely doctrinal dispute would be difficult:

Matthew 26:59. *Now the chief priests . . . sought false witness against Jesus, to put him to death;*
Matthew 26:60. *But found none . . .*

In desperation, they turned to the matter of Messiah-hood itself. Certainly, to claim, falsely, to be the Messiah, was the height of blasphemy and deserved death. And certainly, Jesus' disciples had openly claimed him to be the Messiah, and Jesus had implicitly accepted the role by refusing to rebuke them for doing so (see page 200).

This, however, was not enough. The claims of the disciples might be disowned; implicit acceptance of the claims might be explained away. If, however, Jesus could be maneuvered into an open avowal of Messiah-hood, under oath, in court, they would have him.

In fact, they would have everything they needed. The priesthood could not, at this time in history, pronounce and carry through a death sentence on their own. The approval of the Roman governor of Judea was needed. Such approval might not be obtained for a purely doctrinal matter (for such disputes the Roman rulers avoided involvement as a matter of policy—there was too much chance of sparking a troublesome revolt). However, if Jesus laid claim to Messiah-hood, he simultaneously laid claim to being the rightful and ideal King of the Jews. This, in turn, was a clear form of political revolt against Rome's authority, even if Jesus made not a single overt move against Rome. That meant the Roman authorities could be called in and a death sentence was sure of being carried out.

The crucial question was therefore asked under oath:

Matthew 26:63. . . . *the high priest . . . said unto him, I adjure thee by the Living God, that thou tell us whether thou be the Christ . . .*

Matthew 26:64. *Jesus saith unto him, Thou hast said: nevertheless I say unto you, Hereafter shall ye see the Son of man sitting on the right hand of power, and coming in the clouds of heaven.*

The phrase, "Thou hast said" is, in itself, evasive, meaning "This is something you have said," as though Jesus himself were careful neither to affirm nor to deny. Mark's version of the question and answer makes Jesus present his inquisitor with an open admission:

Mark 14:61. . . . *the high priest asked him, . . . Art thou the Christ . . .*

Mark 14:62. *And Jesus said, I am . . .*

However, even in Matthew's more cautious version of Jesus' answer, Jesus goes on to expand his view with a Messianic quotation. The remark concerning the Son of man is from the Book of Daniel:

Daniel 7:13. . . . *one like the Son of man came with the clouds of heaven . . .*

Daniel 7:14. *And there was given him dominion, and glory, and a kingdom . . .*

That was it. Jesus seemed to be making a clear comparison of himself with the figure in Daniel, one who was commonly accepted at the time as representing the Messiah (see page I-610). The high priest had what he wanted:

Matthew 26:65. *Then the high priest rent his clothes, saying, He hath spoken blasphemy; what further need have we of witnesses? . . .*

Matthew 26:66. *What think ye? They* [the court] *answered and said, He is guilty of death.*

Peter

If Jesus, even at this crisis, maintained a firm belief in his Messiah-hood, this was not so of his disciples. All had fled, and only one is recorded as being present, secretly, at the trial:

> Matthew 26:58. . . . *Peter followed him* [Jesus] *afar off unto the high priest's palace, and went in, and sat with the servants, to see the end.*

After the end of the trial, Peter was recognized three different times as being one of the disciples of Jesus. It was Peter's chance to be as true to his mission as Jesus was, but he failed. Each time he denied knowing Jesus, the third time most emphatically:

> Matthew 26:74. *Then began he* [Peter] *to curse and to swear, saying, I know not the man . . .*

Pontius Pilate

The priestly officials also had what they needed to bring Jesus before the Roman authorities:

> Matthew 27:1. *When the morning was come,* . . . *the chief priests . . .*
> Matthew 27:2. . . . *bound him* [Jesus], . . . *led him away, and delivered him to Pontius Pilate the governor.*

This is the first mention in Matthew of the secular ruler of Judea since the reference to Archelaus at the time of the return of Joseph and his family from Egypt (see page 135).

Archelaus, or Herod Archelaus, ruled as ethnarch over Judea, Samaria, and Idumea after the death of his father, Herod the Great, in 4 B.C. His rule, however, was harsh and oppressive and he succeeded in antagonizing both Jews and Samaritans. Both groups, in a rare exhibition of cooperation, appealed for relief to the Roman Emperor.

Rome was not in the least averse to strengthening its hold upon the unruly province, for Judea had an important strategic significance at the time. Immediately to Judea's east was the powerful kingdom of Parthia, and that kingdom was Rome's most dangerous enemy in New Testament times.

In 53 B.C., for instance, not long after Judea had passed under Roman domination, the Parthians had defeated a Roman army at Carrhae. (This was the Graeco-Roman name for Haran, the city where Abraham and his family had once dwelt. See page I-59.) Seven Roman legions had been destroyed, the worst Roman defeat ever suffered, up to that time, in the east, and a defeat that had not yet been avenged. Then again, in 40 B.C., the Parthians had taken advantage of civil wars in Rome to occupy large sections of Roman territory in the east. They had occupied Judea, which had cooperated with them willingly against Rome, and against the Roman puppet, Herod.

As long as Judea retained even the semblance of independence, then, she was a danger to Roman security for its ruler might at any time decide to intrigue with the Parthians.

Rome therefore took advantage of the complaints of the Jews and Samaritans to depose Herod Archelaus in A.D. 6, allowing him to live out the remaining twelve years of his life in exile.

Neither Judea nor Samaria got independence as a result, of course. Instead the area was made part of a Roman province, complete with a Roman ruler and a well-armed Roman garrison.

Judea, although made part of the province of Syria, was, because of its strategic importance, given special status. A governor was appointed by the emperor, one who was to be responsible directly to himself as well as to the provincial ruler of Syria. The Latin name for such an official was "procurator" ("caretaker"). In Greek, the name given the Roman officials over Judea was "hegemon" ("leader") and in the King James Version, and the Revised Standard Version too, this becomes "governor."

The first four procurators of Judea ruled quietly enough. In A.D. 26, however, Pontius Pilate was appointed. He was a man of obscure birth who owed his advancement to the fact that he was a protégé of Lucius Aelius Sejanus, who was then the leader of the Praetorian Guard (a contingent of soldiers which guarded Rome itself) and the most powerful man in the empire at the moment.

Sejanus was strongly anti-Jewish and Pilate probably took his job on the understanding that he was to keep the Jews in check, weaken them at every opportunity, and prevent them from ever serving as a Parthian cat's-paw against Rome.

Pilate set about this with a will. Where earlier procurators had made their headquarters at Caesarea, a city on the Samaritan coast, fifty miles northwest of Jerusalem, Pontius Pilate stationed troops in the capital itself. This meant the army, with its ensigns bearing the portrait of the emperor, moved into Jerusalem. The excited Jews considered such portraits to be a violation of the commandment against idolatry and protested violently. Eventually Pilate had to remove the objectionable portraits when it seemed that a revolt would be the inevitable result if he didn't. There was no question but that he could crush such a revolt, but disorders that might bring in the Parthians would look bad on his record if it seemed that he had deliberately provoked them.

Pilate may have made it a practice to be in Jerusalem during the Passover season, when the city was crowded, and dangerous emotions ran high. He was undoubtedly ready to take instant action in case such feelings became a revolt. He might even have welcomed the chance. He had already, on one recent occasion, showed no hesitation in slaughtering a Galilean mob that had begun proving disorderly during a festival:

> Luke 13:1. . . . some . . . told him [Jesus] of the Galilaeans, whose blood Pilate had mingled with their sacrifices.

He would have no hesitation in doing so again. The high priest must have known this and his treatment of Jesus must have had, as one of its motives, the desire to forestall this eventuality by any means, to deflect Pilate's anger from the Jews generally to a single man so that "one man should die for the people."

The Potter's Field

Judas Iscariot is pictured, meanwhile, as horrified at the consequences of his betrayal:

> Matthew 27:3. Judas, . . . when he saw that he [Jesus] was condemned, repented himself . . .

If he had planned to force Jesus into Messianic action, he felt now that that plan had failed and that he was going to be responsible for Jesus' death. If he had been seeking to punish Jesus for not being the kind of Messiah that Judas would have liked to see, then apparently he felt that the death penalty was more punishment than he had intended.

He attempted to return the thirty pieces of silver to the priestly officials and when they refused to accept it from his hands, he threw the money down and went off and hanged himself, so that he died on the same night as his betrayal. This remorse tends to relieve the traitor of some of the utter blackness that has gathered about his name.

Unfortunately, the plausibility of Matthew's dramatic tale of the end of Judas suffers from the suspicion that the evangelist was merely trying to introduce yet another Old Testament quotation. With reference to the thirty pieces of silver that Judas had cast aside, Matthew explains that the priests felt that the money, which was the price of treachery, could not be put back in the treasury. It carried a man's blood on it.

Matthew 27:7. *And they . . . bought with them the potter's field, to bury strangers in.*

Matthew 27:8. *Wherefore that field was called, The field of blood, unto this day.*

Matthew 27:9. *Then was fulfilled that which was spoken by Jeremy [Jeremiah] the prophet, saying, And they took the thirty pieces of silver . . .*

Matthew 27:10. *And gave them for the potter's field . . .*

The potter's field was, presumably, a place where one could obtain clay of a kind suitable for the making of pottery. From the verses just quoted, the phrase "potter's field" has come to mean any public burial place for use of the criminal, the homeless, the paupered—anyone who could not afford, or did not deserve, a better resting place.

Matthew's Old Testament quotation, however, is even more than usually unapt, in this case. For one thing, it is not from Jeremiah, but from Zechariah's cryptic tale of the shepherds. (The mistake may have come about because Jeremiah talks about buying a field at one point, see page I-575, and tells a parable about potters at another point, but it is a mistake just the same.)

In the Book of Zechariah, the shepherd who resigned received thirty pieces of silver for his wages (see page I-669)—

Zechariah 11:13. . . . And I took the thirty pieces of silver, and cast them to the potter in the house of the Lord.

But the "potter in the house of the Lord" is by no means the "potter's field." Indeed, the very word "potter" is a mistranslation and may appear in the Old Testament verse as a result of Matthew's misuse of the passage and its effect upon the piety of those who worked on the King James Version. The Revised Standard Version has the phrase read "the treasury in the house of the Lord."

In other words, the money was, in Zechariah, deposited in the Temple treasury, which is precisely what the priests refused to do with Judas' money. The two passages are therefore not parallel, as Matthew apparently felt, but, on the contrary, antithetical.

There is a competing tradition of Judas' death, given in the Acts of the Apostles:

Acts 1:18. Now this man [Judas] purchased a field with the reward of iniquity; and falling headlong, he burst asunder in the midst, and all his bowels gushed out.

Acts 1:19. And it was known unto all the dwellers at Jerusalem; insomuch as that field is called in their proper tongue [Aramaic], Aceldama, that is to say, The field of blood.

According to this competing tradition—which involves no Old Testament prophecies—Judas felt no remorse and committed no suicide. He lived long enough to carry through a business transaction designed to make him a landowner and died afterward of some sort of stroke.

Barabbas

Apparently, Pilate accepted Jesus' evasive answer to the high priest ("Thou hast said") as negative, or at least as not positive, and was therefore uncertain that he merited execution. Or perhaps Pilate wanted to disoblige the high priest, who, Pilate may well have felt, had his own ulterior motives for wanting Jesus dead, quite apart from his actual guilt or innocence:

Matthew 27:18. *For he* [Pilate] *knew that for envy they* [the priests] *had delivered him* [Jesus].

At any rate, he went over the head of the priestly party to the people themselves, and offered to release a prisoner in honor of the Passover festival.

Matthew 27:16. *And they* [the Romans] *had then a notable prisoner, called Barabbas.*

Matthew 27:17. *Therefore . . . Pilate said . . . Whom will ye that I release unto you? Barabbas, or Jesus which is called Christ?*

Barabbas is not further described in Matthew. Mark, however, says:

Mark 15:7. *And there was one named Barabbas, which lay bound with them that had made insurrection with him, who had committed murder in the insurrection.*

It might well be then that Barabbas had been one of the Sicarii, or terrorists, who had led a guerrilla band against the Romans, and had carried through the assassination of some Roman official. He might well therefore be a hero to the Zealots, the very ones who were disenchanted with Jesus for having backed away in the matter of the tribute.

Given their choice between a bandit leader who did not preach but fought against the Romans, and one who preached and called himself a Messiah but took no action and submitted tamely to capture, imprisonment, and trial, the populace (or at least the vocal Zealots among them) called for Barabbas—and got him.

Barabbas is not a proper name but is the Aramaic equivalent of a surname, meaning "son of the father." The word "Christ" or "Messiah" can also be termed as "son of the Father" (though with a capital letter). Oddly enough, tradition asserts that Barabbas' proper name was Joshua or, in Greek, Jesus. Consequently, what Pilate was asking the crowd was whether they wanted Jesus, son of the father, or Jesus, son of the Father.

There have indeed been those who suggested that Barabbas and Jesus are the same person and that the tale of a bandit leader and of a meek and peaceful Messiah somehow got entwined, that Jesus was tried before Pilate but was released as Barabbas, and that the tale of the crucifixion and resurrection is the embroidery of later legend. It is unlikely, however, that this view will ever gain many adherents.

Pilate and Pilate's Wife

Matthew emphasizes the reluctance of Pilate to give the order for execution. Partly, he explains this through the use of his favorite device of a dream:

> Matthew 27:19. When he [Pilate] was set down on the judgment seat, his wife sent unto him, saying, Have thou nothing to do with that just man: for I have suffered many things this day in a dream because of him.

This is the only appearance of Pilate's wife in the New Testament, but tradition has been busy with her. It is said that her name was Claudia Procula and that she was, or later became, a secret Christian. She is even canonized in the Greek Orthodox Church.

Having offered to release Jesus and having had to release Barabbas instead, Pilate is faced with a shouted cry for the execution of Jesus. Pilate protested:

> Matthew 27:23. And the governor said, Why, what evil hath he done? . . .
> Matthew 27:24. When Pilate saw that he could prevail nothing, . . . he took water, and washed his hands before the multitude, saying, I am innocent of the blood of this just person . . .

All the four gospels agree that Pilate was reluctant to order the execution of Jesus, but only Matthew inserts this hand-washing—a dramatic act that makes the English phrase "to wash one's hands of" mean "to disclaim responsibility."

Possibly it was an act of Jewish ritual which the Roman Pilate would not have performed, but it was one which Matthew, who knew a great deal about Jewish ritual and very little about Roman ways, found natural to include.

In the Book of Deuteronomy, it is stated that if a murdered body be found and the murderer not be known, the people of the nearest town go through a certain ritual, involving a heifer, for absolving themselves of guilt:

Deuteronomy 21:6. *And all the elders of that city . . . shall wash their hands over the heifer . . .*

Deuteronomy 21:7. *And they shall . . . say, Our hands have not shed this blood . . .*

Since Pilate thus proclaims his innocence, Matthew has the impatient crowd accept the responsibility themselves, making use of the dramatic Old Testament idiom used for the purpose:

Matthew 27:25. *Then answered all the people, and said, His blood be on us, and on our children.*

This statement, which is found in none of the other gospels, and which may well have arisen merely out of Matthew's penchant for interpreting and describing everything in accordance with Old Testament prophecy, ritual, and idiom, has cost the Jews a fearful price in the two thousand years since Jesus' death.

As for Pilate, his later years are obscure. He remained as Procurator of Judea till A.D. 36, when he was finally recalled because his tactlessness continued to rouse revolts among the Jews and Samaritans.

The manner of his death is not known. Hostile tradition has him executed by the Roman Emperor, or committing suicide to avoid such execution. On the other hand, there are also legends concerning his later conversion to Christianity, based perhaps on the accounts of his reluctance to condemn Jesus. There are apocryphal writings, too, which no longer exist, but which are referred to by some of the early Christian writers. They were supposed to have represented his report concerning the trial and resurrection of Jesus. Pilate is even canonized as a saint in the Abyssinian church.

Crucifixion

Having disclaimed responsibility for Jesus' death, Pilate gave the order for execution:

Matthew 27:26. *Then released he Barabbas unto them: and when he had scourged Jesus, he delivered him to be crucified.*

Crucifixion was neither a Jewish nor a Greek method of execution. Among Jews, it was common to stone people to death; among the

Greeks, to force them to take poison. The Romans, however, used crucifixion as a punishment for treason. (So did other peoples, such as the Persians and Carthaginians.)

A person, nailed to a wooden cross, died slowly of exposure, hunger, and thirst. It was a cruel death; all the more so, since it was so public as to divest the dying man of every shred of dignity, exposing him to the jeers of heartless onlookers.

Yet, the fact remains that Jesus was not condemned to an unusual or uncommon death, but one that was routine by Roman law. In 72 B.C., about a hundred years before the execution of Jesus, a band of gladiators and slaves rebelled against Rome under the leadership of Spartacus. They were eventually defeated by the Roman general Marcus Licinius Crassus (a general who was to be defeated and killed fifteen years later by the Parthians at the battle of Carrhae; see page 223). Crassus captured some six thousand of the slaves and, according to the story, crucified them wholesale along the road from Rome to Capua, so that any traveler would find himself going miles and miles between a seemingly endless row of men slowly dying in painful torture. (Similarly, Darius I of Persia at one time crucified three thousand Babylonian rebels wholesale.)

Crucifixion, as a means of punishment, continued to be part of the Roman law till it was abolished by Constantine I, the Roman Emperor who first legalized the practice of Christianity.

Cyrene

It was customary for a man about to be crucified to carry the heavy cross, or part of it, to the place of execution. Jesus may have been unable to lift the cross after the events of the night and the mistreatment to which he had been subjected.

> Matthew 27:32. And as they [the escorting soldiers] came out, they found a man of Cyrene, Simon by name: him they compelled to bear his [Jesus'] cross.

Presumably, Simon had arrived in Jerusalem in order to attend the Passover festival, and found himself unexpectedly carrying a cross.

Cyrene (see page 91) had a large Jewish colony in New Testament times. Jason, the historian of the Maccabean revolt, on whose works

2 Maccabees was based, was a man of Cyrene. In 117 B.C., Cyrene became independent of Egypt, and in 67 B.C. it was absorbed by Rome.

Golgotha

Jesus was next led to the place of execution:

Matthew 27:33. . . . *they were come unto a place called* [in Aramaic] *Golgotha, that is to say, a place of a skull* . . .

This is a grisly name indeed, deriving perhaps from the fact that some vaguely skull-shaped promontory was in the neighborhood, or from the existence of skulls of previous men executed there. (Both suggestions are mere guesses.)

In Luke the Latin equivalent of the name is given:

Luke 23:33. . . . *they were come to the place, which is called Calvary* . . .

The site of Golgotha/Calvary is not exactly known but it must have been just outside Jerusalem.

There Jesus was crucified, with the record of the crime set above his head, as was customary:

Matthew 27:37. *And set up over his head his accusation written, THIS IS JESUS THE KING OF THE JEWS.*

This is a version of the significance of the name "Jesus Christ" and is a record of the fact that Jesus was executed for the crime of treason against Rome—claiming to be a king without Roman approval.

Vinegar and Gall

Matthew is intent on demonstrating that every aspect of the crucifixion fulfills Old Testament prophecy. Thus, he describes a drink offered Jesus by the soldiers:

Matthew 27:34. *They gave him vinegar to drink mingled with gall* . . .

This sounds like an additional heartless torment inflicted upon a dying man. Actually, it is the reverse. Vinegar (which is derived from

French words meaning "sour wine") can, in this case, be taken literally as the sour wine that was the customary drink for the Roman soldiers. The passage is translated in the Revised Standard Version as "they offered him wine to drink, mingled with gall . . ."

Gall itself is exceedingly bitter, but what may be meant here is some form of deadening anesthetic. Mark, indeed, does not mention gall but describes the incident:

Mark 15:23. And they gave him to drink wine mingled with myrrh . . .

If Matthew bases his description on what is said in Mark, why does he change the humane wine and myrrh, clearly intended as a kindly attempt to anesthetize Jesus and deaden the pain he must suffer, into the heartless vinegar and gall, which sounds so like an additional torment? Why needlessly multiply the apparent sins of the crucifiers? Apparently Matthew introduces vinegar and gall to hark back to a passage in the Psalms where the psalmist describes his own distress with poetic exaggeration:

Psalm 69:21. They gave me also gall for my meat; and in my thirst they gave me vinegar to drink.

Eli, Eli

Death was not long delayed:

Matthew 27:46. And about the ninth hour Jesus cried with a loud voice, saying, Eli, Eli, lama sabachthani? that is to say, My God, my God, why hast thou forsaken me?

It might be suggested that this was the last cry of despair of the "historic Jesus"—the Galilean carpenter who felt the urge to preach, convinced himself at last that he was the Messiah, held to this faith to the last minute, and now—finally—had to realize he was not the Messiah after all and that the whole of his mission had but brought him to this horrible death.

Yet it is not likely that Matthew could possibly have thought this (or Mark, in whom also this dying cry is to be found). Rather, some Old Testament significance is to be sought.

The cry "My God, my God, why hast thou forsaken me?" is the opening of the 22nd Psalm:

Psalm 22:1. *My God, my God, why hast thou forsaken me? why art thou so far from helping me, and from the words of my roaring?*

It is a quotation that is particularly apt for the occasion, since the psalmist describes himself (in the King James Version) as in the extreme of despair and as suffering a fate very like crucifixion:

Psalm 22:16. *For dogs have compassed me: the assembly of the wicked have inclosed me: they pierced my hands and my feet.*
Psalm 22:17. *I may tell all my bones: they look and stare upon me.*
Psalm 22:18. *They part my garments among them, and cast lots upon my vesture.*

Matthew describes the literal fulfillment of the poetic description of the extremity of misfortune in the eighteenth verse and quotes that verse too, pointing to its fulfillment:

Matthew 27:35. *And they crucified him, and parted his garments, casting lots . . .*

The sharpest association of the passage with the crucifixion is the phrase "they pierced my hands and my feet." The Revised Standard Version, which keeps the phrase, points out in a footnote that in the original Hebrew the word which is translated as "pierced" in the Latin versions of the Bible, actually means "like a lion." In the Jewish version of the Bible, the sixteenth verse is given ". . . Like a lion, they are at my hands and my feet." The Jerusalem Bible gives it: ". . . they tie me hand and foot." One wonders if "pierced" was inserted in translation as a reference backward from Jesus' exclamation on the cross.

Joseph of Arimathea

After his death, Jesus was buried:

Matthew 27:57. *When the even was come, there came a rich man of Arimathaea, named Joseph, who also himself was Jesus' disciple:*
Matthew 27:58. *He went to Pilate, and begged the body of Jesus.*

Having obtained the body, he buried it in his own new tomb—dug into the rock—and placed a great stone in the opening.

The town of Arimathea, the birthplace of this disciple of Jesus, is not mentioned in the Bible elsewhere, but it is usually identified with Ramathaim-Zophim, the birthplace of the prophet Samuel (see page I-267).

Joseph of Arimathea does not appear in the Bible except for this one deed, and the reputed site of his tomb is now memorialized by the Church of the Holy Sepulchre in Jerusalem.

Joseph is, however, the subject of a much later legend. He was supposed to have been the custodian of the cup from which Jesus urged his disciples to drink in the course of the last supper:

> Matthew 26:27. *And he took the cup, and gave thanks, and gave it to them, saying, Drink ye all of it;*
> Matthew 26:28. *For this is my blood of the new testament . . .*

This cup came to be called the "Holy Grail." Its possession was supposed to have preserved Joseph of Arimathea through many years of imprisonment. Eventually he was supposed to have brought the cup to the town of Glastonbury in southwestern Britain and there it disappeared. (These legends were very much elaborated and encouraged by the monks at the Abbey of Glastonbury.)

Much of the cycle of legend that surrounded Britain's King Arthur and his knights dealt with the attempts to recover the Holy Grail.

The First Day of the Week

The story of the "historic Jesus" ends here with his burial, for if we are to eliminate the miraculous, then the tale of the resurrection must be put down to legend.

If the burial had really been the end in every way, however, it is very probable that Jesus' disciples would gradually have forgotten their old teacher, that no new disciples would have gathered in his memory, and that the history of the world would have been enormously different.

However, even if we take the rationalist view that there was no resurrection in reality, it cannot be denied that there was one in the belief of the disciples and, eventually, of hundreds of millions of men —and that made all the difference.

Matthew describes the priestly authorities as fearing a coup on the part of Jesus' disciples. They say so to Pilate:

> Matthew 27:63. . . . Sir, . . . that deceiver [Jesus] said, while he was yet alive, After three days I will rise again.
>
> Matthew 27:64. Command therefore that the sepulchre be made sure until the third day, lest his disciples come by night, and steal him away, and say unto the people, He is risen from the dead . . .

The priestly authorities presumably feared that Jesus, even though dead, might still be used as a rallying cry for a revolt against the Romans. A resurrection would be faked and used as proof of the divine Messiah-hood of Jesus. Pilate, also seeing the danger, granted a contingent of soldiers to guard the tomb.

The belief that Jesus would rise on the third day is given by Matthew, characteristically, in terms of an Old Testament analogy. At one point, when Jesus is asked for some sign that he is indeed a heaven-inspired preacher, Jesus refuses, except to point out one analogy (found spelled out only in Matthew):

> Matthew 12:40. For as Jonas [Jonah] was three days and three nights in the whale's belly; so shall the Son of man be three days and three nights in the heart of the earth.

Now the crucifixion had taken place on a Friday, according to all four gospels. Thus Matthew says:

> Matthew 27:62. Now the next day, that followed the day of preparation . . .

The "next day" was the day after the crucifixion and it followed the "day of preparation," which was therefore the day of the crucifixion. By the "day of preparation" is meant the day on which one prepares for the Sabbath. It is the day before the Sabbath (our Saturday) and, therefore, Friday.

It is for this reason that the crucifixion is commemorated by Christians on a Friday ("Good Friday").

Then comes the story of the sequel to the crucifixion:

> Matthew 28:1. *In the end of the sabbath, as it began to dawn toward the first day of the week,*
>
> Matthew 28:2. . . . *there was a great earthquake: for the angel of the Lord descended from heaven, and came and rolled back the stone from the door* . . .

Those guarding the tomb and those coming to mourn are alike astonished, but the angel addresses the latter:

> Matthew 28:5. . . . *Fear not ye: for I know that ye seek Jesus, which was crucified.*
>
> Matthew 28:6. *He is not here: for he is risen, as he said* . . .

With the crucifixion taking place on Friday and the resurrection on Sunday ("the first day of the week") one can suppose that Jesus remained "in the heart of the earth" three days (Friday, Saturday, Sunday). However, Matthew's comparison with Jonah's "three days and three nights" in the whale misses, as so many of Matthew's quotations do.

Jesus died on Friday at the ninth hour, shortly after he cried out, "My God, my God, why hast thou forsaken me?" (See page 232.)

This, counting the hours—in the fashion of the time—from sunrise to sunset, would be about 3 P.M. by the modern scheme of hours. If Jesus rose at dawn on Sunday, say 6 A.M., then while he was in the heart of the earth for parts of three different days, he was there for only two nights and one day.

The fact that the resurrection took place on the first day of the week (Sunday) gave that day a special significance to the followers of Christ. It was the "Lord's Day" to be treated with special significance.

At first, it was distinct from the Sabbath (the Seventh Day, or Saturday), which the early Christians celebrated in the usual manner. However, as hostility grew between Christians and Jews, and as the Christians gathered their numbers more and more from among the Gentiles, Sunday came to take on the attributes of a Sabbath and Saturday was abandoned by the Christians altogether.

The anniversary of the particular Sunday on which Jesus was resurrected is commemorated as Easter Sunday.

Mary Magdalene

Among the women who watched at the site of the crucifixion was one called Mary Magdalene:

Matthew 27:55. *And many women were there beholding* [the crucifixion] *afar off, which followed Jesus from Galilee* . . .
Matthew 27:56. *Among which was Mary Magdalene* . . .

She was also present at the grave at dawn on the Sunday following:

Matthew 28:1. *In the end of the sabbath* . . . *came Mary Magdalene* . . . *to see the sepulchre.*

Mary Magdalene means Mary of Magdala, Magdala being a town on the west shore of the Sea of Galilee. Its exact location is uncertain, but it may have been a suburb of Tiberias.

The only reference to Mary Magdalene in the gospels, other than as a witness of the crucifixion and resurrection, is as a woman cured by Jesus:

Mark 16:9. *Now when Jesus was risen early the first day of the week, he appeared first to Mary Magdalene, out of whom he had cast seven devils.*

This is said also by Luke, though not in connection with the resurrection, but with an earlier period while Jesus was still in Galilee:

Luke 8:1. . . . *he* [Jesus] *went throughout every city and village, preaching* . . . *and the twelve were with him,*
Luke 8:2. *And certain women, which had been healed of evil spirits and infirmities, Mary called Magdalene, out of whom went seven devils* . . .

Mary Magdalene has been considered, in tradition, to have been a prostitute and to have repented as a result of her meeting with Jesus. The seven devils might then be considered devils of lust.

This is probably so only because she is mentioned in Luke almost immediately after a tale about another woman. This one comes into Jesus' presence while he is dining with a Pharisee:

Luke 7:37. *And, behold, a woman in the city, which was a sinner . . .*

Luke 7:38. *. . . stood at his feet behind him weeping . . .*

This sinner was, indeed, a prostitute in all likelihood, but there is no direct identification, anywhere in the Bible, of this woman with Mary Magdalene. To be possessed by devils, as Mary Magdalene was, would be the sign of what we would today call mental illness, rather than anything else. We might much more reasonably consider Mary Magadalene a cured madwoman rather than a reformed prostitute.

Nevertheless, the term "magdalen" is now used to refer to a reformed prostitute, or to a house for reformed prostitutes. And, since Mary Magdalene, as a repentant sinner, is always shown in paintings with her eyes red and swollen with weeping, the word "maudlin" (the British pronunciation of "magdalen") has come to mean tearfully or weakly emotional.

The existence of Mary Magdalene may explain a puzzle concerning the resurrection—why it was believed, and yet not believed.

On the one hand, there seems no question that the disciples accepted the resurrection and that they continued to preach the doctrines of Jesus on that basis, so that their successors, after three centuries, won the empire.

On the other hand, if Jesus did indeed rise from the dead, why was this not the signal for a wild acclamation of the Messiah and a revolt against Rome, as the authorities feared?

One might reconstruct events something like this. Mary Magdalene was the first to see the risen Jesus:

Mark 16:9. *Now when Jesus was risen early the first day of the week, he appeared first to Mary Magdalene, out of whom he had cast seven devils.*

Mark 16:10. *And she went and told them that had been with him, as they mourned and wept.*

Mark 16:11. *And they . . . believed not.*

Nevertheless, the tale of Mary Magdalene must eventually have carried conviction to the mourning disciples, who would, after all, have wanted fervently to believe that Jesus was indeed the Messiah and would rise from the dead.

Once Mary Magdalene's tale of an empty tomb and of a Jesus who appeared to her was believed, confirming tales would naturally arise in later times. There would come tales of Jesus having appeared to this disciple or that, under such circumstances or others, and a number of them would be recorded in the gospels when these came to be written. But all might conceivably have rested entirely upon the word of one witness, Mary Magdalene.

Yet Mary Magdalene had been possessed by "seven devils." She had been a madwoman or, in any case, seriously disturbed, and her behavior might have remained erratic enough to give her the reputation of being "touched." Even if she had shown marked improvement under Jesus' influence, the shock of the arrest, trial and crucifixion might well have unhinged her once more and made her an easy target for hallucination.

Aside from the disciples, who may have accepted her story only after a while, there might have been no one who would lend it credence. The people generally would have shrugged off anything she had to say as the ravings of a madwoman.

It would follow from this that though the disciples might believe (and more and more fervently as time went on), there would be no general acceptance of the tale by the people. And there were no disorders and certainly no revolt against Rome.

The view given in the gospels is, of course, that Jesus did rise, and he appeared not to Mary Magdalene alone but to a number of people on several different occasions, walking and talking with them. Matthew pictures the disciples as returning home after receiving the tale of the resurrection:

Matthew 28:16. *Then the eleven disciples went away into Galilee, into a mountain where Jesus had appointed them.*

. . . .

Matthew 28:18. *And Jesus came and spake unto them . . .*

To explain the disbelief of the Jews generally, Matthew advances a rather unlikely tale that is not found in the other gospels. He says the priestly authorities bribed the guardians of the tomb to say that they had fallen asleep and that while they slept, Jesus' disciples stole the body and that Jesus had not really risen.

What makes the tale unlikely is that sleeping while on patrol is a cardinal sin for soldiers at all times and it is unlikely that the guards would have let themselves be bribed into admitting such a thing. Even though the priests promised to protect them from the consequences if Pilate heard that they had slept on duty, it is doubtful that they would have taken the chance.

Nevertheless, that is what Matthew says and he concludes:

Matthew 28:15. *So they took the money, and did as they were taught* [instructed]: *and this saying is commonly reported among the Jews until this day.*

6. MARK

The Gospel According to St. Mark

It is generally accepted that Mark is the earliest of the four gospels, and it is certainly the shortest.

It has been suggested that this first of the gospels was put into writing in order to circulate among Christians the story of the sufferings of Jesus and his steadfastness under affliction. Perhaps this was in order to encourage Christians at a time when they, generally, were undergoing persecution.

The first serious persecutions of Christianity were initiated in Rome by the Emperor Nero after the great fire of A.D. 64 and it is indeed likely that Mark's gospel may have been written shortly after.

From the fact that Jesus' apocalyptic discourse is included and the destruction of Jerusalem clearly indicated (see page 209), it is thought that it might not have been written till after A.D. 66, when the Jewish rebellion against Rome began. There are even those who feel the final form was attained only after A.D. 70 and the Roman destruction of the Second Temple. It could not, however, have been long after A.D. 70, for the gospel must have been in existence and circulating before Matthew and Luke came to be written—since the two latter borrowed extensively from Mark.

Mark's gospel seems to have been written for Christians of Jewish origin, but apparently not for those with extensive knowledge of Biblical lore. There is none of Matthew's Old Testament pedantry. Perhaps the writer of Mark was not himself a very educated man—at least the Greek of the gospel is not very polished.

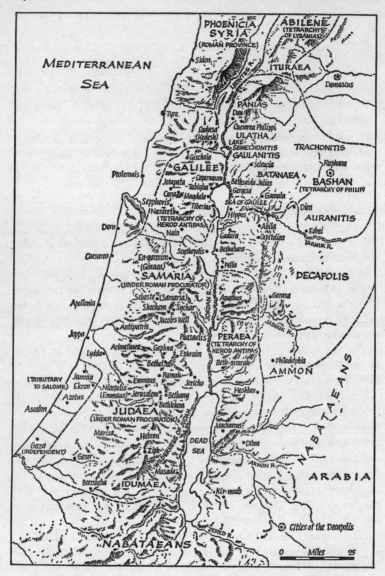

Palestine in the Time of Christ

Mark

Papias, the second-century Christian bishop, stated that someone named Mark had composed a gospel, using information obtained from Simon Peter himself as his source. It is certain that it is this second gospel to which he refers.

Apparently Peter did have a younger associate named Mark (or Marcus, to use the fuller Latin form of the name). He refers to this man affectionately as one would a disciple or follower, in his first epistle:

1 Peter 5:13. *The church . . . saluteth you; and so doth Marcus my son.*

Nor, despite the Latin name, is Mark a Gentile. Mark appears to be only a surname added to the Jewish proper name of John (Johanan). Thus, in Acts:

Acts 12:12. *. . . he* [Peter] *came to the house of Mary the mother of John, whose surname was Mark . . .*

John Mark must have been quite young at the time of the crucifixion and he does not appear by name in the gospels. There is, however, one incident described in Mark but not in the other gospels which may indeed refer to Mark himself. It comes just after the arrest of Jesus, when his disciples fled. One unidentified person is described as remaining for a while:

Mark 14:51. *And there followed him a certain young man, having a linen cloth cast about his naked body; and the young men* [who had come to arrest Jesus] *laid hold on him:*

Mark 14:52. *And he left the linen cloth, and fled from them naked.*

Nothing follows from this event and the young man does not reappear. Tradition has it, though, that this young man is Mark himself, and that the evangelist could not resist mentioning his own presence at a key point in the story of Jesus.

John the Baptist

Mark begins his gospel with John the Baptist. He has nothing to say of the virgin birth in Bethlehem, of any marvels or miracles relating to Jesus' infancy. He does not even make mention of the descent from David. In this gospel, Jesus is referred to as the Son of God (that is, the Messiah) but rarely as the Son of David.

In fact, if we had only the gospel of St. Mark to guide us to the life of Jesus, we would have to assume that Jesus was born in Nazareth after the ordinary fashion of men, into a poor Galilean family of no royal pretensions.

Such an origin is so out of line with Old Testament prophecies concerning the Messiah that Matthew may have written *his* gospel primarily in order to assert such matters as the Davidic descent and the birth in Bethlehem. Only so could Jesus be defended against the claims of Jewish theologians that he could *not* be the Messiah because he was of Galilean birth and of non-royal lineage.

In Mark the first mention of Jesus is in connection with his baptism:

> Mark 1:9. . . . *in those days, . . . Jesus came from Nazareth . . . and was baptized of John in Jordan.*

and thereafter the Spirit of God descended upon him as in Matthew. John the Baptist is described as the forerunner (as he is in all the gospels) and as knowing that to be his function:

> Mark 1:7. And [John the Baptist] *preached, saying, There cometh one mightier than I after me, the latchet of whose shoes I am not worth to stoop down and unloose.*

In Matthew at the time of Jesus' baptism, John is described as specifically recognizing Jesus as that mightier one, but there is none of this in Mark.

The Unclean Spirit

Following the baptism, Mark refers briefly to the episode of the temptation, but without details, certainly without the Old Testament quotations that Matthew introduced for the delectation of his learned audience.

Jesus then chooses his first four disciples and begins his preaching activity. Mark concentrates heavily on his activities as a miraculous healer. Thus, at Capernaum:

Mark 1:23. . . . *there was in their synagogue a man with an unclean spirit . . .*

. . . .

Mark 1:25. *And Jesus* [said] *. . . come out of him.*
Mark 1:26. *And . . . the unclean spirit . . . came out of him.*

Mark quotes the unclean spirit as crying out at the approach of Jesus:

Mark 1:24. . . . *what have we to do with thee, thou Jesus of Nazareth? . . . I know thee who thou art, the Holy One of God.*

Mark uses the phrase "Jesus of Nazareth" since there is no indication in this gospel that Jesus was born anywhere but in Nazareth. The phrase was well enough known to be adopted in the other gospels, despite the tale of the birth at Bethlehem. Furthermore, Mark, who never mentions the Davidic descent, makes use of "Holy One of God" as a phrase signifying the Messiah, rather than "Son of David."

Levi the son of Alphaeus

Mark records Jesus as selecting a publican for a disciple:

Mark 2:14. *And as he passed by, he saw Levi the son of Alphaeus sitting at the receipt of custom, and said unto him, Follow me. And he arose and followed him.*

Matthew tells the same story, but of the disciple Matthew (presumably the Evangelist himself), and says nothing of the publican being the son of Alphaeus.

In Matthew's list of the twelve apostles he lists two pairs of brothers:

Matthew 10:2. . . . *Simon . . . Peter, and Andrew his brother; James the son of Zebedee, and John his brother . . .*

If Levi (or Matthew) were the son of Alphaeus, a third pair of brothers must be found among the apostles, for there is a second James, distinguished, as the son of Alphaeus, from James, son of Zebedee. Ought not Levi (or Matthew) be mentioned together with James the son of Alphaeus? In the list of apostles, Matthew includes:

Matthew 10:3. . . . *Matthew the publican; James the son of Alphaeus, and Lebbaeus, whose surname was Thaddaeus.*

The pattern in Matthew is that the lesser known brother follows the better known (or, perhaps, the younger follows the older) and the father's name is mentioned only for the brother mentioned first. Now Lebbaeus is a Greek form of the name Levi, so that the verse 10:3 might almost seem to include James the son of Alphaeus and Levi, his brother. Yet there is no mention of the brotherhood; Matthew is placed on the other side of James; and Matthew seems to go out of his way to identify himself as "Matthew the publican."

In Mark's list of apostles, brotherhood is less important. Andrew, for instance, is not identified as the brother of Peter (although he is so identified at the time both were accepted as disciples). Andrew is not even placed next to Peter. Mark says:

Mark 3:18. *And Andrew, and Philip, and Bartholomew, and Matthew, and Thomas, and James the son of Alphaeus, and Thaddaeus . . .*

Matthew is not identified. Yet why would Matthew claim to be a publican if he were not; the calling was a disgraceful one (see page 167). Or did Matthew wish to emphasize his rise to grace by blackening his position before that rise?

Abiathar

Mark begins early to describe the gathering dismay of the orthodox among the Jews at Jesus' doctrines; at his claim to have the power to forgive sins and at his cavalier attitude toward the Sabbath (see page 184).

In maintaining that the Sabbath might be broken, when necessary, for the good of men, Jesus pointed out an action of David himself as a precedent. When David was a fugitive from Saul, and suffering the pangs of hunger, the high priest at Nob allowed him to use the special hallowed bread, ordinarily reserved for priests only. Thus human necessity rose above ritual.

In giving this example, however, Mark made a factual error:

> Mark 2:26. . . . he [David] *went into the house of God in the days of Abiathar the high priest, and did eat the shewbread* . . .

But it was not Abiathar who was high priest at the time this incident took place, but Abiathar's father, Ahimelech (see page I-290). It is an understandable slip, however, for Abiathar was the sole survivor of the slaughter of the priests at Nob as a result of their having fed David, and Abiathar was closely connected with David throughout the latter's subsequent reign. It would be almost second nature for a Jew of New Testament times to think of Abiathar in connection with King David.

Matthew and Luke both repeat this story, but neither mentions the name of the high priest, thus avoiding the slip.

Boanerges

In Mark's list of the twelve apostles, an interesting addition is a surname given to the sons of Zebedee:

> Mark 3:17. *And James the son of Zebedee, and John the brother of James; and he* [Jesus] *surnamed them Boanerges, which is, The sons of thunder* . . .

Boanerges is a Greek transliteration of the Aramaic "benai regesh," which means "sons of anger." This may represent a tradition to the effect that James and John were fiery in temper and always ready to take angry action.

A clear example of this is to be found in Luke. There, when Jesus was rebuffed by Samaritans who would not allow him to enter one of their villages, James and John demand retaliation:

> Luke 9:54. *And when his disciples James and John saw this, they said, Lord, wilt thou that we command fire to come down from heaven, and consume them, even as Elias* [Elijah] *did?*

The reference here is to a tale of Elijah, who, when fifty soldiers came to arrest him in the time of Ahaziah, king of Israel, used fire from heaven in his defense:

2 Kings 1:10. *And Elijah answered and said to the captain of fifty, If I be a man of God, then let fire come down from heaven, and consume thee and thy fifty. And there came down fire from heaven, and consumed him and his fifty.*

Jesus, however, rebuked his wrathful disciples:

Luke 9:56. . . . *the Son of man is not come to destroy men's lives, but to save them* . . .

Legion

In Mark's telling of the casting out of devils in the country of the Gadarenes or Gergesenes (see page 176), he has Jesus speaking to the possessing devils:

Mark 5:9. *And he* [Jesus] *asked him* [the possessing spirit], *What is thy name? And he answered, saying, My name is Legion: for we are many.*

Legion is capitalized in the King James Version, and in the Revised Standard Version as well, as though it were a proper name, the name of the inhabiting spirit.

Actually "legion" is the name given to the principal unit of the Roman army and is from a Latin word meaning "to gather together." A legion is a group of soldiers "gathered together." In New Testament times, a legion consisted of some six thousand soldiers, and the word could therefore be used to indicate a great number. The statement "My name is Legion: for we are many" is equivalent to saying, "There are thousands of us."

And, indeed, the spirits are then sent into thousands of swine:

Mark 5:13. . . . *the unclean spirits . . . entered into the swine: . . . (they were about two thousand;)* . . .

Talitha cumi

Mark's account of Jesus' life and death is so like Matthew's in essentials that there remains little to say that has not been said in the previous chapter. One interesting point might be mentioned:

For all that Mark seems to have written in Greek, it is closer to the Aramaic even than Matthew. In fact, part of the imperfection of the Greek of this gospel seems to be that it contains numerous Aramaic forms of expression, literally translated, as though Mark were writing in Greek, but thinking in Aramaic.

Oftener than in the other gospels, Mark gives the actual Aramaic and then translates it, as in the case of "Boanerges." Another example arises in the case of the young daughter of a synagogue official— a girl whom Jesus raises from the dead. All three synoptic gospels tell of this miracle, but only Mark reports Jesus' words, on raising the girl, in the native Aramaic:

Mark 5:41. *And he [Jesus] took the damsel by the hand, and said unto her, Talitha cumi; which is, being interpreted, Damsel, I say unto thee, arise.*

At another time, Mark reports Jesus' curing of a deaf man with a speech impediment:

Mark 7:34. *And looking up to heaven, he [Jesus] sighed, and saith unto him, Ephphatha, that is, Be opened.*

And still again, at Gethsemane, when Jesus prays, addressing God as "Father," the Aramaic word is given first:

Mark 14:36. *And he [Jesus] said, Abba, Father, all things are possible unto thee; take away this cup from me . . .*

7. LUKE

The Gospel According to St. Luke

The third and last of the synoptic gospels seems, like that of St. Matthew, to have been based largely on the gospel of St. Mark, but with additional matter included.

Luke is therefore certainly later than Mark, and is probably later than Matthew as well. Scholars generally seem to agree that Luke was written some time after the crucial year, A.D. 70, when Jerusalem was taken and the Temple destroyed by the Romans. Some have even suggested dates as late as A.D. 100, though A.D. 80 would be more generally acceptable.

If Luke is later than Matthew, it nevertheless seems to have been written independently. The additional matter included in Luke, beyond what is found in Mark, is for the most part quite different from the additional matter found in Matthew.

Partly, this may have arisen out of a difference in intent.

Suppose we begin with the gospel of St. Mark, the earliest of the synoptics, and view it for what it seems to be—the simple story of a prophet and wonder-worker who is viewed by the author as the Messiah, and who is wrongfully accused and executed but triumphantly restored to life. The story as told by Mark is intended for the ordinary Christian of Jewish background.

Matthew, in his rewriting of this gospel, added material designed

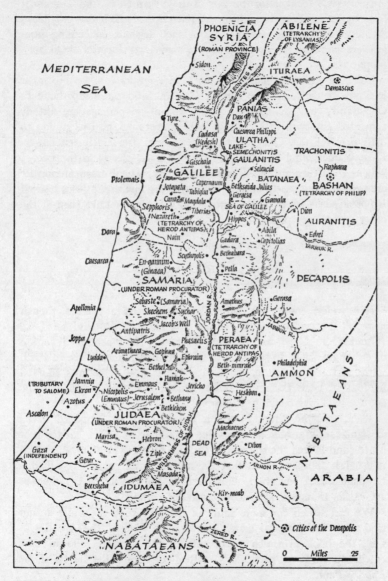

Palestine in the Time of Christ

(in his view) to fit it for the ears of those learned in Old Testament lore, by interlarding it with many references to Biblical prophecies and, for the purpose, making use of such legends concerning Jesus as were common at the time and would lend themselves to such prophecies.

Luke, on the other hand, rewrote Mark's gospel in a way to make it fit, particularly, for the ears of Gentiles who are sympathetic to Christianity and are considering conversion—or perhaps are already converted and wish to know still more concerning the background to their new religion. Old Testament prophecies are largely ignored by Luke as unessential and the Jews are cast more clearly in the role of villains than they are in Matthew and Mark. The Roman authorities are treated more gently than in the first two gospels, and Jesus himself is portrayed as far more sympathetic to Gentiles in Luke than in the other synoptic gospels.

Luke

It is widely considered that Luke was himself a Gentile, though none of the evidence is conclusive. His name is Roman, for Luke ("Loukas" in Greek and "Lucas" in Latin) is a shortened version of either Lucius or Lucanus, both good Roman names. This, in itself, settles nothing, of course, for Roman names were sometimes adopted by Jews in New Testament times. Paul is a Roman name, but the apostle Paul was certainly Jewish.

Then, too, the Greek in which Luke is written is judged to be of significantly greater literary value than that of either Matthew or Mark (and indeed the superiority of Luke seems evident to most even in English translation) so that the author is judged to have had a thorough Greek education. This increases the possibility that he was a Gentile, though it still doesn't make it certain.

We can search for more hints in the fact that the same author who wrote Luke almost certainly wrote the Acts of the Apostles as well, the book in which the events of the decades following the crucifixion are given, particularly matters concerning the travels of the Apostle Paul.

There are indications that the writer of Acts was actually a companion of Paul who accompanied him on his travels. Thus, at one point Paul is described as seeing the vision of a man in Macedonia crying for help:

Acts 16:10. *And after he had seen the vision, immediately we endeavoured to go into Macedonia . . .*

It may be that the writer of Acts has suddenly switched to a quotation from Paul's memoirs, without indicating the fact. (The conventions about the use of quotation marks are modern, of course.) It seems more reasonable, however, to suppose that the use of "we" means that the writer was one of Paul's entourage who tried with him to arrange for passage to Macedonia.

But who might this companion be? Persons particularly close to Paul are mentioned by him several times in his letters. Thus, in the Epistle to the Colossians, Paul brings his letter to a close by sending greetings from those around him:

Colossians 4:14. *Luke, the beloved physician, and Demas, greet you.*

It is usually assumed that Luke was Paul's personal doctor, and the nature of the post alone would assure a close connection of the two throughout Paul's arduous travels. In the Second Epistle to Timothy, Paul specifically states:

2 Timothy 4:10. *. . . Demas hath forsaken me, having loved this present world . . .*
2 Timothy 4:11. *Only Luke is with me . . .*

thus indicating the particular close fidelity of his physician. Luke is also mentioned in the closing of the Epistle to Philemon as one of those from whom greeting is sent.

The tradition is that it is this Luke who was author of both the third gospel and Acts. This tradition dates back to Irenaeus, a bishop who served in Gaul about A.D. 170.

That still doesn't help us decide whether Luke was Jewish or Gentile.

Yet the Book of Acts seems to deal with Antioch in a particularly detailed manner, as though the author were well acquainted with church matters there. The Christians at Antioch were largely of Gentile background (there were relatively few Jews there) and if Luke was a member of the church of that city, the chances are good that he was a Gentile. An early church father, Eusebius of Caesarea, wrote a history of the Church in A.D 324, and he considered Luke to have been a citizen of Antioch of Syrian extraction. This is the tradition generally accepted.

And yet there is a verse in Acts that lists some of the members of the church at Antioch:

Acts 13:1. *Now there were in the church that was at Antioch certain prophets and teachers; as Barnabas, and Simeon that was called Niger, and Lucius of Cyrene* . . .

Can Lucius of Cyrene be the Luke of the Pauline epistles? This has been suggested by some. But Cyrene was an important Jewish center and if Luke were a native of Cyrene rather than of Antioch, the chance that he was Jewish is materially increased.

On the whole, the best evidence in favor of Luke's Gentile origin is his writing itself and its sympathetic attitude toward Gentiles.

Theophilus

Luke begins his gospel in approved Greek fashion by addressing the person for whom it is intended:

Luke 1:3. *It seemed good to me also* . . . *to write unto thee in order, most excellent Theophilus,*
Luke 1:4. *That thou mightest know the certainty of those things, wherein thou hast been instructed.*

This sounds as though Luke were attempting to further the conversion of some specific Greek. Absolutely nothing is known about this prospective convert, but it is usually supposed that he was of good family since Luke refers to him as "most excellent."

Some have suggested that Theophilus was an official of the Roman court that was trying the Apostle Paul, and that the gospel of St. Luke was in the nature of a brief for the defense, prepared by Paul's close friend and associate. It was intended to acquaint the court with the fact that Paul was not a traitor to Rome but a messenger from God.

There are also suggestions that Theophilus (the name means "one who loves God") was not a person at all but represented, allegorically, potential converts generally.

Zacharias

Luke was under no illusion that he was to write the first biography of Jesus, for he was well aware that a number of such biographies already existed. There was Mark, for one, and perhaps a number that were never accepted as canonical and have since been lost:

Luke 1:1. *Forasmuch as many have taken in hand to set forth in order a declaration of those things which are most surely believed among us* . . .

It may well have been, though, that if he was not the first in the field, he intended to be most complete. Mark began with the baptism of Jesus by John, at a time when Jesus was already a grown man, and ends with the resurrection. Matthew goes back to Jesus' birth, but in Luke we go further back still to the birth of John the Baptist.

The purpose, here, may have been to make it perfectly clear that John was a subsidiary element, a forerunner, and one who clearly recognized his own role as a mere herald of the greater man to follow. This may have been particularly important in the light of the doctrinal disputes in decades immediately following the crucifixion, when the followers of John the Baptist maintained for some time a tradition that was apparently independent of the followers of Jesus. Thus, in Acts, a newcomer is introduced as follows:

Acts 18:24. . . . *a certain Jew named Apollos . . . came to Ephesus.*
Acts 18:25. . . . *knowing only the baptism of John.*

He was apparently a follower of the doctrines of John the Baptist who, however, knew of Jesus and quickly joined the followers of Jesus.

Luke, therefore, begins with Zacharias, the father of John the Baptist, an individual not mentioned elsewhere in the New Testament:

Luke 1:5. *There was in the days of Herod . . . a certain priest named Zacharias, of the course of Abia* [Abijah] . . .

The priesthood was divided into twenty-four divisions or "courses," each of which served a week at the Temple so that a given man served for one week at a time, twice each year. These twenty-four courses are each named for an ancestor of Aaronic descent and these are listed in 1 Chronicles. Among them are:

1 Chronicles 24:10. *The seventh to Hakkoz, the eighth to Abijah* . . .

Zacharias was thus a priest of the eighth course.

Elisabeth

The mother of John the Baptist is also introduced:

Luke 1:5. . . . *and his* [Zacharias'] *wife was of the daughters of Aaron, and her name was Elisabeth.*

Elisabeth ("Eleisabet" in Greek) is a good Aaronic name, since it is equivalent to the Hebrew "Elisheba," which was the name of Aaron's wife:

Exodus 6:23. *And Aaron took him Elisheba . . . to wife* . . .

The couple were childless and, as they were advanced in years, it seemed as though that state might be permanent. Elisabeth shared this fate with a number of women in the Old Testament: Sarah, the wife of Abraham; Rachel, the wife of Jacob; the unnamed wife of Manoah; and Hannah, the wife of Elkanah. In each of the cases mentioned, the barrenness was ended through divine intervention and a notable son was born: Isaac, Joseph, Samson, and Samuel, respectively. The story of Elisabeth follows these earlier models.

Zacharias takes his turn at service in the Temple, in a year not specified. The angel Gabriel appears to him, just as an angel appeared to the wife of Manoah. Zacharias is told he will have a son in terms that echo, in part, the words of the earlier tale concerning the wife of Manoah. Shortly thereafter, Elisabeth did indeed become pregnant.

Mary

The story now shifts to the future mother of Jesus:

Luke 1:26. *And in the sixth month* [of Elisabeth's pregnancy] *the angel Gabriel was sent from God unto a city of Galilee, named Nazareth,*

Luke 1:27. *To a virgin espoused to a man whose name was Joseph, of the house of David; and the virgin's name was Mary.*

Luke 1:28. *And the angel . . . said . . .*

. . . .

Luke 1:31. *. . . . behold, thou shalt conceive in thy womb, and bring forth a son, and shalt call his name JESUS.*

Luke stresses the fact that Mary is a virgin, but this is by no means as clear a statement of the virgin birth as is to be found in Matthew. Mary, although a virgin at the time of this "annunciation," was engaged to be married, and Gabriel's words might be taken as meaning that she would conceive after her marriage with Joseph had been consummated, and in the ordinary manner of conception.

To be sure, the story goes on:

Luke 1:34. *Then said Mary unto the angel, How shall this be, seeing I know not a man?*

It is an odd question, considering that she is about to be married, unless, as some commentators suggest, she intends to be a perpetual virgin, even if she marries. (However, Luke doesn't say so.) Another possibility is that Mary conceived at the instant of the annunciation and therefore while she was still a virgin. Yet Gabriel in answering Mary's question uses the future tense:

Luke 1:35. *And the angel answered . . . , The Holy Ghost shall come upon thee . . .*

Though it is hard to say that Luke declares the virgin birth unequivocally and—if Luke is read *alone*—it is easy to argue that a virgin birth is not intended, still Christians generally accept Luke's tale of the annunciation as signifying Jesus' birth of a virgin.

Gabriel also told Mary the news concerning Elisabeth:

Luke 1:36. *And, behold, thy cousin Elisabeth, she hath also conceived a son in her old age: and this is the sixth month with
her . . .*

Mary hastened to visit her cousin ("the visitation"). When she entered the house of Zacharias, Elisabeth greeted her at once:

Luke 1:42. *And she* [Elisabeth] *spake out with a loud voice,
and said, Blessed art thou among women, and blessed is the fruit of
thy womb.*

The first part of her greeting is a duplicate of the last part of the
greeting given Mary by Gabriel:

Luke 1:28. *And the angel . . . said, Hail, thou that art highly
favoured, the Lord is with thee: blessed art thou among women.*

In the Revised Standard Version, the greeting of Gabriel begins
"Hail, O favored one" and in the Catholic version, "Hail, full of
grace."

There is a tendency to think that the phrase "blessed art thou
among women" was accidentally transferred from Elisabeth to Gabriel
in the copying process. It is for this reason that the Revised Standard
Version omits it in Gabriel's greeting.

By combining the two greetings and adding the name of the person
greeted and the name of the child who is to be the fruit of Mary's
womb, we have "Hail, Mary, full of grace, the Lord is with thee.
Blessed art thou among women, and blessed is the fruit of thy womb,
Jesus." The first two words of this greeting, in Latin, are "Ave, Maria"
and this greeting is the famous prayer of that name which is so
prominent in the liturgy of the Roman Catholic Church.

Elisabeth's reference to the fruit of Mary's womb is in the present
tense, which may mean that the evangelist considers Mary to be already pregnant. If so, this is the strongest evidence for the virgin
birth in Luke.

Yet one can't help but wonder if the legend of the visitation was
not chosen by Luke for inclusion in his gospel primarily because it
offered a chance to demonstrate that John the Baptist recognized Jesus'
priority and transcendent importance even in the womb. He has
Elisabeth say to Mary:

Luke 1:44. . . . *as soon as the voice of thy salutation sounded in mine ears, the babe leaped in my womb for joy.*

This would be a strong point for the followers of Jesus and against the competing followers of John.

In the course of the visit of Mary to Elisabeth, Mary chants a hymn of praise to God which begins:

Luke 1:46. *And Mary said, My soul doth magnify the Lord* . . .

The hymn is very much like that ascribed to Hannah on the occasion of her giving birth to Samuel, and is widely considered to be inspired by it.

Actually, it is Elisabeth, rather than Mary, whose case was like Hannah's. It was Elisabeth who, like Hannah, was barren for many years despite marriage, and it was Elisabeth who, like Hannah, had been blessed with conception by God and with vindication in a society that considered barrenness a punishment for sin.

It is to be expected, then, that the hymn, which follows immediately after Elisabeth's greeting to Mary, should be intoned by Elisabeth rather than Mary. In some old manuscripts, indeed, Luke 1:46 reads, "And she said, My soul doth magnify the Lord," where "she" might refer to Elisabeth as easily as to Mary. Perhaps the transfer of the prayer from Elisabeth to Mary is part of the victory of the disciples of Jesus over those of John in the decades when the gospels were written.

The first phrase of the song is, in Latin, "Magnificat anima mea Dominum" and it is therefore referred to as the "Magnificat."

Mary remained with Elisabeth three months, presumably till the birth of Elisabeth's child. Then she returned home.

Luke's choice of legends that centered on Mary rather than, as in Matthew's case, on Joseph, might be significant. The Gentiles knew of goddesses, and their pagan religions often had a strongly feminine cast. If Luke were a Gentile, he would be drawn to the tales of Mary. Matthew, on the other hand, a product of the strongly patriarchal Jewish culture, would automatically deal with Joseph.

Luke's preoccupation with Mary has led to the legend that he knew her personally and learned of the story of Jesus' birth from her in her old age. There is also a tradition to the effect that Luke was an artist and painted a portrait of Mary which was later found in Jerusalem. Such traditions are supported by nothing more than pious belief.

John the Baptist

When Elisabeth's child was born, it was expected he was to be named Zacharias like his father. That Luke should seriously maintain this:

Luke 1:59. . . . *they* [kinsmen] *came to circumcise the child; and they called him Zacharias, after the name of his father.*

is an odd departure from Jewish custom. There is no case in the Bible of a child named for a living father, and it is certainly unheard of for pious Jews to do so today. Perhaps this is the kind of lapse one might expect of a Gentile, as Luke is considered to be.

In any case, Elisabeth objected:

Luke 1:60. *And his mother . . . said, Not so; but he shall be called John.*

Zacharias agreed to this and then intoned a hymn of praise:

Luke 1:67. *And . . . Zacharias . . . prophesied, saying,*
Luke 1:68. *Blessed be the Lord God of Israel; for he hath visited and redeemed his people . . .*

The first word of this hymn is, in Latin, "Benedictus" and it is by that name that the entire hymn is known.

Zacharias does not appear again in Luke, or anywhere else in the Bible. Some early commentators suggested that the reference by Jesus to Zacharias son of Barachias who was "slain between the temple and the altar" (see page 207) was a reference to the father of John the Baptist. This, however, is almost certainly not so, and the Bible makes no reference whatsoever to the death of John's father.

Caesar Augustus

It is now time for Luke to turn to Mary again and recount the tale of the birth of Jesus. There is no sure indication in what is to follow of the time that has elapsed between the birth of John the

Baptist and the birth of Jesus. Luke merely uses a conventionally indefinite phrase:

Luke 2:1. *And it came to pass in those days . . .*

Of course, if Mary's pregnancy followed hard on the annunciation, which came in the sixth month of Elisabeth's pregnancy, then Jesus had to be born just six months after John the Baptist, assuming both pregnancies to have lasted nine months.

But even if this were so and Jesus were half a year younger than John, in what year were both born?

Matthew says only that Jesus was born "in the days of Herod the king" (see page 121), which sets an extreme time limit between 37 B.C. and 4 B.C. Luke, the Gentile, dates the birth by the Gentile emperor and not by the Jewish king:

Luke 2:1. *And it came to pass in those days, that there went out a decree from Caesar Augustus . . .*

Caesar Augustus was born in 63 B.C., in the very year in which Judea was converted into a Roman province by Pompey (see page 122). His name at birth was Caius Octavius; he was the grandnephew of Julius Caesar, and, eventually, that general's adopted heir. When Julius Caesar was assassinated in 44 B.C., Caius Octavius came to Rome to receive his inheritance and changed his name to Caius Julius Caesar Octavianus. At this period in his life he is best known in history as Octavian.

Octavian was a nineteen-year-old boy, sickly and of unimpressive appearance. The most powerful man in Rome at the time was Mark Antony. For fourteen years the two men fought a civil war against each other, sometimes a hot war of spears and swords, sometimes a cold one of propaganda and maneuver. Octavian was immeasurably the greater man of the two and in 30 B.C. the defeated Mark Antony killed himself. Octavian was then sole and absolute ruler of Rome.

Octavian was Imperator ("Commander") of the army, an old title, but one which came to be associated particularly with him and his successors. In English this has been corrupted to Emperor, so that Octavian became the first Roman Emperor and the government over which he and his successors presided came to be known as the Roman Empire.

In 27 B.C. he was voted the title "Augustus" meaning "undertaken

under favorable auguries" or, which is the same thing, "well-omened."
He is commonly known to history by that name.

The period during which Augustus ruled in Rome and Herod in
Jerusalem—the period during which Jesus must have been born according to Matthew and Luke—was from 27 B.C. and 4 B.C.

In 27 B.C. Augustus closed the Temple of Janus, a move indicating
the coming of peace over the vast area that marked the Roman realm.
This was a notable event, for this had taken place in only four or five
brief periods prior to Augustus' time during all the seven warlike centuries in which the dominion of Rome had gradually spread from a
single city to all the Mediterranean world.

The period of peace that began with Augustus' rule lasted for
centuries (the "pax Romana" or "Roman peace"). The Mediterranean world had never seen so long a period of peace before Augustus'
time, or, for that matter, since.

It is sometimes stated that the beginning of this period of peace
was a particularly appropriate time for Jesus to be born. To those who
accept the divine ordering of human affairs, it seems easy to assume
that matters were deliberately arranged in order that a profound peace
should fall over all the world in preparation for the birth of the
"Prince of Peace."

This, however, is a view that is more romantic than justified. To be
sure, there was peace in the settled regions of the empire (including
Judea), where peace had been conspicuously absent in the preceding
century, and, to be sure, this is not a matter to be lightly dismissed.
The peace, however, was not universal.

All through Augustus' reign and, therefore, all through the period
of Jesus' birth and youth, the Roman boundaries to the north were
aflame. Augustus was pushing the boundaries of the empire to the
Danube and eastward across Germany. For the barbarous tribes south
of the Danube and west of the Elbe, there was no peace.

Cyrenius

The period of Jesus' birth might be narrowed by considering the
reference to the nature of the decree of Caesar Augustus:

> Luke 2:1. . . . *a decree from Caesar Augustus, that all the world*
> *should be taxed.*

Luke 2:2. (*And this taxing was first made when Cyrenius was governor of Syria.*)

Cyrenius was indeed an important Roman official in the time of Augustus. His name was Quirinius, actually, which became "Kyrinios" in Greek and "Cyrenius" in English. The Revised Standard Version restores it to the Latin "Quirinius."

Quirinius was in charge of Roman military affairs in Syria, an office which placed him over the legions in Judea as well, on two different occasions: from 6 to 4 B.C. and from A.D. 6 to 9. All commentators agree that Jesus could not have been born as late as A.D. 6 to 9 and that the incidents surrounding Jesus' birth, if they took place while Quirinius was governor of Syria, had to take place during his first term, from 6 to 4 B.C. This would certainly harmonize Luke's account with Matthew's, at least in this respect.

During Quirinius' second administration, there was (according to Josephus) a census initiated for the purpose of determining some fair basis for the assessment of a special tax.

In ancient times, censuses were generally instituted with either taxation or military enrollment in mind, and this was never popular in either case. Even in the time of David himself, a census was viewed with hostility (see page I-318) and, in post-Exilic times, was looked back upon as having been brought about through nothing less than Satanic inspiration:

1 Chronicles 21:1. *And Satan stood up against Israel, and provoked David to number Israel.*

A Judea which thought of a census with such hostility even when carried through by its great king David was not likely to view with equanimity one that was initiated by a group of Gentile oppressors.

Nevertheless, such a census was an obvious necessity in Quirinius' second administration. Herod Archelaus had just been deposed as ethnarch (see page 138) and now Judea was under direct Roman rule. As long as Judea had been under some native ruler under native laws, Rome might have been willing to have its taxes collected in any fashion that pleased the ruler—provided only he turned over an adequate amount to Rome. Once Rome was in direct charge, however, things would have to be done systematically and the first step would be a census, numbering the people and their possessions.

From our point of view, this is an enlightened measure and one that would work in favor of the common people, for Augustus ruled well and enforced a surprising amount of honesty in provincial government. Unfortunately the purpose of a census and its honest intent could not easily be explained. The Jews (and all the peoples of the east) knew only too well of corrupt governments and gouging tax collectors. The only way in which individuals could save themselves from utter ruin when the tax collector came round was by a combination of cheating and bribery. A census that would expose their actual belongings and place the collector under an obligation to collect a known amount would deprive them of their chance of wiggling their way out of some of the tax.

It is not surprising, then, that there was wild rioting over Judea when the Romans began to carry through their census. Luke even mentions such rioting in Acts:

> Acts 5:37. . . . *Judas of Galilee* [rose up] *in the days of the taxing, and drew away much people after him* . . .

The riots were put down bloodily, of course, and the census was carried through. The memory remained green for decades afterward and it is not surprising that Luke used it as a landmark for the birth of Jesus.

This particular census in Quirinius' second administration is not, however, an accurate landmark. Jesus could not have been born as late as that; he had to be born in Quirinius' first administration and unfortunately we have no records of any census carried through in that time.

It has been suggested that there was indeed a census carried through in 6 B.C. in Quirinius' first administration. At that time, the suggestion has it, Herod ruled over Judea and he might have carried the census through in accordance with Jewish custom. There would then be no disorders and nothing for Josephus to remark upon.

This is conceivable, but it seems most unlikely and no one would dream of suggesting such a thing except for the necessity of justifying the reference in the gospel of St. Luke. Herod was not a popular ruler with the Jewish nationalists. The latter considered him, as an Idumean, to be just as foreign as the Romans. It passes the bounds of belief to suppose that a Herodian census would have been carried through without disorders.

Bethlehem

One might suppose, instead, that Luke made use of the well-remembered census merely as a landmark by which to date the approximate time of birth of Jesus, as Matthew used the star of Bethlehem (see page 128). The Biblical writers are rarely concerned with exact dating, in any case, and find other matters of more importance.

But there is a chance that more was involved. We might argue that Luke was faced with a serious difficulty in telling the tale of Jesus' birth and that he had decided to use the census as a device to get out of that difficulty.

In Mark, the earliest of the gospels, Jesus appears only as Jesus of Nazareth. To Mark, as nearly as we can tell from his gospel, the Messiah was a Galilean by birth, born in Nazareth.

Yet this could not be accepted by Jews learned in the Scriptures. Jesus of Nazareth had to be born in Bethlehem in order to be the Messiah. The prophet Micah was considered to have said so specifically (see page I-653) and the evangelist Matthew accepts that in his gospel (see page 132).

In order to make the birth at Bethlehem (made necessary by theological theory) consistent with the known fact of life at Nazareth, Matthew made Joseph and Mary natives of Bethlehem who migrated to Nazareth not long after Jesus' birth (see page 138).

Luke, however, did not have access to Matthew's version, apparently, and it did not occur to him to make use of so straightforward a device. Instead, he made Joseph and Mary dwellers in Nazareth before the birth of Jesus, and had them travel to Bethlehem just in time to have Jesus born there and then had them return.

That Mary, at least, dwelt in Nazareth, and perhaps had even been born there, seems plain from the fact that Gabriel was sent there to make the annunciation:

> Luke 1:26. . . . *the angel Gabriel was sent from God unto a city of Galilee, named Nazareth,*
> Luke 1:27. *To a virgin* [whose] . . . *name was Mary.*

But if that were so, why should Mary, in her last month of pregnancy, make the difficult and dangerous seventy-mile overland journey to

Bethlehem

Bethlehem? Luke might have said it was done at Gabriel's orders, but he didn't. Instead, with literary economy, he made use of the landmark of Jesus' birth for the additional purpose of having Jesus born at Bethlehem. Once Caesar Augustus had issued his decree commanding the census in advance of taxation:

> Luke 2:3. *And all went to be taxed, every one into his own city.*
> Luke 2:4. *And Joseph also went up from Galilee, out of the city of Nazareth, into Judaea, unto . . . Bethlehem; (because he was of the house and lineage of David:)*
> Luke 2:5. *To be taxed with Mary his espoused wife, being great with child.*

Though this device has much to be said for it from the standpoint of literary economy, it has nothing to be said for it in the way of plausibility. The Romans couldn't possibly have conducted so queer a census as that. Why should they want every person present in the town of his ancestors rather than in the town in which he actually dwelt? Why should they want individuals traveling up and down the length of the land, clogging the roads and interfering with the life of the province? It would even have been a military danger, for the Parthians could find no better time to attack than when Roman troops would find it hard to concentrate because of the thick crisscrossing of civilians on their way to register.

Even if the ancestral town were somehow a piece of essential information, would it not be simpler for each person merely to state what that ancestral town was? And even if, for some reason, a person had to travel to that ancestral town, would it not be sufficient for the head of the household or some agent of his to make the trip? Would a wife have to come along? Particularly one that was in the last month of pregnancy?

No, it is hard to imagine a more complicated tissue of implausibilities and the Romans would certainly arrange no such census.

Those who maintain that there was an earlier census in 6 B.C. or thereabouts, conducted under the auspices of Herod, suggest that one of the reasons this early census went off quietly was precisely because Herod ran things in the Jewish fashion, according to tribes and households. Even if Herod were a popular king (which he wasn't) it is difficult to see how he could have carried through a quiet census by requiring large numbers of people to tramp miles under the dangerous and primitive conditions of travel of the times. All through their history, the Jews had rebelled for far smaller reasons than the declaration of such a requirement.

It is far easier to believe that Luke simply had to explain the birth of Jesus in Bethlehem for theological reasons, when it was well known that he was brought up in Nazareth. And his instinct for drama overcame any feelings he might have had for plausibility.

Judging by results, Luke was right. The implausibility of his story has not prevented it from seizing upon the imagination of the Christian world, and it is this second chapter of the gospel of St. Luke that is the epitome of the story of the Nativity and the inspiration of countless tales and songs and works of art.

Christmas

In Bethlehem, according to Luke's account, Mary gave birth:

Luke 2:7. *And she [Mary] brought forth her firstborn son and wrapped him in swaddling clothes, and laid him in a manger; because there was no room for them in the inn.*

Presumably the inn was full of travelers, as all inns in Judea must have been at that time, if Luke's story of the census is accepted. Every town, after all, would have been receiving its quota of families returning from elsewhere.

There is no indication at all at this point concerning the date of the Nativity. The feast is celebrated, now, by almost all Christian churches on December 25. This is Christmas ("Christ's mass").

But why December 25? No one really knows. To Europeans and North Americans such a date means winter and, in fact, many of our carols depict a wintry scene and so do our paintings. Indeed, so close is the association of winter and snow that each year millions irrationally long for a "white Christmas" though snow means a sharp rise in automobile fatalities.

Yet upon what is such wintry association based? There is no mention of either snow or cold in either Luke or Matthew. In fact, in the verse after the description of the birth, Luke says:

Luke 2:8. *And there were in the same country shepherds abiding in the field, keeping watch over their flock by night.*

It is customary, since we have the celebration firmly fixed on December 25, to imagine these shepherds as keeping their watch in bitter cold and perhaps in deep snow.

But why? Surely it is much more likely that a night watch would be kept in the summertime when the nights would be mild and, in fact, more comfortable than the scorching heat of the day. For that matter, it is but adding still another dimension to the implausible nature of the census as depicted by Luke if we suppose that all this unnecessary traveling was taking place in the course of a cold winter time.

To be sure, it is a mistake to think of a Palestinian winter as being as cold as one in Germany, Great Britain, or New England. The usual associations of Christmas with snow and ice—even if it *were* on December 25—is purely a local prejudice. It falls in the same class with the manner that medieval artists depicted Mary and Joseph in medieval clothing because they could conceive of no other kind.

Nevertheless, whether December 25 is snowy or mild makes no difference at the moment. The point is that neither Luke nor Matthew give a date of any kind for the Nativity. They give no slightest hint that can be used to deduce a day or even guess at one.

Why, then, December 25? The answer might be found in astronomy and in Roman history.

The noonday Sun is at varying heights in the sky at different seasons of the year because the Earth's axis is tipped by 23 degrees to the plane of Earth's revolution about the Sun. Without going into the astronomy of this in detail, it is sufficient to say that the noonday Sun climbs steadily higher in the sky from December to June, and falls steadily lower from June to December. The steady rise is easily associated with a lengthening day, an eventually warming temperature and quickening of life; the steady decline with a shortening day, an eventually cooling temperature and fading of life.

In primitive times, when the reason for the cycle was not understood in terms of modern astronomy, there was never any certainty that the sinking Sun would ever turn and begin to rise again. Why should it do so, after all, except by the favor of the gods? And that favor might depend entirely upon the proper conduct of a complicated ritual known only to the priests.

It must have been occasion for great gladness each year, then, to observe the decline of the noonday Sun gradually slowing, then coming to a halt and beginning to rise again. The point at which the Sun comes to a halt is the winter "solstice" (from Latin words meaning "sun-halt").

The time of the winter solstice was the occasion for a great feast in honor of what one might call the "birth of the Sun."

In Roman times, a three-day period, later extended to seven days, was devoted to the celebration of the winter solstice. This was the "Saturnalia," named in honor of Saturn, an old Roman god of agriculture.

At the Saturnalia, joy was unrestrained, as befitted a holiday that celebrated a reprieve from death and a return to life. All public business was suspended, in favor of festivals, parties, singing, and gift-giving. It was a season of peace and good will to all men. Even slaves were, for that short period, allowed license that was forbidden at all other times and were treated—temporarily—on a plane of equality with their masters. Naturally, the joy easily turned to the extremes of licentiousness and debauchery, and there were, no doubt, many pious people who deplored the uglier aspects of the festival.

In the Roman calendar—a very poor and erratic one before the time of Julius Caesar—the Saturnalia was celebrated the seventeenth, eighteenth, and nineteenth of December. Once Caesar established a sensible calendar, the winter solstice fell upon December 25 (although in our own calendar, slightly modified since Caesar's time, it comes on December 21).

In the first centuries of the Roman Empire, Christianity had to compete with Mithraism, a form of Sun-worship with its roots in Persia. In Mithraism, the winter solstice was naturally the occasion of a great festival and in A.D. 274, the Roman Emperor, Aurelian, set December 25 as the day of the birth of the Sun. In other words, he lent the Mithraist holiday the official sanction of the government.

The celebration of the winter solstice was a great stumbling block to conversions to Christianity. If Christians held the Saturnalia and the birth of the Sun to be purely pagan then many converts were discouraged. Even if they abandoned belief in the old Roman gods and in Mithras, they wanted the joys of the holiday. (How many people today celebrate the Christmas season with no reference at all to its religious significance and how many would be willing to give up the joy, warmth, and merriment of the season merely because they were not pious Christians?)

But Christianity adapted itself to pagan customs where these, in the judgment of Christian leaders, did not compromise the essential doctrines of the Church. The Bible did not say on which day Jesus was born and there was no dogma that would be affected by one day rather than by another. It might, therefore, be on December 25 as well as on any other.

Once that was settled, converts could join Christianity without giving up their Saturnalian happiness. It was only necessary for them to joyfully greet the birth of the Son rather than the Sun.

If December 25 is Christmas and if it is assumed that Mary became pregnant at the time of the annunciation, then the anniversary of the annunciation must be placed on March 25, nine months before Christmas. And, indeed, March 25 is the day of the Feast of the Annunciation and is called Annunciation Day or, in England, Lady Day, where "Lady" refers to Mary.

Again, if the annunciation came when Elisabeth was six months pregnant, John the Baptist must have been born three months later. June 24 is the day on which his birth is celebrated.

December 25 was gradually accepted through most of the Roman Empire between A.D. 300 and 350. This late period is indicated by the date alone.

There were two general kinds of calendars in use in the ancient Mediterranean world. One is the lunar calendar, which matches the months to the phases of the Moon. It was devised by the Babylonians, who passed it on to the Greeks and the Jews. The other is the solar calendar, which matches the months to the seasons of the year. It was devised by the Egyptians, who passed it on, in Caesar's time, to the Romans, and, by way of Rome, to ourselves.

The lunar calendar does not match the seasons and, in order to keep it from falling out of line, some years must have twelve lunar months and others thirteen, in a rather complex pattern. To people using a solar calendar (as we do) the lunar year is too short when it has twelve months and too long when it has thirteen. A date that is fixed in a lunar calendar slips forward and backward in the solar calendar, although, in the long run, it oscillates about a fixed place.

The holidays established early in Church history made use of the lunar calendar used by the Greeks and Jews. As a result, these holidays shift their day (by our calendar) from year to year. The chief of these days is Easter. It is the prime example of a "movable holiday" and each year we must look at the calendar to see when it might come. All the other movable holidays are tied to Easter and shift with it.

When Christianity spread throughout the Roman Empire and even became the official doctrine of the land, early in the fourth century, it began to make increasing use of the Roman calendar. It became rather complicated to adjust the date of Easter to that calendar. There were serious disagreements among different portions of the Church as to the exact method for doing so, and schisms and heresies arose over the matter.

Those holidays that came into being comparatively late, when Christianity had become official in the empire, made use of the Roman calendar to begin with. Such holiday dates slid back and forth on the lunar calendar but were fixed on solar calendars such as our own. The mere fact that Christmas is celebrated on December 25 every year and that the date never varies on our calendar is enough to show that it was not established as a religious festival until after A.D. 300.

Simeon

Luke goes on to tell of incidents in Jesus' infancy and youth as Matthew does. However, none of the incidents in Luke are to be found in Matthew, and none in Matthew are to be found in Luke. Thus, Luke says nothing at all concerning the flight into Egypt or the slaughter of the innocents. He also says nothing at all about the star of Bethlehem and the three wise men from the east. Similarly, Matthew says nothing at all about the census, the manger, or the shepherds.

According to Luke, when Jesus was presented at the Temple as a first-born son, he was seen by an old man named Simeon. Simeon, who believed he would not die until he saw the Messiah, recognized that Messiah in the infant and said:

Luke 2:29. *Lord, now lettest thou thy servant depart in peace, according to thy word:*

Luke 2:30. *For mine eyes have seen thy salvation . . .*

In Latin, Simeon's words begin: "Nunc dimittis servum tuum, Domine," and the whole passage is therefore referred to as the "Nunc Dimittis."

Simeon was an example of those who expected the Messiah but were content to do so quietly and patiently, as opposed to the Zealots who actively searched for a Messiah and were willing to fight upon the slightest suspicion of one.

Another aged habitué of the Temple, a woman, is likewise described as recognizing the infant Jesus as the Messiah:

Luke 2:36. *And there was one Anna, a prophetess . . .*

Anna is the Greek form of the Hebrew, Hannah (the name of the mother of Samuel).

The Doctors

One tale of Jesus' boyhood is told by Luke, and it is the only tale of Jesus as a boy that is to be found anywhere in the gospels.

At the age of twelve he is taken with his parents when they make their annual trip to Jerusalem at the time of the Passover. When Joseph and Mary leave Jerusalem, they discover Jesus is not with them, and must return in search of him.

Luke 2:46. *And it came to pass, that after three days they found him in the temple, sitting in the midst of the doctors, both hearing them, and asking them questions.*

Luke 2:47. *And all that heard him were astonished at his understanding and answers.*

That Jesus was twelve at this time is perhaps no accident. In Judaism, the age of thirteen is taken as the time of coming to religious maturity. It is the time when a young man must take on the responsibility of religious observances. Modern Jews have the ritual of the "bar mitzvah" ("son of the commandments," meaning "one who is responsible for obedience to the commandments"), which each young man goes through on his thirteenth birthday. Prior to that there is a lengthy period of instruction and training in order to fit him for his task.

The ceremony of the bar mitzvah, as at present constituted, seems to be of medieval origin, but no doubt religious education prior to the thirteenth birthday was important in New Testament times. One has a picture of the young Jesus fascinated by the "teachers" (the term used in place of "doctors" in the Revised Standard Version) and eagerly listening to instruction. In modern terms, he was preparing for his bar mitzvah.

This incident in Luke may have been included as a way of refuting those who sneered at the early Christians as followers of an ignorant and unlettered Galilean. Luke attempts to demonstrate here that, even as a child, the intelligence of Jesus and his interest in the Law astonished even the learned men of the Temple.

Tiberius Caesar

But now Luke makes the great jump. He has done with legends of the time before baptism and moves up to the period of time covered by Mark.

Luke 3:1. Now in the fifteenth year of the reign of Tiberius Caesar, Pontius Pilate being governor of Judaea, and Herod being tetrarch of Galilee, and his brother Philip tetrarch of Ituraea and of the region of Trachonitis, and Lysanias the tetrarch of Abilene,

Luke 3:2. Annas and Caiaphas being the high priests, the word of God came unto John the son of Zacharias in the wilderness.

Tiberius Claudius Nero was the stepson of the Emperor Augustus, being the son of Augustus' wife by a previous marriage. He was born in 42 B.C. and during the early years of Augustus' reign he served well as a general guiding the Roman armies against the tribes in the Danubian areas, and against the Germans east of the Rhine.

Augustus had no sons and the two sons of his only daughter had died young. He was therefore forced, rather against his will, to adopt Tiberius as his heir. In A.D. 14, when Augustus died, Tiberius became the second Roman Emperor—that is, Tiberius Caesar.

He reigned for twenty-three years, till A.D. 37. The "fifteenth year" of his reign would be A.D. 28/29.

Of the remaining rulers referred to in these verses, Pontius Pilate, Herod Antipas of Galilee, and Philip of Iturea have been mentioned in connection with Matthew's gospel. Trachonitis, a region north of Iturea proper and south of Damascus, is listed here as part of Philip's territory. Abilene is a district farther north still, lying northeast of Damascus.

Two high priests are listed, Annas and Caiaphas, and this cannot be literally correct. It was Caiaphas who was high priest. However, Annas had been high priest some fifteen years earlier and, as father-in-law of Caiaphas, may still have been honored and influential in the high-priestly circles.

Luke also gives Jesus' age at this period, being the only evangelist to do so:

> Luke 3:23. *And Jesus himself began to be about thirty years of age* . . .

Luke says "about." If this were A.D. 29 and if Jesus were exactly thirty years old, then he would indeed have been born in 1 B.C. And if he were born on December 25 in 1 B.C., then the New Year that would start one week later would be A.D. 1. This is roughly the line of reasoning of Dionysius Exiguus, but it is wrong, because Herod the Great had been dead some four years on December 25, 1 B.C.

Dionysius' mistake, apparently, was to ignore the "about" and to assume that the Biblical writers were more accurate about their dating and chronology than they really were. Jesus would have had to be at least thirty-three years old at the time of his baptism, and perhaps thirty-five.

The Son of Joseph

It is at this point that Luke supplies Jesus with a genealogy, one that runs backward in time rather than forward, as does Matthew's.

> Luke 3:23. . . . *Jesus . . . being (as was supposed) the son of Joseph, which was the son of Heli,*
> Luke 3:24. *Which was the son of Matthat . . .*

The parenthetical phrase "as was supposed" would indicate Luke's acceptance of the virgin birth, unless it was inserted by some pious early copyist of the gospel.

The genealogy traces Jesus' line back not merely to Abraham, the point from which Matthew's genealogy starts (see page 111), but further back still, to the beginning:

> Luke 3:38. *Which was the son of Enos, which was the son of Seth, which was the son of Adam, which was the son of God.*

Matthew, writing from the Jewish standpoint, naturally begins with Abraham. Luke, a Gentile, would not be satisfied to trace Jesus' genealogy only as far back as it remained Jewish. By going back to the beginning, he stressed the universality of Jesus' message, for whereas only Jews were descended from Abraham, all men—Jews and Gentiles alike—were descended from Adam.

Luke lists seventy-five generations in going from Jesus all the way back to Adam, the longest continuous genealogy in the Bible. Nor is Luke as preoccupied with numbers as Matthew was. He makes no effort to divide the genealogy into significant sections. He has fifty-five generations counting back to Abraham in place of Matthew's forty-two.

Luke counts twenty generations from Adam to Abraham, whereas the lists in the fifth and eleventh chapters of Genesis count nineteen. The discrepancy occurs as follows. Luke says:

> Luke 3:35. . . . *which was the son of Sala* [Salah],
> Luke 3:36. *Which was the son of Cainan, which was the son of Arphaxad* . . .

whereas we find in Genesis:

> Genesis 11:12. *And Arphaxad lived five and thirty years, and begat Salah* . . .

In other words, an additional generation has crept in between Salah and Arphaxad, so that the former is the son of the latter in Genesis and the grandson of the latter in Luke. This is undoubtedly a copyist's error, for Cainan is the great-grandson of Adam and occurs also in the appropriate place in Luke's genealogy.

> Luke 3:37. . . . *which was the son of Maleleel* [Mahalaleel], *which was the son of Cainan,*
> Luke 3:38. *Which was the son of Enos* . . .

So Cainan is counted twice.

From Abraham to David, the genealogies given in Matthew and in Luke agree. Thereafter, they disagree sharply. Matthew follows the descent from David through Solomon, Rehoboam, and the line of Judean kings. Luke follows the descent from David through a son named Nathan:

Luke 3:31. . . . *which was the son of Nathan, which was the son of David* . . .

Nathan was a son just older than Solomon, if the list of sons mentioned in the Second Book of Samuel are indeed in order of birth:

2 Samuel 5:14. *And these be the names of those that were born unto him* [David] *in Jerusalem; Shammuah, and Shobab, and Nathan, and Solomon* . . .

Luke gives the son of Nathan as Mattatha, and his son as Menan, neither of whom is mentioned elsewhere in the Bible. Indeed, the entire genealogy after Nathan is completely obscure, merely a list of unknown names. Whereas Matthew has virtually every king of Judah listed among the ancestors of Jesus, Luke lists only David himself.

At only one place after David is there even a possibility of coincidence. Matthew lists the fifteenth and sixteenth generations after David as being of Shealtiel and Zerubbabel:

Matthew 1:12. *And after they were brought to Babylon, Jechonias* [Jehoiachin] *begat Salathiel* [Shealtiel]; *and Salathiel* [Shealtiel] *begat Zorobabel* [Zerubbabel] . . .

Luke docs indeed mention these two names, perhaps because of the prominent role played by Zerubbabel in connection with the return from exile:

Luke 3:27. . . . *which was the son of Zorobabel* [Zerubbabel], *which was the son of Salathiel* [Shealtiel], *which was the son of Neri* . . .

But Matthew follows the Book of Ezra in having Shealtiel the son of Jehoiachin, whereas Luke has him descend from Neri, who is nowhere else mentioned in the Bible. Luke, moreover, has Zerubbabel twenty-two generations after David, rather than Matthew's sixteen.

The two genealogies come together only at Joseph, the husband of Mary. They disagree even in the name of Joseph's father:

Matthew 1:16. *And Jacob begat Joseph the husband of Mary* . . .

Luke 3:23. . . . *Jesus . . . the son of Joseph, which was the son of Heli* . . .

Attempts have been made to correlate these wildly differing gene-alogies by supposing that Matthew was tracing the line of Jesus back to David through Joseph, while Luke does so through Mary. It is suggested, for instance, that Joseph was not the "son of Heli" as stated in Luke 3:23, but actually the son-in-law of Heli, so that Heli was Mary's father and the rest of the genealogy was Mary's.

This involves no flat contradictions, for the name of Mary's father is not given directly anywhere in the Bible.

And yet are there grounds for considering Mary to have been de-scended from David? That she was of Davidic descent is a tradition that arose early in the history of Christianity. For instance, when Gabriel is sent to make the annunciation:

Luke 1:26. . . . Gabriel was sent . . .
Luke 1:27. To a virgin espoused to a man whose name was Joseph, of the house of David; and the virgin's name was Mary.

One might argue that the phrase "of the house of David" re-ferred to Mary rather than to Joseph, or to both.

But the argument is a tenuous one. After all, Mary is described as a cousin of Elisabeth, who is herself described as a Levite.

Looking at the two genealogies objectively, it is hard not to think of Matthew's as the more reliable. It includes more names that are to be found in the Old Testament and it carries the list down the line of Judean kings, something one would tend to think more appropriate for a Messiah of Davidic descent.

One might almost think that Luke—a Gentile not acquainted with Jewish genealogical records—might have invented names to fill in the generations after David and Nathan.

Judas the brother of James

Luke now goes on with the tales that are also given in Matthew and Mark. Jesus is tempted by Satan and successfully resists. He preaches in his home town of Nazareth but is rejected by those who knew him too well as a youth and will not accept him seriously as a prophet. He heals the sick and begins to collect disciples.

Luke agrees with Mark in naming the publican disciple Levi (see page 245). However, in Luke's list of the twelve apostles, Levi is not mentioned, but Matthew is. This supports the notion that Levi and Matthew are the same person known by two alternate names.

On the other hand, Luke does not mention Lebbaeus Thaddeus by either name and it is this Lebbaeus who might conceivably be Levi the son of Alphaeus that Mark mentions, and therefore the brother of James the son of Alphaeus. In the place of Lebbaeus, Luke includes:

Luke 6:16. *And Judas the brother of James . . .*

This is by no means a reference to Judas Iscariot, for Luke includes him separately, too, as the last of the list, of course.

Luke 6:16. *. . . and Judas Iscariot, which also was the traitor.*

But if there is a second Judas who is the brother of James (presumably the son of Alphaeus), then is this Judas the son of Alphaeus an alternative name for Levi the son of Alphaeus; and is this Judas the publican, Levi, rather than Matthew?

It is hard to tell. The Greek original of Luke 6:16 says simply "Judas of James" and that might be more naturally translated as "Judas son of James" rather than "brother of James." If this Judas is the son of someone named James, then the connection with Levi is lost.

The Centurion

Luke's account of Jesus' life after the baptism is quite similar to that found in Matthew and Mark, the other synoptic gospels, and much of it can, in consequence, be passed over without comment. However, Luke does add or omit items that significantly illustrate the difference in his point of view. He, after all, is taken to be a Gentile, while Mark and Matthew are certainly of Jewish origin.

Thus, Luke includes material that portrays Gentiles favorably. For instance, Luke tells the story of the centurion who asks Jesus to cure his servant. Matthew, in telling that same story, makes no effort to picture the Gentile centurion as anything but a centurion (see page 173).

Luke, however, draws a picture of the centurion as one of touching faith and humility. The centurion does not consider himself worthy to approach Jesus and, instead, sends Jewish elders on his behalf. Yet so worthy is the centurion that the elders (who can't be conceived as being unduly biased in favor of Gentiles) plead for him:

> Luke 7:4. *And when they* [the elders] *came to Jesus, they besought him instantly, saying, That he* [the centurion] *was worthy* . . .
> Luke 7:5. *For he loveth our nation, and he hath built us a synagogue.*

Luke also demonstrates himself to be sympathetic to women. Thus, in the nativity tale, he concentrates on Mary where Matthew deals primarily with Joseph. Luke portrays a Jesus who can even find room for sympathy toward prostitutes. Thus, when Jesus is dining with a Pharisee:

> Luke 7:37. . . . *behold, a woman in the city, which was a sinner, when she knew that Jesus sat at meat in the Pharisee's house* . . .
> Luke 7:38. . . . *stood at his feet behind him weeping* . . .

The Pharisee shows disdain for the woman but Jesus finds her contrition acceptable and her sins forgiven and reads his host a lesson in which the Pharisee comes off rather poorly.

It is immediately on the conclusion of this episode that Luke mentions the women who follow Jesus. This is characteristic of Luke, for the other synoptic gospels mention only the men at this point:

> Luke 8:1. . . . *the twelve* [apostles] *were with him,*
> Luke 8:2. *And certain women, which had been healed of evil spirits and infirmities, Mary called Magdalene, out of whom went seven devils,*
> Luke 8:3. *And Joanna the wife of Chuza Herod's steward, and Susanna, and many others* . . .

Mary Magdalene is mentioned first and it is sometimes assumed that she was the "woman . . . which was a sinner" of the immediately preceding episode but there is no clear justification for this (see page 238). Neither Joanna nor Susanna is mentioned outside of Luke.

The Good Samaritan

Luke, writing from the Gentile viewpoint, omits those verses in Matthew and Mark which portray Jesus as hostile to non-Jews. Luke does not tell the story of the Canaanite woman who asks that her daughter be cured and who humbly accepts Jesus' designation of Gentiles as "dogs" (see page 172).

And in describing Jesus' sending out of the apostles on their preaching mission, Luke omits the passage in which Jesus forbids them to enter the cities of the Gentiles or Samaritans and declares his own mission to be confined to the Jews (see page 173).

Instead, Luke includes a parable, not found in any of the other gospels, which is among the most popular of all those attributed to Jesus, and which preaches universalism.

The parable is occasioned by the question of a lawyer; that is, a student of the Mosaic Law or a "scribe" as Matthew would call him. He asks of Jesus how one may attain eternal life and Jesus challenges him to answer his own question by citing the Law. The lawyer answers:

> Luke 10:27. . . . *Thou shalt love the Lord thy God with all thy heart, and with all thy soul, and with all thy strength, and with all thy mind; and thy neighbour as thyself.*

The first part of this answer is a quotation from Deuteronomy, one that is held to be a central tenet of Judaism:

> Deuteronomy 6:4. *Hear, O Israel: The Lord our God is one Lord:*
> Deuteronomy 6:5. *And thou shalt love the Lord thy God with all thine heart, and with all thy soul, and with all thy might.*

The last part of the lawyer's quotation is from another section of the Law:

> Leviticus 19:18. *Thou shalt not avenge, nor bear any grudge against the children of thy people, but thou shalt love thy neighbour as thyself . . .*

Jesus approves of the statement, but the lawyer goes on to ask:

> Luke 10:29. . . . *And who is my neighbour?*

The attempt here is to force a nationalist answer, for the remark in Leviticus about loving one's neighbor as one's self, follows immediately after a reference to "the children of thy people." The commandment in Leviticus might therefore be taken as narrowly restricting a man's love to neighbors of his own "people" only.

Jesus might therefore have answered that it was only necessary to love those who were Jews or, a little more broadly, all those, Jews or non-Jews, who worshipped the true God in the approved manner. All others would then be outside the pale of love. (This indeed was what Jesus seemed to be saying in the story of the Canaanite woman in Matthew.)

Jesus does not say this in Luke, however. Instead he tells the famous story of the man (presumably a Jew) who traveled from Jerusalem to Jericho, was beset by thieves and left for dead. A priest and a Levite passed him by, making no effort to help. They were each learned in the Law and undoubtedly knew the verse in Leviticus and were faced with a neighbor (even in the narrow sense of the word) in need. Yet they did nothing.

> Luke 10:33. *But a certain Samaritan . . . came where he was: and when he saw him, he had compassion on him . . .*

The Samaritan saved the man and Jesus asked:

> Luke 10:36. *Which now of these three, thinkest thou, was neighbour unto him that fell among the thieves?*
> Luke 10:37. *And he* [the lawyer] *said, He that shewed mercy on him . . .*

In other words, a man is not a "neighbor" because of what he is but because of what he does. A goodhearted Samaritan is more the neighbor of a Jew, than a hardhearted fellow Jew. And, by extension, one might argue that the parable teaches that all men are neighbors, since all men can do well and have compassion, regardless of nationality. To love one's neighbor is to love all men.

The term "good Samaritan" has been used so often in connection with this parable that one gets the feeling that Samaritans were particularly good people and that it was only to be expected that a Samaritan would help someone in trouble. This loses the point of the story, since to a Jew of the time of Jesus, Samaritans were a hateful and despised people. The hate was returned and it was therefore naturally to be expected that a Samaritan would *not* help a Jew under *any* conditions. The point Jesus was making was that *even* a Samaritan could be a neighbor; how much more so, anyone else.

The flavor of the parable would probably be best captured in modern America, if we had a white southern farmer left for dead, if we then had him ignored by a minister and a sheriff, and saved by a Negro sharecropper. Then the question "Which now of these three . . . was neighbour" would have a sharper point for our time.

The fact that Samaritans could be as narrowly nationalistic as Jews is brought out in Luke, who reports that the Samaritans would not allow Jesus to pass through their territory on his way to Jerusalem, because they would not cooperate with anyone attempting to visit that city so hated by them:

> Luke 9:53. . . . *they* [the Samaritans] *did not receive him* [Jesus], *because his face was as though he would go to Jerusalem.*

Here too Luke seizes the opportunity to display the good will of Jesus as rising above nationalistic considerations, even when he is provoked. James and John, the sons of thunder (see page 247), ask if they ought not to call down a rain of fire on the inhospitable Samaritans, and Jesus answers:

> Luke 9:56. . . . *the Son of man is not come to destroy men's lives, but to save them* . . .

At another point, Luke introduces another tale not found in the other gospels which tends to display a Samaritan in a good light. Jesus cures ten lepers but only one returns to thank him:

> Luke 17:16. . . . *and he was a Samaritan.*
> Luke 17:17. And Jesus . . . *said, Were there not ten cleansed? but where are the nine?*
> Luke 17:18. *There are not found that returned to give glory to God, save this stranger.*

Lazarus the Beggar

Luke retains the anti-rich attitude of Matthew (see page 170). He quotes Jesus' remarks about the dangers of wealth:

> Luke 16:13. *No servant can serve two masters* . . . *Ye cannot serve God and mammon.*
>
> . . . .
>
> Luke 18:25. . . . *it is easier for a camel to go through a needle's eye, than for a rich man to enter into the kingdom of God.*

Indeed, Luke goes even beyond Matthew, for he includes a famous parable (found only in Luke) that seems to illustrate this hard view against riches.

Luke 16:19. *There was a certain rich man* . . .
Luke 16:20. *And there was a certain beggar named Lazarus, which was laid at his gate, full of sores* . . .

The Latin word for rich is "dives," so that in the Latin version of the Bible, the phrase "rich man" is "homo dives." If the verse is left partly untranslated, it becomes, "There was a certain man, Dives . . ." This is what gives rise to the common misconception that the name of the rich man in this parable was Dives, so that one will speak of the parable of "Dives and Lazarus." Actually, the rich man is not named; he is merely a rich man. As for Lazarus, that is a Greek version of the Hebrew name, Eleazar.

When the beggar dies, however, he goes to heaven:

Luke 16:22. . . . *the beggar died, and was carried by the angels into Abraham's bosom* . . .

Because of this verse "Abraham's bosom" has entered the English language as synonymous with heaven, but in connection with Lazarus, it means more than that.

The phrase originates out of the dining customs of the period. The Israelites in the time of the kingdoms sat upon chairs at meals, as we do today. Thus, concerning the feast where Saul grew suspicious of David because of the latter's absence, the Bible relates:

1 Samuel 20:25. *And the king sat upon his seat, as at other times* . . .

The Greeks, however, (at least among the wealthier classes) had the habit of reclining upon their left elbow on low upholstered couches and eating with the right hand. The custom spread among the better-off of other nations, as a sign of genteel and gracious living. This style of eating gave rise to universally understood metaphors.

A host would put the guest of honor to his immediate right at a meal. If both reclined on their left elbows, the guest's head would now be close to the host's breast. In a manner of speaking, the guest would be "in the host's bosom."

If we use the expression today, when Western eating habits, at all levels of society, include sitting rather than reclining, the expression "in his bosom" gives rise to thoughts of one man cradling the head of another, but that is wrong. It would be better if we translated the phrase into our analogous metaphor today and said, "the beggar died, and was carried by the angels to the right side of Abraham." In short, Lazarus not only went to heaven, but to the post of highest honor, at the right hand of Abraham himself.

As for the rich man, his fate was quite different; he went to hell. What's more, this wasn't the Sheol of the Old Testament, the gray place of infinite nothingness, with the chief punishment that of the absence of God (see page I-173). In Old Testament times, hell, or Sheol, had little to do with punishment. Rewards and punishments were viewed by the Israelites as something that was meted out in this world and not in the next.

However, during the centuries when the Jews were under the domination of outsiders, it seemed too clear that the foreign oppressors were flourishing and the Jews were suffering. The whole problem of good and evil, of reward and suffering, grew tremendously complex, theologically speaking. The Book of Job is an example of the controversy that arose in that respect.

Since to most Jews it was unthinkable that God was unjust, it followed that the apparent injustices of this world would have to be redressed in the world to come. Virtuous men would be rewarded infinitely in heaven, while wicked men would be punished infinitely in hell. This latter view makes itself felt in the last verse in Isaiah, which is part of the post-Exilic "Third Isaiah" (see page I-553). Those who are saved, the verse says:

> Isaiah 66:24. . . . *shall go forth, and look upon the carcasses of the men that have transgressed against me: for their worm shall not die, neither shall their fire be quenched* . . .

A contributing factor to the development of the notion of a hell of torture may have been the exposure, in Ptolemaic and Seleucid times, to certain Greek legends. The Greek Hades, generally, was very much like the Israelite Sheol, a gray place of negativeness. A portion of it, Tartarus, was, however, reserved for notable criminals, and there the Greek imagination exhausted itself in imagining ingenious tortures—such as Sisyphus endlessly rolling a rock uphill only to have it roll down again as soon as the top was gained, or thirsty Tantalus forever up to his chin in water which swirled away whenever he stooped to drink.

The less ingenious men of Judea clung to external fire as a means of torture and by New Testament times that was fixed. Thus Mark quotes Jesus as warning men not—

Mark 9:43. . . . *to go into hell, into the fire that never shall be quenched . . .*

The rich man of the parable of Lazarus the beggar descends into just such a hell:

Luke 16:22. . . . *the rich man also died, and was buried;*
Luke 16:23. *And in hell . . . being in torments, . . .*
Luke 16:24. . . . *he cried . . . , Father Abraham, . . . send Lazarus, that he may dip the tip of his finger in water, and cool my tongue; for I am tormented in this flame.*

Abraham refuses, for there is an impassable gulf between heaven and hell. Moreover, Abraham is described by this parable in Luke as justifying the presence of Lazarus in heaven and the rich man in hell without reference to virtue and wickedness. No sins of the rich man are recalled, merely the fact of his being rich:

Luke 16:25. *But Abraham said,* [to the rich man] *Son, remember that thou in thy lifetime receivedst thy good things, and likewise Lazarus evil things: but now he is comforted, and thou art tormented.*

It is this dramatic turnabout, this promise to the poor and down-trodden of the world, that they would have their revenge in the after-world, that may have helped make this parable particularly popular. Because of its popularity, the term "Lazarus" has come to be applied to diseased beggars. Since the sores mentioned are often presumed to be those of leprosy, the term, particularly in the shortened form "lazar," has come to be synonymous to "leper."

A Far Country

Luke has Jesus relate the parable of the talents (see page 210), though here the units of money are referred to as "pounds." A change is introduced. Instead of, as in Matthew, the mere mention of a man traveling to a far country, the purpose of the journey is given:

Luke 19:12. . . . *A certain nobleman went into a far country to receive for himself a kingdom, and to return.*

. . . .

Luke 19:14. *But his citizens hated him, and sent a message after him, saying, We will not have this man to reign over us.*

Luke 19:15. . . . [But] *he . . . returned, having received the kingdom . . .*

In the context of modern times, this would be puzzling. Why should one travel to a far country to receive a kingdom? In New Testament times, however, this was not odd at all, for the far country was Rome.

Around the perimeter of the Roman Empire were a number of puppet kingdoms, each theoretically independent, but all completely under Rome's thumb. No one could succeed to the throne of any of these kingdoms without Rome's permission, and that was not always possible to get without a healthy bribe. And if a claimant hurried to Rome to negotiate such a bribe, it might happen that his subjects at home would send a counter-deputation to plead against it, if the claimant were unpopular.

Just this seems to have happened in the case of Herod Archelaus in 4 B.C., after the death of Herod the Great, and it is to him that the parable seems to refer. Archelaus was confirmed in his rule, but as ethnarch only, not as king, and ten years later, as a result of the persistent pleadings of his subjects, he was deposed.

Herod Antipas

The account of Jesus' climactic week in Jerusalem, as given in Luke, differs little, in general, from the accounts of Matthew and Mark. But Luke is a Gentile and he seems anxious to diminish even further the share of Pilate, the Gentile governor, in the crucifixion of Jesus, and to increase the share of the Jewish secular authorities.

As in Matthew and Mark, Pilate, in Luke, is pictured as unwilling to condemn Jesus, but he declares his belief in Jesus' innocence three times, rather than once as in Matthew or twice as in Mark. Further-

more, in Luke, and in Luke only, Pilate is described as attempting to
deny jurisdiction altogether:

> Luke 23:6. . . . *Pilate . . . asked whether the man* [Jesus] *were a
> Galilaean.*
>
> Luke 23:7. *And as soon as he knew that he belonged unto Herod's
> jurisdiction, he sent him to Herod, who himself also was at Jerusalem
> at that time.*

This, of course, is Herod Antipas, tetrarch of Galilee, who was in
Jerusalem, presumably, for the Passover season. The trial before Herod
comes to nothing, really, because Jesus would not speak in his own
behalf. Herod refused to make any judgment:

> Luke 23:11. *And Herod . . . sent him again to Pilate.*

But it would seem that whatever blame falls upon Pilate, in Luke's
eyes, falls also upon Herod Antipas.

The Crucifixion

The details of the crucifixion as given by Luke differ in some ways
from those given by Matthew and Mark. In Matthew and Mark
we have the picture of the "historic Jesus" abandoned and reviled by
all, and seeming to die in despair.

In Luke this has largely disappeared and Jesus is pictured as much
more clearly the Messiah. He forgives his crucifiers in a noble phrase
that is not found in the other gospels:

> Luke 23:34. *Then said Jesus, Father, forgive them; for they know
> not what they do.*

As in Mark and Matthew, Luke describes three as being crucified at
this time, with Jesus on the middle cross between two thieves. Mark
says nothing more about this, while Matthew describes even these
thieves as reviling Jesus:

> Matthew 27:44. *The thieves also, which were crucified with him,
> cast the same* [mockery] *in his teeth.*

In Luke, however, Jesus is described as forgiving again. One of the
thieves accepts Jesus as Messiah:

Luke 23:42. *And he said unto Jesus, Lord, remember me when thou comest into thy kingdom.*

Luke 23:43. *And Jesus said unto him, Verily I say unto thee, To day shalt thou be with me in paradise.*

This thief is known in tradition as "the good thief" or "the penitent thief." He is not named in the gospels, but tradition supposes his name to be Dismas.

Finally, Luke does not describe Jesus' final despairing cry of "My God, my God, why hast thou forsaken me?" It does not easily fit the Messianic picture, nor can Luke count on his Gentile readers appreciating the subtlety of the application of the psalm whose first phrase that cry is (see page 233). Instead, he has Jesus' last words the much more formal and undramatic:

Luke 23:46. . . . *Jesus . . . said, Father, into thy hands I commend my spirit: and having said thus, he gave up the ghost.*

That too, as it happens, is a quotation from the psalms:

Psalm 31:5. *Into thine hand I commit my spirit: thou hast redeemed me, O Lord God of truth.*

Then follows the tale of the resurrection, told at much greater length and in much more circumstantial detail than in either Matthew or Mark. With that, the gospel of St. Luke ends.

8. JOHN

The Fourth Gospel

The details of Jesus' life, as given in the fourth gospel, are quite
different from those which the first three synoptic gospels have in
common.

There are some who endeavor to accept as correct all four gospels
and who therefore must explain apparent inconsistencies. It is possible
to argue, for instance, that the synoptic gospels deal primarily with
Jesus' preachings to the common people of Galilee and ignore his work
in Jerusalem itself, except for the final climactic week of his life. The
fourth gospel, it could then be suggested, rounds out the picture by
concentrating on Jesus' work in Jerusalem, which it describes as lasting
three years, rather than one week. Jesus' discourses now tend to be long
and argumentative (rather than simple and parable-laden) as would
suit disputes with learned priests and theologians.

On the other hand, it might also be argued that the fourth
gospel was written quite late, for a community that was already
Christian but was involved in doctrinal disputes. Its purpose might
then have been, not to present a realistic picture of Jesus, but rather to
use him as a figure through whom to present the author's theology, as
opposed to the conflicting views of others. It might, from that standpoint, seem that the fourth gospel could be considered a form of
didactic fiction, roughly analogous to the dialogues in which Plato
placed his own philosophy into the mouth of Socrates.

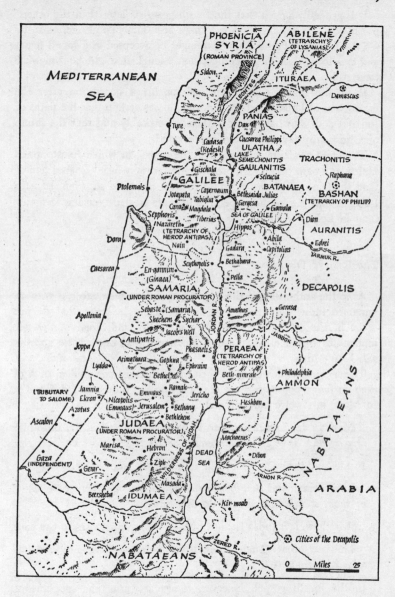

Palestine in the Time of Christ

It is generally agreed that the fourth gospel is later than the others, but by A.D. 150 it seems already to have been known and referred to by Christian writers. Perhaps A.D. 100 might be accepted as a round figure and as a likely date for its composition, though it might be somewhat later still.

If so, the fourth gospel appeared roughly a generation after the destruction of Jerusalem, by which time it was certain that the paths of Judaism and Christianity had diverged irrevocably and that the future of Christianity lay with the Gentile world.

This state of affairs is reflected in the gospel, in which Jesus appears far less as a parochial Jewish prophet and far more as a universal Son of God than in any of the synoptic gospels, far more so, even, than in Luke. And in the fourth gospel, the Jews are treated even less favorably than in Luke.

The Beloved Disciple

As to the authorship of the fourth gospel, that seems to rest with an unnamed individual who is mentioned therein in terms that do not occur in the synoptic gospels. We meet this individual at the last supper, for instance, when Jesus announces that one of the apostles will betray him.

The incident is described in each of the four gospels and in each of the four the response on the part of the apostles is described differently. In Mark, all twelve are troubled:

Mark 14:19. *And they began to be sorrowful, and to say unto him one by one, Is it I? and another said, Is it I?*

In Luke, all twelve are troubled, but discuss it among themselves:

Luke 22:23. *And they began to enquire among themselves, which of them it was that should do this thing.*

In Matthew, it is Judas Iscariot himself who guiltily rises to the bait:

Matthew 26:25. *Then Judas, which betrayed him, answered and said, Master, is it I? . . .*

In the fourth gospel, however, things are not that spontaneous. Jesus is presented as a divine and Godlike figure whom it is far less easy to approach. Since he did not spontaneously reveal the name of the mysterious traitor, it might be that he did not wish to reveal it and that there might therefore be a danger involved in trying to penetrate the secret. Presumably, then, the one to take the risk of inquiring ought to be that disciple who was Jesus' favorite and who might therefore most safely presume on the Master's patience.

John 13:23. *Now there was leaning on Jesus' bosom one of his disciples, whom Jesus loved.*

John 13:24. *Simon Peter therefore beckoned to him, that he should ask who it should be of whom he* [Jesus] *spake.*

We must not assume, of course, that the disciple in question was actually being cradled by Jesus. The phrase "leaning on Jesus' bosom" was merely the common metaphor used to signify that the disciple was seated in the place of honor on Jesus' right (see page 284).

In none of the synoptic gospels is reference made to some particular apostle "whom Jesus loved"; only in the fourth.

The Beloved Disciple is mentioned as witnessing the crucifixion, as being the first apostle to reach the sepulcher from which Jesus had been resurrected, and as recognizing the resurrected Jesus.

Most significantly, he appears at the very end of the gospel when the risen Jesus is giving his final instructions to Peter:

John 21:20. *Then Peter, turning about, seeth the disciple whom Jesus loved following; which also leaned on his breast at supper . . .*

With reference to this, an editorial comment, added a few verses later, reads:

John 21:24. *This is the disciple which testifieth of these things, and wrote these things . . .*

Is this the signature of the Beloved Disciple? Does this mean that the Beloved Disciple actually wrote the fourth gospel as we have it today? Or did someone else write the fourth gospel, after having used the reminiscences of the Beloved Disciple as his source material, and did he then attribute the authorship to that source, considering himself only a secretary? Or was the verse added by a later copyist or commentator who was expressing his own theory that the Beloved Disciple had written the fourth gospel?

It is difficult to see how these questions can ever be answered in

such a way as to satisfy everybody. Christian tradition, however, has it
that the Beloved Disciple was indeed the author.

It seems odd, perhaps, and even unpleasantly vain, that the Beloved
Disciple, if he is the author of the fourth gospel, should so stress his
favored position with Jesus each time he mentions himself. But perhaps
there is a purpose beyond vanity in this. If the fourth gospel were
written to expound a theological viewpoint against strong competing
forces, it would be important that the writer stress, as forcefully as he
could, his own authority to speak. He was not only one of the apostles,
but of all the apostles, Jesus' favorite and the one most likely to be "in
the know."

And if the gospel were actually written by a secretary from words or
writings of the disciple, it may have been the secretary who kept stressing
the favored position of the source for the purpose just given.

John Son of Zebedee

The question next arises as to who the Beloved Disciple might be?
To begin with, it seems reasonable to suppose he was one of the
apostles, since the Beloved Disciple was at the last supper and, as the
synoptic gospels agree, only Jesus and his twelve apostles were at this
supper:

> Matthew 26:20. *Now when the even was come, he sat down with
> the twelve.*
> Matthew 26:21. *And . . . they did eat . . .*

To be sure, however, the fourth gospel, alone of the gospels, does not
specifically list the names of the twelve apostles, and does not specifically state that only the apostles joined Jesus at the last supper. Within
the context of the fourth gospel, then, the Beloved Disciple might not
have been one of the twelve apostles, and several nonapostles have been
suggested for the role. Nevertheless, Christian tradition makes the
Beloved Disciple one of the apostles.

But which one?

He is the favorite, and it does seem from the synoptic gospels that
among the apostles there is an inner group of three, who share more
intimately with Jesus the crucial moments of his life. These three,

Peter and the sons of Zebedee, James and John, are described as witnessing the transfiguration, for instance:

> Matthew 17:1. . . . *Jesus taketh Peter, James, and John his brother, and bringeth them up into an high mountain apart,*
> Matthew 17:2. *And was transfigured before them . . .*

The other nine apostles were not vouchsafed this sight.

Again it was Peter, James, and John who were alone with Jesus at the time of the prayer in Gethsemane just before the arrest:

> Matthew 26:37. *And he [Jesus] took with him Peter and the two sons of Zebedee . . .*

One might argue that Jesus would scarcely omit the disciple he loved best from these climactic moments, so that the Beloved Disciple must be one of these three: Peter, James, or John.

Of these three, Peter would seem the almost automatic choice since all the gospels agree that he was the leading apostle who always took the initiative among them. Yet it is precisely Peter who must be eliminated, since on three of the occasions on which the Beloved Disciple is present, Peter is present also, and the two are distinguished as separate individuals. Thus it is Peter who motions to the Beloved Disciple to inquire about the traitor.

This makes it seem that the Beloved Disciple was either James or John, one of the two sons of Zebedee. (Could it be for this reason that the two made so bold as to ask for favored positions with Jesus when the Messianic kingdom was established—see page 196—presuming on his favoritism toward one of them?)

In choosing between James and John, let us return to the final appearance of the Beloved Disciple on the occasion of the resurrected Jesus' last discourse with Peter. Peter turns, sees the Beloved Disciple (see page 293), and asks:

> John 21:21. . . . *and what shall this man do?*
> John 21:22. *Jesus saith unto him, If I will that he tarry till I come, what is that to thee? follow thou me.*

Peter, in other words, is to follow instructions and not worry about the Beloved Disciple. The Beloved Disciple will have his own tasks, which may include anything, even up to and including remaining alive on Earth till the second coming.

The writer of the fourth gospel then goes on to correct a misapprehension, pointing out that Jesus did not say flatly that the Beloved Disciple would not die till the second coming; but that he would not die *if* Jesus chose to arrange it so.

John 21:23. *Then went this saying abroad among the brethren, that that disciple should not die: yet Jesus said not unto him, He shall not die; but, If I will that he tarry till I come, what is that to thee?*

There is important significance here. The early Christians believed that Jesus would soon return and that the kingdom of God would quickly be established. There are verses that would seem to bear them out. Thus, in each of the three synoptic gospels there is repeated what seems to be a definite promise on the part of Jesus to that effect.

Matthew 16:28. *Verily I say unto you, There be some standing here, which shall not taste of death, till they see the Son of man coming in his kingdom.*

Clearly, the Beloved Disciple must have been standing there at the time and if that disciple had an extended lifetime, Jesus' remark must have begun to take on specific meaning. One by one, those who had known and heard Jesus died, but the Beloved Disciple lived on. Surely, then, many must have thought it was he to whom Jesus referred as the someone who "shall not taste of death" till the second coming.

The fourth gospel as the latest-written (seventy years or more after the crucifixion) would have to be less certain than the synoptic gospels on the matter of the imminent second coming. In particular if the Beloved Disciple died without the second coming having taken place, it would be necessary for his secretary or some later commentator to insert a remark to the effect that Jesus *had* made a statement with reference to the Beloved Disciple, but that it had been a conditional and not an absolute one.

(Of course, the reference to some who would not die before the second coming might be taken to refer not to the Beloved Disciple but to some quite obscure person who was standing within earshot of Jesus at the time. This thought probably contributed to the rise of the tale of the so-called "Wandering Jew." This was a Jew who committed some crime or offense against Jesus at the time of the crucifixion and was condemned to wandering the Earth, immortally, until the second coming. Concerning this figure, a vast array of legends has arisen, all of which are entirely without Biblical foundation except for the distant support of this one verse.)

Returning to the Beloved Disciple, however, we can see that this final passage in the fourth gospel can be used to argue that he must have been long-lived. And, indeed, if he wrote the fourth gospel in A.D. 100 or somewhat later, this must be so.

But of the two sons of Zebedee, James was not long-lived. He died a martyr's death not many years after the crucifixion:

> Acts 12:1. *Now about that time Herod the king stretched forth his hands to vex certain of the church.*
> Acts 12:2. *And he killed James the brother of John with the sword.*

The leaves John the son of Zebedee, and he is the only one of the apostles concerning whom where is no widely accepted tradition of martyrdom. Rather, legend supposes him to have lived to the age of ninety and beyond.

According to legend, John, in later life, engaged in missionary work in Ephesus, a city on the coast of Asia Minor. During the reign of Domitian (A.D. 81–96), when Christians were persecuted, he retired for safety's sake to the island of Patmos, about fifty miles southwest of Ephesus. After Domitian's death he returned to Ephesus and there died sometime in the reign of Trajan (A.D. 98–117).

If these are indeed the facts and if he were twenty at the time of the crucifixion, John son of Zebedee would have been born A.D. 9 and would have been ninety-one years old in A.D. 100 when the fourth gospel might have been written. That is a great age, but certainly not an impossible one.

Another point in favor of this theory is that John is never mentioned by name in the fourth gospel, so there is no possibility of distinguishing him from the Beloved Disciple. The closest approach comes when some of the disciples are listed among those who witnessed the resurrected Jesus on one occasion:

> John 21:2. . . . *Simon Peter, and Thomas called Didymus, and Nathanael of Cana in Galilee, and the sons of Zebedee, and two other of his disciples.*

And at this point there is no mention of the Beloved Disciple.

There are thus no glaring inconsistencies in supposing the Beloved

Disciple to be John son of Zebedee, and indeed it is the strong tradition of the early Church that this John was the author of the fourth gospel. By A.D. 200 the tradition was universal and it can be traced back to Irenaeus.

His testimony is considered particularly valuable, since he claims to have known Polycarp, a Christian bishop of Asia Minor, who lived from about A.D. 70 to 155 and who, in turn, was supposed to have been a disciple of John himself.

In modern times there have been theories that the John mentioned by Irenaeus as the author of the fourth gospel was some other John, not the son of Zebedee, but the matter is never likely to be settled to the complete satisfaction of everyone. We can say simply that Christian tradition makes John son of Zebedee the author of the fourth gospel and there is no clear and simple way of refuting that tradition. The fourth gospel is therefore called "The Gospel According to St. John."

The Word

The gospel of St. Mark begins with the baptism of Jesus by John the Baptist as the period at which the Holy Spirit entered Jesus. Matthew and Luke begin with the birth of Jesus as that period.

John goes further back still. Whereas in the synoptic gospels Jesus is seen primarily as a human being (although he is the Messiah also), in John, Jesus is seen in much more exalted fashion, as clearly and manifestly divine to all but the villains of the piece. And to stress that point, John begins his gospel with a hymn in praise of "the Word" (or, in Greek "Logos") which carries matters back to the very beginning of time.

John 1:1. *In the beginning was the Word, and the Word was with God, and the Word was God.*

The use of the term "the Word" in its capitalized sense, as an aspect of God, is not found anywhere in the Old Testament, or, for that matter, anywhere in the New Testament except in the gospel of St. John and a couple of other books attributed to the same author.

The term "Logos" is to be found, however, in the writings of the

Greek philosophers, and is used in something of the sense in which it is found in John.

The term dates back to the sixth century B.C., at the time the Kingdom of Judah was coming to an end, and the Jews were being carried off into Babylonian Exile. In that century, a new way of looking at the universe arose among certain scholars on the western coast of Asia Minor.

The first of these was Thales of Miletus, who was born about 640 B.C. (when Manasseh was rounding out his long reign over Judah). He is thought to have first devised the methods of abstract geometry; to have studied electric and magnetic phenomena; to have brought Babylonian astronomy to the Greek world; and to have suggested that water was the fundamental material of the universe.

However, the most important contribution made by Thales and those who studied under him and followed him was the assumption that the universe was not erratic in its workings; and was not at the mercy of impulsive gods or demons who interfered with nature to suit their own whims and who could be swayed by human entreaty or threats. Rather, Thales and his group supposed that the universe ran according to certain fixed rules, which we might term "laws of nature" and that these laws were not forever unknowable but could be worked out by man through observation and reason. This assumption of the rationality and knowability of the universe was established by these Greeks as the foundation of science and it has remained the foundation ever since.

It was not so much that Thales and the rest necessarily denied the existence of gods or the fact that the world was created by superhuman agency. It was just that the gods, in creating the world, did so according to some rational principle and then abided by that principle, without arbitrary interference in the day-to-day workings of the universe.

One of those who followed Thales in this view of the universe was Heraclitus of Ephesus, who taught about 500 B.C. He seems to have used the word "Logos" to represent the rational principle according to which the world was created. (Is it entirely a coincidence that the Logos-permeated gospel of St. John was, according to legend, written in the very city of Ephesus which, in a way, had seen the first introduction of that term?)

Literally, "Logos" means "Word" in English, but the Greek term has implications far beyond the simple significance of "word." "Logos" refers to the whole rational structure of knowledge. We use it in the names of our sciences: "zoology" ("words concerning animals," or, more properly, "the rational structure of knowledge concerning animals"); "geology" ("words concerning the Earth"); "biology" ("words concerning life"); and so on.

As "Logos" came to be used more and more by Greek thinkers, some of them rather mystical, it came to stand not merely for an abstract principle but for a personified entity that had created the world. "Logos" came to be considered a kind of god in its own right; a rational, creative god.

In post-Exilic times, as the Jews came under the influence of Greek philosophy, they felt impelled to try to justify "Logos" in terms of the Jewish God. Often they used a Hebrew word, which we translate as "Wisdom," to represent something like the Greek "Logos." The Wisdom so referred to is not merely worldly learning but, more than that, a kind of inner, spiritual learning that transcends the world of matter.

The use of the term as a substitute for "Logos" was quite apt. As a matter of fact, in the course of the sixth century B.C., the term "philosopher" began to be applied to the Greek scholars and this is a Greek term which can be translated as "lover of wisdom."

It was divine Wisdom, in the eyes of some of the post-Exilic Jewish writers, that created the world and set it upon its rational foundation. Some of the books of the Apocrypha and even some of the later canonical books of the Old Testament contain hymns to Wisdom that almost sound as though it is a formal aspect of God, to be worshipped, rather than a mere abstraction being praised. Its eternal existence is emphasized and in the Book of Proverbs, Wisdom is pictured, at one point, as speaking in the first person and as saying:

> Proverbs 8:22. *The Lord possessed me in the beginning of his way, before his works of old.*
>
> Proverbs 8:23. *I was set up from everlasting, from the beginning, or ever the earth was.*

Ecclesiasticus has a similar passage in which Wisdom is again speaking in the first person:

> Ecclesiasticus 24:9. *He* [God] *created me* [Wisdom] *from the beginning before the world, and I shall never fail.*

In the Wisdom of Solomon, Wisdom is sometimes presented in terms usully reserved for God:

Wisdom of Solomon 1:6. *For wisdom is a loving spirit; and will not acquit a blasphemer of his words . . .*

The role of Wisdom as the creative aspect of God is also referred to:

Wisdom of Solomon 7:22. . . . *wisdom . . . is the worker of all things . . .*

There is a reference to Wisdom in the gospel of St. Luke, where Jesus is quoted as saying:

Luke 11:49. *Therefore also said the wisdom of God, I will send them prophets and apostles . . .*

In Jesus' lifetime, there lived in Alexandria a Jew named Philo (usually called Philo Judaeus, or "Philo the Jew"). He was learned not only in Jewish thought, but in Greek philosophy as well and he labored, in his writings, to explain the former through the words and concepts of the latter.

Philo, writing in Greek, makes use of the term "Logos" rather than "Wisdom" and has it representing the rational and creative aspect of Yahveh. To explain its relationship to God, he speaks of it, metaphorically, as the "image of God" or the "son of God."

John adopts this Philonian view, a view which is particularly fitting, if the gospel were written in Ephesus at the very center of the Greek philosophic tradition and the place where the term "Logos" was first used.

John therefore opens with a hymn to Logos (that might, conceivably, have been adapted from some pagan hymn) which is expressed in such a way as to fit the theological view expressed by the gospel.

There were views concerning Logos which, it seems, John considered incompatible with the true faith.

There were, for instance, philosophers and mystics who tried to separate the notions of God and of Logos. They felt that there was a God who was indeed personified Wisdom, but he was far and remote and unknowable to man. He was pure spirit and had nothing to do with anything material. To these philosophers, this divine, spiritual, and unknowable principle was "Gnosis," which is Greek for "knowledge." Such philosophers are therefore called "Gnostics."

But if Wisdom or Gnosis is remote from matter and unconcerned with it, how did the world come to be created? Here the Gnostics took a turning opposed to that of Thales. It was not a rational principle (divine or otherwise) that created the world, but a sub-divine and evil principle. Where Thales found the world rational and supposed that a rational principle had created it, the Gnostics found the world evil and supposed that an evil principle had created it.

The Greek philosopher Plato had made use of the term "demiourgos" for the creative principle, and this becomes "demiurge" in English. The word means "worker for the people" or, so to speak, "civil servant." It was used in the Greek cities for certain officials who were viewed as serving the public. The Demiurge was looked upon, in other words, as a superhuman civil servant who served mankind by first creating and then governing the world.

To the Gnostics, this Demiurge was an inferior principle who had created an evil world with deliberate malice. What's more, the spiritual essence of man, which was akin to the distant Gnosis, was trapped by the Demiurge in a body which, being made of matter, was evil. For a man to aspire to salvation, it was necessary, somehow, to transcend the evil body and to attain the distant spirituality of Gnosis.

In the early days of Christianity, certain Gnostics adapted their thought to Christianity. Gnosis was still the unknowable, unreachable God. The "God" of the Old Testament, on the other hand, who had created the world, was viewed by the Gnostics as really the Demiurge. It was Yahveh's demonic influence that was responsible for all the evil in the world.

Jesus, on the other hand, was, by the Gnostic view, the Logos, a son or derivative of the spiritual Gnosis. Jesus was himself pure spirit since he could not involve himself with the created matter of the evil Demiurge, but he took on the illusion of a material body in order to help guide men away from the Demiurge of matter to the Gnosis of spirit.

The gospel of St. John sets itself firmly against the Gnostic interpretation. John makes God and Logos equal in all respects. Not only did Logos exist from the very beginning so that Logos was with God, but Logos *was* God.

Furthermore, this God was not a mysterious Gnosis, but was the very God of the Old Testament who had created the world:

John 1:2. *The same [Logos] was in the beginning with God.*
John 1:3. *All things were made by him; and without him was not any thing made that was made.*

and the Logos was the rational, creative aspect of that God.

What's more, this same God of the Old Testament was not merely an entity of matter, while something else was spirit. God was both spirit and matter; God was the "light" toward which men could strive and that was the inner essence of things:

John 1:4. *In him [God/Logos] was life; and the life was the light of men.*
John 1:5. *And the light shineth in darkness . . .*

Nor was Jesus a mere thing of spirit clothed in the illusion of matter. John made it clear that the Logos was to be considered as having been incarnated in a real and actual material body:

John 1:14. *And the Word was made flesh, and dwelt among us . . .*

John the Baptist

The hymn to Logos is interrupted with an emphatic assertion that the Logos is *not* to be interpreted as John the Baptist. In the early decades following the crucifixion there were those who maintained that John the Baptist had been of particular importance and that perhaps he, rather than Jesus, was the Messiah. These may have represented a considerable group even as late as A.D. 100 and they had to be countered.

John 1:6. *There was a man sent from God, whose name was John.*
John 1:7. *The same came for a witness, to bear witness of the Light . . .*
John 1:8. *He was not that Light . . .*

Then, after the conclusion of the hymn to Logos, the fourth gospel quotes John the Baptist himself as denying any pretensions to Messiah-hood:

John 1:19. *. . . when the Jews sent priests and Levites from Jerusalem to ask him [John the Baptist], Who art thou?*
John 1:20. *. . . he confessed . . . I am not the Christ.*

The fourth gospel goes still further than that.

The synoptic gospels, written at a time when Christianity was still in its infancy and when it needed allies in its fight against Jewish orthodoxy, seem willing to allow John the Baptist the lesser, but still considerable, role of the incarnated Elijah. The fourth gospel, written at a time when Christianity was a couple of decades stronger, seemed to feel no need for such a compromise:

John 1:21. *And they asked him* [John the Baptist], *What then? Art thou Elias* [Elijah]? *And he saith, I am not. Art thou that prophet? And he answered, No.*

. . . .

John 1:23. *He said, I am the voice of one crying in the wilderness, Make straight the way of the Lord . . .*

As for "that prophet" referred to in John 1:21, this is usually thought of as referring to a passage in one of the Deuteronomic discourses attributed to Moses. There, God is quoted as saying:

Deuteronomy 18:18. *I will raise them up a Prophet from among their brethren, like unto thee* [Moses], *and will put my words in his mouth . . .*

It would seem that the Book of Deuteronomy was actually written in the reign of Josiah or shortly before (see page I-195) and it may be that this passage was used to refer to someone contemporary with the Deuteronomist. Josiah may even have been persuaded that the passage referred to one of those who brought him the book after its "discovery" in the Temple, and this may have encouraged him to institute the thorough Yahvist reform that he then carried through.

Nevertheless, by post-Exilic times, this passage seems to have been accepted by the Jews as Messianic in nature, and it was so accepted by the Christians, of course, who saw in it a reference to Jesus. That is why the King James Version capitalizes the word "Prophet" although the Revised Standard Version does not.

John the Baptist is pictured by the fourth gospel as denying an identity with that prophet and as therefore denying Messiah-hood once again.

The Lamb of God

The fourth gospel proceeds, remorselessly, still further. Not only is John quoted as denying the Messiah-hood for himself, but, after baptizing Jesus, he accepts the latter as the Messiah, and proclaims him as such:

John 1:29. *The next day John seeth Jesus coming unto him, and saith, Behold the Lamb of God, which taketh away the sin of the world.*

John 1:30. *This is he of whom I said, After me cometh a man which is preferred before me . . .*

. . . .

John 1:32. *And John bare record, saying, I saw the Spirit descending from heaven like a dove, and it abode upon him.*

. . . .

John 1:34. *And I saw, and bare record that this is the Son of God.*

In Mark and Luke, there is no reference to any such recognition at all on John's part. In Matthew there is a single verse which refers to John's realization of Jesus' role; for when Jesus comes to be baptized:

Matthew 3:14. . . . *John forbad him, saying, I have need to be baptized of thee, and comest thou to me?*

Later, however, Matthew, and Luke too, report that John sent disciples to inquire as to whether Jesus were the Messiah, something that would certainly be unnecessary if John had witnessed the Spirit of God descending upon Jesus like a dove. (And certainly the fourth gospel at no time makes mention of any such uncertainties on the part of the Baptist.) The synoptic gospels each report this descent of the Spirit of God but none of the three indicates in any way, then or later, that this descent was witnessed by John, or by anyone besides Jesus.

Indeed, the synoptic gospels show the realization of the Messiah-hood to have developed slowly among Jesus' disciples and, moreover, clearly record Jesus' carefulness in making no specific and open claim to the role. It is only at the very end, before Caiaphas, that he admits he is the Messiah (see page 221) and this, considered by the Jewish authorities to be blasphemy, is at once sufficient to condemn Jesus to death. This view seems, indeed, to be in accord with the historical reality of the times, for to lay claim to Messiah-hood without a proof that would satisfy the authorities was virtually sure death. (Just as in later centuries, to have laid claim to be the new incarnation of Jesus would have paved the way to the stake or, in modern times, to the madhouse.)

In the fourth gospel, however, everyone, from John the Baptist on, is pictured as recognizing Jesus as the Messiah at once. Not only does Jesus not deny the role but he, himself, proclaims it. Thus, when a Samaritan woman speaks to Jesus of the Messiah, Jesus answers quite frankly:

> John 4:26. . . . I that speak unto thee am he.

This open admission of Messiah-hood by Jesus and by others is pictured in the fourth gospel as continuing through a period of three years, in Jerusalem and elsewhere, before Jesus is arrested, condemned, and executed.

From the standpoint of realistic history, this view is quite impossible. However, the gospel is presenting theology and not history, and the theological Jesus, as opposed to the "historical Jesus," is divinity manifest.

In acclaiming Jesus as the Lamb of God, John the Baptist is not only referring to his Messiah-hood but to the actual form that Messiah-hood is to take. He is pictured as recognizing Jesus not as the royal Messiah who will lead the Jews to the ideal kingdom by defeating their enemies with the weapons of war, but rather as the suffering and tortured "servant" of Second Isaiah (see page I-551).

The reference to Jesus as the Lamb of God seems to turn upon a particular verse in one of these suffering servant passages:

> Isaiah 53:7. He [the servant of God] was oppressed, and he was afflicted, yet he opened not his mouth: he is brought as a lamb to the slaughter . . .

Nathanael

The manner in which Jesus collects his disciples is described in the fourth gospel, in quite a different way than in the synoptic gospels. In the synoptic gospels the disciples are selected by Jesus in Galilee; in

John, where Jesus is throughout treated with greater dignity, it is the disciples who come seeking after him.

Thus, John the Baptist acclaims Jesus as the Lamb of God a second time in the presence of two of his disciples and they instantly leave the Baptist and follow Jesus:

John 1:40. *One of the two which heard John* [the Baptist] *speak, and followed him* [Jesus], *was Andrew, Simon Peter's brother.*

The other is not named and he is traditionally assumed to be John son of Zebedee, the Beloved Disciple and the author of the gospel. His modesty is viewed as causing him to refrain from naming himself.

There is no indication in the synoptic gospels that any of the apostles were originally followers of the Baptist. Still, this clearly fits the purpose of the fourth gospel, since it shows that the Baptist's followers, guided by the Baptist himself, clearly prefer Jesus to John, and this further weakens the Baptist party among the evangelist's opponents.

The first two disciples spread the word:

John 1:41. *He* [Andrew] *first findeth his own brother Simon, and saith unto him, We have found the Messias* [Messiah] . . .

This quite negates one of the great moments in the synoptic gospels —where Peter confesses his belief in Jesus as the Messiah (see page 194), a confession which turns Jesus toward Jerusalem and the crucifixion. Here, instead, Peter is told at the outset that Jesus is the Messiah and there is no room later in this gospel for any slowly attained realization of this belief by either Peter or any other disciple. The nature of Jesus in the view of the fourth gospel is too exalted to admit of any such slow or gradual realization; the realization must come at once.

Furthermore, the acceptance of these first disciples does not take place in Galilee, but on the site in the Trans-Jordan where John the Baptist was conducting the baptismal rite:

John 1:28. *These things were done* . . . *beyond Jordan, where John was baptizing.*

And as though to emphasize that fact, Jesus is then described as being on his way to return to Galilee:

John 1:43. *The day following Jesus would go forth into Galilee, and findeth Philip, and saith unto him, Follow me.*

John 1:44. *Now Philip was of Bethsaida, the city of Andrew and Peter.*

Presumably, Philip had been told of the Messiah by Andrew and Peter and he in turn spreads the news still further:

John 1:45. *Philip findeth Nathanael, and saith unto him, We have found him, of whom Moses in the law, and the prophets, did write . . .*

Nathanael is not listed among the apostles in the synoptic gospels; indeed, his name does not occur outside the fourth gospel. On the other hand, Bartholomew, who is listed among the apostles in all three of the synoptic gospels, is not mentioned in John. Since in all three of the synoptic gospels, Bartholomew is named directly after Philip:

Mark 3:18. *And Andrew, and Philip, and Bartholomew . . .*

and since here in John there seems a special relationship between Philip and Nathanael, it is customary to identify Nathanael with Bartholomew. Since Bartholomew means "son of Talmai" and may be a patronymic only, Nathaniel may be the actual given name. The apostle would then be Nathanael Bartholomew ("Nathaniel, son of Talmai").

It may also be that Nathaniel is not one of the twelve disciples but is some disciple outside this inner circle of twelve.

The fourth gospel does not list the twelve apostles at all, the only gospel not to do so. The very word "apostle" does not occur in the fourth gospel. It may well be that John soft-pedals the tradition of the twelve apostles as far as possible, since the analogy there is to the twelve tribes of Israel, an analogy long outmoded by events, at the time the gospel was written.

The Son of Joseph

Philip identifies Jesus clearly and unmistakably, when he reports of him to Nathanael:

John 1:45. *Philip findeth Nathanael, and saith unto him, We have found him, . . . Jesus of Nazareth, the son of Joseph.*

No attempt is made, in this gospel, to refer to the virgin birth at Bethlehem. This is not because John is unaware that among the Jews the birth at Bethlehem was a necessary requirement for a true Messiah, for upon hearing this identification of the Messiah "of whom Moses in the law, and the prophets, did write," Nathanael is at once dubious:

John 1:46. *And Nathanael said unto him* [Philip], *Can there any good thing come out of Nazareth?* . . .

This might have been the contempt of a man of Jerusalem for a Galilean provincial, but it wasn't. Nathanael is himself a Galilean according to John. At one point, where several disciples are listed, John says:

John 21:2. . . . *Simon Peter, and Thomas called Didymus, and Nathanael of Cana in Galilee* . . .

Or Nathanael's remark might simply imply that no prophet ever came out of Galilee, as is stated later in the gospel, when the Pharisees are quoted as saying to one of their own number who spoke in defense of Jesus:

John 7:52. . . . *Art thou also of Galilee? Search, and look: for out of Galilee ariseth no prophet.*

But that isn't so, either. The prophet Jonah (the historical prophet of the time of Jeroboam II, on whom the fable with the whale was later grafted) was from the region, even though it was not called Galilee at the time:

2 Kings 14:25. . . . *Jonah, the son of Amittai, the prophet, which was of Gath-hepher.*

In fact, Gath-hepher was not only in Galilee but it is usually identified with a town only three miles from Nazareth.

Or it might be (as is sometimes suggested) that Nazareth itself had a bad reputation among Galileans generally. Perhaps it was considered a city of fools, like the Gotham of English folk tales. And perhaps this reputation was particularly strong in Nathanael's home town of Cana which was close enough to Nazareth to allow of the kind of neighborly rivalry one gets between Minneapolis and St. Paul, or between Fort Worth and Dallas. There is, however, nothing concrete on which to base such a belief.

It seems most likely that the remark simply refers to the fact that Jews did not expect the Messiah to come from anywhere but Bethlehem. This, too, is stated flatly later in the gospel where the opinions of the people generally are given.

John 7:41. . . . But some said, Shall Christ come out of Galilee? John 7:42. Hath not the scripture said, That Christ cometh of the seed of David, and out of the town of Bethlehem, where David was?

It seems logical to suppose that Nathanael, at first hearing that Jesus was of Nazareth, had the same doubt. The evangelist does not bother to counter these doubts by any remark concerning the birth at Bethlehem. Perhaps he felt the birth at Bethlehem was something that concerned only Jews and he intended his own gospel to have a universal importance.

Once Nathanael meets Jesus, he is at once brought over:

John 1:49. Nathanael . . . saith unto him [Jesus], Rabbi, thou art the Son of God; thou art the King of Israel.

The word "rabbi" used here means "my master" or "my teacher." It is precisely the term of respect one would use for another more learned than himself. In the theocratic society of Judea, it bears somewhat the same aura of respect that the title "professor" does in our own more secular society. Earlier in the chapter, John translates the word. When the first two disciples approach Jesus:

John 1:38. . . . They said unto him, Rabbi, (which is to say, being interpreted, Master,) where dwellest thou?

In the other gospels, the King James Version usually gives the Greek equivalent only, so that Jesus is routinely addressed as "Master." Thus, Peter addressing Jesus at the sight of the transfiguration, is quoted as saying:

Mark 9:5. And Peter . . . said to Jesus, Master, it is good for us to be here . . .

The equivalent verse in Matthew uses another term of respect, one of more secular tang and perhaps more suitable to the divinity that was gathering about Jesus in the eyes of his disciples:

Matthew 17:4. . . . Peter . . . said unto Jesus, Lord, it is good for us to be here . . .

Another form of addresses is "rabboni," meaning "my great master" or "my lord and master." This is used of the resurrected Jesus, by Mary Magdalene:

John 20:16. . . . She turned herself, and saith unto him, Rabboni; which is to say, Master.

Cana

Once back in Galilee, Jesus performs his first miracle—one which is found only in John. It takes place at a wedding festival:

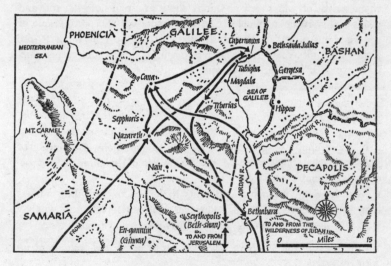

Early Journeys of Christ

John 2:1. . . . there was a marriage in Cana of Galilee; and the mother of Jesus was there:

John 2:2. And both Jesus was called, and his disciples, to the marriage.

Cana, mentioned only in John, is close to Nazareth. It is usually identified with a site about four miles northeast, though some favor a site some nine miles north of Nazareth. It is this town of which Nathanael is a native.

Oddly enough, John's reference to "the mother of Jesus" is characteristic of him. Not only does he not refer to the virgin birth and make Jesus the son of Joseph without qualification, but he never names Mary. His is the only gospel in which Mary is not named; she is referred to only as "the mother of Jesus."

Mary appears in the legends of Jesus' birth and childhood in Matthew and Luke. On one occasion she is mentioned by all three synoptic gospels. This is when she and other members of the family of Jesus try to see him when he is surrounded by his disciples, and Jesus turns them away. That is all.

In John, however, Mary plays a somewhat greater role; and, as is characteristic of John's view of things, she is aware of her son's role and of his ability to work miracles. She tells Jesus that the party is out of wine and instructs the servants to do whatever he tells them to do. Jesus then proceeds to turn water into wine (and, as the gospel carefully explains, into very good wine indeed).

The Jews' Passover

In the synoptic gospels only one visit to Jerusalem is recorded of Jesus, and that takes place in the last week of his life, on the occasion of a Passover.

John, however, records several visits to Jerusalem, including no less than three Passovers. The first Passover visit takes place immediately after the miracle of turning water into wine.

John 2:13. *And the Jews' passover was at hand, and Jesus went up to Jerusalem* . . .

John refers to the festival as "the Jews' passover," for his Gentile audience needed the qualifying adjective to understand what was being spoken of. He is even more carefully explanatory at other times:

John 6:4. *And the passover, a feast of the Jews, was nigh.*

Luke, also writing to a Gentile audience, must also explain:

Luke 22:1. *Now the feast of unleavened bread drew nigh, which is called the Passover.*

Matthew, on the other hand, writing for Jews, feels the need of no explanation:

Matthew 26:2. *Ye know that after two days is the feast of the passover . . .*

A more important point is that John is writing in a time when Christianity has become almost entirely Gentile and completely withdrawn from Judaism and out of sympathy with the Jews.

In the synoptic gospels, it is the Pharisees, Sadducees, and scribes who oppose Jesus on doctrinal points who conspire against him and bring about his crucifixion. It is they who are blamed and not the Jews generally, for it is from the Jews that Jesus' disciples are also drawn.

John, however, seems to feel that party distinctions would be lost on his audience, and usually refers to Jesus' opponents simply as "Jews." Thus, it is the "Jews," rather than the Sadducees of the Temple, who are pictured as questioning John the Baptist:

John 1:19. . . . *the Jews sent priests and Levites from Jerusalem . . .*

And it is the "Jews" rather than the scribes and Pharisees, who question Jesus on the first visit to Jerusalem:

John 2:18. *Then answered the Jews and said unto him [Jesus], What sign shewest thou unto us, seeing that thou doest these things?*

Even Jesus' disciples are described as referring to Jesus' opponents simply as "Jews," as though they themselves were not also Jews. Thus, when Jesus planned to go once more into Judea:

John 11:8. *His disciples say unto him, Master, the Jews of late sought to stone thee; and goest thou thither again?*

Then, too, parents whose son had been cured by Jesus deny knowing how the cure came about, and the reason is presented by John as follows:

John 9:22. *These words spake his parents, because they feared the Jews . . .*

although the parents were themselves Jews, of course.

This general reference to Jews in John, where the synoptics speak of specific parties among the Jews, helped rouse antipathy against Jews on the part of Christians in later centuries. It helped give rise to the common oversimplification that "the Jews killed Christ," as though all Jews of Jesus' time were equally responsible and as though all of Jesus' early disciples from Peter to Paul were not themselves Jews.

To be sure, John does on occasion speak of Jews who follow Jesus:

John 8:31. *Then said Jesus to those Jews which believed on him . . .*

The Temple

On the occasion of this first visit to Jerusalem, John describes Jesus as driving the money-changers from the Temple, placing that event near the beginning of his mission rather than at the end, as in the synoptic gospels. Those who refuse to admit inconsistencies among the gospels are forced to conclude that there were two such episodes, one near the beginning, and one near the end.

The "Jews" (that is, the Sadducee officials of the Temple) are naturally upset over this action of Jesus, and demand some evidence from him that he is indeed acting under divine inspiration.

John 2:19. *Jesus answered . . . , Destroy this temple, and in three days I will raise it up.*

Jesus is not quoted as making any such statement in the synoptic gospels. In fact, quite the reverse. Mark and Matthew record that a similar statement was *falsely* attributed to Jesus as part of the attempt to condemn him as a blasphemer before Caiaphas.

Mark 14:57. *And there arose certain, and bare false witness against him, saying,*
Mark 14:58. *We heard him say, I will destroy this temple that is made with hands, and within three days I will build another made without hands.*

Then, when Jesus was on the cross, he was mocked with this statement:

Mark 15:29. *And they that passed by* [the cross] *railed on him . . . saying, Ah, thou that destroyest the temple, and buildest it in three days,*

Mark 15:30. *Save thyself, and come down from the cross.*

But John accepts this as a true saying of Jesus and interprets it as a reference to the resurrection:

John 2:21. *But he* [Jesus] *spake of the temple of his body.*

In connection with this remark concerning the Temple, John mentions the literal-minded retort of the priests—a retort which has been used for chronological purposes:

John 2:20. *Then said the Jews, Forty and six years was this temple in building, and wilt thou rear it up in three days?*

Actually, construction of the Second Temple was begun in 538 B.C. in the reign of Cyrus of Persia and completed in 516 B.C. in the reign of Darius (see page I-449), so that it was only twenty-two years in building.

Herod the Great, however, in his attempt to gain the good will of his subjects, initiated a vast restoration and enlargement of the Temple, one which amounted, virtually, to a rebuilding. This restoration was begun in 19 B.C. and it was not actually completed until A.D. 63—three years before the beginning of the war that was to destroy that same Temple forever. The Temple was eighty-two years in the restoring.

But suppose it had been continuing for forty-six years at the time of Jesus' first Passover visit to Jerusalem and that the priests were saying, in essence, "So far just the temple restoration alone has been proceeding for forty-six years and here you offer to build it from scratch in three days!"

If so, then the year of the visit would be A.D. 27. The next two Passover visits recorded in John would then be in A.D. 28 and 29 and if the last of the three were the one of the crucifixion, that would agree with the chronology as given in Luke in terms of the reign of Tiberius (see page 274).

Nicodemus

Oddly enough, on the first occasion in which John does specify a
Pharisee, it is one that he depicts as sympathetic to Jesus (and one who
is nowhere mentioned in the synoptic gospels):

> John 3:1. *There was a man of the Pharisees, named Nicodemus,
> a ruler of the Jews:*
> John 3:2. *The same came to Jesus by night, and said unto him,
> Rabbi, we know that thou art a teacher come from God . . .*

He asked questions of Jesus and listened to the answers which were
not given in the form of parables as in the synoptic gospels, but rather
in philosophic discourse that Nicodemus found difficult to follow.

Nicodemus was apparently swayed by Jesus' statements, however,
for later when the Pharisees planned to put Jesus out of the way for
blasphemy, Nicodemus rose and insisted on a fair trial, thus blunting
the purpose of Jesus' opponents for the time. (It was Nicodemus who
was mockingly asked if he too were from Galilee.)

After the crucifixion, Nicodemus, according to John, took care of
Jesus' body, along with Joseph of Arimathea (see page 233), and saw
to its proper burial. In early Christian tradition, Nicodemus is supposed
to have turned Christian. An apocryphal "Gospel According to Nicodemus" is attributed to him. It dealt with the trial and execution of
Jesus, his descent into hell, and his resurrection.

Samaria

Apparently, Jesus' success in attracting followers in Judea attracted
the attention of the Pharisees and Jesus thought it best to return to
Galilee.

> John 4:3. *He left Judaea, and departed again into Galilee.*
> John 4:4. *And he must needs go through Samaria.*

In Matthew and Mark, gospels written for Jewish audiences, Jesus
is depicted as sharing the general Jewish hostility to Samaritans. Even

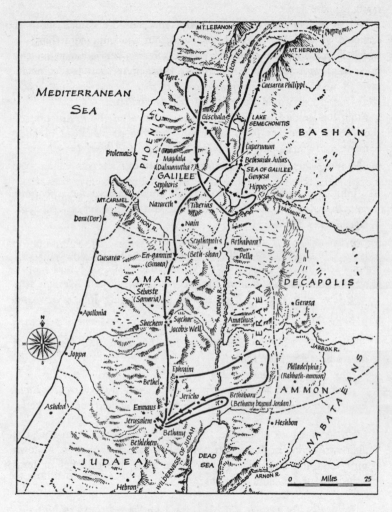

Samaria

in Luke, written for Gentiles and depicting individual Samaritans with sympathy, it is indicated (see page 282) that the Samaritans, generally, oppose Jesus.

Not so in John. Here, in the most Gentile of the gospels, Jesus is depicted as speaking freely to a Samaritan woman (something at which his disciples are shocked) and as offering her salvation on the same basis with Jews. This fits John's thesis that Jesus has come to save all men, and not the Jews alone. If that thesis were not made clear, his gospel would be valueless to his audience.

From the vantage point of a full generation after the destruction of the Temple, John has Jesus point out that the parochialism of both Samaritans (worshipping on Mount Gerizim) and Jews (worshipping on Mount Zion) was soon to have no meaning:

John 4:21. *Jesus saith unto her, Woman, believe me, the hour cometh, when ye shall neither in this mountain, nor yet at Jerusalem, worship the Father.*

Jesus calmly announces himself as the Messiah, and the Samaritan woman tells others of her people. As is characteristic of John's gospel, the Samaritans at once believe, and accept Jesus not as a Messiah sent to the Jews only, but to all the world (again fitting John's view and his audience).

John 4:40. . . . *the Samaritans . . . besought him* [Jesus] *that he would tarry with them . . .*
John 4:41. *And many more believed . . .*
John 4:42. *And said unto the woman, Now we believe . . . and know that this is indeed the Christ, the Saviour of the world.*

Once Jesus is back in Galilee, the evangelist mentions in an aside the well-known saying of Jesus that a prophet had no honor in his own country and also later states, again as an aside, the disbelief in Jesus on the part of his close relations:

John 7:5. *For neither did his* [Jesus'] *brethren believe in him.*

John does not, however, include the account (found in all the synoptic gospels) of Jesus' failure to impress his townsmen at Nazareth. Such a failure would not fit the picture of Jesus as drawn by John.

Jewry

A second trip is then made to Jerusalem, where Jesus heals a crippled man on the Sabbath and gets in trouble with the conservative elements among the Jews for having violated the Sabbath. In the discussion thereafter, John has Jesus implying himself to be the Messiah, and driving the conservative elements into a fury at this seeming blasphemy.

Again, Jesus returns to Galilee as a matter of prudence and there, near the time of a second Passover, performs other miracles, including the feeding of thousands of people by means of five loaves of bread and two fish—the only miracle described in all four gospels.

Jesus remains in Galilee for a time—

John 7:1. . . . *for he would not walk in Jewry, because the Jews sought to kill him.*

The expression "Jewry" is used only three times in the King James Version. Only one of these is in the Old Testament—in the very late Book of Daniel, where the Babylonian king asks Daniel:

Daniel 5:13. . . . *Art thou that Daniel, which art of the children of the captivity of Judah, whom the king my father brought out of Jewry?*

The second occasion is in Luke, where Jesus is accused of sedition before Pilate:

Luke 23:5. . . . *He stirreth up the people, teaching throughout all Jewry . . .*

"Jewry" is an archaic term for Judah or Judea and in the Revised Standard Version, the word is rendered "Judah" in the verse from Daniel, and as "Judea" in the two verses from the gospels.

"Jewry" in modern ears does not have quite the same connotation as Judea. The latter is a geographical term and it was politically distinct from Galilee in Jesus' time. Jesus' priestly enemies were powerful in Judea ("Jewry") but not in Galilee, and Jesus was clearly safer in his home province.

But if "Judea" is clear in its meaning, "Jewry" is so no longer. In modern ears, it sounds rather analogous to the word "Christendom." It seems to cover all the area in which Jews live; it seems indeed to be a way of saying "all the Jews." Place this in conjunction with the following phrase, "because the Jews sought to kill him" (the synoptic gospels would have said, "because the Pharisees sought to kill him"), and the impression is given of the malignant hostility toward Jesus on the part of all the Jews—something that is clearly not the case.

Abraham

But Jesus did return to Jerusalem for a third time, at the time of the Feast of the Tabernacles, and his teachings became ever more bold. Indeed, he finally pronounced himself to be the Messiah in the plainest terms.

John 8:54. *Jesus answered, . . .*

. . . .

John 8:56. *Your father Abraham rejoiced to see my day: and he saw it, and was glad.*

John 8:57. *Then said the Jews unto him, Thou art not yet fifty years old, and hast thou seen Abraham?*

To the Jewish leaders, blasphemy had reached the ultimate, for Jesus was claiming to be not merely the Messiah, but God himself. The deliberate use of the words "I am" in Jesus' climactic answer:

John 8:58. *Jesus said unto them, Verily, verily, I say unto you, Before Abraham was, I am.*

harks back to God's announcement of his own name to Moses:

Exodus 3:14. *And God said unto Moses . . . Thus shalt thou say unto the children of Israel, I AM hath sent me unto you.*

With that, many Jews must have felt perfectly justified in attempting to stone Jesus, for stoning was the traditional method of execution for blasphemers:

Leviticus 24:16. *And he that blasphemeth the name of the Lord, he shall surely be put to death, and all the congregation shall certainly stone him . . .*

Deductions are made concerning Jesus' age from the comment to the effect that Jesus was "not yet fifty years old" and some suppose that he was not far short of fifty at this time. It is even possible to argue that he was forty-six years old by beginning with John's comment that when Jesus spoke of re-erecting the Temple, he was speaking of his own body (see page 315). Therefore, when the Pharisees said it had taken forty-six years to build the Temple, might they not have meant that Jesus was forty-six years old? It is difficult to take this argument seriously, however, for surely, even if Jesus were speaking of his body, the Pharisees weren't, and to use their statement as a basis for deducing Jesus' age is a great deal to ask of a conversation that was supposedly going on at cross-purposes. It seems much more natural to accept Luke's flat statement (see page 275) that Jesus was about thirty years old when he began his mission.

Still, if Jesus were forty-six at the time of his death, and if the crucifixion did take place in A.D. 29, as Luke indicates (see page 274), then Christ must have been born in 17 B.C. There is nothing clearly impossible about this, except that basing it on the comment "Thou art not yet fifty" offers a very thin foundation. The expression might merely be a metaphoric way of saying, "You have not yet attained to years of wisdom," or "You are not even an old man"—and this can be said of a thirty-three-year-old even more forcefully than of a forty-six-year-old.

Jesus goes on to make additional claims to Messiah-hood and divinity. At one point he says:

John 10:11. *I am the good shepherd . . .*

This harks back to a passage in the writings of the prophet Ezekiel in which God is quoted as denouncing the wickedness of the Jewish leaders, who are described metaphorically as wicked shepherds:

Ezekiel 34:2. *Son of man, prophesy against the shepherds of Israel . . . Woe be to the shepherds of Israel that do feed themselves! should not the shepherds feed the flocks?*

Ezekiel goes on to quote God as offering himself to be the shepherd who would save his people:

Ezekiel 34:11. . . . *I, even I, will both search my sheep, and seek them out.*

Ezekiel 34:12. *As a shepherd seeketh out his flock . . . so will I seek out my sheep . . .*

Then in speaking of the Messianic kingdom, the Messiah is spoken of with the same metaphor:

Ezekiel 34:23. *And I will set up one shepherd over them, and he shall feed them, even my servant David . . .*

In speaking of himself as the good shepherd, then, Jesus is naming himself either the Messiah or God, or both. If the point is not clear, he makes it flatly a little later:

John 10:30. *I and my Father are one.*

and again he narrowly escapes a stoning, and retires to the Trans-Jordan.

Lazarus

It is serious news that now calls Jesus back to Judea for a fourth time as the third and last Passover of John's gospel approaches. A friend was seriously ill.

John 11:1. *Now a certain man was sick, named Lazarus, of Bethany, the town of Mary and her sister Martha.*
. . . .
John 11:3. *Therefore his sisters* [Mary and Martha] *sent unto him, saying, Lord, behold, he whom thou lovest is sick.*

This Lazarus is not mentioned anywhere in the synoptic gospels, which is odd, for the event that is to follow is pictured by John as the very climax of Jesus' miracles on Earth. Yet if it is indeed the climax, why the total silence of the other gospels?

Some have suggested that the story of Lazarus is an allegorical one, intended to show, in concrete form, the power of Jesus' teaching. For that reason, it might be argued, John simply borrowed material for the purpose. The name Lazarus he might have adopted from the beggar in Luke's parable (see page 284), the one who went to heaven while the rich man went to hell.

Why the beggar? Well, when the rich man is in hell, he asks that

Lazarus be sent back to Earth to warn the rich man's five brothers of the torment awaiting them. But Abraham, from heaven, assures the rich man that:

Luke 16:31. . . . *If they hear not Moses and the prophets, neither will they be persuaded, though one rose from the dead.*

There is thus a connection between Lazarus the beggar, and the notion of being raised from the dead, and the tale, in John, of Lazarus of Bethany who is raised from the dead by Jesus.

There are raisings from the dead in the other gospels. In Luke, for instance, there is the tale of Jesus' raising the dead son of a widow:

Luke 7:14. . . . *And he [Jesus] said, Young man, I say unto thee, Arise.*

Luke 7:15. *And he that was dead sat up, and began to speak . . .*

The story in Luke is told quickly, however, and is placed near the beginning of Jesus' career. It is no more than on a par with Jesus' other miracles of healing.

In John, however, the analogous story of a raising from the dead is told in much more dramatic detail and is placed at the end of Jesus' career, as a fitting climax to the gathering force of his miracles and self-manifestation.

By the time Jesus reaches Bethany, Lazarus is dead and buried and has remained in the tomb for days. Jesus has the stone blocking the tomb rolled away.

John 11:43. *And . . . he [Jesus] cried with a loud voice, Lazarus, come forth.*

John 11:44. *And he that was dead came forth . . .*

There are those who suspect that since Lazarus is defined as "he whom thou lovest," that he is none other than the Beloved Disciple and the author of the fourth gospel. It might be possible to argue from that that Lazarus knew the events of the raising firsthand and included them, whereas the other evangelists did not.

This, however, seems weak, for the episode is described as having been public and as having achieved such fame as to be the final straw that determined the Pharisees to have Jesus convicted and executed. How could the synoptic gospels overlook such a thing?

Caiaphas

The Jewish religious leaders see clearly now that if Jesus is not stopped, those who flocked to him in the aftermath of the Lazarus miracle would become uncontrollable. They feared a rebellion and a consequent catastrophe to follow:

John 11:48. *If we let him* [Jesus] *thus alone, all men will believe on him: and the Romans shall come and take away both our place and nation.*
John 11:49. . . . *Caiaphas . . . said unto them . . .*
John 11:50. . . . *it is expedient for us, that one man should die for the people, and that the whole nation perish not.*

This statement of Caiaphas' is to be found only in John, who uses it to fit his own scheme of things. He points out that Caiaphas, who was, after all, high priest, was engaging in unconscious prophecy; that Jesus would indeed die in order that salvation might be brought to all people—but not to the Jews only:

John 11:52. *And not for that nation only, but that also he* [Jesus] *should gather together in one the children of God that were scattered abroad.*

Of course, by the "children of God that were scattered abroad" one might suppose that John meant the Jews dwelling outside Judea. It is equally possible, however, to suppose it to refer to the Gentiles who lived all over the world and who, by accepting Jesus, would become the "children of God"—the spiritual heirs of Abraham.

If there is doubt here, it is removed by an incident described shortly afterward. Even while the Jewish leaders are planning to have Jesus executed, the first Gentile disciples arrive:

John 12:20. *And there were certain Greeks among them that came up to worship at the* [Passover] *feast:*
John 12:21. *The same came therefore to Philip . . . and desired him, saying, Sir, we would see Jesus.*

Sometimes the word "Greeks" in English translations of the Bible means Jews from Egypt or elsewhere who have Greek as their native language. The original Greek of the New Testament, however, uses slightly different forms to distinguish between men of Jewish birth who speak Greek, and men of Greek birth who had been converted to Judaism. In this case, it seems to be men of Greek birth—converted Gentiles—who are meant.

And they ask to see Jesus. The Gentiles begin to turn toward Jesus, in John's picture of events, just as the Jews are about to turn finally away from him. And it is this decisive turn that marks to Jesus the time of the death and resurrection. The disciples bring word to him that the Greeks wish to see him:

John 12:23. *And Jesus answered them, saying, The hour is come, that the Son of man should be glorified.*

John indicates plainly, then, that the direction of Christianity is toward the Gentile and away from the Jew—as is the theme of his entire gospel, in fact, from the very hymn that opens it:

John 1:11. *He came unto his own, and his own received him not.*
John 1:12. *But as many as received him, to them gave he power to become the sons of God, even to them that believe on his name . . .*

And that, surely, is what John's audience wanted to hear.

The Comforter

John describes the triumphant entry into Jerusalem, though the passage is not as convincing as in the synoptic gospels, where it seems to be the *only* entry.

John does not, however, describe a last supper during Jesus' final night of freedom, or the prayer at Gethsemane. He does not have Jesus pray that the fated cup might be allowed to pass from him (see page 218). That would be not in accord with the divine Jesus pictured by John. Indeed, John has Jesus speak in such a way as to seem to contradict, deliberately, that passage in the synoptic gospels:

John 12:27. *Now is my soul troubled; and what shall I say? Father, save me from this hour: but for this cause came I unto this hour.*

Jesus washes the feet of his disciples (as a lesson in humility, not found in the synoptic gospels) and then continues to deliver self-

assured philosophical discourses. During these, he makes statements
that helped give rise to thoughts of an imminent second coming
among the early Christians. Thus, he tells them, with reference to his
forthcoming death:

> John 14:2. . . . I go to prepare a place for you.
> John 14:3. And . . . I will come again, and receive you unto
> myself . . .

This might be interpreted as meaning he would come, unseen, for
each disciple, as that disciple lay dying, to lead him to his prepared
place in heaven. There was, however, certainly a tendency to assume
that this (and other verses in the gospels) implied a return of Christ in
glory, and one that was not long delayed either. This return would
fulfill the same purposes as the Jews had believed would be fulfilled by
the Messiah.

Jesus is quoted as making another promise:

> John 14:16. And I will pray the Father, and he shall give you
> another Comforter, that he may abide with you for ever;
> John 14:17. Even the Spirit of truth . . .

This is usually interpreted as meaning that Christians would be
guided by the Holy Spirit once Jesus was taken away from them and
that this Spirit would comfort them and guide them aright.

Nevertheless, there were not lacking those among the early Christians
who personified the Comforter (or "Paraclete" as the word is in Greek).
It seemed to them that Jesus was promising a new and still later
Messiah who would take on human appearance, just as Moses was
considered to have prophesied Jesus in his reference to a Prophet (see
page 304).

Thus, somewhere about A.D. 160 (about half a century after the gospel
of St. John had been written) a Christian of Asia Minor named
Montanus claimed to be the incarnation of the Comforter.

Montanus was rejected as a false Messiah by the Christian leadership,
just as Jesus had been rejected by the Jewish leadership. And just as
Jesus slowly gathered disciples who grew in numbers after his death, so
did Montanus. The sect of Montanists, puritanical in doctrine, was
particularly strong in Carthage and its environs, and among them was
Tertullian, the first important Christian leader to write in Latin.

However, Christianity was wider spread than Judaism had been in Jesus' time, and Christianity was not weakened by a catastrophe analogous to the Roman destruction of Judea. Consequently the Montanists were kept in check. Furthermore, they expected an imminent second coming of some sort, and as this did not take place, they slowly withered. Still, some remained until the days of the Moslem conquest of North Africa in the seventh century wiped out Christianity in that region altogether.

Pilate

The story of Jesus' capture and trial is essentially the same in John as in the synoptic gospels, but with an important change in atmosphere. The divine Jesus portrayed by John is by no means the mute and suffering servant pictured by the Second Isaiah and the synoptic gospels. Instead, Jesus is completely self-possessed and in control of events at all times. He goes to his death deliberately.

Thus, he boldly faces those who have come to arrest him and calmly announces his identity even before Judas has a chance to indicate him. And when Pilate asks him if he is the King of the Jews, Jesus questions Pilate in turn and has no difficulty in dominating the exchange:

John 18:34. *Jesus answered him, Sayest thou this thing of thyself, or did others tell it thee of me?*

John 18:35. *Pilate answered, Am I a Jew? Thine own nation and the chief priests have delivered thee unto me: what hast thou done?*

Thus Pilate is clearly forced to confess that he knows nothing of the affair and that he is merely a mouthpiece of the Jewish priesthood. In this way, John, writing for his Gentile audience, does more than any of the synoptic gospels (even Luke) to lift the blame for the crucifixion from the Gentiles and place it on the Jews.

This is made even plainer at a later stage of the trial when Pilate questions Jesus again. Jesus is now silent and Pilate says desperately:

John 19:10. . . . *Speakest thou not unto me? knowest thou not that I have power to crucify thee, and have power to release thee?*

John 19:11. *Jesus answered, Thou couldest have no power at all against me, except it were given thee from above: therefore he that delivered me unto thee hath the greater sin.*

In other words, Pilate is again pictured as a puppet who can do only what he must do, in accordance with the Roman law (or with the will of God). In either case, since he has not been taught the Scriptures, since he knows nothing of the Messiah, and since he has not been exposed to Jesus' preaching, he cannot know what he is doing. The greater sin belongs to those who, knowing of the Scriptures, the Messiah, and Jesus' teaching, nevertheless handed Jesus over to the implacable grinding of Roman law. The expression "he that delivered me" is singular and it may indicate Caiaphas the high priest (though some suggest Judas Iscariot, or even Satan).

If the reader takes the expression to refer to Caiaphas, then here again would be a statement from Jesus that it is the Jewish authority, rather than the Roman authority, that is truly responsible for the crucifixion.

To make this still clearer, John has Pilate show even greater reluctance to carry through the task than even Luke does, and has him yield to the priestly party only after political threats which are not found in the synoptic gospels, but which John's Gentile audience would thoroughly understand:

John 19:12. . . . *the Jews cried out, saying, If thou let this man go, thou art not Caesar's friend: whosoever maketh himself a king speaketh against Caesar.*

In other words, the priestly party is prepared to accuse Pilate of treason if he acquits Jesus. An accusation of treason in the days of the suspicious Tiberius was often equivalent to conviction.

John even has the priests making what the nationalist Jews of the time would consider a treasonable statement to their own cause in their anxiety to enforce the crucifixion. Jesus is mockingly produced to the crowd as the Messianic king:

John 19:15. . . . *Pilate saith unto them, Shall I crucify your King? The chief priest answered, We have no king but Caesar.*

They are thus pictured as denying the Messianic hope altogether and the case against them, as carefully constructed by John, is complete.

The Spear

John's version of the crucifixion differs from that pictured in the synoptic gospels in a number of respects. Jesus bears his own cross. No one is described as having to help him. The humiliating aspects of the crucifixion—including the jeering of the crowd—are omitted. Jesus' mother, Mary, is at the site of the crucifixion (though her presence there is not mentioned in any of the other gospels) and Jesus is sufficiently self-possessed, even on the cross, to place her in the charge of the Beloved Disciple, who is also there.

John, like Luke, omits the last cry of despair (see page 232). Such despair would be unthinkable in the picture of Jesus drawn by John. Instead, John has Jesus merely announce the completion of his mission:

John 19:30. . . . *he said, It is finished: and he bowed his head, and gave up the ghost.*

Certain events following Jesus' death are given in John, but not in the synoptic gospels. John explains that the priests want the crucified individuals (Jesus and the two robbers) down from the cross that very evening, in order not to profane the coming Passover. For that reason, soldiers are sent to break the legs of the crucified men in order that they might be thus killed and taken down. (Actually, however it sounds to us, such leg-breaking seems to be intended as an act of mercy. Those who were crucified might otherwise linger a number of days in gradually increasing torment.)

Jesus, however, had died already, apparently sooner than was expected; sufficiently soon, indeed, to make one soldier suspicious that Jesus might be playing possum:

John 19:33. *But when they* [the soldiers] *came to Jesus, and saw that he was dead already, they brake not his legs:*

John 19:34. *But one of the soldiers with a spear pierced his side, and forthwith came there out blood and water.*

John introduces these items to make a very important theological point; one, apparently, which was disputed by some factions among the early Christians. He therefore emphatically defends the truth of what he has just said:

> John 19:35. *And he that saw it bare record, and his record is true: and he knoweth that he saith true, that ye might believe.*

John then goes on to explain the significance of this vehemently defended account of the leg-breaking that did not come to pass and the spear thrust that did:

> John 19:36. *For these things were done, that the scripture should be fulfilled, A bone of him shall not be broken.*
>
> John 19:37. *And again another scripture saith, They shall look on him whom they pierced.*

The first quotation is from the Book of Psalms. In one which praises the care of God for those who trust in him, there is the verse:

> Psalm 34:20. *He* [the Lord] *keepeth all his* [the righteous one's] *bones; not one of them is broken.*

And in the later, apocalyptic chapters of Zechariah, reference is made to some not clearly defined person who is mistreated:

> Zechariah 12:10. . . . *they shall look upon me whom they have pierced, and they shall mourn for him . . .*

But this anxiety to fit the events of Jesus' life into the various utterances found in the Old Testament is not really characteristic of John. He is not Matthew and he is not writing for Matthew's audience.

The reference must be wider still. Jesus was crucified at the Passover festival, and at the beginning of the fourth gospel John the Baptist has referred to Jesus as the "Lamb of God" (see page 305). Well, there is an association of the lamb and Passover.

In God's instructions to Israel on the occasion of the first Passover, on the eve of the Exodus from Egypt, Moses is told:

> Exodus 12:3. *Speak ye unto all the congregation of Israel, saying, In the tenth day of this month they shall take to them every man a lamb . . .*

The lamb is to be sacrificed on the eve of Passover and its blood smeared on the doorposts:

Exodus 12:13. . . . *and when I see the blood, I will pass over you, and the plague shall not be upon you* . . .

Later, in the same chapter, a further instruction is given concerning the lamb:

Exodus 12:46. . . . *neither shall ye break a bone thereof.*

This is in accordance with the general rule that all animals sacrificed to God must be in perfect condition and without blemish:

Deuteronomy 17:1. *Thou shalt not sacrifice unto the Lord thy God any bullock, or sheep, wherein is blemish, or any evilfavouredness* . . .

John's analogy seems to be clear. The crucifixion of Jesus on the eve of Passover is a new and greater sacrifice. In place of the unblemished lamb, always a symbol of the pure and innocent, there is the unblemished Lamb of God, the pure and innocent Jesus. Not a bone of Jesus was broken but the blood of Jesus had to be seen in accordance with Exodus 12:13 and 12:46 respectively. Hence the soldiers did not break Jesus' legs and did draw blood with the spear.

The fact that the sacrifice was so much greater—Jesus rather than an ordinary lamb—could be argued as indicating the purpose to be equivalently greater, all mankind rather than the Jews only. This would fit John's scheme of things and would account for the manner in which he insists his account of the spear is true.

Another connotation of this analogy is that a lamb was sometimes used as a sin offering; a sacrifice meant to atone for the sin and clear the sinner before God:

Leviticus 4:27. *And if any one of the common people sin* . . .
. . . .
Leviticus 4:32. *And if he bring a lamb for a sin offering* . . .

Jesus is the unblemished Lamb sacrificed as a sin-offering for all mankind and this gives a further significance to the manner in which John the Baptist first greets Jesus (according to the fourth gospel):

John 1:29. . . . *John seeth Jesus coming unto him, and saith, Behold the Lamb of God, which taketh away the sin of the world.*

Thomas

The story of the resurrection is told by John in greater detail than is found in any of the other gospels. (Apparently, the later the gospel, the more detailed the story of the resurrection.)

The most dramatic account of the initial doubts of the apostles is given here in connection with Thomas:

> John 20:24. *But Thomas, one of the twelve, called Didymus, was not with them when Jesus came.*
>
> John 20:25. *The other disciples therefore said unto him, We have seen the Lord. But he said unto them, Except I shall see in his hands the print of the nails, and put my finger into the print of the nails, and thrust my hand into his side, I will not believe.*

Thomas was granted his desire and accepted the resurrection, but it is this passage which adds the phrase "doubting Thomas" to our language, a phrase that has come to be used for any notorious skeptic.

The surname Didymus means "twin," and it would seem then that "Thomas the Twin" must have had a twin brother or sister. The Bible does not mention any such twin, though legend has been busy (some even maintaining that Thomas was a twin brother of Jesus).

It may be significant that only John uses this surname. Thomas is merely Thomas when he is mentioned in the synoptic gospels. Perhaps the "twin" is not a physical reference at all, but refers to Thomas being "of two minds"; that is, of skeptical tendencies, generally. Perhaps then, "Thomas called Didymus" is merely the evangelist's way of saying "Doubting Thomas."

9. ACTS

THEOPHILUS · MATTHIAS · PENTECOST · TONGUES · PARTHIANS AND MEDES · ANANIAS · GAMALIEL · STEPHEN · PHILIP · SIMON MAGUS · CANDACE · SAUL OF TARSUS · DAMASCUS · BARNABAS · JAMES THE LORD'S BROTHER · LYDDA · CORNELIUS · ANTIOCH · CLAUDIUS CAESAR · HEROD AGRIPPA I · CYPRUS · PAPHOS · PAUL · PAMPHYLIA · PISIDIA · LYCAONIA · ATTALIA · SILAS · TIMOTHY · PHRYGIA AND GALATIA · TROAS · MACEDONIA · PHILIPPI · LYDIA · THESSALONICA · BEREA · ATHENS · EPICUREANS AND STOICS · DIONYSIUS THE AREOPAGITE · CORINTH · AQUILA · GALLIO · EPHESUS · APOLLOS · DIANA OF THE EPHESIANS · MILETUS · RHODES · FELIX · ANTIPATRIS · DRUSILLA · FESTUS · HEROD AGRIPPA II · MYRA · CRETE · MELITA · SYRACUSE · RHEGIUM · ROME

Theophilus

Following the four gospels—the four versions of the life of Jesus—comes a book which is for the most part a straightforward history and is particularly valuable for that reason.

It deals with the slow growth of Christianity during the generation that followed the crucifixion of Jesus—from its beginnings in Jerusalem until its slowly widening influence finally reached Rome itself. In so doing, it indicates the steady shift of Christianity away from its national Jewish foundation to the status of a universal Gentile religion, and the hero of that shift is the apostle Paul.

Although the second half of the book is essentially a biography of Paul, the first half gives some details concerning the other important disciples, so that the book is fairly named "The Acts of the Apostles" (rather than "The Book of Paul").

The author of Acts is generally considered to be the same as that of the third gospel. Acts begins, for instance, with a dedication similar to that which introduces the third gospel (see page 254), and it refers to an earlier book:

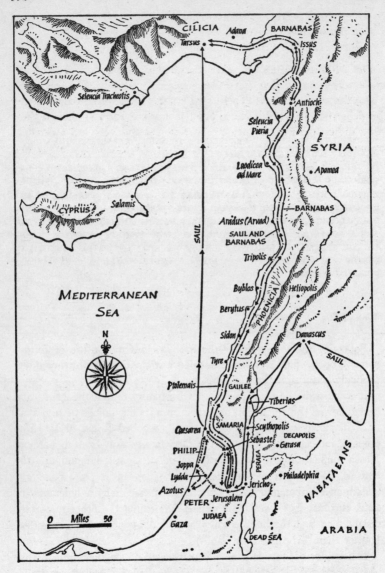

Journeys of the Apostles

Acts 1:1. *The former treatise have I made, O Theophilus, of all that Jesus began both to do and teach,*

Acts 1:2. *Until the day in which he was taken up . . .*

This "former treatise" is taken to be the third gospel, and it is universally assumed that Luke (see page 252) wrote that gospel and is also the author of Acts. To be sure, a later hand might have added the dedication to Theophilus in order to make it seem as though the same author had written both the third gospel and Acts, but a careful examination of the style and vocabulary of the two books seems to back up the theory of common authorship.

Indeed, one wonders if Luke and Acts might not originally have formed a single treatise which was divided only when it was decided to gather the various canonical gospels into a group.

The events dealt with in Acts end just prior to the Neronian persecution of Christians in A.D. 64, and some have suggested that the book was written at about that time. Others have favored dates as late as A.D. 100. However, it seems very likely that Acts was written about the same time as Luke and A.D. 80 seems a nice even date for both.

No one knows where Acts was written. The last events recorded take place in Rome, so it might have been written there. If it were written some fifteen years after those events it might well have been composed elsewhere. Some suggest Asia Minor and, in particular, the city of Ephesus. Christian missionary work was especially successful in Ephesus in the first century. Tradition places the composition of other New Testament books there, notably the fourth gospel (see page 297).

Matthias

As Acts begins, the resurrected Jesus is still with his small band of disciples and is giving them his final instructions over a fairly extended period of time:

Acts 1:3. *To whom* [the disciples] *also he* [Jesus] *shewed himself alive . . . , being seen of them forty days . . .*

After this, Jesus was taken up to heaven (the ascension):

Acts 1:9. *. . . while they beheld, he* [Jesus] *was taken up; and a cloud received him out of their sight.*

It was now up to the disciples to continue their work on their own, and their first act was to reconstitute the inner circle of twelve, which had been broken by the defection of Judas Iscariot. The remaining apostles are listed—the fourth list in the New Testament. The other three are in Matthew, Mark, and Luke, respectively; John does not give a list.

> Acts 1:13. . . . *Peter, and James, and John, and Andrew, Philip, and Thomas, Bartholomew, and Matthew, James the son of Alphaeus, and Simon Zelotes, and Judas the brother of James.*

Naturally, Judas Iscariot is omitted, but if we consider these eleven, we find it to include precisely those names listed in Luke, but not precisely those in Matthew and Mark. Only Luke of the three synoptic gospels contains Judas the brother of James as one of the twelve apostles; only Luke identifies Simon as Simon Zelotes. This is an additional piece of evidence in favor of the theory that Luke wrote Acts as well as the third gospel.

Peter arranged to have a new individual selected to take the place of Judas Iscariot in order to bring the number of the inner circle back to the mystical twelve that matched the twelve tribes of Israel. Two were nominated, Joseph Barsabbas and Matthias. To choose between the two, lots were used:

> Acts 1:26. . . . *and the lot fell upon Matthias; and he was numbered with the eleven apostles.*

Neither Joseph Barsabbas nor Matthias are mentioned anywhere else in the New Testament.

But the twelve apostles were by no means the only ones with whom Christianity made its start. Others, in addition, were gathered together in these very early days:

> Acts 1:15. . . . *Peter stood up in the midst of the disciples . . . (the number of names together were about an hundred and twenty,) . . .*

Among them, Acts lists:

> Acts 1:14. . . . *Mary the mother of Jesus, and . . . his brethren.*

This is the last act recorded of Mary in the New Testament. Luke, in common with the other synoptic gospels, had recorded her and Jesus' brothers as having vainly tried to see Jesus (see page 188) and she is never mentioned again. (Her appearance at the crucifixion is to be found only in John.) However, if the evidence of Acts is accepted, she joined the Christian fellowship after her son's death, whatever her doubts might have been in his lifetime.

Pentecost

After the ascension, the second of the three great harvest festivals of Judaism was approaching. This was, in Hebrew, Hag ha-Shabuoth ("feast of weeks") or simply Shabuoth. The significance of the name arises from the manner of determining the time of its observation. That determination was based upon Passover, the first of the harvest festivals:

Leviticus 23:15. *And ye shall count unto you from the morrow after the sabbath* [of the Passover] . . . ; *seven sabbaths shall be complete:*

Leviticus 23:16. *Even unto the morrow after the seventh sabbath shall ye number fifty days* . . .

In other words, Shabuoth comes seven weeks and a day after the Passover Sabbath and hence it is the "feast of weeks." The Greek name refers to the number of days that had elapsed; it is "Pentecost" from a Greek word meaning "fiftieth" since it comes on the fiftieth day after Passover. The festival is mentioned by both names in 2 Maccabees:

2 Maccabees 12:31. . . . *so they* [certain Jews] *came to Jerusalem, the feast of the weeks approaching.*

2 Maccabees 12:32. *And after the feast, called Pentecost, they went forth* . . .

Since the account in Acts makes the ascension take place forty days after the resurrection, which in turn took place the day after the Passover Sabbath, Pentecost must have come ten days after the ascension.

The twelve apostles, still completely Jewish in background and religion, made ready to celebrate the festival:

Acts 2:1. *And when the day of Pentecost was fully come, they* [the apostles] *were all with one accord in one place.*

Because of what then took place Pentecost remains an important day in the Christian calendar, and is celebrated on the seventh Sunday after Easter.

Tongues

The apostles, gathered to celebrate Pentecost, were overcome by a religious ecstasy, which they attributed to the entry into them of the Holy Spirit—a manifestation promised them by Jesus just before the ascension, for Acts quotes Jesus as saying:

Acts 1:5. . . . *ye shall be baptized with the Holy Ghost not many days hence.*

The manifestation of the Holy Spirit at Pentecost took the form of ecstatic utterances:

Acts 2:4. *And they* [the apostles] *were all filled with the Holy Ghost, and began to speak with other tongues, as the Spirit gave them utterance.*

The utterance of incoherent sounds under the influence of religious ecstasy is an effect common to many religions. As an example, the Pythia, the priestess of Apollo at Delphi, gave forth incoherent utterances under the influence of the narcotic leaves she chewed and of the gases that issued from a volcanic vent. These were then interpreted by priests in such a way as to yield the oracles that the Greeks so valued.

This "gift of tongues" or, in Greek, "glossolalia" was a common feature of the ecstatic frenzies of the bands of prophets that were a feature of Israelite religious practices under the judges and the kings. In fact, such ecstatic and incoherent speech was what was usually meant by the term "to prophesy" in the early books of the Bible. The best known case, perhaps, is that of Saul, who, on meeting a band of prophets, caught their fervor (religious ecstasy is contagious) and joined them:

1 Samuel 10:10. . . . *a company of prophets met him* [Saul]; *and the Spirit of God came upon him, and he prophesied among them.*

Nor is the "gift of tongues" an ancient phenomenon only. In the emotion-filled gatherings of some Christian sects today, ecstatic events of one sort of another are common. The "Shakers," for instance, a sect that achieved some prominence in nineteenth-century America but is almost extinct today, were so called because they frequently went into convulsions in the course of their prayers and shook as they cried out incoherently. Sects in which exhibitions of the "gift of tongues" is frequent are often referred to as the "Pentecostal Churches" because of the fact that this incident during the apostles' celebration of Pentecost offered them their Biblical justification.

Parthians and Medes

The account in Acts brings the miraculous into this account of the "tongues" spoken by the apostles, by declaring that their utterances were understood by every one who heard them as being spoken in the listeners' native laguage. The audience is described:

Acts 2:5. *And there were dwelling at Jerusalem Jews, devout men, out of every nation under heaven.*

. . . .

Acts 2:9. *Parthians, and Medes, and Elamites, and the dwellers in Mesopotamia, and in Judaea, and Cappadocia, in Pontus, and Asia,*
Acts 2:10. *Phrygia, and Pamphylia, in Egypt, and in the parts of Libya about Cyrene, and strangers of Rome . . .*
Acts 2:11. *Cretes and Arabians . . .*

This list of nations represents, for the most part, a systematic sweep from east to west. First are the provinces of the Parthian Empire (then at the peak of its power), the borders of which lay not far to the east of Judea. The Parthians, who were the ruling group within the empire, had, as their native province, the northeastern section of what is now modern Iran, a province just southeast of the Caspian Sea.

Immediately to the west of Parthia proper, was Media, and south of Media was Susiana, the ancient Elam (see page I-455). To the west of Media and Elam was Mesopotamia, the ancient Babylonia. These various provinces made up the main portions of the Parthian Empire, and that brought the listing to Judea itself.

The list moves westward into Asia Minor, where five different **regions** are named: Cappadocia and Pontus are to be found in the eastern portion of that peninsula, while Asia, Phrygia, and Pamphylia are in the western portion.

Asia is a term which, in modern use, is applied to the entire vast continent of which Asia Minor is part. In Roman times, however, the "province of Asia" referred to the western third of the peninsula only, the area that had once been the kingdom of Pergamum (see page 74). Throughout the Book of Acts, the word "Asia" is to be understood in this sense. As for Phrygia, it had once been an independent kingdom centuries before, but now it was merely a name given to portions of the Asia Minor interior.

At the time of the apostles' Pentecost, all the regions of Asia Minor but Pontus were parts of the Roman Empire. Pontus remained in nominal independence under a puppet king for another generation. In A.D. 63, however, Nero made Pontus into a Roman province outright.

With the regions of Asia Minor northwest of Judea mentioned, the list moves to the southwest, to Egypt and Cyrene, and then to the far west—Rome. Crete and Arabia seem to be added as an afterthought.

While the list is lengthened as though to make extremely impressive the manner in which the apostles spoke (or, at least, were understood) in the language of "every nation under heaven," it might be argued that the list is not as impressive as it seems.

In Roman times, the Greek language had spread widely throughout the east and local native languages had been submerged into a kind of peasant patois. Jews living in those areas learned Greek. As an example, the Jews of Alexandria spoke Greek, not Egyptian.

It followed then that the Jews from Cappadocia, Pontus, Asia, Phrygia, Pamphylia, Egypt, Cyrene, Crete (and from Rome, too), all spoke Greek. Those from the Parthian provinces probably all spoke Aramaic, which was the language of trade and commerce in the regions to the east of the Greek-speaking areas, and which was the native language of Judea itself. In short, if the apostles knew at least some Greek in addition to their native Aramaic (and in those days it is very likely they did), and if, in their ecstasy, they uttered phrases in both languages, then all those who listened to them from the various nations listed, would have understood something. And in this way the account could be accepted without the necessity of a miracle.

Nevertheless, of course, believing Christians accept the incident as miraculous. So did the onlookers, if we accept the account in Acts, for many were converted to the belief in Jesus as Messiah following a speech by Peter:

Acts 2:41. *Then they that gladly received his [Peter's] word were baptized: and the same day there were added unto them about three thousand souls.*

Ananias

The early Christian community practiced a communism of property:

Acts 4:32. . . . *they had all things common.*
. . . .
Acts 4:34. *Neither was there any among them that lacked: for as many as were possessors of lands or houses sold them, and brought the prices of the things that were sold,*
Acts 4:35. *And laid them down at the apostles' feet: and distribution was made unto every man according as he had need.*

This idyllic picture of union and selflessness was not, however, without its flaws. Apparently, there were cases where some could not resist holding back at least a little from the common fund, though claiming, falsely, to have delivered the whole.

Acts 5:1. *But a certain man named Ananias, with Sapphira his wife, sold a possession,*
Acts 5:2. *And kept back part of the price, his wife also being privy to it, and brought a certain part, and laid it at the apostles' feet.*

Peter saw through the deception and rebuked first Ananias and then Sapphira, accusing each of lying. Each dropped dead upon being rebuked, and Ananias lives on in colloquial speech as a name applied to any liar.

Ananias is the Greek form of the Hebrew name Hananiah. It is an interesting coincidence that, of the fourteen individuals of that name mentioned in the Old Testament, the most considerable is a lying prophet. In the time of Jeremiah, the prophet Hananiah predicted the speedy liberation of the Jews from Babylonian imprisonment. Jeremiah quoted God as threatening Hananiah with death for lying:

Jeremiah 28:17. *So Hananiah the prophet died the same year in the seventh month.*

Gamaliel

That the Christians survived and expanded their influence under Peter was due, at least in part, to a division among the Jewish sects. The aristocratic Sadducees, pro-Roman and opposed to anything that might give rise to political or social unrest, viewed the activities of the apostles with alarm. The religious enthusiasms they aroused, and the atmosphere of revivalist intensity, seemed most dangerous to them.

Acts 5:17. *Then the high priest rose up, and all they that were with him, (which is the sect of the Sadducees,) and were filled with indignation . . .*

More than one attempt was made to imprison the apostles, especially their leader, Peter, and even condemn them to death.

Standing against the Sadducees, however, were the Pharisees. In almost all respects, the religious views of the early Christians were those of the Pharisees. The great dividing line at this time consisted chiefly of the fact that the Christians accepted Jesus as the Messiah and the Pharisees did not. It is quite likely that many of the Pharisees of the time felt that this belief in Jesus was an aberration that would soon die out and that the greater danger within Judaism was the Sadducee sect with whom the Pharisees had been feuding bitterly for about a century and a half.

To defend the apostles against the Sadducee-controlled council, there arose a leader among the Pharisees:

Acts 5:34. *Then stood there up one in the council, a Pharisee, named Gamaliel, a doctor of the law, had in reputation among all the people . . .*

Gamaliel was a grandson of Hillel (see page 145) and carried on the gentle teachings of his renowned grandfather. Gamaliel pointed out that there had been other leaders of popular uprisings in recent decades whose followers had been filled with Messianic hopes and that nothing had come of any of them:

Acts 5:36. *For before these days rose up Theudas, boasting himself to be somebody; . . . and all, as many as obeyed him, were scattered, and brought to nought.*

Acts 5:37. *After this man rose up Judas of Galilee in the days of the taxing . . . : he also perished . . .*

Gamaliel pointed out that the Christians would die out too, if their beliefs in Jesus were false, without the council having to take any action, any more than they did in the earlier cases. And if the Christian beliefs were indeed divinely inspired, then any action against them by the council would not only be futile, but also dangerous.

The council was persuaded and the apostles were allowed to continue their work. However, there was no permanent alliance between Christians and Pharisees. The issue of the Messiah-hood of Jesus was insuperable.

Gamaliel led the Pharisees till his death in A.D. 52. A number of his descendants continued to head the shattered Jewish community in Judea after Rome had wiped out all Jewish political power. The last of the line was Gamaliel VI, who died about A.D. 425.

Stephen

The growth of the Christian fellowship was bound to bring problems, and quite early two parties were formed.

One party consisted of Jews of Judea and Galilee, whose language was Aramaic and who carried on their religious observances in the traditional Hebrew. The other party consisted of Jews from outside Judea and Galilee and whose language was Greek, both in their daily lives and their devotions. These two parties can be distinguished on the basis of the language in which they worshipped and are referred to in Acts as Hebrews and Grecians, respectively.

It is understandable that the two groups should misunderstand each other. The Hebrew party could not help but feel that the age-old holy language of Hebrew was the proper one in which to pray and that the holy land of Israel was the proper surrounding in which to pray. To them, the Grecians would naturally seem like foreigners, half corrupted by the Gentiles, speaking a heathen language and tolerant toward pagan ways. The Grecian party, on the other hand, knowing more of the great outside world, would look upon the Hebrews as backward provincials whose narrow outlook was unfitting for the tasks ahead.

Acts 6:1. *And in those days, when the number of the disciples was multiplied, there arose a murmuring of the Grecians against the Hebrews, because their widows were neglected in the daily ministration.*

In other words, the Grecians claimed they were not receiving their fair share of the community income. Since the twelve apostles were all of the Hebrew group there might have been grounds for this complaint.

Had the apostles chosen to override these objections and to maintain a strictly Hebrew stand, the Grecians might have fallen away, and Christianity might have withered.

The apostles did not, however, do this. In a decision which, through hindsight, can be seen to have been statesman-like, they offered the Grecians special representation within the Christian fellowship by

allowing them seven leaders who would see to their fair treatment:

Acts 6:5. *And the saying pleased the whole multitude: and they chose Stephen . . . and Philip, and Prochorus, and Nicanor, and Timon, and Parmenas, and Nicolas . . .*

The leader of the Grecian seven was Stephen and he immediately began to be active in missionary labors among his Grecian fellows. Here he met with much opposition:

Acts 6:9. *Then there arose certain of the synagogue, which is called the synagogue of the Libertines, and Cyrenians, and Alexandrians, and of them of Cilicia and of Asia, disputing with Stephen.*

While the Temple was the one place of worship in Jerusalem, there were a number of synagogues in which Jews could gather to discuss the Law, dispute various points, and perhaps carry on their social affairs. It may not have been too different in essence from modern clubs.

Naturally, one would expect Jews of common background to group themselves into a particular synagogue. The Grecians would be happier with others who spoke Greek. Indeed, it might be that those from

Cilicia or Asia, speaking Greek with an Asia Minor accent, would frequent one, while those from Cyrene and Alexandria, speaking with an African accent, would frequent the other. (Cilicia, not mentioned earlier in the Bible, is a region occupying the eastern half of the southern coast of Asia Minor.)

It is not clear whether the "synagogue of the Libertines" represents still a third group, or whether it is the one to which (as the translation in the Jerusalem Bible would have it appear) the Jews of Cyrene and Alexandria belonged.

The word "Libertines," in modern English, refers to those who carry liberty to excess and allow no inhibitions to restrain their unbridled desires. We tend to think of libertines as wicked and lustful, and might consider it quite natural, therefore, for such people to oppose Stephen.

However, "Libertine" has an older meaning; it is applied to a person who has been enslaved but who has been freed, one who is more commonly called in modern terms a "freedman." And, indeed, the Revised Standard Version refers to the "synagog of the Freedmen" rather than to that of the Libertines.

It is thought that the synagogue may have consisted of descendants of Jews who had been taken prisoner by Pompey when he besieged and occupied Jerusalem a century before, and who had later been liberated. They or their descendants may have made their homes in Cyrene and Alexandria, the largest and most flourishing Jewish centers in all the Greek world, and this may have given the name to the synagogue of the Jews of Africa.

Stephen was brought before the council on the charge of blasphemy and, in his defense, he recited the early history of the Jews through the time of Moses, emphasizing the manner in which people in every age had rejected the prophets—even Moses himself—and ending in a furious outcry:

> Acts 7:51. *Ye stiffnecked and uncircumcised in heart and ears, ye do always resist the Holy Ghost; as your fathers did, so do ye.*
> Acts 7:52. *Which of the prophets have not your fathers persecuted? . . .*

Such a defense could scarcely win over his audience and, to top that off, Stephen then committed that which seemed clear blasphemy in the view of his audience. He virtually repeated Jesus' statement under similar conditions. Jesus had said:

Matthew 26:64. . . . *Hereafter shall ye see the Son of man sitting on the right hand of power . . .*

referring to Daniel's statement which had been accepted as Messianic (see page I-610).

And Stephen said:

Acts 7:56. . . . *Behold, I see the heavens opened, and the Son of man standing on the right hand of God.*

Stephen was promptly condemned to death by stoning and the sentence was carried through.

This event may have taken place in A.D. 31, two years after the crucifixion, and Stephen ranks as the first Christian martyr. The first man recorded as dying for the new faith, which held Jesus to be the Messiah predicted by the Old Testament prophets, was of the Grecian party. The pendulum was beginning its swing.

Philip

Stephen's death was followed by vigorous action against the Christians in Jerusalem. Many were forced to leave, for safety's sake. Included among these was Philip, the second of the seven leaders of the Grecian party. (He is the only one besides Stephen of whom the Bible has anything more to say than an inclusion in the list of the seven.)

The Philip mentioned here is the second of the two prominent Philips of the New Testament. The first is Philip the apostle, a Galilean and therefore of the Hebrew party. He is mentioned in all four lists of the apostles, including the one in the first chapter of Acts. Except for these listings, he does not appear in the synoptic gospels or in Acts, but is involved in several incidences in the gospel according to St. John.

The second Philip, the one who figures in Acts, is called Philip the evangelist because he preached the gospel outside Judea and won converts. Thus, in the immediate aftermath of Stephen's stoning:

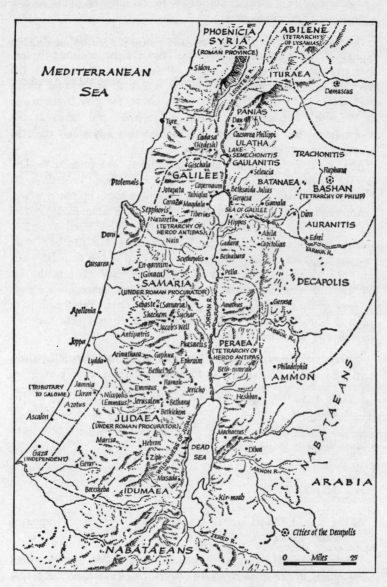

Palestine: The Time of Christ

Acts 8:5. . . . *Philip went down to the city of Samaria, and preached Christ unto them.*

If this verse refers to the city of Samaria that had been the capital of the Northern Kingdom of Israel eight centuries before, that city no longer existed as such. It had been destroyed by the Assyrians and had dragged on thereafter as a small and squalid village until it was finally rebuilt by Herod the Great. He gave it the name of "Sebaste," a Greek word meaning "revered" and taken as the equivalent of the Latin "Augusta," so that that city was named in honor of the emperor, Augustus.

Actually, though, it is not likely that Philip went to Sebaste. The Revised Standard Version translates the verse "Philip went down to a city of Samaria"; some unnamed Samaritan city, in other words.

Apparently, the followers of Jesus had by now been made to feel such heretics by the Jewish authorities, that they found a certain kinship with those other heretics, the Samaritans. The situation is no longer what it was in Jesus' lifetime (as depicted in the gospels) when any approach to the Samaritans on the part of Jesus was a matter for surprise and even disapproval on the part of his disciples.

Now, when Philip began to garner conversions, Peter and John went to Samaria, without apparent hesitation, to complete the conversions and make them official:

Acts 8:17. *Then laid they* [Peter and John] *their hands on them* [the Samaritan converts], *and they received the Holy Ghost.*

In this way, the Samaritans were accepted as Christians in the fullest sense, on a plane of complete equality with Christians of orthodox Jewish origin. This was an important step in the growth of Christianity out of its Jewish swaddling clothes.

Simon Magus

At the time of Philip's arrival, the Samaritans were already impressed with another leader:

Acts 8:9. *But there was a certain man, called Simon, which beforetime in the same city used sorcery, and bewitched the people of Samaria, giving out that himself was some great one.*

Because of this verse, this man is usually identified as Simon the Sorcerer, or Simon Magus (to distinguish him from Simon Peter). We might suppose that he was some healer, preaching much as the apostles did. Such activities are always called divinely inspired by friends, and sorcery by foes. (The Pharisees accused Jesus of sorcery and if their views had won out, he might conceivably have gone down in history as Jesus Magus.)

Simon Magus was himself converted to Christianity by Philip and underwent baptism. When Peter and John arrived as the accepted authorities, by virtue of their rank as apostles, to make such conversion official, Simon attempted to gain equal rights and privileges. Perhaps he felt that as apostolic representative in Samaria, with full powers, he could continue his older activities under a new name and retain whatever worldly power and prestige that had given him. He offered, therefore, to buy the right:

Acts 8:18. .... he [Simon] offered them [Peter and John] money,

Acts 8:19. Saying, Give me also this power, that on whomsoever I lay hands, he may receive the Holy Ghost.

It was not after all an uncommon practice to buy religious office. The high priesthood in Jerusalem was bought and sold in Seleucid times (see page 98) and in the times of the Romans; and the practice was undoubtedly common in all religions.

But Simon is roundly rebuked on this occasion by Peter. Nevertheless, the practice of buying religious office has not been unknown in the history of Christianity, and a special name has been given this practice —"simony," from Simon Magus, because of this passage.

The Bible says nothing more about Simon Magus, but he figures largely in the tales transmitted by the early Christian writers. He is supposed to have fallen out of the mainstream of Christianity, to have founded Christian Gnosticism (see page 301), to have continued to use magic and to have opposed Peter and Paul, in later years, by his sorcerers' tricks, with consequences fatal to himself.

The Simonians, a heretical sect that endured for some two centuries, are traced back to Simon Magus. We have only the writings of the early Christians as testimonials to Simonian beliefs and, as can easily be imagined, those testimonials are unfavorable indeed.

Candace

Feeling himself to have completed his task in Samaria, Philip traveled southward to Gaza, which had once been one of the five chief cities of the Philistines in the time of David. There he met a stranger from a far land:

> Acts 8:27. . . . *a man of Ethiopia, an eunuch of great authority under Candace queen of the Ethiopians, who had the charge of all her treasure, and had come to Jerusalem for to worship* . . .

Ethiopia was the name given by the Greeks to the land along the Nile immediately south of Egypt, beyond the river's first cataract. That name is applied nowadays to Abyssinia, which is actually some five hundred miles southeast of the ancient Ethiopia. The region known as Ethiopia to the ancients makes up the northernmost portion of the modern nation of Sudan and might best be termed Nubia.

Philip met, in other words, a Nubian, from the land south of Egypt.

Nubia's earliest history is that of an appendage of Egypt. The Egyptians traded with Nubia and under the strong Egyptian pharaohs, Nubia was conquered and occupied for centuries at a time. Nubia, under pharaonic domination, accepted Egyptian culture and religion but never quite gave up its memory of political independence.

After the disastrous invasions of the Peoples of the Sea (see page I-131), which occurred at the time of the Exodus, Egypt's power shrank permanently, and Nubia broke free. It formed an independent kingdom (still Egyptian in culture and religion) with its capital at Napata, a city on the Nile River about four hundred miles upstream from Egypt's southern boundary.

About 750 B.C. (toward the end of Uzziah's reign in Judah), Nubia came under the rule of a chieftain named Kashta. Under him, Nubia reached the peak of its power and this came just as Egypt was sinking toward a low point. Kashta conquered southern Egypt and established himself as a new pharaoh of what historians call the Twenty-fifth Dynasty. (This is sometimes known as the Ethiopian Dynasty, though Nubian Dynasty would be better.) Kashta's successor, Piankhi, conquered the rest of Egypt in 736 B.C.

This Nubian Dynasty played a significant role in Judean history.

When Sennacherib was laying siege to Jerusalem in 701 B.C., Egypt (in its own self-interest) raised an army against the Assyrian monarch. This army was under the leadership of Taharqa, a prince of the Nubian Dynasty, who, eleven years later, was to ascend the throne of Egypt. He is referred to in 2 Kings as Tirhaka (see page I-384). His campaign against Sennacherib could not be considered as better than a draw, but that was enough to induce the Assyrian (fighting at the end of a long line of communications) to withdraw and attend to pressing needs closer to home. The Nubian Dynasty, therefore, helped in a very material way to preserve Jerusalem.

Sennacherib's successor, Esarhaddon, did better. He reduced Judah to the role of a quiet tributary under Manasseh and then, by 661 B.C., drove the Nubian Dynasty out of Egypt. For twenty years Assyrian garrisons ruled Egypt. Egypt then regained its independence, but under native monarchs. The Nubians never returned.

To make sure that they would not, the native pharaohs of the Twenty-sixth Dynasty established the fort at Elephantine, manned by Jewish mercenaries (see page I-571). These guarded the Nile against incursions by Nubians from the south. Indeed, the Egyptians took the offensive and, about 590 B.C., sacked Napata itself.

From that point on, Nubia remained in isolation (except for a possible Persian raid in 522 B.C.) and slowly declined. Although Nubia continued to cling to the Egyptian religion, Judaism must have penetrated somewhat. Jews from Elephantine may have settled in Nubia or gained converts there. Some of these, whether Jews by birth or conversion, may have undertaken the long trip to Jerusalem to worship at the Temple, as the one true place of worship, just as Moslems today undertake the pilgrimage to Mecca as often as they can.

The eunuch met by Philip was, therefore, a Jew, though whether by birth and descent, or by conversion, the Bible does not say.

In Roman times, Nubia maintained its independence and was ruled by several energetic queens. The Nubian word for queen was rendered by the Greeks as Kandake and by the Romans and ourselves as Candace. This name was applied to all the queens of Nubia at this time.

The most important of these was one who, at the time that Augustus took over Egypt and made it a Roman province, dared invade Egypt. Perhaps she thought that the confusion of the Roman takeover would render Egypt easy pickings.

If so, she was wrong. A Roman army under Gaius Petronius marched southward and sacked Napata in 22 B.C. It would have been Roman policy in the days before Augustus to annex Nubia, but Augustus favored a policy of peace whenever possible. Nubia was evacuated and allowed to retain its independence. It did not attempt any futher adventures northward, however.

A successor of this Candace who had opposed the Romans (a successor also known as Candace) was the "queen of the Ethiopians" of Acts 8:27. She employed a Jewish eunuch as treasurer, and it was this Jewish treasurer of Nubia that Philip met.

The Nubian Jew was reading a passage from Isaiah when Philip met him. Philip interpreted the passage for him in a Messianic sense, applying it to Jesus. The Nubian forthwith asked to be converted and, presumably, carried the Christian message with him to his homeland.

It is interesting that in this case, Peter and John were not there to make the conversion official. The situation was beginning to slip out of the control of apostolic leadership and of the Hebrew party whose power centered in Jerusalem. It was to continue to do so.

Saul of Tarsus

But the greatest Grecian of all was at hand, one who far surpassed Stephen and Philip in his impact upon history. He was a man named Saul, and he began his career as a firm opponent of the followers of Jesus.

Saul was a member of the tribe of Benjamin and had his share of the Jewish stock of nationalist pride, as can be seen from his self-description in his Epistle to the Philippians:

> Philippians 3:4. *Circumcised the eighth day, of the stock of Israel, of the tribe of Benjamin, an Hebrew of the Hebrews* . . .

It is not surprising that, as a child of a staunch Benjamite family, he was given the name of the greatest Benjamite in history, King Saul. At least King Saul had been the greatest Benjamite till the coming of this new Saul.

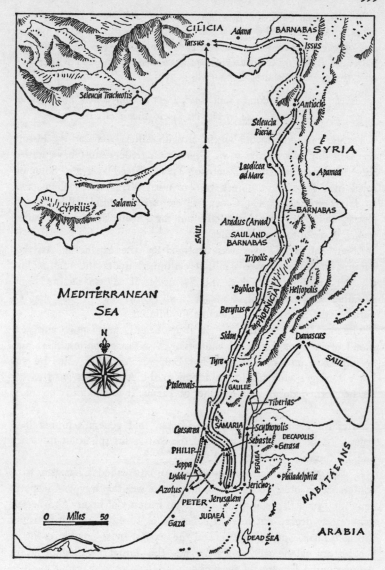

Journeys of the Apostles

Yet although Saul describes himself as a "Hebrew of the Hebrews" (that is, not only a Jew but a Jew by birth—the son of Jews) he was not of the Hebrew group of the early Christians for he was not a native of Judea or Galilee. He was born instead in Asia Minor and was, therefore, of the Grecian group:

Acts 21:39. . . . *Paul* [Saul] *said, I am a man which am a Jew of Tarsus, a city in Cilicia, a citizen of no mean city* . . .

Tarsus was indeed the largest city in Cilicia. Its earliest history was probably as a Hittite town. Phoenician traders must have settled there in the great days of Hiram of Tyre (when David and Solomon ruled over Israel) and Greek traders must have arrived there, too. In later centuries, when Greek culture became fashionable, Tarsus always claimed to be a Greek city, but the Phoenician tinge remained strong down into Roman times.

About 850 B.C. Tarsus was captured by the expanding Assyrian Empire, and after Assyria's fall, it continued under the rule of first the Persian kings and then the Seleucids. It always retained considerable self-government, however, and in 171 B.C. it was granted virtual independence by Antiochus IV himself.

The next two centuries saw it at its height, prosperous, cultured, proud of its Greekness, and containing a group of philosophers and an important university as well. The Emperor Augustus, when he was but a teenager, studying on an island in the Aegean Sea, had as his teacher, Athenodorus, a philosopher of Tarsus. It was indeed "no mean city."

After the assassination of Julius Caesar, that general's former lieutenant, Mark Antony, was awarded the east as his sphere of influence and he took up residence in Tarsus.

It was while at Tarsus that Mark Antony called Cleopatra to a conference in order to extract money from wealthy Egypt. Cleopatra came to Tarsus in a ship fitted out to an extreme of luxury and herself deliberately decked out in such a fashion as to entrance the pleasure-loving Roman. She succeeded, and the second most notable event in the history of the city of Tarsus was this initial meeting of Mark Antony and Cleopatra in its harbor.

More important still was a happening that went completely unnoticed in its time. Since Tarsus was an important trading center, it gathered a colony of Jews which grew and prospered. In a particular year which is completely unknown but which we might venture to guess to have been A.D. 10, Saul of Tarsus was born there, and that was indeed the most notable event in the city's history.

Saul's family was apparently of considerable account. They were, for one thing, Roman citizens, and they may have been rich enough to purchase the citizenship. The citizenship was often awarded for some service rendered Rome, but it might also be sold—as has been the case, for instance, with knighthoods in English history. The Bible does not say which was true in the case of Saul's family, but whatever the situation, Saul himself inherited the status and was a citizen by birth.

Roman citizenship was worth having in New Testament times, for it carried not only prestige and status, but certain important privileges as well.

Thus, at one time, when Saul was on the point of being whipped, he took advantage of a Roman citizen's immunity to corporal punishment without trial. He said to the Roman soldier with the whip:

Acts 22:25. . . . *Is it lawful for you to scourge a man that is a Roman, and uncondemned?*

The centurion at once reported this to his captain, who promptly questioned the prisoner:

Acts 22:27. *Then the chief captain came, and said unto him* [Saul], *Tell me, art thou a Roman? He* [Saul] *said, Yea.*

The chief captain proudly announced that he too was a Roman, having paid through the nose for it, and Saul quietly topped him by announcing himself as a citizen by birth:

Acts 22:28. *And the chief captain answered, With a great sum obtained I this freedom. And Paul* [Saul] *said, But I was free born.*

Saul was promptly spared the whipping, saved by his citizenship.

Very little is known of Saul's relatives. He himself seems never to have married and so had no children. He did, however, have at least a sister and a nephew, for they are referred to:

Acts 23:16. . . . *when Paul's* [Saul's] *sister's son heard of their lying in wait, he . . . told Paul* [Saul].

The prosperity of Saul's family might well be further indicated by the fact that they could afford to send their son to Judea for a thorough religious training in Jerusalem itself.

As a result of this, Paul gained a good knowledge of Aramaic (unlike many of the Grecian faction); good enough so that he could not only understand Aramaic commentaries on the Scripture but could actually converse and preach in the language. This bilingual ability gained him considerably more influence with the native population of Judea than he might otherwise have had:

Acts 21:40. . . . *Paul* [Saul] *. . . beckoned with the hand unto the people. And where there was made a great silence, he spake unto them in the Hebrew tongue* [Aramaic] *. . .*

. . . .

Acts 22:2. (*And when they heard that he spake in the Hebrew tongue to them, they kept the more silence . . .*

In Jerusalem, Saul attached himself to none other than Gamaliel, the leading Pharisee of the time and the one who had advocated toleration for the Christians (see page 342). Thus, Saul says:

Acts 22:3. *I am . . . a Jew, born in Tarsus . . . yet brought up in this city* [Jerusalem] *at the feet of Gamaliel, and taught according to the perfect manner of the law of the fathers . . .*

And, of course, Saul became a Pharisee in consequence, as he himself admits, for in the same verse in which he describes himself as an Hebrew of the Hebrews, he adds that he is:

Philippians 3:4. . . . *as touching the law, a Pharisee.*

In the course of his career, Saul did not scruple to gain the support of the Pharisees by declaring himself to be one of them in philosophy, as opposed to the Sadducee factions. Standing before the council, he shrewdly gained the support of the Pharisee group by saying:

Acts 23:6. . . . *Men and brethren, I am a Pharisee, the son of a Pharisee . . .*

Perhaps his family's wealth was not quite sufficient to maintain Saul in idleness throughout his years as a student. He may well have had to, at least in part, "work his way through college" so to speak. If he did so, it was through labor at a craft. He was a working-man as well as a scholar. This craft is referred to when, in his travels, Saul is housed by certain members of the same craft:

Acts 18:3. . . . *because he was of the same craft, he abode with them, and wrought; for by their occupation they were tent-makers.*

This line of work may perhaps more properly be termed that of "weaver," for it is unlikely to have been so specialized as to be limited to tents alone, particularly since he practiced his calling in Greek towns, where there could scarcely have been much call for tents as such. The craft may even have been that of Paul's family generally, for Tarsus was famous for the weaving of cloth made from goat's hair, a cloth known as "cilicium" after the region in which Tarsus was located.

Saul, in his youth, was a thoroughgoing Pharisee and completely opposed to the views of those who believed Jesus to be the Messiah. Presumably, Saul attended the synagogue which was attended by "them of Cilicia and of Asia" (see page 344), for he was himself of Cilicia by birth. No doubt, he disputed with Stephen, and may even have been foremost among those who denounced him. Certainly he was a prominent member of the executing crowd.

The witnesses against Stephen had the duty of casting the first stones, according to the Mosaic Law:

Deuteronomy 17:7. *The hands of the witnesses shall be first upon him* [the condemned] *to put him to death . . .*

The witnesses, in taking care of this duty, discarded their outermost garments in order that their arms might be free to throw.

Acts 7:58. . . . *and the witnesses laid down their clothes at a young man's feet, whose name was Saul . . .*
. . . .
Acts 8:1. *And Saul was consenting unto his* [Stephen's] *death . . .*

This is the first mention of Saul in Acts and quite clearly he must have cast his share of the stones after the witnesses had cast the first.

What's more, Saul led those forces which then instituted a persecution of the Christians:

Acts 8:3. *As for Saul, he made havock of the church, entering into every house and haling men and women committed them to prison.*

In his later life, he refers on a number of occasions to this early period when he persecuted the sect of which he was afterward to be the greatest supporter. He says, for instance, in the Epistle to the Galatians:

> Galatians 1:13. *For ye had heard . . . how that beyond measure I persecuted the church of God, and wasted it.*

Damascus

Saul was not content to carry on his zealous hounding of the Christians in Jerusalem, or even in Judea. Apparently the new sect was making its appearance among Jewish congregations in cities outside Judea. Saul wanted authority to travel to such cities and wipe out Christianity there:

> Acts 9:1. *And Saul . . . went unto the high priest,*
> Acts 9:2. *And desired of him letters to Damascus to the synagogues, that if he found any of this way* [Christians] *. . . he might bring them bound unto Jerusalem.*

In this way, Damascus re-enters the stream of Biblical history. In the time of the kingdoms it had been the capital of a nation that had been an important enemy of Israel, but after its destruction by Assyria in 732 B.C., its importance vanished. It came under the control, successively, of the Assyrians, Chaldeans, and Persians. After the time of Alexander the Great, it was held sometimes by the Ptolemies, sometimes by the Seleucids.

The Romans took it in 64 B.C., but in A.D. 31 they allowed it considerable autonomy under the control of the Arabian kinglet, Aretas —the same one who fought with Herod Antipas over the latter's divorce and remarriage (see page 152) and who now, in Saul's time, was approaching the end of a long, half century reign.

Near Damascus, however, Saul underwent an unusual experience:

> Acts 9:3. *. . . as he* [Saul] *. . . came near Damascus . . . there shined round about him a light from heaven:*
> Acts 9:4. *And he fell to the earth, and heard a voice saying unto him, Saul, Saul, why persecutest thou me?*

Acts 9:5. *And he* [Saul] *said, Who art thou, Lord? And the Lord said, I am Jesus whom thou persecutest* . . .

Saul was blinded by the vision and had to be led into Damascus, where he remained blind for three days. His sight was then restored at the touch of a Christian disciple in Damascus.

As a result, Saul was converted to Christianity, becoming as fanatical an upholder of the belief as, earlier, he had been fanatical in opposing it. (This is by no means uncommon in conversions.) The year in which this conversion took place is not known; estimates range from A.D. 32 (the year after Stephen's death) to A.D. 36.

Saul at once began to preach Christian doctrine in Damascus, to the surprise of all who knew of his reputation as an anti-Christian fanatic. His successes were apparently great; great enough to cause those Jews who remained unconverted to believe Saul deserved death for blasphemy.

Acts 9:23. *And after that many days were fulfilled, the Jews took counsel to kill him* . . .

Acts does not say how long Saul remained in Damascus beyond the vague "many days." In the Epistle to the Galatians, however, Saul says of this period:

Galatians 1:17. *. . . I went into Arabia, and returned again unto Damascus.*

Galatians 1:18. *Then after three years I went up to Jerusalem* . . .

So we may take it that for three years, Saul pondered the new doctrine (spending some time in quiet introspection in the semidesert region east of Damascus—referred to here as "Arabia"). Gradually he developed his own approach.

Perhaps he might have remained longer in Damascus and its environs, were it not that danger was growing acute. Saul eventually had to go into hiding in order that the indignant Jews of Damascus might not arrest him and place him on trial. In fact, it grew necessary to get him out of the city altogether and this was a rather difficult task.

Acts 9:24. *. . . they* [Saul's enemies] *watched the gates day and night to kill him.*

Acts 9:25. *Then the disciples took him by night, and let him down by the wall in a basket.*

The matter must have been more, however, than a purely doctrinal dispute between Jews and Christians. Damascus may have had a strong contingent of Jews but it was largely a Gentile city and it was under Gentile rule. The Jews could not, of their own authority, have guarded the gates. Apparently Paul's activities also disturbed King Aretas, and it was his soldiers who searched for Saul.

Saul himself, in describing this episode, says:

2 Corinthians 11:32. *In Damascus the governor under Aretas the king kept the city of the Damascenes with a garrison, desirous to apprehend me:*
2 Corinthians 11:33. *And through a window in a basket was I let down by the wall and escaped his hands.*

Barnabas

Saul returned to Jerusalem now and tried to join the Christian community there. He failed at first, since the disciples were very naturally suspicious of the erstwhile persecutor. Saul needed a sponsor and found one:

Acts 9:27. *But Barnabas took him [Saul] and brought him to the apostles and declared unto them how he [Saul] had seen the Lord . . .*

Barnabas was mentioned earlier in Acts in connection with the communism of the early Christian fellowship. In contradistinction to Ananias, who tried to gain the credit of a total contributor to the welfare fund, while secretly holding back some, Barnabas gave all:

Acts 4:36. *And Joses [Joseph], who by the apostles was surnamed Barnabas, (which is, being interpreted, The son of consolation,) a Levite, and of the country of Cyprus,*
Acts 4:37. *Having land, sold it, and brought the money, and laid it at the apostles' feet.*

It was perhaps this act that caused him to receive the surname of Barnabas, since in those infant days of the community, both the money itself and the appreciation of the feeling of confidence that lay behind the award, must have been consolation indeed.

Barnabas was another of the Grecian group, having been born on the island of Cyprus. He may well have felt a strong feeling of kinship to Saul, for their birthplaces were not very far apart. Cyprus is just off the Cilician seacoast, and the northeastern tip of the island is only about a hundred miles south of Tarsus.

James the Lord's Brother

Acts says little about what Saul did, specifically, after being introduced to the apostles, but Saul himself in his Epistle to the Galatians says:

> Galatians 1:18. . . . I went up to Jerusalem to see Peter, and abode with him fifteen days.
> Galatians 1:19. But other of the apostles saw I none, save James the Lord's brother.

Paul, in other words, saw the two leading Christians. Peter, as the chief of the original band of twelve apostles, might be considered the nearest worldly representative of the memory of Jesus. It was James "the Lord's brother," however, who seems to have been the actual administrative head of the Jerusalem branch of the fellowship—of the "Mother Church," so to speak.

James was not one of the original apostles. Indeed, on the testimony of the fourth gospel, he was a doubter during Jesus' ministry:

> John 7:5. For neither did his [Jesus'] brethren believe in him.

Nevertheless, he apparently came to be a believer by the time of the crucifixion or immediately afterward, for the gathering of the early disciples before the great day of Pentecost included:

> Acts 1:14. . . . the women, and Mary the mother of Jesus, and . . . his [Jesus'] brethren.

James's conversion to belief may have come about through a sight of the resurrected Jesus. At least Paul, in his First Epistle to the Corinthians lists him among the witnesses to the resurrection:

> 1 Corinthians 15:5. And . . . he was seen of Cephas [Peter], then of the twelve:
> . . . .
> 1 Corinthians 15:7. After that, he was seen of James; then of all the apostles.

Presumably, the James mentioned here might be James son of Zebedee or James son of Alphaeus, each one a member of the original band of twelve. However, it is generally accepted that when Acts refers to James, without qualification, they mean Jesus' younger brother. (Again, it should be pointed out that those Christians who accept the belief that Mary, the mother of Jesus, was a perpetual virgin, consider James to be Jesus' cousin or half brother, rather than his brother.)

From Peter and James, Saul, it may be assumed, gathered many details concerning Jesus' ministry and person.

There is always dispute as to whether Saul ever actually saw Jesus in the latter's lifetime. It is not known when Saul arrived in Jerusalem for his education. If he arrived three or four years before his appearance at the stoning of Stephen, as is not at all unlikely, then he would have been in Jerusalem in the hectic week preceding the crucifixion. If he did, it would be almost certain that he would have been among the crowds listening to Jesus' words (and Saul, it might reasonably be assumed, would have been loud in his angry denunciations of Jesus).

And yet even if Saul had been in Jerusalem at that time, and had been among the crowds around Jesus, he might always have been far back and unable to catch a real glimpse. Certainly, if he had met Jesus face to face in the course of the latter's ministry, Saul would have said so in one of his epistles, and he does not.

Most commentators conclude that Saul never actually met Jesus in the flesh, and, if so, the meeting with Peter and James must have been particularly important to Saul. We can well imagine him asking eagerly after the personal memories of these two close associates of the Jesus whom Saul now accepted as the Messiah.

In Jerusalem, Saul continued to preach Christian doctrine ardently and was soon in danger again. The anti-Christian elements must have been particularly resentful over the loss of so valued a member and have chafed at the Christian victory in gaining so notable a defector. Again it was felt that Saul could gain safety only in flight:

Acts 9:30. . . . *the brethren . . . brought him* [Saul] *down to Caesarea, and sent him forth to Tarsus.*

This may have been anywhere from A.D. 34 to 38, depending on when it was that Saul's conversion occurred. Saul remained in Tarsus a lengthy time but exactly how lengthy a time can only be deduced from fragmentary evidence. The best guess seems to be from eight to ten years.

Nothing is known concerning this period except that Saul presumably carried on his preaching in Cilicia. He himself says merely:

> Galatians 1:21. *Afterwards I came into the regions of Syria and Cilicia;*
>
> Galatians 1:22. *And was unknown by face unto the churches of Judaea . . .*
>
> Galatians 1:23. *But they had heard only, That he which persecuted us in times past now preacheth the faith . . .*

Lydda

The general persecution of the followers of Jesus that had been set off after the stoning of Stephen had by now eased up, and apparently there were groups of Christians in Galilee, as well as in Samaria and Judea:

> Acts 9:31. *Then had the churches rest throughout all Judaea and Galilee and Samaria . . .*

Peter, as the spiritual leader of the Christians, felt it safe now to travel through the area, visiting the various groups:

> Acts 9:32. . . . *as Peter passed throughout all quarters, he came down also to . . . Lydda.*

Lydda is the Greek form of the Hebrew, Lod, and is a town mentioned only a few times, and then inconsequentially, in the Old Testament. It is on the main road from Jerusalem to the seaport of Joppa, about twenty-two miles from the former and only ten miles from the latter.

Although Lydda was only an unimportant village in Old Testament times, and was to become an unimportant village again after the Jewish rebellion, it was passing through a brief period of consequence in New Testament times. It was large and prosperous and was a respected seat of learning.

Perhaps Lydda's most important claim to fame (aside from this mention in Acts) is that it was the home of a legendary Christian hero who slew a dragon and saved a young lady whom the dragon was about to eat, some time during the period of the Roman Empire. (Oddly enough, this is very like the Greek tale of Perseus and Androm-eda—see page I-414—which was supposed to have taken place at Joppa. Could the Christian legend have been borrowed from the Greek?) In any case, the dragon-slaying hero is the St. George who is now con-sidered the patron saint of England.

Lydda exists today as a sizable town of twenty-one thousand in modern Israel.

Cornelius

The most significant event in Peter's journey took place at Caesarea. This was Judea's chief port, about thirty miles north of Joppa. There the Roman power was chiefly concentrated, and there the procurators generally held their seat.

> Acts 10:1. *There was a certain man in Caesarea called Cornelius, a centurion . . .*
>
> Acts 10:2. *A devout man, and one that feared God . . . gave much alms . . . and prayed to God alway.*

Apparently, although Cornelius was strongly attracted to Jewish doc-trine, he was not accepted fully into the Jewish fellowship because he had not yet undergone circumcision, the indispensable initiating rite to Judaism. That this is so is indicated by the fact that when Cornelius hears that Peter is in Joppa and sends for him, Peter hesitates about accepting the invitation. He says:

> Acts 10:28. . . . *Ye know how that it is an unlawful thing for a man that is a Jew to keep company, or come unto one of another nation . . .*

This does not include ordinary contact, of course, but does involve the matter of dining with a Gentile. The complex dietary laws of the Jews are not followed by the Gentiles and for a Jew to dine with a Gentile would cause him to eat food that was ritually unclean and this would be a grave infraction of the Mosaic Law.

Peter, we can well imagine, was torn between two courses. As a good Jew, he was horrified at the thought of eating with a Gentile. On the other hand, as a good Christian, it was quite apparent that a conversion was in the air and a conversion that was too good to turn down lightly. Cornelius is described in Acts as a pious man and he was a Roman soldier. For a Roman soldier to become Christian would be a great victory for the cause and as a centurion, an officer, he could doubtless influence other conversions. Did Peter have a right to toss away such an opportunity lightly—and perhaps even make an enemy of an important soldier in so doing?

The decision was in favor of the centurion despite his status as Gentile, and Acts explains that decision in terms of a vision seen by a Peter in which the Jewish division of food into ritually clean and unclean is abolished. Now Peter could freely eat with a Gentile. And Peter did more:

Acts 10:48. *And he [Peter] commanded them to be baptized in the name of the Lord* . . .

This was an important and even crucial step. Until this point, all Christians had taken the Mosaic Law as the basis of their faith. To them Jesus had appeared as the climax and fulfillment of that Law. In Matthew's version of the gospel, Jesus is quoted as saying:

Matthew 5:17. *Think not that I am come to destroy the law* . . . *I am not come to destroy, but to fulfil.*

Those who had accepted Christianity until now, had been Jews either by birth or by conversion, or Samaritans. The Samaritans might be heretics who did not believe in worshipping at Jerusalem but they did accept the Mosaic Law. Even the Nubian eunuch baptized by Philip accepted the Mosaic Law, since he worshipped at the Temple at Jerusalem and no one could do so without being circumcised.

Here, though, Peter had eaten with a heathen who, however devout and well disposed toward Judaism and Christianity, was not circumcised. Furthermore, Peter had allowed a man to become a Christian without having first become a Jew—he had short-circuited the Mosaic Law, so to speak.

This did not sit well with the Christians of Jerusalem:

Acts 11:2. . . . *when Peter was come up to Jerusalem, they that were of the circumcision contended with him,*
Acts 11:3. *Saying, Thou wentest in to men uncircumcised, and didst eat with them.*

Peter explained his side of the matter and Acts makes it appear that this explanation won over the rest:

> Acts 11:18. When they [the dissatisfied disciples] heard these things, they held their peace, and glorified God, saying, Then hath God also to the Gentiles granted repentance unto life.

But this may not be a fair representation of events. The writer of Acts is Luke, a Gentile, and he presents a pro-Gentile view which would tend to minimize the role of the Hebrew group and soft-pedal their anti-Gentile prejudices. It may well be that Peter was not so easy a victor and that he was forced to back-track by the Hebrew group under James, the brother of Jesus. Thus, in the Epistle to the Galatians, Peter is criticized for weakness:

> Galatians 2:12. For before that certain [emissaries] came from James, he [Peter] did eat with the Gentiles: but when they were come, he withdrew and separated himself, fearing them which were of the circumcision.

Even if Peter backed down, it is scarcely likely that the conversion of Cornelius and his friends was revoked. Perhaps we might speculate that the conversion was allowed to stand provided that those converted submitted to circumcision and to other necessary ritual. And perhaps Peter promised to be more careful in the future. Certainly, no further conversions by Peter are mentioned.

Nevertheless, a Gentile had been converted and Christianity had made its first cautious step beyond the bounds of the Mosaic Law.

Antioch

What was difficult for Peter to do within Judea under the strict eyes of the Jerusalem community of Christians, was easier for those Christians who were far away. Those who had been scattered after the stoning of Stephen had been baptizing, as Philip had done, but sometimes in a carefully limited way:

> Acts 11:19. Now they which were scattered abroad . . . travelled as far as Phenice [Phoenicia] and Cyprus and Antioch, preaching the word to none but unto the Jews only.

Others, however, did more:

Acts 11:20. *And some of them were men of Cyprus and Cyrene, which, when they were come to Antioch, spake unto the Grecians* . . .

Acts 11:21. . . . . *and a great number* [of the Grecians] *believed* . . .

Here the word "Grecians" in 11:20 is clearly intended to be opposed to the "Jews only" of the verse before, so that it can be taken that Greeks, or perhaps Greek-speaking Syrians, were being proselytized and were being converted directly to Christianity.

In Antioch, the church began to take on, for the first time, not only a Grecian, but a Gentile tinge. It is not surprising, then, that it was in Antioch that the followers of Jesus were first really noticed by the Gentiles and were first given a distinct Greek name:

Acts 11:26. . . . . *And the disciples were called Christians first in Antioch.*

Antioch, the capital city of the Seleucid king, Antiochus IV, the great villain of the Maccabean revolt, thus became the first major center of Christianity outside Judea, and the birthplace of the word by which the world's dominant religion of today came ever after to be known. The name may have first been applied to the followers of Jesus as a derisive insult shouted out by unconverted Gentile opponents. If so, the call of derision came to be accepted by the disciples as a badge of honor. It is not the only time in history that an insult has been accepted by the insulted and made clean. The name of the modern sect of "Quakers" is an example of that phenomenon too. "Quaker" originated as a term of ridicule.

The developing church at Antioch quickly grew to be of crucial importance. Although Antioch was no longer the capital of a great independent kingdom, it remained a huge and wealthy city of some half million population. In New Testament times, it was the third largest city in the empire, with only Rome itself and Alexandria larger. The church in Antioch was bound to be more prosperous than the churches in Judea, for even Jerusalem, however important it might seem to Biblically minded Jews, was only a provincial town in comparison to a place like Antioch.

As a matter of fact, Antioch remained a great city throughout the

period of the Roman Empire, but it never recovered from an earthquake and a Persian sack in the sixth century A.D. Today it is part of
the modern nation of Turkey, bearing the still-recognizable name of
Antakya and with a population of nearly fifty thousand.

The leaders at Jerusalem, upon hearing reports of growing numbers
of conversions in Antioch, might well have felt uneasy. Were these
conversions, far from their own careful oversight, only of Gentiles who
agreed to be circumcised and uphold the Mosaic Law, or were they
not?

Then, too, we might imagine them wondering whether it was wise
to allow Antioch to go its way uncontrolled. A swelling Christian
community in a city fully three hundred miles north of Jerusalem
might develop traditions of its own and begin to represent a competing center. Internal quarrels between the Christians of different cities
would certainly be bad for Christians as a whole.

The leaders of the Jerusalem church therefore sent Barnabas as
their emissary to Antioch, to serve as a connecting link. Barnabas,
recognizing that the task was more than he could himself carry through,
remembered his old friend, whose fiery spirit, he felt sure, was equal
to any task:

Acts 11:25. Then departed Barnabas to Tarsus, for to seek Saul:
Acts 11:26. And when he had found him, he brought him unto
Antioch.

In this way, Saul was restored to activity after his years of vegetation
in Tarsus.

Claudius Caesar

When, however, was it that Saul came to Antioch? Speculation with
regard to this question is tempting for at this point Acts refers to two
historical events that can be independently dated.

First, there was a famine in Judea:

Acts 11:27. And in these days . . .
Acts 11:28. . . . there . . . [was prophesied] great dearth through-
out all the world: which came to pass in the days of Claudius
Caesar.

Tiberius, Rome's second emperor, under whom Jesus had been crucified, died in A.D. 37, about eight years after the crucifixion and perhaps not more than a couple of years after Saul's conversion. Tiberius was followed by his grandnephew, who, under the name Caligula, became Rome's third emperor.

Caligula ruled for four years only, and for at least half this time was quite mad. He is not mentioned in the Bible, but from Josephus we know that in his lunatic desire to be worshipped as a God, he ordered that his statue be set up in the Temple at Jerusalem. The Jews refused vehemently and completely; undoubtedly if Caligula had insisted on erecting such a statue, there would have been a bloody rebellion. Undoubtedly Caligula would have insisted anyway, but before things could come to the final break, the emperor was assassinated in A.D. 41.

He was succeeded by his uncle, Claudius, a much gentler and saner man, though rather weak and not really a successful ruler. However, he did rule for thirteen years, from 41 to 54 A.D., so that merely to say that a famine occurred "in the days of Claudius Caesar" gives unsatisfactory leeway.

To be sure, no famine occurred at this time "throughout all the world" but allowance must be made for Jewish nationalism. The phrase was probably used to mean "throughout all Judea"—that is, throughout all the world that counted.

Josephus does speak of hard times in Judea in A.D. 46–48, but how close is that to the time of Saul's arrival in Antioch? The Biblical phrase "in those days" is not necessarily precise but can be used to signify a very rough contemporaneity. The famine certainly came after Saul's arrival in Antioch, for later he is one of those from Antioch who carries relief to Judea on the occasion of the famine.

The famine, however, may have come fully two or three years after Saul's coming to Antioch.

Herod Agrippa I

A second reference to something that can be used chronologically follows almost at once:

Acts 12:1. *Now about that time Herod the king stretched forth his hands to vex certain of the church.*

Acts 12:2. *And he killed James the brother of John with the sword.*

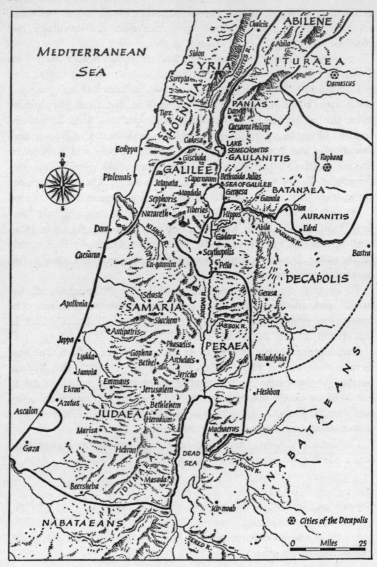

Dominions of Herod Agrippa I

This is not Herod Antipas, or any of the Herods of the gospels, but a new member of the family altogether, one not previously referred to in the Bible. It is Herod Agrippa.

He was born about 10 B.C. and was the son of Aristobulus, who was in turn the son of Herod the Great by his second wife, Mariamne the Maccabean. The little boy received his name in honor of Agrippa, the son-in-law of the Roman emperor, Augustus. Agrippa had died shortly before but he had been a favorite of both the emperor and the Roman people, and a close friend besides of Herod the Great. Through his grandmother, be it noted, Herod Agrippa was of Maccabean descent.

In 6 B.C. Herod Agrippa's father, Aristobulus, and his uncle, Alexander, were executed by Herod. They were the last two adult sprigs of the Maccabean line, and all that were left were three children. There was Herod Agrippa and a younger brother (who was eventually to be known as Herod of Chalcis) and also a sister, Herodias (who was later to be the death of John the Baptist).

In view of Herod the Great's pathologically suspicious nature, it was thought best to take the young Herod Agrippa to Rome. There, as an Eastern princeling, he was treated with every consideration. Indeed, he became quite a favorite with Antonia, sister-in-law of the Emperor Tiberius and mother of the future Emperor Claudius.

As a grown man, Herod Agrippa returned to his homeland, and there he found his sister the wife of Herod Antipas, tetrarch of Galilee. His sister obtained a lucrative position for him in the capital, but Herod Agrippa was a happy-go-lucky man who found that his expenses always outran his income. He soon became too expensive a luxury for his sister, quarreled with Herod Antipas, and had to leave for Rome again in A.D. 36.

In Rome he became friends with the young Caligula, heir to the throne. He became so friendly in fact that the old emperor, Tiberius (as suspicious as Herod the Great), suspected him of conniving to hasten Caligula's accession to the throne. Herod Agrippa was thrown into prison, but within six months Tiberius was dead anyway and Caligula at once liberated his friend.

Caligula made Herod Agrippa king of the realm that had been formerly held by his half uncle, Philip the Tetrarch (see page 136), who had died three years earlier in A.D. 34.

Herod Antipas, who still ruled in Galilee, was annoyed at this elevation of his scapegrace half nephew, and demanded the title of king for himself, too. Herod Agrippa's friendship for the new young emperor, however, was more than enough to counterbalance Antipas' maneuvering and the latter was relieved of his post in A.D. 39 after having ruled for thirty-three years. Galilee was added to Herod Agrippa's dominions and Antipas died soon after in banishment.

When Caligula was assassinated, Herod Agrippa found himself no worse off. His sponsorship by Antonia meant that he had known Claudius, the new emperor, for a long time. Furthermore, the bumbling Claudius found himself uncertain in his initial dealings with the Senate and the smooth and sophisticated Herod Agrippa helped him out. The grateful Claudius appointed Herod Agrippa as king of the entire realm that had once been ruled by Herod the Great. This was in A.D. 41.

For the last time, Judea bore the appearance, at least, of independence and greatness and, indeed, for a short time, the land stood at the peak of prosperity and was materially better off than ever it had been since the days of Solomon. It had no foreign enemies and the danger of war did not threaten. It could relax in profound peace under the benevolent shadow of the Roman Empire as ruled by a weak but well-intentioned emperor.

Herod Agrippa I felt it politic to try to ingratiate himself with his Jewish subjects. He had already gained popularity with them by trying to persuade the mad Caligula not to place the imperial statue in the Temple. Even for a good friend of Caligula that was a rash move and might have been the end of him if Caligula had lived. Caligula died and Herod Agrippa I was safe, but the Jews appreciated the risk he had taken.

Herod Agrippa I scrupulously adhered to all the tenets of Judaism, hoping to make the Jews forget his Idumean origins (for his Maccabean descent was through women while the Idumean descent was through men). This he apparently succeeded in doing for when, during a Passover feast, he wept that he was not a full Jew by birth, the spectators, weeping in sympathy, are supposed to have called out that he *was* a Jew, and their brother.

Clearly, it would be politically profitable for him to display his Jewish zealousness by cracking down on the Christian church which was offending the mainstream of Judaism more than ever by their admission of uncircumcised Gentiles. When James the son of Zebedee was executed, that was the first recorded death of one of the original twelve (barring that of Judas Iscariot).

Herod Agrippa I also imprisoned Peter, who, according to Acts, was miraculously liberated, and who then hastened to a friend's house:

Acts 12:12. . . . *he came to the house of Mary the mother of John, whose surname was Mark . . .*

It is this John Mark who, according to tradition, was the author of the earliest gospel, the second in order in the New Testament (see page 243).

The time in which this persecution took place can be set fairly closely, for Herod Agrippa I had only a short reign, dying suddenly in A.D. 44, in the course of games at Caesarea being held in honor of Claudius. That the Herod referred to in this chapter is indeed Herod Agrippa I is shown by the description (in miraculous terms) of that sudden death:

Acts 12:21. . . . *Herod, arrayed in royal apparel, sat upon his throne . . .*

. . . .

Acts 12:23. And . . . *the angel of the Lord smote him . . . and he . . . gave up the ghost.*

His death was an unparalleled disaster for the Jews. Had he lived another twenty years, as he might have done, his shrewd ability to placate both Jews and Romans might have kept the peace between them and might have established a stable dynasty that would have lasted far beyond his time. The Jewish rebellion might, just possibly, not have come to pass.

As it was, he died leaving a teen-age son, whom Claudius would not trust on the difficult throne of Judea. The land passed under the rule of procurators once more—and under them, Judea chafed more and more until it erupted in the disastrous rebellion of A.D. 66.

For the Christians, on the other hand, Herod Agrippa's sudden death was just as unparalleled a blessing. Had he lived, his strong hand might slowly have beaten down Christianity within his dominions and his influence with the Roman government might have served to see to it that Christianity was suppressed outside Judea, too.

His death made that impossible and, furthermore, by removing the only possible man who could conceivably have prevented the Jewish rebellion, the permanent weakening of Judaism came to pass and on the ruins of Judea, Christianity was able to flourish, grow, and, eventually, conquer Rome and the Western world.

Since Herod Agrippa I reigned from A.D. 41 to 44, it follows that the death of James son of Zebedee took place during this interval, possibly in 43. Perhaps Saul's coming to Antioch also took place about then.

Cyprus

The fact that the daughter church at Antioch was outstripping the mother church at Jerusalem was clear by the time of Herod Agrippa I. The Jerusalem church, plagued by famine and by the heavy hand of

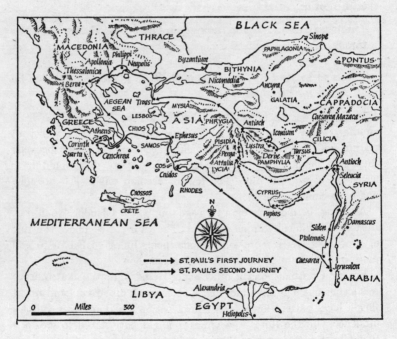

St. Paul's First and Second Journeys

the king, was impoverished, and the church at Antioch, wealthy and secure in comparison, sent relief:

Acts 11:29. . . . *the disciples* [at Antioch], *every man according to his ability, determined to send relief unto the brethren which dwelt in Judaea:*

Acts 11:30. *Which also they did, and sent it to the elders by the hands of Barnabas and Saul.*

The verse which tells of the return to Antioch of Barnabas and Saul, after their mission to Jerusalem, comes immediately after those relating the death of Herod Agrippa I. Perhaps the return to Antioch took place in A.D. 46, when the famine, according to Josephus, was first making its effects seriously felt.

Barnabas and Saul did not go back to Antioch alone:

Acts 12:25. . . . *Barnabas and Saul returned from Jerusalem,* . . . *and took with them John, whose surname was Mark.*

John Mark was, apparently, a nephew of Barnabas, for he is so referred to in the Epistle to the Colossians:

Colossians 4:10. *Aristarchus my fellowprisoner saluteth you, and Marcus, sister's son to Barnabas* . . .

The vigor of the Antioch church is also indicated by its readiness to engage in missionary activities. Immediately upon the return of Barnabas and Saul, perhaps before A.D. 46 was over, the two were sent across the sea, with John Mark as their assistant.

Acts 13:4. So *they* [Barnabas and Saul] . . . *departed unto Seleucia; and from thence they sailed to Cyprus.*

Acts 13:5. *And when they were at Salamis, they preached the word of God in the synagogues of the Jews: and they had also John to their minister.*

Thus, Saul set forth on what was to be his first missionary voyage. It began in Seleucia, a western suburb of Antioch. Seleucia was on the Mediterranean coast and served as Antioch's seaport. It had been founded in 300 B.C. by Seleucus I (who had also founded Antioch) and it had been named in honor of himself.

Cyprus may have been one of the sites from which the Philistines launched their invasions of Egypt and the Canaanite coast at the time of the Exodus (see page I-201), but it had played no further part in pre-Exilic Jewish history.

Cyprus was early colonized both by Phoenicians and Greeks, though it was politically dominated first by Assyria and then by Persia. After the death of Alexander the Great, Cyprus moved into the orbit of the Ptolemies and remained under rulers of that line for two and a half centuries. It was in this time, undoubtedly, that Jews entered Cyprus in sizable numbers, under the protection of the tolerant Ptolemies. In 58 B.C., Cyprus was annexed by Rome.

Salamis, on the eastern shore of the island, was its chief city in ancient times. It was Greek, and was reputedly settled by colonists from the small Greek island of Salamis near Athens (the Salamis that is famous as the site of the battle at which the Greek fleet defeated the Persians under Xerxes). This tradition may be the result of nothing more than the coincidence of names, however.

Salamis had an important Jewish colony and it was reasonable that the church at Antioch send a mission there. The city was not very far off, only 130 miles by sea. Furthermore, Barnabas was himself a Cypriote Jew and, very possibly, although the Bible does not say so, a native of Salamis. He was, in a sense, returning home. (His reputed tomb is located near the site of that city and also there is the "monastery of St. Barnabas.")

Paphos

Barnabas and Saul then traveled the full width of Cyprus:

Acts 13:6. . . . *they had gone through the isle unto Paphos . . .*

Paphos was best known in ancient times as the site of religious fertility rites in connection with a goddess whom the Greeks identified with Aphrodite (who was therefore sometimes called the "Paphian goddess").

It was second only to Salamis in size among the Cypriote cities. In 15 B.C. it had been virtually destroyed by an earthquake but it had been rebuilt by Augustus and had recovered to the point of serving as the seat of the Roman proconsul, Sergius Paulus, at the time of the missionary voyage of Barnabas and Saul.

Paul

Sergius Paulus, the proconsul, was, apparently, interested in Judaism. He was, perhaps, being instructed in that faith by a Jew attached to his court; a Jew who is described in Acts with a natural lack of sympathy:

Acts 13:6. . . . *they* [Barnabas and Saul] *found* [in Paphos] *a certain sorceror, a false prophet, a Jew, whose name was Bar-jesus:*

Acts 13:8. . . . *the sorcerer . . . withstood them* [Barnabas and Paulus . . .

Sergius Paulus was curious to meet these new men, concerning whom he must have heard reports to the effect that they were preaching a novel and interesting variety of Judaism. Bar-jesus attempted to dissuade the proconsul from this step, since Barnabas and Saul must have seemed, in his eyes, dangerous heretics, and individuals who would compete with him for favor in the eyes of the Roman official.

There may even have been a dispute between them with Sergius Paulus as an interested onlooker and audience:

Acts 13:8. . . . *the sorcerer . . . withstood them* [Barnabas and Saul], *seeking to turn away the deputy from the faith.*

Saul, however, denounced Bar-jesus and had him miraculously stricken with blindness, thus securing the conversion of the proconsul.

This act is an important turning point in Saul's life. Many Jews in New Testament times had Gentile names, either Greek or Roman. Among the apostles, for instance, there were Andrew and Philip, both excellent Greek names. The seven Grecian leaders (see page 344) all had Greek names; the name "Stephen" means "crown." Sometimes an individual had both a Jewish name and a Gentile name in addition, the latter for use in official dealings with Gentile representatives of the government perhaps. Thus, we have John [Hebrew] Mark [Roman].

The case was the same with Saul, who apparently had a second name for use with Gentiles—Paulus or, in English, Paul. At the time of the confrontation with Bar-jesus, the author of Acts makes the transition from one to the other:

Acts 13:9. *Then Saul, (who also is called Paul,) . . . set his eyes on him* [Bar-jesus] . . .

Up to this point Saul/Paul was called nothing but Saul; after this point he is called nothing but Paul, and it is as Saint Paul that he is known to us.

The transition would seem significant. It comes at a time when Paul (as we shall now call him) was engaged for the first time in converting a Gentile, and in so doing, was opposed by a Jew.

It may even be that Paul was faced with a crucial decision. Sergius Paulus may have been hesitating over conversion to Judaism because of his reluctance to undergo circumcision and undertake the duties and rites (strange to his own culture) of the Mosaic Law. If Paul could require of him faith in Jesus as the Messiah, without circumcision and the Mosaic Law, the conversion might be won.

It was certainly an important conversion since Sergius Paulus was the most important man on the whole island, and would have meant a triumph for Paul. Acts, which throughout tends to minimize the dispute among Christians over the manner of converting Gentiles, does not go into detail here, but the supposition that Sergius Paulus was converted without circumcision (and, what is more important, without the stipulation of later circumcision) is a reasonable one, in the light of later events.

The change from the Hebrew Saul to the Roman Paul may therefore be symbolic of Paul's shift away from the Mosaic Law and toward what we might call the Gentilization of Christianity.

Then, too, the change in name may have been influenced by the name of the proconsul. The Bible does not say that Paul was always the apostle's Roman name from birth, or even from youth. It is never referred to until this point. Could it have been adopted at this point, in honor of Sergius Paulus, or in honor of Paul's victory in securing the conversion of the proconsul? Perhaps so.

Another significance to the change in name may be that now Paul finally felt that he had left his origin behind him. The handicap of having once been a persecutor of Christians had been a heavy one, even after Paul had convinced the disciples of the sincerity of his conversion. When Barnabas had called him to Antioch, he had still had to take a back seat. When the five leaders of the Antioch church are named, Paul is named last:

Acts 13:1. *Now there were in the church that was at Antioch certain prophets and teachers; as Barnabas, and Simeon . . . and Lucius of Cyrene, and Manaen . . . and Saul.*

(Some have wondered if this Lucius of Cyrene might not be the Luke who wrote the third gospel and Acts, see page 254.)

Again, Paul's activities in the church up to and including the start of this first missionary voyage were only under the sponsorship and continuing protection of Barnabas, as though without the presence of that dedicated Christian, Paul could not maintain himself against the memory in the mind of the fellowship of what he had done at the time of the stoning of Stephen.

Even Paul himself finds forgiveness hard:

1 Corinthians 15:9. *For I am the least of the apostles, that am not meet to be called an apostle, because I persecuted the church of God.*

Perhaps, then, Paul felt that the conversion of Sergius Paulus finally tipped the scales in his favor and his early sins had been made up for. The offending Saul could now be wiped away and the newborn and triumphant Christian, Paul, could be put in his place.

Pamphylia

Leaving Paphos, the missionaries crossed the sea again, and here a new change appears, following hard upon the change in name from Saul to Paul.

Acts 13:13. *Now when Paul and his company loosed from Paphos . . .*

Until this point, whenever Paul and Barnabas had been mentioned together it had always been as "Barnabas and Saul." There is no question but that Barnabas was the older man, the leader, the sponsor, the more considerable.

Now, however, it is "Paul and his company." Paul emerges as the leader and everyone else falls back into subsidiary place. This continues throughout the rest of Acts. It is Paul, Paul, and Paul. When Paul's associates are mentioned they are little more than names that appear and disappear, the details of their comings and goings not being given, while all attention is paid to Paul.

How did this come about? How is it that just at the place of the name change and of the conversion of Sergius Paulus, the apostle became dominant?

We might argue that when Paul and Barnabas were put to the task of wresting Sergius Paulus from the grasp of the Jewish teacher, Bar-jesus, Barnabas flinched away from Paul's suggestion that circumcision be put aside. He fell back, uncertain, and it was Paul who then advanced to combat with Bar-jesus. In taking the initiative at this crucial point, Paul established his ascendancy over Barnabas, an ascendancy Barnabas could never retake.

That this may well be so would appear from Paul's statement in the Epistle to the Galatians. When he is scolding those Christians who clung to the Mosaic Law and who were reluctant to take the chance of eating and otherwise consorting with Gentiles, Paul says:

Galatians 2:13. . . . *Barnabas also was carried away with their dissimulation.*

Barnabas, like Peter, wanted to accept Gentiles, but could not quite bring himself to do so in the face of his early training and the disapproval of the conservatives under James.

Paul and his group reach the coast of Asia Minor:

Acts 13:13. . . . *they came to Perga in Pamphylia* . . .

Pamphylia is the section of the Asia Minor seacoast just to the north-west of Cyprus. To reach Perga, the chief city of Pamphylia, from Paphos in Cyprus, is about a two-hundred-mile sea journey. Pamphylia lay immediately to the west of Cilicia (Paul's home province) and was very like it in culture. In 25 B.C., Pamphylia had been annexed by Rome.

Apparently the quarrel between Paul and other members of the group intensified in the course of this voyage. At least we might assume so from the fact that one important member of the party left and returned home.

Acts 13:13. . . . *and John departing from them returned to Jerusalem.*

It may be that John Mark was simply homesick or ill. Acts gives no reason for the departure. Yet the separation seems to have been viewed with anger by Paul and was the occasion later for a quarrel between Paul and Barnabas, and that would indicate something serious.

It is easy to assume a doctrinal dispute. John Mark was of the Hebrew group of Christians, apparently. If he were indeed the author of the second gospel, we would have to assume that he was conservative with respect to the Mosaic Law, for Mark stresses Jesus' contempt for Samaritans and Gentiles and portrays him in the strict light of Judaism.

Pisidia

From Perga (the capital of Pamphylia, a town situated ten miles north of the coast), Paul traveled northward to a town where there was an important Jewish colony:

Acts 13:14. . . . *when they departed from Perga, they came to Antioch in Pisidia, and went into the synagogue on the sabbath day* . . .

Pisidia was the district just north of Pamphylia. Its chief city had been founded by Seleucus I, who named it Antioch after his father, just as he had named the other city he had founded in Syria. It was the latter which grew into a metropolis and came to be the Antioch meant when that name was used without qualification. The Pisidian capital must be identified as "Antioch in Pisidia." Like Pamphylia, Pisidia became Roman in 25 B.C.

Paul was invited to preach in the synagogue and he promptly told the audience the tale of Jesus, much as Stephen had done in Jerusalem a decade and a half before. Many of the congregation were impressed by the speech, sufficiently so to want to hear more the next Sabbath. The King James Version expresses this in, apparently, a mistranslated manner, for it says:

Acts 13:42. *And when the Jews were gone out of the synagogue, the Gentiles besought that these words might be preached to them the next sabbath.*

This makes it seem that the Gentiles were readier to accept Paul's message than the Jews were, but what would Gentiles be doing in the synagogue?

The Revised Standard Version makes no mention of Gentiles at all but translates the verse as follows: "As they [Paul and Barnabas] went out, the people begged that these things might be told them the next sabbath." The Jerusalem Bible translates it similarly as "As they [Paul and Barnabas] left they were asked to preach on the same theme the following sabbath."

It was not Gentiles that were attracted to Paul's teachings, but some of the congregation, some of the Jews. This is admitted by the King James Version in the very next verse:

Acts 13:43. *Now when the congregation was broken up, many of the Jews and religious proselytes followed Paul and Barnabas . . .*

The Jewish leaders, however, apparently argued strenuously against the Messianic thesis of Paul, insisting that Jesus could not have represented the fulfillment of the Messianic dream. Their authority swung opinion away from Paul once more.

To Paul, this must have been extremely irritating. He had scored a great victory with the conversion of Sergius Paulus, a Gentile, and now he was experiencing nothing but frustration with the stubborn Jews—his fellow religionists—who, it must have seemed to him, should most naturally have turned to Jesus. Paul, therefore, lost his temper:

Acts 13:46. *Then Paul and Barnabas waxed bold, and said, It was necessary that the word of God should first have been spoken to you: but seeing ye put it from you, and judge yourselves unworthy of everlasting life, lo, we turn to the Gentiles.*

It is this decision to turn to the Gentiles that caused the translaters of the King James Version (perhaps) to drag in, most unjustifiably, the earlier approval of Gentiles of Paul's teachings.

Paul did not turn to the Gentiles exclusively. His ultimatum was for that city alone and in every new city that Paul entered, he always approached the Jews first. But always, when they rejected him, he turned to the Gentiles of that city. What had been perhaps an impulsive act, under the temptation of snagging a rich catch in Paphos, was now becoming a settled policy.

Paul justified this by pointing out a passage in the Second Isaiah, where the suffering servant is said to be intended for more than merely to restore Israel and Judah from exile. The ideal Messianic kingdom is to shed its glory over all the Earth, that Gentiles might admire and, perhaps, undergo conversion:

Isaiah 49:6. . . . *I will also give thee for a light to the Gentiles, that thou mayest be my salvation unto the end of the earth.*

Apparently Paul was beginning to view himself as that light to the Gentiles of whom Second Isaiah had spoken.

Lycaonia

Despite the winning of converts, Jewish opposition was formidable enough to drive Paul and Barnabas out of Antioch in Pisidia. They headed southeastward some eighty miles:

Acts 13:51. . . . *and came unto Iconium.*

Iconium was the chief city of the Asia Minor region called Lycaonia, which lay east of Pisidia and north of Cilicia and which, like the latter two, had become Roman in 25 B.C. Of the cities that Paul visited in the first missionary voyage, Iconium survived best. It is the eighth largest city of modern Turkey, under the recognizable name of Konya, and has a population of over 120,000.

Paul and Barnabas preached in Iconium, and the conversions they succeeded in making again roused the dangerous ire of the leading Jews. The missionaries moved again, southward this time:

Acts 14:6. *They . . . fled unto Lystra and Derbe, cities of Lycaonia . . .*

These cities, fifty and thirty miles, respectively, south of Iconium, are important in history only because of the visits now paid them by Paul.

In Lystra, Paul heals a cripple and the missionaries are promptly hailed as gods by the pagan crowds:

Acts 14:12. *And they called Barnabas, Jupiter; and Paul, Mercurius, because he was the chief speaker.*

It was common in later Greek myths to tell of trips to Earth by
Zeus (Jupiter, in Latin) and Hermes (Mercurius, in Latin, which
becomes Mercury in English). The best-known such tale in modern
times is that of Philemon and Baucis, a poor old couple, who lived in
Asia Minor. When Zeus and Hermes appeared in humble guise, the
old couple offered them their bit of hospitality when their neighbors
turned the gods away. As a result the neighbors were punished, but
the poor hut of Philemon and Baucis was converted into a beautiful
temple in which they served as priest and priestess, and they were
further granted the boon of ending their life together and remaining
united in death.

The tale was told by the Roman poet Ovid a generation earlier
and must have been known throughout the Roman world and been
of particular interest to those of Asia Minor.

The fact that Barnabas is considered Zeus and Paul Mercury, is
often interpreted as meaning that Barnabas presented a distinguished
appearance, while Paul did not. In fact, it is common to suppose that
Paul was of small stature and unprepossessing appearance, and sickly,
too.

Paul himself was given to stressing his own physical shortcomings,
perhaps out of modesty, and perhaps as a shrewd, strategic device.
Thus, in his Second Epistle to the Corinthians, he describes his
opponents as saying:

> 2 Corinthians 10:10. . . . *his* [Paul's] *bodily presence is weak,
> and his speech contemptible.*

This may be Paul's Socratic irony, which, by deliberately making
himself out to be clearly worse than he really is, produces a reaction
which makes him seem better than he would otherwise appear. This
must be true concerning his reference to his speech, since his speech
had to be anything but contemptible, judging from the effects it had.

The very fact that he was called Hermes "because he was the
chief speaker" shows this. Indeed, naming Paul Hermes may be taken
to be in his favor rather than the reverse. In the visits of Zeus and
Hermes to Earth, as told in Greek legends, Zeus, as the chief god,
may have felt it beneath his dignity to do much more than look
stately and benign, leaving the actual activity to Hermes. Presumably
this now was the position with the missionaries. Barnabas, still titular
head of the group, but worried about Paul's activities among the

Gentiles, may have withdrawn more and more into a grave silence, while his supposed subordinate, Paul, must have talked with ever-increasing assurance on every occasion.

To be sure, Paul occasionally speaks of some infirmity he has:

2 Corinthians 12:7. *And lest I should be exalted above measure* . . . *there was given to me a thorn in the flesh, the messenger of Satan to buffet me* . . .

What that "thorn in the flesh" might be is not explicitly stated. Paul seems to dislike talking about it and seems to feel that his listeners know all about it anyway and don't need to have it detailed to them.

It is supposed that it is some sort of recurrent illness, which periodically "buffeted" him, and incapacitated him from work. Thus, he says at one point:

1 Corinthians 2:3. *And I was with you in weakness, and in fear, and in much trembling.*

This may be a metaphorical way of saying he came into the Christian fellowship to preach, not in a vainglorious, self-confident way, but with diffident shyness, afraid to pit himself against those who must know so much more than he. If so, this, too, must be Socratic irony, for there is no trace of diffident shyness in any of the words or acts attributed to Paul, either before or after his conversion.

On the other hand, some interpret this as referring to a sickness, perhaps to the trembling fits induced by recurrent malaria.

It is also suggested by some that Paul suffered from epileptic fits. These would be periodic, of course, and since epilepsy was widely supposed to be caused by demonic possession, Satan could be regarded as buffeting him in the course of these seizures in all literal truth.

Lending this thought some support is Paul's remark in the course of a speech to the Jews of Jerusalem, describing his religious experiences. He said that at one point:

Acts 22:17. . . . *when I was come again to Jerusalem, even while I prayed in the temple, I was in a trance* . . .

Of course, there are many reasons besides epilepsy for trances, but if Paul is considered an epileptic, it becomes possible to argue that what happened near Damascus was a severe epileptic fit that involved a hallucination which Paul interpreted as representing Jesus. If so, epilepsy changed the course of the world in this case at least.

Yet all such arguments concerning Paul's physical appearance and the state of his health rest on very insecure foundations. If, instead, we go by Paul's endless energy, the travelings he endured, the tribulations he surmounted, we can only suppose that he was a man of phenomenal strength and health.

Thus, after Paul had, with difficulty, persuaded the pagans of Lystra not to worship himself and Barnabas as gods, Jews from Antioch in Pisidia and from Iconium roused the people against them and the situation changed at once. From gods they became blasphemers, and Paul was stoned and left for dead. To be stoned until one appears dead is to be battered indeed, yet Paul managed to struggle to his feet and the next day to leave Lystra with Barnabas and to travel to Derbe. No weak and sickly man could have managed that.

Attalia

Paul and Barnabas were now ready to return to Antioch, and from Derbe they might easily have traveled southeastward a hundred and twenty miles or so to the Cilician seacoast and there taken ship for Antioch. They might even have struck farther eastward and visited Paul's home at Tarsus.

Paul did not do this. In fact, he does not appear to have done much in Cilicia in the course of his missionary labors. Could he have completed the job as far as possible during his years in Tarsus before Barnabas called him to Antioch? Or (more likely) was he, like Jesus, a prophet without honor in his own country?

In any case, the missionaries chose, instead, to retrace their steps, visiting again the churches they had founded in the various cities they had visited:

Acts 14:25. *And when they had preached the word in Perga, they went down into Attalia:*

Acts 14:26. *And thence sailed to Antioch . . .*

Attalia was the seaport of Perga. It had been founded by Attalus II of Pergamum and named for its founder. Thus ended Paul's first missionary voyage.

Silas

Paul's report of his activities, particularly of his acceptance of Gentiles directly, without requiring them to undergo the full yoke of the Mosaic Law, was apparently accepted by the church at Antioch:

Acts 14:27. . . . *they* [Paul and Barnabas] . . . *gathered the church* [at Antioch] *together,* [and] *they rehearsed all that God had done with them, and how he had opened the door of faith unto the Gentiles.*

There was, however, considerable disapproval of this when word reached the Christian elders in Jerusalem. The faction led by James considered the Mosaic Law essential:

Acts 15:1. *And certain men which came down* [to Antioch] *from Judea . . . said, Except ye be circumcised after the manner of Moses, ye cannot be saved.*

Who these men might have been is not stated, but one of them could have been Peter. In the Epistle to the Galatians, Paul may be referring to this episode, when he said:

Galatians 2:11. *But when Peter was come to Antioch, I withstood him to the face, because he was to be blamed.*

Paul taunted Peter with having been willing to eat with Gentiles, as in the case of Cornelius (see page 364), yet veering away under pressure from James and his group.

The dispute waxed hot and there seemed real danger of infant Christianity breaking up into two mutually hostile sections. It was decided, therefore, for representatives of the two wings to get together and thrash matters out and come to some general conclusions:

Acts 15:2. . . . *they* [the Christian leaders at Antioch] *determined that Paul and Barnabas, and certain other of them, should go up to Jerusalem unto the apostles and elders about this question.*

There followed what is termed the Council of Jerusalem, which is supposed to have taken place in A.D. 48. It may be that James took up the extreme Mosaic position, Paul the extreme anti-Mosaic position, while Peter and Barnabas strove for compromise. Thus:

> Acts 15:5. *But there rose up certain of the sect of the Pharisees which believed* [in Jesus], *saying, That it was needful to circumcise them, and to command them to keep the law of Moses.*

Peter rose, however (perhaps with Paul's sarcastic words in Antioch ringing in his ears), to admit that in the case of Cornelius he himself had accepted an uncircumcised Gentile. He said:

> Acts 15:7. . . . *ye know how that a good while ago God made choice among us, that the Gentiles by my mouth should hear the word of the gospel, and believe.*

That pulled the rug out from under the Mosaic group. Paul recited the achievements of his first missionary voyage, probably describing his actions as following the tradition of Peter. James was forced to capitulate, giving his reason for doing so, too:

> Acts 15:13. . . . *James answered . . .*
> Acts 15:14. *Simeon hath declared how God at the first did visit the Gentiles . . .*

(James refers here to Peter by his full Aramaic name, Simeon, as though the writer of Acts was at pains to demonstrate James's Semitism even through the Greek in which he was writing.)

Nevertheless, James held out for a compromise by insisting on at least four ritual abstentions to which converting Gentiles must agree:

> Acts 15:20. . . . *they* [must] *abstain from pollutions of idols, and from fornication, and from things strangled, and from blood.*

But they were not to be required to undergo circumcision, or to adhere to the complex dietary laws (not even to abstain from pork, a cause for which martyrs in Maccabean times had willingly died under torture).

It was actually a stunning victory for Paul's view. It may have been on this occasion that Paul (and through him the church at Antioch) was granted equality with the leaders of the church at Jerusalem. Paul refers to such an occasion in the Epistle to the Galatians:

Galatians 2:9. . . . *James, Cephas* [Peter], *and John . . . gave to me and Barnabas the right hands of fellowship; that we should go unto the heathen, and they unto the circumcision.*

In this way, two wings of Christianity were indeed formed; a Mosaic wing under James and a Gentile and non-Mosaic wing under Paul. They were not, however, to be at enmity, but with a negotiated truce between them. When Paul and Barnabas returned to Antioch, men of the church at Jerusalem were selected to accompany them, almost as though they were to serve as ambassadors of one wing to the other:

Acts 15:22. *Then pleased it the apostles and elders . . . to send chosen men of their own company to Antioch with Paul and Barnabas; namely, Judas surnamed Barsabas, and Silas . . .*

Judas Barsabas is not mentioned elsewhere than in this chapter, but Silas plays an important later role for he accompanied Paul on later missionary voyages.

Silas, like Paul, may have been a Roman citizen. At least, when both later undergo flogging by the Roman authority, Paul speaks of their citizenship in the plural:

Acts 16:37. . . . *Paul said unto them, They have beaten us* [himself and Silas] *openly uncondemned, being Romans . . .*

If Silas were a Roman citizen, he too might be expected to have a Latin name, equivalent to the Paul of his companion. In Acts, Silas is never referred to by any other name, but in some of the epistles, there is reference to someone of similar name:

1 Thessalonians 1:1. *Paul, and Silvanus, and Timotheus, unto the church of the Thessalonians . . .*

It is usually accepted that Silvanus is the Latin name used by Silas.

Timothy

Some time after the Council of Jerusalem, Paul suggested to Barnabas that they revisit the churches they had founded in Cyprus and Asia Minor. Barnabas agreed and suggested they take John Mark again.

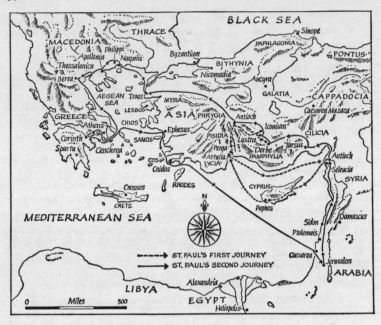

St. Paul's First and Second Journeys

Here, Paul disagreed violently, for he felt that John Mark had deserted them on the first journey:

> Acts 15:39. *And the contention was so sharp between them, that they* [Paul and Barnabas] *departed asunder one from the other* . . .

It may well have been that Paul strongly disapproved of John Mark's tendencies toward the Mosaic view, and may even have distrusted Barnabas' own stand in this matter. He felt the latter to be too ready to compromise with James's group (see page 388). Barnabas, on the other hand, could not so easily condemn his own nephew and may even have resented the fashion in which Paul had gained the upper hand.

In the end, the itinerary was split between Paul and Barnabas:

Acts 15:39. . . . *Barnabas took Mark, and sailed unto Cyprus;*
Acts 15:40. *And Paul chose Silas . . .*
Acts 15:41. *And he went through Syria and Cilicia . . .*

Each, in other words, visited his home territory. With this separation, Barnabas disappears from view and is not further mentioned.

When Paul and Silas reached Lystra in Lycaonia (for Paul merely passed through Cilicia and, presumably, Tarsus, and there is no mention of his preaching there) they picked up a new companion:

Acts 16:1. . . . *a certain disciple was there, named Timotheus, the son of a . . . Jewess* [who] . . . *believed; but his father was a Greek.*

Apparently Timotheus (Timothy, in English; a name meaning "honoring God") was a third-generation Christian after a fashion, for his mother and grandmother had both been converted in the course of Paul's first missionary visit to Lystra. In Paul's Second Epistle to Timothy, Paul speaks of:

2 Timothy 1:5. . . . *the unfeigned faith . . . which dwelt first in thy grandmother Lois, and thy mother Eunice . . .*

The shaky nature of the truce between Paul's wing of Christianity and that of James was here displayed. Paul wanted to take Timothy along with him on his trip but Timothy was uncircumcised and the Christians of Lystra knew it. Apparently, enough of them were of the Mosaic wing to force Paul into an action of expediency rather than conviction; especially if there were taken further into consideration the view of the unconverted Jews:

Acts 16:4. *Him* [Timotheus] *would Paul have to go forth with him; and took and circumcised him because of the Jews which were in those quarters . . .*

Phrygia and Galatia

Paul visited the churches he had founded:

Acts 16:6. . . . *they had gone throughout Phrygia and the region of Galatia . . .*

Phrygia and Galatia lay in the very center of Asia Minor, north of Pisidia and Lycaonia. Phrygia did not actually form a distinct political division in Paul's day. It derived its name from a people who had dominated Asia Minor over a thousand years before, at the time of the Trojan War and the Hebrew Exodus from Egypt. It was applied to a region that formed the eastern section of the kingdom of Pergamum during the time of the Seleucids. After 133 B.C., it formed the eastern part of the province of Asia.

Galatia was a comparatively recent formation. It gained its name from the Gauls who invaded Asia Minor about 278 B.C. By 235 B.C. they had been defeated and forced to settle down in peace in central Asia Minor in a region which came to be called Galatia after them. They were quickly hellenized. In 25 B.C., Galatia was made into a Roman province and, as a province, its boundaries were altered from time to time.

Because Galatia, at one time or another, included various districts of inner Asia Minor, the word came to be used in common speech to describe the interior of the peninsula generally.

Troas

Having visited the churches he had already established, Paul headed outward to new pastures. These, however, were not to border on the old ones, and he passed through western Asia Minor without preaching:

Acts 16:6. . . . they . . . were forbidden of the Holy Ghost to preach the word in Asia,

Acts 16:7. After they were come to Mysia, they assayed to go into Bithynia: but the Spirit suffered them not.

Acts 16:8. And they passing by Mysia came down to Troas.

Paul decided not to preach in the cities of the province of Asia but passed through its northwestern section (Mysia) quickly. Nor did he turn aside to preach in Bithynia, a section of Asia Minor which lies to the northeast of Mysia and takes up much of the Black Sea coast of the peninsula. Bithynia, which is separate from the province of Asia, became Roman in 65 B.C.

Finally, Paul reached Troas, that part of Mysia which forms the northwestern tip of Asia Minor. The name is given to a small peninsula, which bore its name because, twelve centuries before, the city of Troy had existed there—the city destroyed by the Greeks after the most famous siege in history.

Troas is a name applied also to a city founded in the vicinity of the site of ancient Troy. By 300 B.C. it had come to be called Alexandria Troas (in honor of Alexander the Great), or Troas in brief. It is to this city rather than to the peninsula that the Biblical mentions of Troas refer.

It would seem then that having left the churches he had founded, Paul traveled westward in a great hurry (if we may judge by the manner in which the journey is compressed into three verses). He must have traveled with a firm purpose in mind, for he did not veer to either the left or the right; that is, to preach in either Asia or Bithynia. He moved, instead, straight into Troas and there found himself six hundred miles west of Antioch.

Naturally, in the language of the times, this firm purpose driving Paul onward would be ascribed to the working of the Holy Spirit forbidding him to preach in either Asia or Bithynia. Some speculate that this reference to the Spirit is a way of saying that Paul was in poor health and unable to preach, but there seems no need to indulge in this supposition. If he were strong enough to travel hundreds of miles under the arduous conditions of the times, he would be strong enough to preach. It is easier to suppose that Paul's firm decision, his strong desire to do what he was planning to do, and nothing else, could only be interpreted by others, and by himself, too, as the driving force of the Holy Spirit.

But what was he planning to do? It is tempting to suppose that when Paul was given official sanction at the Council of Jerusalem to go to the Gentiles, it occurred to him that he ought to travel to the very core and fount of Gentile-dom. Why not leave Asia Minor altogether and penetrate into Europe. The port of Troas was what he wanted, for from it there would be many ships to take him across the Aegean and into Macedonia, or even into Greece itself.

Might it not even be that this was his main purpose from the beginning of his second missionary voyage? That the suggested purpose to revisit the churches of central Asia Minor was a blind to secure the blessing of the Antioch community, which might otherwise have flinched away from too bold a project. Could Paul have confided these plans to Barnabas, and had Barnabas flinched, too, and was this the true cause of the quarrel between them?

Barnabas, according to this view, lacked the bold vision of Paul, contented himself with the narrow bounds of Cyprus and stepped off the stage of history. Paul went onward without Barnabas, and the future of Christianity went with him.

Macedonia

Once in Troas, Paul lost no time in moving into Europe; a move which the writer of Acts explains in appropriate Biblical terms:

Acts 16:9. *And a vision appeared to Paul in the night; There stood a man of Macedonia, and prayed him, saying, Come over into Macedonia, and help us.*

Acts 16:10. *And after he had seen the vision, immediately we endeavoured to go into Macedonia . . .*

Macedonia, which in the reign of Alexander the Great had conquered a vast empire, had since 146 B.C. been merely part of the Roman realm. For two centuries it had remained peacefully somnolent under Rome's vast shadow and virtually lacked a history. In the eyes of later generations (but not of contemporaries, of course) it was only Paul's coming that finally brought back Macedonia into significance with respect to the currents of world history.

In Acts 16:10 there is the sudden use of the pronoun "we"—"we endeavoured to go into Macedonia."

The usual conclusion is that Luke, the writer of Acts, is now part of Paul's party. We cannot say, however, how this came to be. The author of the book, with frustrating modesty, never says anything of himself. Was Luke a native of Troas who, like Timothy, was converted and then drawn into the entourage?

In view of the early traditions that he was a Syrian from Antioch, could he have been an emissary from the church at Antioch sent after Paul with messages, or, possibly, to bring back news? Did he overtake Paul in Troas and decide to accompany him?

There is no way of telling from the Biblical account.

Philippi

It was about A.D. 50 that Paul crossed over into Europe:

Acts 16:11. . . . *loosing from Troas, we came with a straight course to Samothracia, and the next day to Neapolis;*
Acts 16:12. *And from thence to Philippi* . . .

From Troas to the nearest important seaport of Macedonia was a 125-mile sea journey to the northwest. This was accomplished in two stages, with a stopover at Samothrace, a small island in the northern Aegean Sea (sixty-six square miles in area) which lay approximately midway from point of embarkation to point of destination.

The Macedonian seaport Neapolis ("New Town"), which lay on the northern coast of the Aegean Sea, served the town of Philippi, which lay ten miles inland and was one of the largest of the Macedonian cities. Originally, Philippi had been a Greek settlement called Crenides ("fountains"). In 356 B.C., however, it had been captured by Philip of Macedon and renamed Philippi in his own honor. Its importance to Philip lay in the fact that its possession secured him control of nearby gold mines and Philip used the gold liberally in the subversion of Greek politicians. It was as much Philip's gold as Philip's army that helped the Macedonian gain control of Greece.

Between the time of Philip's capture of the city and Paul's arrival there, only one incident served to bring it into the full glare of history. After the assassination of Julius Caesar, armies led by the assassins Brutus and Cassius faced other armies led by Mark Antony and Octavian. The battle was fought near Philippi in 42 B.C. It was drawn and uncertain at first, but Cassius, prematurely fearful of defeat, killed himself, and thereafter Antony and Octavian won a clear victory.

Through their victory at the battle of Philippi, Antony and Octavian were able to divide the Roman realm between themselves, and, a dozen years later, Octavian defeated Mark Antony, took over sole control, and became the Emperor Augustus.

Lydia

In Philippi, Paul made some conversions:

> Acts 16:14. *And a certain woman named Lydia, a seller of purple, of the city of Thyatira, which worshipped God, heard us . . .*
> Acts 16:15. *And . . . she was baptized . . .*

Lydia was not in use in ancient times as a feminine name and it is suggested that the woman was not named Lydia, but that she was from the region of Lydia and that the verse might better be translated: "And a certain Lydian woman . . ."

Lydia was the name of a kingdom ruling over the western half of Asia Minor during the period when the Jews were in Babylonian Exile. From 560 to 546 B.C. it was ruled by Croesus, whose wealth has become proverbial. In 546 B.C. Croesus was defeated by Cyrus (see page I-434) and Lydia became part of the Persian Empire. After the death of Alexander the Great, the region was fought over by his generals and finally had a rebirth in Greek form as the kingdom of Pergamum. In 133 B.C., this became Rome's province of Asia, but the name Lydia could still be applied to the west-central portion of the province.

The capital of Lydia had been the city of Sardis in west-central Asia Minor about fifty miles from the Aegean Sea. Thyatira was a northwestern suburb founded by Seleucus I. It had a thriving trade in the purple dye that had made the Phoenician city of Tyre famous. (It was one of the very few dyes known to the ancient world that would retain its bright color even under the effect of water and sunlight and it was therefore a most valuable product. Nowadays, of course, we have any number of synthetic dyes.) The Lydian woman from Thyatira had brought her trade to a new market and was probably quite well-to-do as a consequence, for she could afford to put up Paul's party during their stay in Philippi.

Thus it came about that Paul, who came to Macedonia in search of new fields for conversion, had as his first convert a woman of Asia Minor after all.

Paul also found that Gentiles could be persecutors too, and that it was not only the Jews who were his enemy. The pagans did not, at that time, distinguish between Jews and Christians and they put into action a law that forbade Jewish proselytization among Greeks. Paul and Silas were brought before the magistrate and the accusation was:

Acts 16:20. . . . *These men, being Jews . . .*
Acts 16:21. . . . *teach customs, which are not lawful for us to receive, neither to observe, being Romans.*

Paul and Silas were flogged and imprisoned for a while and were released, according to the account in Acts, by a miraculous earthquake. Apologies were added when it was discovered they were Roman citizens and had been flogged without a proper trial. No doubt, the claim to citizenship, once verified, would have sufficed for freedom even without the earthquake.

Thessalonica

Paul's party left Philippi after that and traveled westward across Macedonia:

Acts 17:1. *Now when they had passed through Amphipolis and Apollonia, they came to Thessalonica, where was a synagogue of the Jews:*

Amphipolis is a city twenty-five miles southwest of Philippi, and had been founded as an Athenian colony in 436 B.C. when Athens was at the height of its Golden Age. It was captured by Sparta in 424 B.C. and was taken by Philip of Macedon in 357 B.C. In New Testament times it was the seat of the Roman governor of that section of Macedonia, even though it was not actually part of the province but was considered a free city.

Twenty miles farther southwest was Apollonia, a comparatively unimportant town, and forty miles due west of that was Thessalonica.

Thessalonica is located at the northwestern corner of the Aegean Sea. It was originally named Therma, from the Greek word meaning "hot" because of the hot springs in the vicinity. The inlet of the Aegean Sea, at the end of which it was located, was therefore called the Thermaic Gulf.

After the death of Alexander the Great, Cassander, the son of one of his generals, seized control of Macedonia. This was in 316 B.C. and he retained his power until his death twenty years later. He married a half sister of Alexander, a girl named Thessalonica, and in 315 B.C. he built a new city near Therma and named it Thessalonica in her honor.

Because of its advantageous position with respect to trade, Thessalonica grew rapidly and eventually became one of the most important cities in Macedonia. Through all historical vicissitudes, it has remained large and important. After the Turkish conquest of Greece in the fifteenth century, the first syllable dropped away and it became better known as Salonica.

Even today Salonica is a large city. It is, indeed, the second largest city of modern Greece, with a population of 250,000.

Thessalonica was the first Macedonian city in which Paul found a Jewish population large enough to maintain a synagogue. He gained some conversions but (as, very likely, he had anticipated) many more from among the Greeks than from among the Jews. The Jewish leaders, annoyed at this, rioted and claimed that Paul was preaching treason, proclaiming Jesus as a king in opposition to the Roman Emperor. (It was just this view of the matter which had led Pontius Pilate to condemn Jesus to crucifixion.) Paul and Silas found it prudent, therefore, to leave Thessalonica.

Berea

The next move was thirty miles to the westward:

Acts 17:10. *And the brethren immediately sent away Paul and Silas by night unto Berea* . . .

In Paul's time, Berea was a large city, on a par with Thessalonica, or even larger. It has declined since but it exists in modern Greece, under the name Verroia, as a sizable town of twenty-five thousand.

It too contained a synagogue and the Jews there are recorded as having been more sympathetic to Paul than were those of Thessalonica. Nevertheless, the Thessalonian Jews sent deputations to Berea to rouse the Jews there to the dangers of this new heresy.

Silas and Timothy remained in Berea for a time, but Paul was sent away.

Athens

This time Paul traveled some two hundred miles southward to the greatest of all the Greek cities, in reputation and glory, if not in size:

Acts 17:15. . . . *they that conducted Paul brought him unto Athens . . .*

In the fifth century B.C., Athens had experienced a Golden Age in art, literature, and philosophy that in some ways has never been surpassed. It was one of a number of small Greek city-states, and Athens, even though one of the largest among them, was no bigger than the state of Rhode Island in area or population.

For a while Athens dominated Greece politically and militarily, but it was defeated in the long and disastrous Peloponnesian War with Sparta, which lasted from 431 to 404 B.C. A century later, Athens led the futile opposition to Philip of Macedon.

But Greek city-states were no longer matches for the larger monarchies that were growing up on all sides. Athens fell farther and farther behind, and although it was saved from destruction time and time again by the universal respect for its great past, it gradually lost all political importance.

For two centuries it retained its self-government and control over its own internal affairs, while under the domination of Macedonia. And after 146 B.C., when Rome established itself as completely dominant over Greece, it nevertheless continued as a free city.

Only once did it waver. In 88 B.C., Mithridates VI of Pontus (a kingdom in northeastern Asia Minor) dared fight against Rome. He won initial victories and swept up all the Roman possessions in the peninsula. Athens, discontented with Roman rule, and misjudging the situation, declared for Mithridates.

However, Rome sent Sulla, one of its competent generals, eastward, and a grim Roman army followed him. Athens tried to resist and withstood a siege but Mithridates did not come to its help and in 86 B.C. Sulla took the city and sacked it. Never again did Athens attempt any independent action of its own.

It settled down to complete submission to the Roman power for as long as that power existed. It remained with its dreams of the past

as a quiet "college town" where Romans and Greeks came for an
education in philosophy.

While Paul waited in this college town for Silas and Timothy to
join him, he disputed with the Jews of the area and stared in horror
and revulsion at the beautiful temples and great works of art by which
he was surrounded, for all seemed to him but wicked objects given
over to idolatry.

Epicureans and Stoics

The Athenian specialty was philosophy. The city had a tradition
of absolutely free speech and it welcomed all sorts of views. Various
philosophers, then, hearing of a stranger in their midst, one who
possessed odd and novel views, sought to know more:

Acts 17:18. *Then certain philosophers of the Epicureans, and of
the Stoicks, encountered him* . . .

The Epicureans and Stoics were two of the important schools of
philosophy current in Athens at the time.

The former was founded by Epicurus, who had been born on the
Greek island of Samos in 341 B.C. He had established a school in
Athens in 306 B.C. and it remained extremely successful until his death
in 270 B.C. Epicurus adopted the beliefs of certain earlier Greek
philosophers and viewed the universe as made up of tiny particles
called atoms. All change, he maintained, consisted of the random
breakup and rearrangement of groups of these atoms and there was
little room in the Epicurean philosophy for any purposeful direction
of man and the universe by gods. The philosophy was essentially
atheistic, although the Epicureans were not fanatic about that; they
would cheerfully go through rituals they considered meaningless in
order to avoid giving unnecessary offense or creating useless trouble
for themselves.

In a universe consisting of atoms in random movement, man could
be conscious of two things: pleasure and pain. It stood to reason
that man should behave in such a way as to enjoy a maximum of
pleasure and a minimum of pain. It remained only to decide what
was actually a maximum of pleasure. To Epicurus, it seemed that if
a little of something gave pleasure, a lot of it did not necessarily give

more pleasure. Starvation through undereating was painful, but indigestion through overeating was also painful. The maximum of pleasure came from eating in moderation, and so with other joys of life. Then, too, there were the pleasures of the mind; of learning; of improving discourse; of the emotions of friendship and affection. These pleasures, in the view of Epicurus, were more intensely pleasant and desirable than the ordinary pleasures of the body.

Not all those who followed the Epicurean philosophy were as wise and moderate as Epicurus himself. It was easy to place the pleasures of the body first and hard to set any limit to them. So the word "epicurean" has entered our language as meaning "given to luxury."

So popular did the Epicurean philosophy become in Seleucid times that to the Jews of the period all Greeks seemed Epicurean. Any Jew who abandoned his religion for Greek ways became an "Epicurean" and to this very day, the Jewish term for a Jewish apostate is "Apikoros," a quite recognizable distortion of the old term.

The second famous school of Greek philosophy was founded by Zeno, a Greek (with possibly some Phoenician blood) who was born on the island of Cyprus at about the time of Epicurus' birth.

Zeno, like Epicurus, founded a school in Athens and taught from a place where a porch or corridor was adorned with paintings of scenes from the Trojan War. It was called the "Stoa poikile" ("painted porch") and Zeno's teachings came therefore to be known as "Stoicism" and his followers "Stoics" (or "Stoicks" in the King James Version).

Stoicism recognized a supreme God and seemed to be on the road to a kind of monotheism. It also contended, however, that divine powers might descend upon all sorts of minor gods and even upon those human beings who were deified. In this way, stoics could adjust themselves to prevailing polytheistic practices.

Stoicism saw the necessity of avoiding pain but did not feel that choosing pleasure was necessarily the best way of avoiding pain. One could not always choose pleasure correctly and even if one did, that merely opened the way for a new kind of pain—the pain that arose when a pleasure once enjoyed was lost. Stoics believed in putting one's self beyond both pleasure and pain, by cultivating indifference and lofty detachment of mind, serving justice without emotion. If you desire nothing, you need fear the loss of nothing. All that counted lay within a person. If you are master of yourself, you can be the slave to no one. If you live a life that rigidly follows a stern moral code, you need not fear the agonized uncertainty of day-to-day decisions. To this day, the word "stoic" is used in English to mean "indifferent to pleasure and pain."

At its height, both Epicureanism and Stoicism could produce men of lofty moral fiber and admirable ethical behavior. This was particularly true of Stoicism. Thus, the most famous Stoic of all was the Roman Emperor Marcus Aurelius, who ruled a little over a century after Paul's time and who, although a pagan, had many of the qualities usually associated with a Christian saint.

Dionysius the Areopagite

Apparently Paul's words were sufficiently interesting, or curious, for the philosophers to bring him to a place where as many of the important people of the town could hear him as possible:

Acts 17:19. *And they took him, and brought him unto Areopagus, saying, May we know what this new doctrine . . . is?*

The word "Areopagus" means "Hill of Ares" (or "Hill of Mars" in the Latin version) and was the place where the Athenians maintained their chief court. It had been the stronghold of the aristocrats in the days just prior to Athens' greatness, but as Athens grew more and more democratic in the course of its Golden Age, the Areopagus lost more and more of its power. Under Roman domination, the Areopagus regained some of its prestige and served as the instrument through which much of the city's internal affairs were conducted.

If Paul had confined himself merely to preaching matters of ethics and morality he would undoubtedly have received a sympathetic, if patronizing, hearing from the sophisticated and self-consciously superior Athenians. However, when he approached his great theme, the resurrection of Jesus (a theme that fills his epistles) the Athenians could not help but laugh:

Acts 17:32. *And when they heard of the resurrection of the dead, some mocked . . .*

. . . .

Acts 17:34. *Howbeit certain men clave unto him and believed: among the which was Dionysius the Areopagite . . .*

Apparently Dionysius is mentioned because he was a member of Athens' ruling council and, therefore, the most prestigious of Paul's converts there.

This is the only mention of this convert in the Bible and yet later tradition built enormously upon this single verse. Possibly it was unavoidable Greek snobbery to find an Athenian convert particularly important just because he was an Athenian.

By the time a century had passed, the tradition arose that Dionysius the Areopagite had served as the first bishop of Athens.

In the sixth century A.D., the Frankish historian Gregory of Tours spoke of a bishop named Dionysius who had been sent to Gaul about A.D. 250. He became bishop of Paris, was martyred, and was eventually considered the patron saint of France under the French version of his name, Saint Denis. A century later, Gregory's reference was misinterpreted to read that Dionysius was sent to Gaul in A.D. 90 and he was thereupon identified with Dionysius the Areopagite.

And about A.D. 500 some writings appeared in Syria which were attributed to Dionysius the Areopagite. The forgery was patent and clear, for it referred to matters that must have taken place many years after Dionysius' death. The author (who will probably never be known) is referred to as the pseudo-Dionysius. Despite the clumsiness of the forgery, it was accepted as genuine by important church leaders in the east and had great influence over the doctrinal disputes of the day.

Corinth

Upon leaving Athens, Paul traveled some fifty miles westward:

Acts 18:1. *After these things Paul departed from Athens, and came to Corinth.*

Corinth is situated on the narrow peninsula connecting the Peloponnesus (the southernmost peninsula of Greece) with the remainder of the land. Because of this, it has access to the sea on the east and the west and was a great trading center. It was prosperous and wealthy in the days of Greek greatness but it was a trading rival of Athens and therefore fought on the Spartan side in the Peloponnesian War.

After 338 B.C., Corinth was dominated by a Macedonian garrison but it remained prosperous. Indeed, by the time Macedonia was defeated by Rome, and the latter power succeeded to the rule of Greece, Corinth was the most prosperous city on the Greek mainland.

In 149 B.C., however, Macedonia, taking advantage of Roman military preoccupation elsewhere, attempted a revolt. This was quickly crushed, but Roman tempers were short and it seemed to them that the Greek cities had encouraged Macedonia. Deliberately they decided to make an example and sent an army against the richest of them, Corinth.

The city, terrified, hastily surrendered, but that did no good. The Roman commander was out to teach the Greeks a lesson and he did. In 146 B.C. the city was pillaged, its men killed, and its women and children sold into slavery.

For exactly a century Corinth lay in devastated ruins until, in 46 B.C., Julius Caesar had it rebuilt. The new Corinth rose and was flourishing again in Paul's time. It served, indeed, as the capital of the Roman province of Achaea, which included Greece proper.

Corinth had other disasters to contend with in its later history, but it survives to this day as a town of sixteen thousand.

Aquila

In Corinth, Paul remained for a year and a half, and there he settled down to earn his living by means of his craft:

> Acts 18:2. And [Paul] found a certain Jew named Aquila, born in Pontus, lately come from Italy, with his wife Priscilla; (because that Claudius had commanded all Jews to depart from Rome:) and came unto them.

It is they who were the tentmakers, or weavers, referred to earlier in this chapter (see page 357).

Apparently Paul arrived in Corinth shortly after Claudius, in a fit of irritation at disorders involving Jews, ordered them all out of Rome. This order, which only held in effect a few years, took place in A.D. 49 and this offers another peg on which to hang the chronology of Paul's voyages.

Gallio

The Corinthian Jews objected strenuously to Paul's activities but, apparently, could do nothing against him under the government then in power. They saw their opportunity, however, when a new governor arrived to begin his term of office. The new governor, they hoped, would sympathize with their point of view.

Acts 18:12. *And when Gallio was the deputy of Achaia, the Jews . . . brought him* [Paul] *to the judgement seat . . .*

Achaia or Achaea (the former is the Greek spelling, the latter the Latin) is the region skirting the northern shore of the Peloponnesus. During the great days of Greece it played only a very minor role, for it was under the thumb of mighty Sparta, just to the south. After the death of Alexander the Great, however, with Sparta long since rendered powerless, the cities of Achaea began to combine for the common defense and formed the "Achaean League." For over a century, the Achaean League preserved a shred of Greek freedom.

It came to an end, however, in 146 B.C. when Corinth was destroyed by the Roman forces. The last bit of Greek independence vanished, but the memory of the Achaean League lingered in the name the Romans gave their Greek province. It was the province of Achaea, or Achaia.

As for the Roman who now came to Corinth to govern the province, he was Junius Annaeus Gallio, though this was only his adopted name, taken after he had been accepted by a well-to-do Roman family. He had been born in Spain and his original name was Marcus Annaeus Novatus.

He was the older brother of Lucius Annaeus Seneca, the most noted Stoic philosopher among the Romans of the early empire, and the tutor of the young man who later became the Emperor Nero.

Gallio's nephew was a young man named Lucan (Marcus Annaeus Lucanus, to be precise) who, later, under Nero, became a poet of considerable reputation.

It is known that Gallio became proconsul of the province of Achaea in A.D. 52 and that fixes the date during which Paul was concluding his stay in Corinth. Gallio listened to the Jewish complaints against Paul with distaste and impatience. To him, it was merely:

Acts 18:15. . . . *a question of words and names, and of your law . . .*

It was a tedious matter of alien semantics to him, in other words, and he refused to involve himself in it. Paul was therefore safe.

The end of Gallio's life, by the way, was tragic. His younger brother, Seneca the philosopher, and his nephew, Lucan the poet, were both forced to commit suicide a dozen years later during the cruel and tyrannical reign of Nero, simply because they had incurred the emperor's displeasure and the suspicion of involvement in a conspiracy against him. (This was true in the case of Lucan, who turned state's evidence against his fellow conspirators but was condemned anyway.) Upon hearing this news, Gallio committed suicide too.

Ephesus

When Paul finally left Corinth, he took Aquila and Priscilla with him and sailed eastward 250 miles, across the center of the Aegean Sea to the Asia Minor coast:

Acts 18:19. *And he came to Ephesus, and left them* [Aquila and Priscilla] *there: but he himself entered into the synagogue, and reasoned with the Jews.*

Ephesus was first settled by Greeks, according to tradition, in 1087 B.C., at a time when all of Greece was experiencing a "Dark Age." A group of uncivilized Greek-speaking tribes, the Dorians, had entered Greece a century before and had been ravaging and dominating the land ever since. This was part of the same group of barbarian migrations that flung the Peoples of the Sea against the nations bordering the eastern Mediterranean. The colonization of Ephesus was carried through by Greeks seeking escape from the misery of home.

Indeed, in that period (when the Israelites in Canaan were themselves undergoing similar suffering under Philistine domination) the entire western coast of Asia Minor was colonized by the Greeks. Ephesus and other cities nearby were colonized by men from Athens and from other regions where the Ionian dialect of Greece was spoken. For that reason, the region around Ephesus was called Ionia.

Under the mild rule of the Lydians in the sixth century B.C., Ionia experienced an amazing cultural growth. It was there that philosophers such as Thales first introduced the basic assumptions of modern science and one of the great Ionian philosophers was Heraclitus of Ephesus (see page 299).

All of Ionia gradually decayed after Persia conquered Lydia, particularly after 500 B.C., when a disastrous revolt of the Ionians against the ruling empire was pitilessly crushed. Ephesus managed to cling to its prosperity more than did the others, however, and, in the centuries after Alexander the Great, it became the most important Greek city in Asia Minor. The prosperity continued under Roman rule, which began in 133 B.C., and Ephesus may not have been far behind Alexandria and Antioch in population and wealth. It survived a sack by Sulla in 84 B.C. and in 6 B.C. it became the capital of the province of Asia.

In Ephesus, Paul disputed with the Jews, but did not remain long. He sailed to Caesarea on the Judean coast:

> Acts 18:22. *And when he had landed at Caesarea, and gone up, and saluted the church, he went down to Antioch.*

It is usually assumed that by "gone up, and saluted the church" is meant a quick trip to Jerusalem. And thus Paul ended his second missionary journey.

Apollos

It was not long after his return to Antioch that the restless and fiery Paul, who could not seem to endure the settled life of a secure Christian community, left (perhaps in A.D. 54) on his third missionary journey.

> Acts 18:23. . . . *after he had spent some time there* [in Antioch], *he departed, and went over all the country of Galatia and Phrygia in order* . . .

Once again he was making the rounds of the churches he had founded in the Asia Minor interior. But meanwhile someone else had arrived in Ephesus, at the western rim of the peninsula:

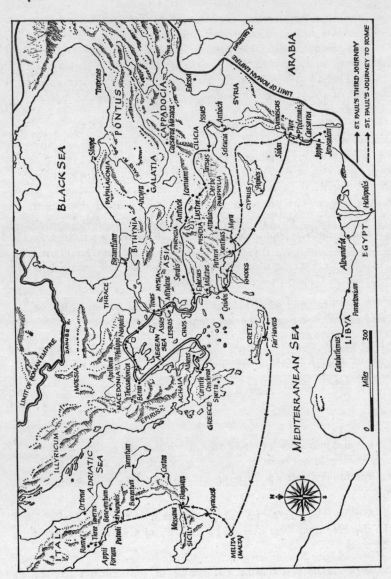

St. Paul's Third Journey and His Journey to Rome

Acts 18:24. *And a certain Jew named Apollos, born at Alexandria, an eloquent man . . . came to Ephesus.*
Acts 18:25. *. . . knowing only the baptism of John.*

Even now, a quarter century after the death of John the Baptist and of Jesus, there remained a sect that looked back to John the Baptist as their teacher and inspiration, rather than to Jesus.

Nevertheless, since John had preached the imminent coming of a Messiah, the Baptist's disciples seemed readier than other Jews to be converted to Christianity. Some instruction from Aquila and Priscilla (whom Paul had brought to Ephesus from Corinth) quickly brought Apollos into the Christian fold, and he moved on to Corinth to labor there.

Paul himself, in his travels through Asia Minor on this third journey, reached Ephesus and encountered disciples of John the Baptist, who readily submitted to baptism in the name of Jesus.

Paul remained in Ephesus for two to three years, till A.D. 57 perhaps, and under his influence the Christian church there flourished greatly. Indeed, as Jerusalem was the first Christian center, and Antioch the second, so Ephesus became the third. Later Christian tradition elaborated the early history of the church at Ephesus. The apostle John son of Zebedee was supposed to have spent his later life there and written the fourth gospel (see page 297). The Virgin Mary was supposed to have gone there too, and also, Mary Magdalene, and the apostles Andrew and Philip.

Diana of the Ephesians

The growth of the church at Ephesus was not entirely without untoward incident. The most spectacular of these came about as the result of the demagoguery of a silversmith:

Acts 19:24. *. . . a certain man named Demetrius, a silversmith, which made silver shrines for Diana, brought no small gain unto the craftsmen;*
Acts 19:25. *Whom he called together with the workmen of like occupation . . .*

The reference to Diana is to a goddess to whom Ephesus, at least in part, owed its relative immunity to the vicissitudes of history. It was a respected religious center and its conquerors tended to be in a certain awe of it.

The religion centered about a fertility goddess of a type familiar in Asia Minor, Syria, and Babylon. The goddess was much like the Ashtaroth so denounced by the Old Testament Yahvists (see page I-232). The rites were orgiastic, though undoubtedly intended, in all seriousness, to encourage the fertility of the soil.

The worship dated back to before the coming of the Greeks to that part of the world and may have centered about the falling of a meteorite originally. Thus, a city official is quoted as saying:

> Acts 19:35. . . . *what man is there that knoweth not how that the city of the Ephesians is a worshipper of the great goddess Diana, and of the image which fell down from Jupiter?*

Meteorites, if seen to fall from the sky, are a natural object of worship for primitive men, who know nothing of astronomy and see them merely as objects hurled down by the sky-god.

If the meteorite was perhaps in the crude shape of a human being (or something that might be imagined to be such a shape) the effect would be all the more impressive. And, in the end, there would not be lacking artisans to hew something that was closer to a recognized form. In New Testament times the goddess worshipped by Ephesus was usually shown as a woman closely draped from the waist down but seeming naked from the waist up and bearing many breasts. These breasts would seem to symbolize the overflowing fertility of the soil which the goddess symbolizes.

The Greeks, finding themselves with this primitive fertility goddess, had to identify her with some more familiar member of the Greek pantheon and they chose Artemis, the goddess of the hunt. It was a remarkably poor choice since the classical Artemis is a chaste and virginal huntress; anything but a many-breasted Earth-mother.

Nevertheless, the choice struck and the many-breasted goddess became "Artemis of the Ephesians" or, in the Roman equivalent, "Diana of the Ephesians."

When Ephesus was under the control of Lydia, a temple was built to Artemis of the Ephesians, under the generous sponsorship of the rich king Croesus. It was called the "Artemision." This temple was burnt down, accidentally, about 400 B.C., but it was quickly rebuilt.

Then, one night in 356 B.C., the Artemision was burnt down again.

This time it was no accident, but was a case of deliberate arson. The culprit was quickly seized and before execution for the crime of sacrilege was passed, he was asked what possible motive he could have had for so senseless an act. He replied that he had done it in order to make his name immortal. Immediately it was decreed that his name be expunged from all records and that no one ever pronounce it. In vain! His name (or some name that purports to be his) is known. It is Herostratus and it is, indeed, immortal. At least it is still remembered over two thousand years later.

Afterward, Greek historians were fond of repeating the story that the night on which the Artemision was burnt down was the very night on which Alexander the Great was born—though in view of the lack of accurate records in those days, it seems doubtful that this interesting coincidence can ever be verified.

Eventually the Artemision was rebuilt, this time under the direction of, among others, an architect who had been in the employ of Alexander the Great himself. The world of Macedonian monarchies was far richer than the earlier world of Greek city-states had been, and the temple was rebuilt on a much larger scale and with much more elaborate ornamentation. Such was its splendor that it came to be considered one of the Seven Wonders of the World.

This Wonder was to endure for seven centuries and it was standing when Paul was in Ephesus. Naturally, the magnificent temple made Ephesus a tourist center and the silversmiths who made trinkets for the tourist trade cleaned up. These silversmiths viewed with the utmost suspicion this Jewish missionary who was convincing more and more men that the great Ephesian goddess was just an idle lump of stone and that the silver trinkets were valueless.

The silversmiths were thrown into fury by the denunciations of Demetrius and in no time at all there was a full-blown riot in the streets:

Acts 19:28. And when they [the silversmiths] heard these sayings, they were full of wrath, and cried out, saying, Great is Diana of the Ephesians.

Acts 19:29. And the whole city was filled with confusion . . .

The city authorities, however, kept the situation in hand, and the riot blew over without real damage.

Miletus

Paul had been intending to visit the churches in Greece again and after the Ephesian riots he left. Perhaps the fact that the church withstood those riots so well led him to feel that he could safely leave it for a time. Or perhaps he felt that his own absence might prevent the recurrence of more dangerous riots.

He spent several months, therefore, in Greece, then, perhaps in A.D. 58, returned to Troas via Macedonia. Again there follows a "we" passage as though Luke had once again joined the party in Troas.

> Acts 20:13. . . . *we went before to ship, and sailed unto Assos . . .*
> Acts 20:14. *And when he* [Paul] *met with us at Assos, we took him in, and came to Mitylene.*
> Acts 20:15. *And we sailed thence, and came the next day over against Chios; and the next day we arrived at Samos, and tarried at Trogyllium; and the next day we came to Miletus.*

Assos was a town on the southern shore of the Troas peninsula, about twenty miles south of Alexandria Troas. The only incident of note in its history is the fact that Aristotle the philosopher spent three years there studying natural history.

Paul's companions rounded the Troas peninsula by sea, while Paul himself traveled to Assos overland. Paul then boarded the ship and all traveled southward along the Asia Minor west coast, passing three large islands: Lesbos, Chios, and Samos.

Lesbos, the largest of the three (623 square miles) had, as its capital city, Mitylene, located on its eastern shore. The period of Lesbos' greatest prosperity was about 600 B.C. It was then politically strong and contributed great names to music and literature, the greatest being that of the poetess Sappho, whose lyrically phrased praise of girls has given us "Lesbianism" as a word to signify female homosexuality.

Chios and Samos (the former 355 square miles in area, the latter 180) were each firm allies of Athens during the Golden Age of the latter city. Earlier than that, Samos had had a period of power of its own, when its fleet under its pirate-ruler, Polycrates, was the strongest in the eastern Mediterranean. Two great philosophers, Pythagoras and

Epicurus, were Samians by birth. All three islands are now part of the modern kingdom of Greece.

The party, on leaving Samos, remained at Trogyllium overnight; that being the promontory on the Asia Minor coast just south of the eastern edge of Samos. Then they went on to Miletus.

Miletus is on the Asia Minor mainland, about thirty miles south of Ephesus. From 600 to 500 B.C. it was the foremost city of the Greek world. Modern science began in Miletus, for Thales and his pupils, Anaximander and Anaximenes, were natives of that city. Its glories came to an end soon after 500 B.C., after it had led a furious revolt against the Persian Empire. Despite help from Athens (which led to the Persian invasion of Greece) the revolt was crushed, and Miletus as the ringleader was punished with particular severity. It survived, but leadership among the cities of the Asia Minor coast passed to Ephesus.

Miletus always had to fight to keep its harbor open against the tendencies to silt up. In the later centuries of the Roman Empire, the fight was gradually lost. Miletus has been nothing but deserted ruins for many centuries and the same fate, for that matter, has befallen Ephesus, Assos, and Troas.

In Miletus, Paul found himself close to Ephesus but he had no intention of stopping there lest church affairs delay him and keep him from his determination to spend Pentecost in Jerusalem. (Some thirty years had now passed since that first Pentecost.)

He therefore sent for the Ephesian elders and contented himself with giving a farewell address, urging them to selfless labors for the church and concluding with a well-known passage:

Acts 20:35. . . . *remember the words of the Lord Jesus, how he said, It is more blessed to give than to receive.*

As it happens, though, this saying did not come to be recorded in any of the gospels.

Rhodes

The journey southward then continued:

Acts 21:1. . . . *we came with a straight course unto Coos, and the day following unto Rhodes, and from thence unto Patara.*

Coos, or (better) Cos, is a fourth island off the Asia Minor coast and is about forty miles south of Samos. It is 111 square miles in area and was the home of the most important medical school of ancient times. Hippocrates, the "father of medicine," was born in Cos about 460 B.C., while Apelles, the greatest of the painters of antiquity, was born there a century later.

Rhodes, still another island off the west coast of Asia Minor (and the southernmost), is sixty miles southeast of Cos. Rhodes is a considerably larger island, with an area of 545 square miles. The city of Rhodes, on the northeastern tip of the island, was founded in 408 B.C.

After the time of Alexander the Great, Rhodes experienced a period of great prosperity that lasted for a century and a half. In 305-304 B.C., it withstood a long and terrible siege by Demetrius, the son of one of Alexander's generals. In celebration afterward, it erected the most famous great statue of the Greek world, a huge carving of the Sungod. This stood in the harbor, looking out to sea, but it did not, as later legend had it, bestride the harbor, with ships passing between its legs. This statue, the Colossus of Rhodes, was considered one of the Seven Wonders of the World. It stood for less than a century, however, for about 225 B.C. it was overthrown by an earthquake and was never re-erected.

In modern times, Rhodes was Turkish for centuries but was taken by Italy in 1912 and held for a generation. In 1945, after World War II, it and nearby islands were ceded by Italy to Greece.

From Rhodes, Paul and his party went to Patara, a town on the southwestern shore of Asia Minor, fifty miles east of Rhodes. It was the chief seaport of Lycia, a small district of Asia Minor which had managed to retain its nominal independence long after surrounding regions had been annexed to the Roman Empire.

It was not until A.D. 43—about fifteen years before Paul touched down in Patara—that the Emperor Claudius annexed it to the empire and made it part of Pamphylia.

Felix

Paul took another ship at Patara, which carried him to Tyre, and from there he made his way to Jerusalem, stopping at Caesarea to visit Philip the evangelist (see page 346).

In Jerusalem, Paul met with James and other leaders of the church. These, despite the concessions they had made at the Council of Jerusalem a decade earlier, were troubled at reports of the mass conversion of pagans without circumcision and without the requirement of obedience to the Mosaic Law. Even if the Jerusalem leaders were willing to accept this as a matter of practical politics, there were many among the congregation who were not willing at all. The leaders explained to Paul:

Acts 21:20. . . . *Thou seest, brother, how many thousands of Jews there are which believe; and they are all zealous of the law:*

Acts 21:21. *And they are informed of thee, that thou teachest all the Jews which are among the Gentiles to forsake Moses* . . .

Actually, it might be argued that Paul only invited Gentiles to become Christians without the Law, while urging Jews to keep the Law, but it could also be argued that if some Christians were free of the Law, other Christians could scarcely be kept to it. James might well have feared that the Christian community at Jerusalem, with their fervent Jewish heritage, on hearing that the Pauline version of Christianity was non-Jewish and even anti-Jewish, might disintegrate, and Christianity would become a Gentile religion altogether. (And this is exactly what did happen in the end.)

Furthermore, the Christian community was working out a record of coexistence with the non-Christian Jews. At least there is no record of James being in trouble with the Jewish authorities after the death of Herod Agrippa I. By proving themselves strict Jews in terms of ritual, the Christians of Jerusalem could perhaps look forward to, first, toleration by the Jews, then the acceptance of Jesus as a prophet at least, and eventually the acceptance of Jesus as the Messiah.

If Christianity came to seem anti-Jewish all such hopes must be gone and the Christians of Jerusalem might even be persecuted, driven out, or hunted down. Paul's very presence in Jerusalem could give rise to this danger. Reports of his missionary activity must have made him notorious as a violator of the Law, and he might be persecuted for this rather than for being a Christian, but the consequences might turn out to be against Christians generally.

James therefore urged Paul to go through an elaborate ritual of purification in the Temple in order to demonstrate his own adherence to the Law. Paul obeyed, but it did not help. He was recognized in

the Temple by some Jews from Asia who might have encountered him
on his missionary journeys, and who might therefore know of his work.
The cry was immediately raised:

Acts 21:28. . . . *Men of Israel, help: This is the man, that teacheth
all men every where against the people, and the law, and this place*
[the Temple] . . .

Paul was even accused of bringing Gentiles into the Temple and
defiling it in that manner. (There were indeed Gentiles in Paul's
entourage, but he did not bring them into the Temple.)

For a time it seemed that Paul might be lynched, but a Roman
captain and his troop, hearing of the disorders, hurried to the spot and
Paul was taken into protective custody. (The Roman captain's name
is later given as Claudius Lysias.)

With the captain's permission, Paul addressed the crowd in Aramaic
(after speaking to the captain in Greek), recounting the details of his
conversion. The audience grew unruly, however, when Paul began to
talk about his work among the Gentiles.

The captain, puzzled by all this, decided to get down to basics
by questioning Paul under torture, a routine procedure in those days.
Paul, however, saved himself from this by announcing his Roman
citizenship (see page 355).

Paul next faced the Jewish council and escaped from their hands by
announcing himself to be a Pharisee. He maintained that he was being
persecuted for his belief in the doctrine of resurrection—a cardinal
point in Pharisaic doctrine and one that was bitterly opposed by the
Sadducees.

To be sure, Paul's belief in resurrection applied specifically to that
of Jesus after the crucifixion, something the Pharisees did not accept.
However, in the heat of debate, the magic word "resurrection" was
enough to cause the Pharisees in the council to turn upon the Sadducees and opt for Paul's innocence.

Nevertheless, Paul's life remained in danger and somehow Acts does
not mention any part played by the Christians in Jerusalem generally
in all this. Perhaps they were too few in number to make their influence felt or to do anything but make Paul's position worse if they
tried. It is tempting, however, to wonder if perhaps the Jerusalem
Christians might not have been just a little pleased at Paul's troubles.
They might well have considered him a perverter of Christian doctrine
and his troubles might have been viewed as a judgment upon him.

Salvation for Paul came from the Roman captain, Claudius Lysias, who had apparently grown friendly with his prisoner. He decided to get Paul out of Jerusalem and assure his physical safety by sending him to Caesarea to be tried, legally, by the Roman authorities and provided an escort—

Acts 23:24. . . . *that they may . . . bring him* [Paul] *safe unto Felix the governor.*

After the death of Herod Agrippa I, Judea was placed under procurators once more, and each had to deal constantly with bandit leaders claiming to be messiahs and leading rebellions against the authorities.

Indeed, when Claudius Lysias had first taken Paul, he thought his prisoner to be one of these rebels; one who happened to be a Jew from Egypt.

Acts 21:37 . . . *the chief captain . . . said, Canst thou speak Greek?*

Acts 21:38. *Art not thou that Egyptian, which . . . madest an uproar, and leddest out into the wilderness four thousand men that were murderers?*

The first procurator to follow Herod Agrippa I was Cuspius Fadus, and he was succeeded by Tiberius Alexander, a Jewish apostate who was supposed to have been a nephew of Philo Judaeus himself (see page 301). In A.D. 48, about the time of the Council of Jerusalem, Ventidius Cumanus became procurator and governed for four years, through a constant haze of riots and insurrections. In A.D. 52 he was replaced by Antonius Felix, under whom the situation grew steadily worse.

Felix was a freedman (someone who had been born a slave but had been freed) and it was quite unusual for a freedman to become a royal governor. However, under Claudius, freedmen had been given important civil service posts, and one of the most important of these functionaries was Pallas.

This Pallas was not only influential with Claudius, but was also friendly with Claudius' fourth and last wife, Agrippina, who was intriguing for the succession to go to her son, Nero. Felix was the brother of Pallas and it is not surprising therefore that, although a freedman, he should be made procurator of Judea.

In A.D. 54 Agrippina finally won her victory. According to the story, she poisoned Claudius and her son, Nero, succeeded to the throne as the fifth Roman Emperor—a reign most fateful to both Jews and Christians.

Antipatris

Paul was taken out of Jerusalem, which he was never to see again:

> Acts 23:31. *Then the soldiers . . . took Paul and brought him by night to Antipatris.*

Antipatris, which is roughly halfway between Jerusalem and Caesarea, is thought to have been built on the site of ancient Aphek, where the Israelite army had been shattered by the Philistines in the time of the high priest Eli (see page I-271).

The city had been built anew by Herod the Great and it had been named Antipatris after the king's father, Antipater the Idumean.

Drusilla

Felix sat in judgment. The Jewish authorities accused Paul of stirring up dissension and profaning the Temple. Paul maintained that he was a Pharisee and again insisted he was being persecuted merely for believing in the Pharisaic doctrine of the resurrection.

Felix listened with considerable interest. He was no Claudius Lysias, and was apparently acquainted with Jewish doctrine, perhaps through his wife.

> Acts 24:24. . . . *Felix came with his wife Drusilla, which was a Jewess, . . . [and] sent for Paul, and heard him concerning the faith in Christ.*

Drusilla was the youngest of the three daughters of Herod Agrippa I, and was twenty-one years old at this time. She had divorced her previous husband under Felix's pressure and had been forced to marry this Roman Gentile in defiance of Jewish law. Felix lost interest in Christian doctrines, however, when Paul discoursed on its ethical content:

> Acts 24:25. *And as he [Paul] reasoned of righteousness, temperance, and judgement to come, Felix trembled, and answered, Go thy way . . .*

Felix kept Paul imprisoned for two years, more to prevent disorders in Jerusalem, perhaps, than out of any conviction of Paul's guilt. The terms of the imprisonment were not harsh. At the end of the two years, Pallas, the procurator's brother, had fallen from favor at the court of Nero, and Felix was relieved of his duties. Since this took place, most likely, in A.D. 61, we can place the time of Paul's visit to Jerusalem, his seizure, and his trial at Caesarea, in A.D. 59.

Festus

A new procurator took office:

Acts 24:27. . . . *after two years Porcius Festus came into Felix' room . . .*

The case of Paul was reopened before this new procurator, whose chief aim was to prevent unnecessary trouble with the increasingly troublesome people of the province. He therefore offered to have the apostle tried in Jerusalem. In order to quiet Paul's fears that such a trial might be an unfair one, the procurator offered to preside over it himself.

Paul did not think that Festus would, merely by his presence, insure a fair trial. Indeed, he probably suspected that Festus would be successfully pressured into a conviction, as had been the case with Pontius Pilate thirty-two years before.

Paul, therefore, appealed to the emperor, which was his right as a Roman citizen, and thus made it impossible for the procurator to do anything but send him to Rome.

Herod Agrippa II

Meanwhile, members of the house of Herod were on hand:

Acts 25:13. *And after certain days king Agrippa and Bernice came unto Caesarea to salute Festus.*

The Agrippa referred to here is Herod Agrippa II, the only son of Herod Agrippa I. He was born about A.D. 27, shortly before the crucifixion of Jesus. The young prince was brought up in Rome, where

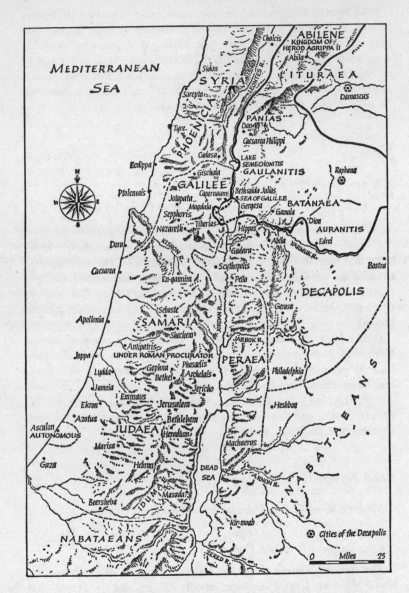

The Kingdom of Herod Agrippa II

his father was at that time such a favorite with the imperial family. Herod Agrippa was a boy of ten when his father began to rule over sections of Judea, and he was only seventeen when his father died. He was too young for Claudius to be willing to entrust him with the very difficult task of ruling all of Judea and the surrounding territory.

Agrippa's uncle, a younger brother of Herod Agrippa I, was still ruling a small section of land north of Galilee, having been made king there by Claudius in A.D. 41. The area was called Chalcis and Agrippa's uncle was therefore known as Herod of Chalcis.

Herod of Chalcis died in A.D. 48 and a year later Herod Agrippa II was appointed king in his place. In A.D. 53 Nero made him king, in addition, over sections of Galilee and Trans-Jordanian territories. He was the last of the Herodian line to rule anywhere in Jewish territories.

Now, in A.D. 61, Herod Agrippa II was coming to Caesarea from his capital, Tiberias, to convey formal greetings to Festus.

Five years later, he was to be in Jerusalem, when the disorders and fury of the Zealots were mounting toward the suicidal rebellion. Herod Agrippa II counseled patience and moderation but he was (and with justification) scorned as a Roman puppet, and ignored. In the rebellion, he sided with the Romans. In consequence he was able to retire to Rome after the destruction of Jerusalem and to live out the remainder of his life in comfort.

About A.D. 100 Herod Agrippa II, the great-great-grandson of Antipater the Idumean, and the great-great-great-great-great-great-great-grandson of Mattathias, the priest who had sparked the Maccabean rebellion, died. He was the last member of either family to be of any consequence at all.

Bernice, or Berenice, was his sister, the oldest of the three girls born to Herod Agrippa I. (Her youngest sister, Drusilla, had been married to Felix, the previous procurator.) Berenice had been married several times, the first time to her uncle, Herod of Chalcis. She left her third husband, a prince who ruled in Cilicia, to live with her brother at Tiberias. Gossip implied an incestuous relationship, but gossip then, as now, invariably placed the most scandalous possible interpretation on any event.

She too took the Roman side in the rebellion. In fact, she became the mistress of Titus, the young Roman general who finally captured and destroyed Jerusalem in A.D. 70. She went to Rome, along with

Titus and her brother, and remained there the rest of her life. She did not, however, remain Titus' mistress. The Romans were quite anti-Jewish in sentiment at this time and Titus was forced to put her aside. The year of her death is not known.

Paul now had still another hearing before Festus and Agrippa. His defense, couched entirely in Jewish terms, touched Agrippa, who said to Paul:

> Acts 26:28. . . . *Almost thou persuadest me to be a Christian.*

It was agreed that Paul had done nothing deserving of condemnation, but since he had appealed to the emperor, he would have to be allowed to go to Rome.

Myra

Under the guard of a centurion, Paul set sail for Rome, in what amounted to a fourth missionary voyage. Luke, if he is taken to be the author of Acts, was apparently one of the company:

> Acts 27:5. . . . *when we had sailed over the sea of Cilicia and Pamphylia, we came to Myra, a city of Lycia.*

Myra was thirty miles east of Patara, the port at which Paul had disembarked on his way to Jerusalem three years before. It was an important and populous city at the time and one of the chief towns of Lycia, but there is little but ruins left today. Paul's party took another ship and left, and Paul was never to see Asia Minor again.

Crete

And now the journey was beset by bad weather:

> Acts 27:7. . . . *we had . . . scarce . . . come over against Cnidus, the wind not suffering us, we sailed under Crete, over against Salmone;*
> Acts 27:8 And . . . *came unto . . . The fair havens; nigh whereunto was the city of Lasea.*

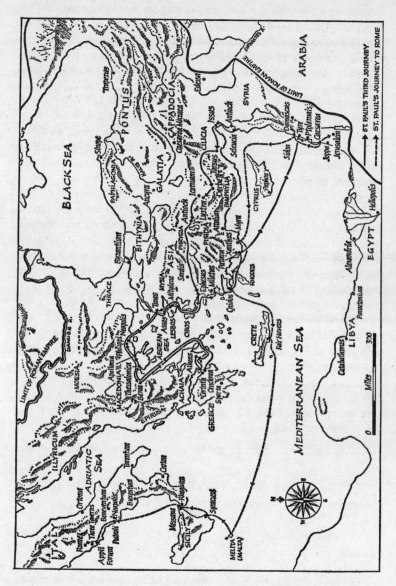

St. Paul's Third Journey and His Journey to Rome

Cnidus (or Cnidos) is a long promontory on the southwest coast of Asia Minor that juts out just south of the eastern edge of the island of Cos (see page 414). The city of Cnidus was at the tip of the promontory. It played no great role in Greek history, but one of the most famous mathematicians and astronomers of antiquity, Eudoxus, was born there.

Contrary winds did not allow a landing on Cnidus but drove them toward Crete, a hundred twenty miles toward the southwest. This is one of the large islands of the Mediterranean, 3200 square miles in area. It is about 160 miles long from east to west, but only 20 miles, on the average, from north to south.

In very ancient times—long before the time of Abraham, even—Crete was the seat of a high civilization. By 1400 B.C., while the Jews were in Egyptian slavery, Crete was taken by raiders from the Greek mainland and began a slow decline. It could still play an important role in the Trojan War about 1200 B.C., but after that it virtually vanishes from historic annals. All during the centuries in which the Greek cities were great, the Cretan cities were sunk in mutual warfare and banditry. It was a haunt of pirates at various periods when warfare preoccupied other powers and permitted piracy to flourish. In 67 B.C., Rome put an end to that by annexing it.

Paul's ship was driven southward around Cape Salmone at the northeastern tip of the island and came to rest in a harbor midway along the southern shore.

This harbor, Fair Havens, despite its name, was not suitable for any long stay. The captain of the ship therefore tried to make for a second and better harbor, some fifty miles westward along Crete's southern shore. A storm struck and beat the ship wildly along:

Acts 27:16. . . . *running under a certain island which is called Clauda . . .*

This island (called Gavdas nowadays) is a small bit of land some twenty-five miles south of the west end of Crete.

Melita

After most difficult times, the ship and its company was cast ashore on an island:

Acts 28:1. *And when they were escaped, then they knew that the island was called Melita.*

Melita is the island now known as Malta, about ninety-five square miles in area and nearly five hundred miles west of Crete. The island was first colonized by Phoenicians and, in the sixth century B.C., came under the control of Carthage, the greatest of all Phoenician colonies. In 218 B.C., at the very start of the second war between Rome and Carthage, Rome took over control of Malta and it remained part of the Roman realm thereafter.

The bay which the ship was supposed to have entered, near the northern tip of the island, is known as Saint Paul's Bay to this day.

Syracuse

Paul and his party stayed in Malta for three months, during the winter of A.D. 61–62. At the end of that time they left in a ship from Alexandria which had been wintering there.

Acts 28:12. *And landing at Syracuse, we tarried there three days.*

Syracuse was the largest and most notable city on the island of Sicily, which is, itself, not mentioned by name in the Bible. Sicily is the largest island in the Mediterranean, and is just about ten thousand square miles in area. It is about fifty miles north of Malta, and its northern tip is separated from the "toe" of the Italian peninsula by a strait that is, in spots, only two miles wide.

In the eighth century B.C. the eastern portion of Sicily was colonized by Greeks and the western portion by Carthaginians. For five hundred years, Greeks and Carthaginians fought each other on the island, without either being able to drive the other completely out.

It was only in 264 B.C. that the Romans finally reached the island. Their intrusion was the occasion of the first of three wars between Rome and Carthage. At the end of that war, Carthage was finally forced to abandon the island altogether.

The city of Syracuse on the east-central shore of Sicily was the oldest Greek settlement on the island. It was founded, according to tradition, in 734 B.C. (when Ahaz sat on the throne of Judah, and when the Kingdom of Israel had only a dozen years to live).

Syracuse took the lead in fighting the Carthaginians and, on several occasions, reached great heights of power. In 415 B.C., Syracuse had to face the unprovoked attack of a great Athenian fleet. That fleet was completely destroyed and this, more than anything else, helped break Athenian power and lead to the ultimate victory of Sparta over Athens.

In 390 B.C., under Dionysius I, Syracuse was at its peak. It drove Carthage from all but the westernmost tip of the island, and it took over the southern shores of mainland Italy as well. After Dionysius, however, there was a decline and the Carthaginians recovered.

When Rome took over the island after the first war with Carthage, Syracuse was left independent under its king, Hiero II. During his long reign of over half a century, Syracuse was more prosperous than ever, even though it was a Roman puppet. The greatest scientist of antiquity, Archimedes, lived there then.

On the occasion of the second war between Rome and Carthage, it seemed at first that Rome would lose. Syracuse hastily switched to the Carthaginian side and Rome sent out a fleet to occupy it. For three years, Syracuse fought desperately with the help of Archimedes' war weapons. In the end, however, in 212 B.C., Syracuse was taken and Archimedes died during the sack that followed.

After that Syracuse and all the rest of Sicily remained securely Roman, though the island was shaken by slave rebellions now and then.

Rhegium

Paul's party sailed north from Syracuse:

> Acts 28:13. *And from thence we . . . came to Rhegium: and . . . the next day to Puteoli . . .*

At the time that the Greeks were colonizing Sicily, they were also settling along the shores of the southern portion of Italy. On the tip of the "toe" of Italy, just across from Sicily, for instance, they founded the town of Rhegion (or Rhegium, in the Latin spelling) in 720 B.C., according to tradition.

It was ruled by Dionysius I when Syracuse was at the height of its power. Beginning in 280 B.C. the Romans took over the Greek cities in southern Italy one by one. Rhegium was the last to fall, becoming

Roman in 270 B.C. Throughout the Roman period, however, Rhegium retained its Greek language and culture and retained its self-government.

From Rhegium, Paul's party went to Puteoli, a city on Italy's southwestern shore, somewhat north of modern Naples. It was founded by the Greeks in 512 B.C. and taken over by the Romans in 215 B.C. It was a large trading center.

Rome

And so, finally, Paul came to Rome:

Acts 28:16. And . . . we came to Rome . . .

In A.D. 62, when Paul arrived in Rome, that city was great and prosperous, the most important city in the world. Nero was just about at the midpoint of his reign, and while he was pleasure-loving, wasteful, and autocratic, the city and the empire continued to be well governed in general.

The Book of Acts says little about the progress of Paul's appeal to the emperor. It records only that he attempted to convert the Jews of Rome to his way of thinking and failed again. After two years of house imprisonment he was freed and the last verse of the book records that he was:

Acts 28:31. Preaching the kingdom of God . . . with all confidence, no man forbidding him.

That was A.D. 64.

It is curious that the book ends there, since there was to follow that very year a terrible persecution of the Christians and since there is some evidence that Paul may have set out on his travels even further west. What's more, to carry the story only three years further would have brought it to the reputed year of Paul's death, A.D. 67.

One possibility is that Acts was written in A.D. 64, but this is pretty well discounted. The year of authorship is much more likely to have been something like A.D. 80. A second possibility is that Luke died before he had a chance to complete the book.

Most likely, though, the point chosen for the ending of Acts is deliberate. It represents a high spot.

Thirty-eight years had passed since the crucifixion of Jesus; thirty-three years, perhaps, since Paul's conversion. When Paul began his career, the Christian fellowship consisted of a small group of disciples gathered in Jerusalem, a group in danger of being wiped out by the opposition of the Jewish authorities.

When Paul ended his career, strong, well-organized, and vigorously proselytizing churches dotted Cyprus, Asia Minor, Macedonia, and Greece, and there were Christians even in Rome.

Very much of all this had been accomplished by one remarkable man—he who had been born Saul of Tarsus and who had become Saint Paul. Luke, his friend and physician, may well have wanted to end his biography of Paul at that moment when, having accomplished all this, he was resting secure in Rome, preaching as he wished and "no man forbidding him."

The darkness was soon to close in again, but Luke chose to leave Paul at this sunlit peak.

10. ROMANS

THE EPISTLE TO THE ROMANS • ROME • SPAIN • CIRCUMCISION • PRISCILLA
AND AQUILA • RUFUS • JASON • TERTIUS • GAIUS AND ERASTUS

The Epistle to the Romans

Following the Book of Acts in the New Testament are twenty-one
letters sent by various apostles to Christians generally, or to various
churches or individuals. The majority of these, as many as fourteen
according to some traditions, were written by Paul. These letters are
referred to as "epistles" (from a Greek word meaning "to send to").
The word is closely related to "apostle" (who is "sent away"). The
relationship is the same as that of "missive" to "missionary."

The various epistles include the earliest writings in the New Testament. Some of them may have been written as early as A.D. 50, almost
twenty years before even the first of the gospels we now possess reached
its present form, and fifty years, perhaps, before the fourth gospel
was written.

The Pauline epistles do not appear in the Bible in chronological
order. They seem, rather, to be placed in order of length, with the
longest first.

The first and longest epistle is listed in the King James Version as
"The Epistle of Paul the Apostle to the Romans" but it can be called
simply "Romans." Partly because of its length, it contains the most
complete exposition of Paul's religious thinking, which is a second
reason for placing it first. Then, too, since it is addressed to the
Christians of the empire's capital and largest city, the matter of prestige
might also have influenced the placing of the epistle.

The letter is not dated in the modern fashion or, for that matter,
in any formal fashion at all (nor is any other epistle). We must therefore seek its date (and those of the others) through indirect hints.

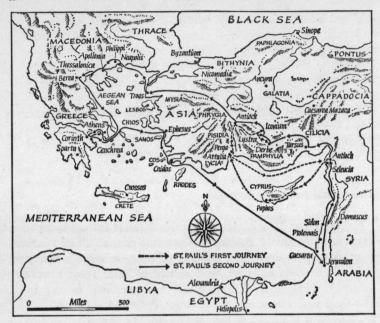

St. Paul's First and Second Journeys

Toward the end of the epistle, for instance, Paul tells the business that currently engages him:

> Romans 15:25. *But now I go unto Jerusalem to minister unto the saints.*
> Romans 15:26. *For it hath pleased them of Macedonia and Achaia to make a certain contribution for the poor saints which are at Jerusalem.*

This, apparently, is just the situation as it was described in the twentieth chapter of Acts:

> Acts 20:2. . . . *he* [Paul] *came into Greece,*
> Acts 20:3. *And . . . purposed to return through Macedonia.*
> . . . .
> Acts 20:6. *And . . . sailed away from Philippi . . .*
> . . . .
> Acts 20:16. . . . [*and*] *hasted . . . to be at Jerusalem the day of Pentecost.*

Paul was anxious, presumably, to bring the contributions sent by the relatively wealthy churches of Greece and Macedonia to the beset Christians of the mother church in Jerusalem.

This was at the end of Paul's third missionary voyage and if the letter were written while he was still getting ready to make the trip to Jerusalem, it should have been written in 58.

One guess is that at the time of writing, Paul was completing his stay at Corinth where there was a flourishing church which he had established in the course of his second journey. Thus, at the end of Romans, Paul says:

Romans 16:1. *I commend unto you Phebe our sister, which is a servant of the church which is at Cenchrea.*

Apparently Phebe is the bearer of the letter and this is to serve as her introduction to the Christian leaders in Rome. (She is mentioned as Paul's sister only in a figurative sense, of course.)

Cenchrea is a suburb of Corinth, five miles east of the city proper, on the eastern shore of the isthmus. Presumably, if Phebe is a native of Cenchrea, Paul is himself in the vicinity and, therefore, very likely at Corinth.

However, the sixteenth (and last) chapter of Romans is only questionably part of the original epistle and deductions based on its contents are therefore shaky ones.

Rome

The elaborate address with which Romans starts gives the name of the sender and those who are to receive it:

Romans 1:1. *Paul, a servant of Jesus Christ, called to be an apostle* . . .

. . . .

Romans 1:7. *To all that be in Rome . . . called to be saints . . .*

At the time the letter was written, Paul had never been to Rome, yet obviously Christianity had reached the city without him. No specific missionary activity on the part of any individual is described in the Bible as having carried the gospel to Rome, but that poses no problem.

There were Jews all over the empire, and there was definitely a colony of them in Rome. Jews from all over the empire, including the city of Rome, traveled to Jerusalem to be present at the Temple during the great feasts, whenever possible, and some of them undoubtedly brought back with them the new doctrines.

Spain

To be sure, Paul intended to visit Rome. Indeed, he hoped to carry the gospel throughout the empire and expressed that hope by projecting a visit to Spain. Jerusalem was in the empire's far east and to plan a visit to Spain in the empire's far west would be to state an intention of traveling throughout the empire:

> Romans 15:24. *Whensoever I take my journey into Spain, I will come to you* [the Romans] . . .

This, and another mention four verses later, is the only place in the Bible where Spain is directly referred to.

To be sure, there was the city of Tartessus, located on the Spanish coast beyond the Strait of Gibraltar (then called the Pillars of Hercules) near the site of modern Cadiz. It was a prosperous trading center, usually identified with the Tarshish mentioned in the Old Testament. King Solomon traded with it (see page I-332) and it is referred to in the Book of 1 Kings as an example of the worldwide spread of his power.

Tartessus, or Tarshish, became proverbial as a kind of "end of the world." After all, it was twenty-five hundred miles west of Jerusalem, and in Biblical times such a distance was almost the equivalent, in modern terms, of a trip to the Moon. Thus, when Jonah decided to run away from God rather than undertake the dangerous task of preaching in Ninevah (see page I-646) he decided to flee as far as possible; to the end of the Earth, in fact.

> Jonah 1:3. . . . *Jonah rose up to flee unto Tarshish from the presence of the Lord* . . .

Tarshish, however, is but very dimly known to us. Spain enters the full light of history only in the sixth century B.C.—at about the time the Jews were being carried off to Babylon.

In that century, both Greeks and Carthaginians were colonizing the Spanish coast and establishing towns. In 480 B.C., Tartessus (Tarshish) was destroyed by the Carthaginians.

After the first war with Rome, Carthage, which had been defeated and driven out of Sicily, turned her attention westward. In 237 B.C. she established her rule over a large section of southeastern Spain. That land was the base of the capable Carthaginian, Hamilcar, whose son, Hannibal, was one of the greatest generals of all time.

Hannibal forced a second war on Rome and nearly defeated her, but Rome endured and by 201 B.C. Carthage was utterly crushed. Rome took over the Carthaginian dominion in Spain, but the takeover was not a peaceful one and chronic warfare against the natives occupied Roman forces for the better part of a century. Indeed, even when Augustus founded the Roman Empire, there were still sections of northern Spain that maintained a stubborn independence of Rome. It was not until 19 B.C. that every bit of the Spanish peninsula could be considered securely Roman.

Paul did not visit Rome as soon as he planned, however, for the trip to Jerusalem which he was ready to undertake at the time of Romans, ended in his imprisonment by Felix (see page 417). It was not until five years after Romans that Paul finally came to Rome and then it was only as a prisoner appealing his case to the emperor.

Whether Paul then went on to Spain is not known. There is a reference in an early writing, dating back to about 95, that Paul reached the "limits of the west," presumably Spain, but such evidence is weak.

Circumcision

Paul deals in Romans with the problem which was paramount in the first decades after Jesus' crucifixion—whether Gentiles converted to Christianity had to be circumcised and observe all the ritual of the Law.

Paul's attitude toward circumcision and the Law was like Jeremiah's attitude toward the Temple (see page I-562). Circumcision, in Paul's view, could not be made use of as a magic talisman to bring automatic salvation to people who were sinful. Nor, by extension, could the absence of circumcision and the Law be considered as losing salvation for people who are otherwise righteous:

Romans 2:25. *For circumcision verily profiteth, if thou keep the law: but if thou be a breaker of the law, thy circumcision is made uncircumcision.*

Romans 2:26. *Therefore if the uncircumcision keep the righteousness of the law, shall not his uncircumcision be counted for circumcision.*

. . . .

Romans 2:29. . . . *he is a Jew, which is one inwardly; and circumcision is that of the heart, in the spirit, and not in the letter . . .*

Furthermore, Paul differentiates between the ritualistic aspects of the Law and its ethical aspects. Even if the Christian is freed from circumcision and other time-honored ritual, he is not freed from its ethics. The name of Christian is not an automatic shield against unrighteousness either:

Romans 6:15. . . . *shall we sin, because we are not under the law, but under grace? God forbid.*

Paul also makes a plea for tolerance.

In most of the churches established in the east, the converted Jews made up the majority at first and they accepted with difficulty, if at all, those converted Gentiles who would not be circumcised. Paul's weight was placed firmly on the side of the Gentile in those cases.

In Rome, however, the Gentile group may well have been the stronger almost from the first. The Emperor Claudius had expelled the Jews from Rome for a brief period about seven years or so before Romans was written. The Christian community in Rome would have had to get along with its Gentile members only. When the Jews returned, those among them who were Christians may have found themselves outsiders in the Church, opposed by those who had had nothing to do with the ritual of the Law and did not want the matter brought up.

Paul, in considering this situation, does not forget he himself is Jewish:

Romans 11:1. *I say then, Hath God cast away his people? God forbid, For I also am an Israelite, of the seed of Abraham, of the tribe of Benjamin.*

He argues that Jews will be converted; that if they show resistance to Christianity at the first, it is part of God's plan to make it easier for Gentiles to be converted. And he seems to plead with the Gentile Christians of Rome to tolerate the Christians of Jewish origin who are scrupulous with respect to such ritualistic matters as the dietary laws:

Romans 14:13. *Let us not therefore judge one another any more* . . .

Romans 14:14. *I know . . . that there is nothing unclean of itself; but to him that esteemeth any thing to be unclean, to him it is unclean.*

Priscilla and Aquila

The last chapter of Romans is very largely a list of names. There is Phebe, who apparently is the bearer of the letter, and then there is mention of over two dozen men and women to whom Paul sends greetings.

It seems unlikely that Paul would know a great many people by name in Rome, a city he had never visited, containing a fellowship with whom he had never dealt directly. There is some suggestion, therefore, that since Romans dealt with matters of interest and importance to Christians generally, and not merely to those of Rome, that copies of it may have been made for use by other churches. It may be, then, that the final chapter of greetings was attached to such a copy rather than to the original letter that made its way to Rome.

It is Ephesians, perhaps, rather than Romans who are being greeted, as might appear from the first to be greeted:

Romans 16:3. *Great Priscilla and Aquila* . . .
Romans 16:4. *Who have for my life laid down their own necks* . . .

Paul had brought Priscilla and Aquila from Corinth to Ephesus at the conclusion of his second missionary voyage (see page 406) and had left them there when he returned to Antioch. When Paul came again to Ephesus in the course of his third missionary journey, Priscilla and Aquila were still there, apparently, for it was during his stay in Ephesus at this time that he wrote epistles to the church at Corinth, and he mentions them there as sending their greetings along with his:

1 Corinthians 16:19. *The churches of Asia salute you. Aquila and Priscilla salute you . . .*

The reference in Romans to Priscilla and Aquila risking their life for Paul may refer to the occasion of the riot of the silversmiths (see page 411). There is no mention of a specific life-saving incident in Acts, but it is not difficult to imagine that Aquila and Priscilla may have done something to protect Paul from the fury of the mob at the risk of their own lives.

Since Romans was written within a year of Paul's leaving Ephesus after the silversmiths' riot, it seems quite likely that Priscilla and Aquila were still there and that the last chapter of greetings is indeed appended to a copy of the epistle which was sent to the Ephesian church.

Rufus

Most of the names in the final chapter of Romans are completely unknown except for their listing here. There is a natural attempt to identify as many of them as possible with those of the same names mentioned elsewhere in the New Testament. Thus, Paul says:

Romans 16:13. *Salute Rufus . . . and his mother . . .*

There is one other Rufus mentioned and that is in Mark. When Jesus is on the way to crucifixion, Mark says:

Mark 15:21. *And they compel one Simon a Cyrenian . . . the father of Alexander and Rufus, to bear his cross.*

Neither Matthew nor Luke, in telling of Simon of Cyrene, mentions his sons. That Mark does so would lead one to suppose that he knows them and expects his readers to know them, so that through them Simon of Cyrene might be identified.

After all, Mark (if he is indeed the author of the second gospel) did accompany Paul on at least part of his first missionary voyage, and might have known various other companions of Paul. If so, the Rufus whom Paul greets at the end of Romans and the Rufus who was the son of Simon of Cyrene may be one and the same.

On the other hand, Luke (if he is indeed the author of the third gospel) seems to have been a much closer associate of Paul than Mark was and he does not mention Rufus in connection with Simon of Cyrene.

And then, Rufus would be a common name. It means "red" and may well have been applied to a good percentage of those who happened to have red hair. It would be quite easy to suppose that Mark's Rufus and Paul's Rufus were two different people.

Jason

With his own greetings out of the way, Paul sends the greetings also of the close co-workers who were with him in Corinth at the time Romans was being written:

Romans 16:21. *Timotheus my workfellow, and Lucius, and Jason, and Sosipater, my kinsmen, salute you . . .*

Timotheus (a name more familiar, in English, as Timothy) is the young man who joined Paul in Lystra, on the latter's second missionary voyage (see page 391) and who remained a close associate of the apostle for the remainder of Paul's life. Lucius would seem to be the Luke who is considered to be the author of the third gospel and of Acts.

As for Jason, he is usually identified with a man of Thessalonica, who may have offered Paul and Silas the hospitality of his house when the apostle arrived at that city in the course of his second missionary voyage (see page 397). In Thessalonica, Paul and Silas were in considerable danger from a mob and Jason found himself in the midst of a riot:

Acts 17:5. *But the Jews which believed not . . . set all the city on an uproar and assaulted the house of Jason, and sought to bring them out to the people.*

Jason was dragged before the authorities and had to deposit bail in order to regain his freedom. Paul and Silas were, in the meantime, ushered safely out of the city and to Berea.

In Berea, they apparently gained another convert, Sopater, with whom the Sosipater of Romans 16:21 is usually identified. He is mentioned in Acts toward the close of the third missionary voyage, just after Romans was written. Paul is leaving Greece, and two of those mentioned at the close of Romans are going with him.

> Acts 20:4. *And there accompanied him into Asia Sopater of Berea . . . and Timotheus . . .*

Tertius

Apparently Paul commonly used a secretary to transcribe his words. This can be deduced from the fact that at the end of some epistles, Paul specifically mentions that the signature is his own, placed there by his own hand, as a sign of the authenticity of the letter. The remainder of the letter is therefore to be presumed to be by another's hand, written at Paul's dictation:

> 1 Corinthians 16:21. *The salutation of me Paul with mine own hand.*

This is, of course, not for a moment to be taken as indicating Paul to be illiterate. A learned Jew could not possibly be illiterate. Nevertheless, the use of a secretary leaves one free to think without the disturbance of having to form the words physically as one thinks. Then, too, there is the very practical point that a professional secretary is bound to cultivate a neat and legible handwriting, and it would not reflect on Paul's literacy to suppose that he (like many great men in history) may well have had a poor handwriting.

Romans is the one epistle in which the secretary is named, or, rather, names himself; and adds his own greetings:

> Romans 16:22. *I Tertius, who wrote this epistle, salute you . . .*

Or, it may be, Tertius is the man who made the copy that was sent on to the Ephesians.

Gaius and Erastus

Tertius adds the greetings of still others:

> Romans 16:23. *Gaius mine host . . . saluteth you. Erastus the chamberlain of the city saluteth you . . .*

Gaius is apparently offering Paul and his party the hospitality of his house at this time. If the epistle were indeed written in Corinth, then Gaius is a Corinthian and, indeed, a man of his name is mentioned in Paul's letters to the Corinthians:

1 Corinthians 1:14. . . . *I baptized none of you but Crispus and Gaius.*

Again, if Erastus is a city official, the city in question ought to be Corinth; and indeed in Paul's Second Epistle to Timothy, an Erastus is mentioned:

2 Timothy 4:20. *Erastus abode at Corinth . . .*

as though he were remaining behind in his home town. Thus, a number of points combine to make Corinth more probable as the place at which Romans was written.

11. 1 CORINTHIANS

The Epistles to the Corinthians

Following the Epistle to the Romans are two epistles to the Corinthians which can be referred to as "1 Corinthians" and "2 Corinthians." The first of these is almost the length of Romans, and the second is not much shorter.

The church at Corinth has been founded by Paul about 51, in the course of his second missionary voyage. He had reached Corinth after his unsuccessful stay in Athens (see page 402), and in Corinth he had met Priscilla and Aquila.

He returned to Antioch by way of Ephesus, taking Priscilla and Aquila with him and leaving them at Ephesus while he went on to Antioch. In the course of his third missionary voyage, Paul returned to Ephesus and remained there from 55 to 57. It was during this interval that he wrote 1 Corinthians for he says in it:

1 Corinthians 16:8. . . . *I will tarry at Ephesus until Pentecost.*

This cannot refer to his brief stay at Ephesus at the conclusion of the second missionary voyage for events are referred to in the epistle which must have taken place after that time.

In 1 Corinthians, Paul refers to a still earlier letter he had written to the men of that city:

1 Corinthians 5:9. *I wrote unto you in an epistle not to company with fornicators.*

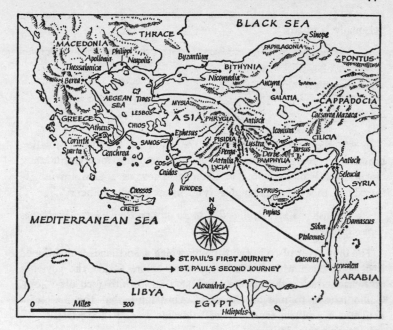

St. Paul's First and Second Journeys

This early letter (which we might call "0 Corinthians") is not, however, necessarily lost. Parts of it may have been combined by later editors with the two epistles we do have.

Stephanus

This very first letter, 0 Corinthians, which is not preserved separately in the canon, apparently elicited some sort of response, and a letter was brought to Paul in Ephesus by some of the leading men of the Corinthian church. At least Paul alludes to their coming:

> 1 Corinthians 16:17. *I am glad of the coming of Stephanus and Fortunatus and Achaicus* . . .

There are no other Biblical references to Fortunatus and Achaicus, but the fact that they are Corinthians seems evident from a reference made by Paul earlier in the epistle to people in Corinth whom he had personally baptized:

> 1 Corinthians 1:16. . . . *I baptized also the household of Stephanus . . .*

Sosthenes

It was the letter, and perhaps the word of mouth information brought by these Corinthian emissaries in response to o Corinthians, that caused Paul to write the letter we know as 1 Corinthians. He introduces this letter as coming from himself and another:

> 1 Corinthians 1:1. *Paul, called to be an apostle . . . and Sosthenes our brother . . .*

The only other place in the Bible in which a Sosthenes is mentioned is in connection with Paul's arraignment before Gallio the governor of Achaea, during the apostle's first stay at Corinth (see page 405). Gallio refused to rule on the case, maintaining that the matter of Paul was a problem for the Jews to decide among themselves.

Following this decision:

> Acts 18:17. . . . *all the Greeks took Sosthenes, the chief ruler of the synagogue, and beat him before the judgment seat . . .*

But there was no reason for the Greeks to beat him after Gallio had dismissed the case, and the King James translaters seem to have introduced the word unnecessarily. The Revised Standard Version has the phrase read: "And they all seized Sosthenes, the ruler of the synagogue, and beat him in front of the tribunal."

The "they all" might very likely refer to the Jewish conservatives who had come to the courtroom to hear sentence pronounced against Paul, and who were disappointed and frustrated over Gallio's action. They may have turned against their own leader, who, as "prosecutor," had mishandled and muffed the case.

Indeed, it might even be argued that the Jews felt that Sosthenes was "soft on Christianity" and had deliberately refrained from prosecuting Paul with full vigor. At least, there is a tradition that Sosthenes did turn Christian afterward and eventually joined Paul and was with him in Ephesus at the time 1 Corinthians was written. If this were so, Sosthenes would be a logical person to add his weight to the epistle, for he would be a Corinthian of note addressing Corinthians.

Apollos

Apparently one piece of news that disturbed Paul was the tale of dissensions and doctrinal disputes within the Corinthian church:

> 1 Corinthians 1:11. . . . *it hath been declared unto me of you . . . by them which are of the house of Chloe, that there are contentions among you.*

There is no other mention of Chloe in the Bible, but it is possible that Stephanus and the other emissaries met for worship in the house of a woman named Chloe. Perhaps there were other houses in which small groups gathered (the infant church at Corinth could very well have had no formal meeting house) and the emissaries were identified by naming their particular house.

Paul details the nature of the dissensions:

> 1 Corinthians 1:12. . . . *every one of you saith, I am of Paul; and I of Apollos; and I of Cephas; and I of Christ.*

This might be taken as referring to specific doctrinal difference that had already grown up around the leaders of the church. Cephas (the Aramaic name of which "Peter" is the Latin equivalent—see page 162) might represent the more conservative element of Jewish origin, holding to the Law; while Paul represented the liberal attitude that de-emphasized the importance of ritual.

Those who claimed to follow Christ might be "fundamentalists" who wished to adhere only to the reported sayings of Jesus himself and not to the added teachings of either Peter or Paul.

This leaves Apollos. Apollos had arrived in Ephesus after Paul had left it toward the conclusion of his second missionary journey. He had been a follower of John the Baptist, but Priscilla and Aquila had converted him to Christianity (see page 409).

After Apollos had become a Christian, he decided to go to Greece and work for the cause there:

Acts 18:27. . . . *he was disposed to pass into Achaia* . . .

. . . .

Acts 19:1. *And it came to pass, that, while Apollos was at Corinth* . . .

At Corinth, Apollos worked well, for Paul says:

1 Corinthians 3:6. *I have planted, Apollos watered* . . .

It is because Paul refers in this epistle to Apollos' work in Corinth, which had to come after Paul's first stay in Ephesus, that we know the epistle had to be written during Paul's second, and more extended, stay in that city.

Apollos' work in Corinth was sufficiently effective for him to win a personal following who admired him and considered him as their leader, as opposed to those who spoke of Paul. In what way Apollos' teachings differed from Paul's we don't know. The teachings might not have differed at all and the dispute may have rested on purely personal grounds; one group might have admired Apollos' style of preaching more than Paul's.

At least there seems to have been no animosity between Paul and Apollos. Some time before 1 Corinthians had been written, Apollos must have come back to Ephesus from Corinth and there he and Paul remained friends, for he is always referred to in friendly manner in Paul's letters:

1 Corinthians 16:12. *As touching our brother Apollos, I greatly desired him to come unto you* . . . *he will come when he shall have convenient time.*

The friendship remains, for in one of Paul's last letters, he commends Apollos to the care of the one he addresses:

Titus 3:13. *Bring Zenas the lawyer and Apollos on their journey diligently, that nothing be wanting unto them.*

Charity

Paul recommends unity to the Corinthian church and proceeds to answer questions concerning such things as the role of sex among

Christians. Paul believes sexual abstinence to be most desirable, but marriage is not sinful and is indeed necessary if that is the only way to keep a man from being driven into irregular unions by the whips of desire.

Paul clearly regrets that marriage should be necessary, for he, in common with the Christian fellowship generally, was convinced that the second coming was soon to take place (the new Messianic hope) and that worldly matters would come to an end, anyway:

> 1 Corinthians 7:29. *But this I say, brethren, the time is short . . .*
> . . . .
> 1 Corinthians 7:31. *. . . the fashion of this world passeth away.*

After dealing with such minor matters as the necessity for a man worshipping with his head uncovered and a woman doing so with her head covered, Paul passes on to the matter of spiritual gifts:

> 1 Corinthians 12:1. *Now concerning spiritual gifts, brethren, I would not have you ignorant.*

The phrase "spiritual gifts" is a translation of the Greek "charisma" which means "gift."

The Greeks had three goddesses that personified all that was delightful and charming. They were known by the related word "Charites" because the desirable qualities of person that made one attractive to others was considered to be a gift of these goddesses.

In Latin, these goddesses were the "Gratiae," which again carries the notion of "gifts" freely given without question of payment (that is "gratis," for which we are "grateful").

The goddesses become in English, the "Graces." A narrow use of the word has come to signify that gift of the Graces which is characterized by smooth and harmonious physical movement. This is "grace" and a person blessed with it is "graceful." More broadly, it can refer to a variety of gifts, and someone who is capable of making such gifts with an air of pleasure is "gracious."

Christians placed emphasis on the graciousness of God. In the old Jewish view, the relationship between God and "his chosen people" was that of a covenant or contract. God would take care of his people in return for their obeying the Law. But Christians now abandoned the Law and argued that in any case no return made by man was adequate as payment for the care taken of him by God. All that man received was the free gift of God without return. Thus, Paul says:

Romans 6:15. . . . *we are not under the law, but under grace.*

Paul lists some of the spiritual gifts awarded men by the grace of God; gifts including wisdom, faith, the working of miracles, prophecy, and the gift of tongues (see page 338). Paul admits all these to be useful gifts, but maintains one gift to be superior to all the rest:

1 Corinthians 13:1. *Though I speak with the tongues of men and of angels, and have not charity, I am become as sounding brass, or a tinkling cymbal.*
1 Corinthians 13:2. *And though I have the gift of prophecy, and understand all mysteries, and all knowledge: and though I have all faith . . . and have not charity, I am nothing.*

But what is charity? The Greek word used by Paul, which is here translated as "charity," is "agape," a word which is usually translated "love." In the Revised Standard Version, in fact, the passage begins: "If I speak in the tongues of men and of angels, but have not love . . ."

The Latin version of the Bible translates "agape" as "caritas" meaning "dear." Something is "dear" if it can be attained at a great price, or if it cannot be obtained even for a great price. If you love something you hold it dear regardless of its intrinsic worth.

For that reason "agape" meaning "love" and "caritas" meaning "holding dear" have much in common. The King James Version uses the closest English analogue of the latter and makes it "charity."

Unfortunately, the translation of "agape" leaves something to be desired in either case. Charity has come to be applied specifically to one aspect of "holding dear"—the ability to hold the poor and unfortunate so dear as to be willing to share one's own wealth and fortune with them. Charity has therefore been narrowed to mean almsgiving and since alms are often given grudgingly and with disdain, and are accepted with humiliation and muffled resentment, the word "charity" has even come to carry a somewhat tainted flavor.

Similarly "love" has come to be applied to that variety of "holding dear" which implies sexual attraction. It becomes almost embarrassing to those who are used to the occurrence of the word "love" in its popular-song sense, to hear Paul praise it. Sometimes there is the impulse to qualify it and translate "agape" as "divine love," "holy love," "spiritual love," or even "Christian love." However, those who experience "agape" even faintly know what Paul means.

As for the remaining spiritual gifts, Paul finds that of prophecy superior to that of tongues; indeed, he seems rather impatient with those possessing the latter gift. To have them too freely encouraged produces pandemonium at service. Paul therefore recommends that they speak only one at a time and even then only when someone with the corresponding gift of interpretation is present. It is interesting that Paul distinguishes between prophecy and tongues, because originally the two were the same (see page I-283).

For the further sake of order at worship, Paul recommends that prophets, too, speak only one at a time and that women not speak at all.

Ephesus

At the end of the epistle, Paul earnestly preaches the doctrine of the resurrection of the body. He points out that if there were no resurrection, then Jesus could not have been resurrected. And if Jesus were not resurrected, all Christian doctrine falls to the ground. And if that is the case what is the purpose of all their efforts? Why should not everyone live for the moment?

1 Corinthians 15:32. *If after the manner of men I have fought with beasts at Ephesus, what advantageth it me, if the dead rise not? let us eat and drink; for to morrow we die.*

The phrase about fighting with beasts may have been meant purely allegorically. Paul may have referred to his labors against the beasts of paganism and sin.

Perhaps, though, there is also something of the literal in it. Can Paul have in mind the rioting sparked by the silversmiths? Were these rioters the beasts? Or might he have considered the possibility of being condemned for blasphemy as an aftermath of the affair and made to undergo a punishment such as facing wild animals in the public arena? We can't tell.

12. 2 CORINTHIANS

Timotheus

The First Epistle to the Corinthians was given, presumably, to Stephanus and the others to take back to Corinth with them. Along with them, however, as a personal emissary, Paul was sending his beloved friend, Timothy; to instruct them in the Pauline doctrine anew:

1 Corinthians 4:17. *For this cause have I sent unto you Timotheus, who is my beloved son, . . . who shall bring you into remembrance of my ways, . . . as I teach every where in every church.*

He urges the Corinthians to accept Timothy kindly:

1 Corinthians 16:10. *Now if Timotheus come, see that he may be with you without fear . . .*

This sending of Timotheus is recorded in Acts. During Paul's stay in Ephesus in the course of his third missionary voyage, and just before the silversmiths' riot is described, he sends his emissaries:

Acts 19:22. *So he [Paul] sent into Macedonia . . . Timotheus and Erastus; but he himself stayed in Asia for a season.*

If this Erastus is the same referred to at the end of Romans (see page 438), he is a Corinthian and is going home.

Corinth

Eventually, Paul himself plans to go to Corinth:

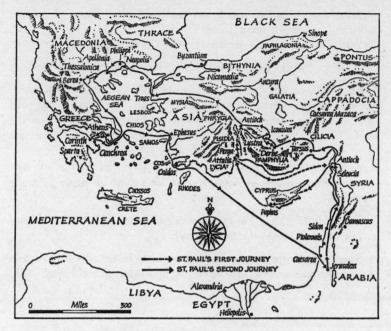

St. Paul's First and Second Journeys

1 Corinthians 16:5. *Now I will come unto you, when I shall pass through Macedonia* . . .

1 Corinthians 16:6. *And it may be that I will* . . . *winter with you.*

This, too, according to Acts, was done, for after the silversmiths' riots:

Acts 20:1. . . . *Paul* . . . *departed for to go into Macedonia.*

Acts 20:2. *And when he had gone over those parts* . . . *he came into Greece,*

Acts 20:3. *And there abode three months* . . .

If he abode three months in Corinth specifically, as seems very likely, this would be the second visit to that city mentioned in Acts. It is apparently while en route to Corinth in 57 that 2 Corinthians (or a part of it) was written. Both epistles to the Corinthians were thus written before Romans, which was composed after Paul had reached Corinth and settled down there.

With reference to his journey toward Corinth, Paul says:

> 2 Corinthians 13:1. *This is the third time I am coming to you* . . .

Apparently in between the first and second visits to Corinth which are mentioned in Acts, there was another visit. It is usually suggested that Timothy's mission met with failure and strong opposition on the part of those Corinthians who followed apostles other than Paul (see page 443). It was this which made Paul try a personal visit.

Apparently Paul's flying visit was a failure (and perhaps that was why it was not mentioned in Acts) and on his return he wrote an angry letter:

> 2 Corinthians 2:4. *For out of much affliction and anguish of heart I wrote unto you with many tears* . . .

This letter, written in anguish, is thought to be actually contained in 2 Corinthians as we now have it, making up the last four chapters.

Titus

The angry letter was sent to Corinth by the hand of Titus, a companion of Paul who is never mentioned in Acts, but is spoken of on several occasions in the epistles.

Titus is a Gentile, for in the Epistle to the Galatians, Paul describes his own coming to Jerusalem in 48 to attend the Council of Jerusalem and says:

> Galatians 2:3. . . . *neither Titus, who was with me, being a Greek, was compelled to be circumcised* . . .

Since the central issue facing the council was this very point of Paul's non-circumcision of Gentiles after conversion (see page 388) Paul was making his attitude quite plain in the heart of the territory of the opposition.

It was by this Titus that Paul sent his angry letter to Corinth and made up his mind to let that letter do its work and not go to Corinth again:

2 Corinthians 2:1. *But I determined . . . that I would not come to you in heaviness.*

However, when he left Ephesus after the silversmiths' riot, and traveled westward to Troas, he was worried over the fact that Titus had not returned:

2 Corinthians 2:13. *I had no rest in my spirit, because I found not Titus my brother . . . [so] I went from thence into Macedonia.*

There the news was good. He met Titus, who brought word that the pro-Paul faction at Corinth had won out:

2 Corinthians 7:6. . . . *God . . . comforted us by the coming of Titus;*

2 Corinthians 7:7. *And not by his coming only, but by the consolation wherewith he was comforted in you . . .*

. . . .

2 Corinthians 7:9. *Now I rejoice . . . that ye sorrowed to repentance . . .*

Part of the repentance, apparently, was the punishment of some individual who had offended Paul, perhaps on the occasion of his short second visit, by stubbornly opposing him. The person is not named and the occasion not described, but the punishment is sufficient.

Paul, apparently anxious not to allow his victory to engender such bitterness as to bring about an irrevocable split, urges forbearance. He writes a conciliatory letter (the first nine chapters of 2 Corinthians), again delivered by Titus, and in it he urges moderation, saying of the leader of the anti-Paul faction:

2 Corinthians 2:5. . . . *he hath not grieved me, but in part . . .*

2 Corinthians 2:6. *Sufficient to such a man is the punishment . . .*

2 Corinthians 2:7. . . . *ye ought rather to forgive him, and comfort him . . .*

And, eventually, Paul visited Corinth, sending 2 Corinthians in the course of this trip there, and nothing is said of further dissension.

13. GALATIANS

Galatia

The fourth of the epistles is addressed:

Galatians 1:1. *Paul, an apostle . . .*
Galatians 1:2. *. . . unto the churches of Galatia . . .*

The problem arises at once as to what is meant by "Galatia." Galatia proper was the region settled by the Gauls three centuries before Paul's time (see page 72). This was a relatively small area in north-central Asia Minor. After the Romans took over central and southern Asia Minor a century before Paul's time, the areas known as Lycaonia and Pisidia were combined with Galatia proper and the whole became the Roman "province of Galatia."

The original Galatia can therefore be called "North Galatia" and the Roman additions to it "South Galatia."

On Paul's first missionary journey, he and Barnabas traveled from Pamphylia through Pisidia and Lycaonia ("South Galatia"), then retraced their steps, so that cities such as Lystra, Derbe, and Antioch in Pisidia were probably visited twice.

On Paul's second missionary journey, he and (this time) Silas visited South Galatia:

Acts 16:1. *Then came he to Derbe and Lystra . . .*

Having done so Acts goes on later to say:

Acts 16:6. *. . . they had gone throughout Phrygia and the region of Galatia . . .*

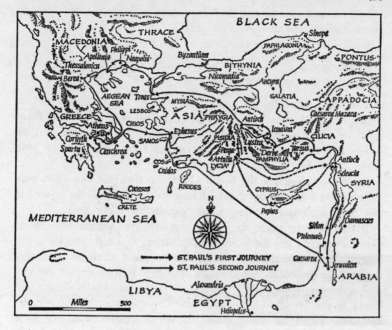

St. Paul's First and Second Journeys

It is possible that this includes portions of North Galatia, though no city in that region is specifically mentioned.

On Paul's third missionary journey, again it is said:

Acts 18:23. . . . *he departed, and went over all the country of Galatia and Phrygia in order.*

Again this may refer to North Galatia.

In short, there are four passages through Galatia mentioned in Acts:

(1) the first half of the first missionary voyage through cities of South Galatia specifically;

(2) the second half of the first missionary voyage through cities of South Galatia specifically,

(3) the second missionary voyage through cities of South Galatia specifically, but possibly also through North Galatia.

(4) the first part of the third missionary voyage, possibly through South Galatia, North Galatia or both.

In Galatians, Paul says:

> Galatians 4:13. *Ye know how through infirmity of the flesh I preached the gospel unto you at the first.*

The usual interpretation is that Paul is referring to a first visit in which he preached while quite ill. And if there was a first visit there must be a second, else why bother to identify the particular visit he is referring to by saying, to paraphrase the verse, "on that first visit when I was sick."

If Paul is addressing the South Galatians, then the two visits may be numbers 1 and 2 above, both having taken place in the course of the first missionary journey, which concluded about 47.

It was then the controversy broke out over the non-circumcision of Gentile converts and the Council of Jerusalem was called to settle the matter. Apparently the conservative view in favor of circumcision was particularly virulent in the Galatian churches. Indeed, during the second missionary voyage when Paul visited Derbe and Lystra (visit number 3 in the list above) and accepted Timotheus as his disciple, he cautiously urged his young friend to accept circumcision (see page 391).

Presumably, there was a strong party in the Galatian churches who denounced Paul's views and denied his authority to grant immunity from circumcision. Galatians is Paul's defense against this and his strong maintenance of his authority.

If Galatians were indeed written soon after the first missionary voyage, then it would have been written from Antioch in 47 and might well be the earliest of Paul's epistles to be preserved and, indeed, possibly the earliest of all the books of the New Testament to achieve written form.

Paul summarizes his early life, indicating the manner in which he was converted to Christianity, and of his labors since. He refers to Peter's coming to Antioch prior to the calling of the council and he refers also to Barnabas who was with him only on the first missionary voyage:

> Galatians 2:11. *But when Peter was come to Antioch, I withstood him to the face* . . .

. . . .

Galatians 2:13. . . . *Barnabas also was carried away with their* [those fearing the conservatives] *dissimulation.*

Paul does not specifically refer to the decision of the Council of Jerusalem (held in 48) which supported his views and which, one might think, ought therefore to be quoted. This backs the possibility of an early date for the epistle.

On the other hand, Paul speaks of reaching a private agreement with James, Cephas [Peter], and John:

Galatians 2:9. . . . *James, Cephas, and John . . . gave to me and Barnabas the right hands of fellowship; that we should go unto the heathen, and they unto the circumcision.*

This might have taken place prior to the first missionary voyage. But it might also have taken place after the council. With Paul's views having won out, James, Peter, and John were merely accepting the inevitable. And the agreement would be made with both Paul and Barnabas, even though it were after the first missionary journey, for although the two never joined forces again, they had planned to.

Acts 16:36. *And some days after Paul said unto Barnabas, Let us go again and visit our brethren in every city where we have preached . . . and see how they do.*

It was only after the subsequent quarrel concerning John Mark that Paul and Barnabas parted and that Paul went through Asia Minor with Silas instead.

If Paul speaks of a first visit to the Galatians, that might be the first of three, as well as the first of two. Or perhaps visits one and two are considered a single visit since they took place within the limits of a single missionary journey, and visit three, on the second missionary voyage, is counted as the second.

If Galatians were written after the Galatian visit in the course of the second missionary voyage, it might have been written from Corinth, where Paul stayed for an extended period after having passed through Asia Minor. The epistle would then have been written in 51 rather than 47.

If the late date is accepted, one must ask why the Galatian churches did not accept the decision of the Council of Jerusalem. Why were they still so turbulent on the matter of circumcision that Paul had to send a strong letter of rebuke?

As it happens, decisions by the head of organizations are not always accepted by every one in the organization. There might well have been a strong conservative party who rejected the council's decision.

And if Paul does not refer to the council's decision in the epistle to bolster his own view it might well be that he scorned to reply on the authority of James, Peter, and John, but insisted on something more than this. There are several places in Galatians where he goes out of his way to stress his lack of debt to the Galilean apostles.

Thus, he starts off proudly:

> Galatians 1:1. *Paul, an apostle, (not of men, neither by man, but by Jesus Christ, and God the Father* . . .

Furthermore, he insists that he need submit to no other authority, for his doctrine was not something he learned from the other apostles who had known the living Jesus, but something he had learned directly by revelation:

> Galatians 1:12. *For I* [Paul] *neither received it* [his doctrine] *of man, neither was I taught it, but by the revelation of Jesus Christ.*

If, however, Paul is addressing the people of North Galatia, then he couldn't possibly have visited them twice until after the first part of his third missionary journey. He might therefore have written Galatians during his stay in Ephesus, shortly before he wrote 1 Corinthians, or even in Corinth in 58, shortly before he wrote Romans. Some commentators prefer this late date because they view the subject matter of Galatians and Romans to be much alike, with Romans a more detailed and thoughtful version.

14. EPHESIANS

Epistle to the Ephesians

Whereas the first four epistles are universally admitted to have been written by Paul, there is a dispute about the fifth, even though in the version that has reached us, Paul's authorship is stated:

> Ephesians 1:1. *Paul, an apostle of Jesus Christ . . . to the saints which are at Ephesus . . .*

Included in the reasons for doubting Paul's authorship are certain differences in style between this epistle and those which are undoubtedly Paul's, and the use of numerous words not characteristic of Paul's other writings. Furthermore, although written to the Ephesians, presumably late in Paul's life, after he had spent some years in the city, it contains no personal greetings.

It is possible, of course, that the letter was not written to the Ephesians specifically, for at least one very early manuscript does not contain the words "at Ephesus" in the first verse. Perhaps it was an epistle meant for churches generally, with copies sent to specific areas with appropriate place names added; and perhaps the one that has survived was the Ephesian copy.

Traditionally, Ephesians was one of a group of epistles written in 62 while Paul was in prison in Rome, but this, too, can be disputed. Even those who agree that the epistle was written in prison may argue, in some cases, that the imprisonment was the one at Caesarea, prior to the voyage to Rome (see page 419), and that the epistle was written in 59. Others even argue for an imprisonment at Ephesus, not mentioned in Acts, at the time of the silversmiths' riot, about 57.

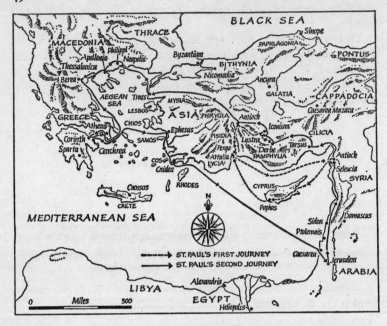

St. Paul's First and Second Journeys

Tychicus

The bearer of the letter, whether a circular one to a number of
churches, or indeed a specific one to the Ephesians, was Tychicus.

> Ephesians 6:21. . . . *Tychicus, a beloved brother and faithful
> minister in the Lord, shall make known to you all things . . .*

In the Book of Acts, Tychicus is mentioned toward the close of
the third missionary journey, when Paul was leaving Macedonia for
Asia Minor:

> Acts 20:4. *And there accompanied him into Asia Sopater of
> Berea . . . and of Asia, Tychicus and Trophimus.*

Tychicus, being a native of the province of Asia, may well have
been an Ephesian (Ephesus was the capital of the province) and

could have been taking the epistle with him on the occasion of a visit home.

Tychicus may have been left behind in Asia Minor after leaving Macedonia with Paul, while the apostle went on to Jerusalem and imprisonment. If so, he rejoined Paul later on, for he is mentioned in several of Paul's later epistles, and could have been the bearer of Ephesians even if it were written as late as 62.

15. PHILIPPIANS

THE EPISTLE TO THE PHILIPPIANS * BISHOPS AND DEACONS * EPAPHRODITUS
* TRUE YOKEFELLOW

The Epistle to the Philippians

This, like Ephesians, is supposed to have been written from prison. Paul alludes to his being in chains:

Philippians 1:13. . . . *my bonds in Christ are manifest in all the palace* . . .

The phrase "in all the palace" is given in the Revised Standard Version as "throughout the whole praetorian guard." Since the praetorian guard was stationed in Rome, the site of the imprisonment would seem to be fixed there. This is further evidenced by a reference toward the end of the epistle:

Philippians 4:22. *All the saints salute you, chiefly they that are of Caesar's household.*

Presumably those of Caesar's households are those servants or slaves of the emperor who had been converted to Christianity. Caesar is a common title for the Roman Emperor, in this case, Nero, and this would seem to make it definite that the epistle was written at Rome some time between 62 and 64. (Nero's violent persecution of the Christians after the fire of 64 could scarcely have left any Christians among his own household.)

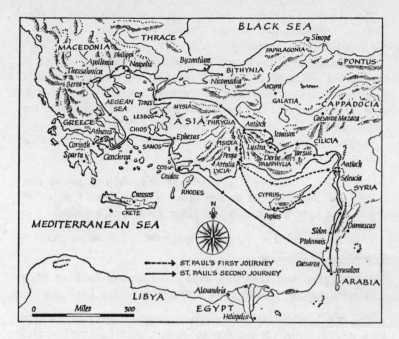

St. Pauls' First and Second Journeys

Bishops and Deacons

The epistle begins:

> Philippians 1:1. *Paul and Timotheus . . . to all the saints which are at Philippi, with the bishops and deacons.*

Philippi is the Macedonian city which Paul visited in the course of his second missionary voyage (see page 395). It was there that Paul founded a European church for the first time.

The faithful Timotheus is with Paul, but is not apparently under formal imprisonment himself, or, if he is, he is soon to be released, for the apostle hopes to send his friend to Philippi:

> Philippians 2:19. . . . *I trust in the Lord Jesus to send Timotheus shortly unto you . . .*

The reference to bishops and deacons gives us a tantalizing glimpse as to the organization of the early Church, just enough to rouse curiosity, without even beginning to satisfy it.

The first leaders of the church were the apostles themselves, but as the number of Christians increased, other leaders were appointed. It is only natural that these were chosen from among those men preeminent for experience and wisdom. These were most likely to be the older men and they would naturally be called "elders."

Thus, when the dispute arose as to the noncircumcision of Gentile converts:

> Acts 15:2. . . . . *they* [the church at Antioch] *determined that Paul and Barnabas, and certain other of them, should go up to Jerusalem unto the apostles and elders about this question.*

What's more, elders were regularly appointed in the various churches founded by missionaries:

> Acts 14:23. *And when they* [Paul and Barnabas] *ordained elders in every church . . . they commended them to the Lord . . .*

This rule by elders was so universally accepted a matter that the Bible scarcely bothers to mention the matter. Such rule was accepted in secular governments as well as in religious bodies. Sparta was ruled by a body called the "Gerusia" (from a Greek word for "old man") and Rome was ruled by a body called the "Senate" (from a Latin word for "old man").

(It should be mentioned, however, that we need not visualize the elders as necessarily ancient graybeards. In ancient societies, where the average life expectancy was thirty-five at best, anyone over forty qualified as an "elder.")

The Greek word for "elder" is "presbyter" (from another Greek term for "old man"). This was corrupted into "prester" (as in the legendary Prester John) and in English has become "priest."

Paul uses the term "episkopos" (or "episcopus" in the Latin spelling) as a synonym for presbyter. It means "overseer," someone who is in charge and guides the way. "Episcopus" has become, in English, "bishop." The word "deacon" is from the Greek "diakonos" and means "servant." Consequently, when Paul's words are translated as "bishops and deacons" what is really meant are "the elders and their helpers."

After New Testament days the Church developed a complicated hierarchy ("sacred government") of many levels. The basic groupings were in order of decreasing authority: bishops, priests, and deacons. A church in which bishops hold authority over wide areas is "episcopalian" in character. The Roman Catholic Church is episcopalian, as is the Greek Orthodox Church and several Protestant churches, such as the Lutherans and Anglicans. The American analogue of the Anglicans calls itself the Protestant Episcopal Church.

The Presbyterian Church is one in which bishops are not recognized but in which the elders ("presbyters") in each church hold authority on an equal basis.

None of the present significance of bishops, priests, and deacons can safely be read back into the New Testament, however.

Epaphroditus

Apparently, Paul's relationship with the Philippian church was a good one and the letter is an affectionate one of gratitude and of warm exhortation. Indeed, the occasion of the letter is the arrival of a messenger from Philippi with a contribution of money for Paul:

Philippians 4:18. . . . *I am full, having received of Epaphroditus the things which were sent from you . . .*

Furthermore, this was not the only time that the Philippians had contributed to Paul's needs:

Philippians 4:15. . . . *when I departed from Macedonia, no church communicated with me as concerning giving and receiving, but ye only.*

Philippians 4:16. *For even in Thessalonica ye sent once and again unto my necessity.*

While in Rome, Epaphroditus fell sick, but recovered and now was returning to Philippi with Paul's letter:

Philippians 2:27. . . . *he was sick nigh unto death: but God had mercy on him . . .*

Philippians 2:28. *I sent him therefore the more carefully, that, when ye see him again, ye may rejoice . . .*

True Yokefellow

At the end of the epistle, Paul raises the matter of some small dispute between two women of the Philippian church:

> Philippians 4:2. *I beseech Euodias, and beseech Syntyche, that they be of the same mind in the Lord.*
> Philippians 4:3. *And I intreat thee also, true yokefellow, help those women which laboured with me in the gospel . . .*

Nothing further is known of Euodias or Syntyche or what their quarrel was about. However, the phrase "true yokefellow" is of interest. Whom could it mean?

There are some suggestions that it referred to Paul's wife and a number of early commentators on the Bible supposed that Paul had married Lydia, the seller of purple dye whom he met in Philippi and with whom he stayed (see page 396). This does not seem very likely since Paul speaks as though he were unmarried. For in 1 Corinthians, when he reluctantly allows marriage in preference to irregular sexual unions, he wishes that this were not necessary:

> 1 Corinthians 7:7. *For I would that all men were even as I myself . . .*

This would certainly imply that Paul had never had relations with a woman. One might argue, perhaps, that he might have married for companionship, even if sex were out of the question. Indeed, Paul claims the right to do so if he chose:

> 1 Corinthians 9:5. *Have we not power to lead about a sister, a wife, as well as other apostles . . .*

But did he actually do so? It is generally assumed he did not.

But if the "true yokefellow" is not Paul's wife (and the phrase is, in any case, masculine in form in the Greek) it could refer to a close fellow worker in Philippi. A number of names have been suggested—Luke, for instance—but there is no really convincing argument in favor of any of those suggested.

One interesting possibility is that what is intended here is a personal name. The word "yokefellow" is the translation of the Greek

"Syzygos." Could there be a man with that name? Could Paul, by "true Syzygos" mean that Syzygos is well named for he is a Syzygos ("yokefellow," "co-worker") in nature and deed as well as in name. The trouble with that theory is that Syzygos is not known to have been used as a personal name by the Greeks.

The mystery will probably never be solved.

16. COLOSSIANS

Colosse

The next epistle (apparently also written from Rome in 62) is addressed to a city which Paul had never visited and which is not mentioned in Acts:

> Colossians 1:1. *Paul . . . and Timotheus . . .*
> Colossians 1:2. *To the saints . . . which are at Colosse . . .*

Colosse, or, more properly, Colossae, is a city in the province of Asia, about 125 miles east of Ephesus. In the time of the Persian Empire, it had been a great city on an important trading route. Since the time of Alexander the Great, it had been declining.

Epaphras

If Paul had not himself visited Colossae and founded its church, a close co-worker apparently did so. He speaks of the Colossians knowing the gospel:

> Colossians 1:7. *As ye also learned of Epaphras our dear fellow-servant, who is for you a faithful minister of Christ . . .*

Paul mentions Epaphras again at the close of the epistle as one of those who sent his regards, so that Epaphras must have been with him in Rome. This is made even more explicit at the close of the brief

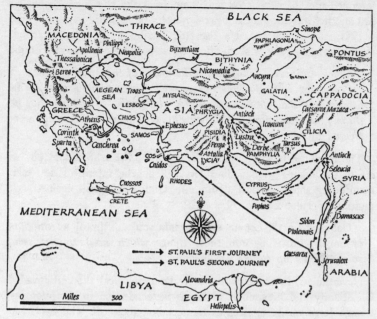

St. Paul's First and Second Journeys

Epistle to Philemon, which was written about the same time as Colossians. There he says:

> Philemon 1:23. *There salute thee, Epaphras, my fellowprisoner in Christ Jesus* . . .

The term "fellowprisoner" might merely be a metaphorical expression for two individuals who are both completely obedient (and, therefore, slaves) to the Christian doctrine. Or it might mean that Epaphras was not merely with Paul but that he was also in chains.

Thrones, Dominions, Principalities, and Powers

The occasion for the epistle was the news that had come to Paul that the Colossians were falling under the influence of Gnosticism (see page 301). Some of the Colossians were coming to accept mystical doctrines concerning vast heavenly hierarchies of angels, all serving as intermediaries between God and man. Jesus, by this view, would be just another intermediary and perhaps not a particularly important one. This Paul denounces. He lists the attributes of Jesus, insisting, eloquently, that Jesus is all in all and that nothing can transcend him:

> Colossians 1:15. . . . [Jesus] *is the image of the invisible God . . .*
> Colossians 1:16. *For by him were all things created, that are in heaven, and that are in earth, visible and invisible, whether they be thrones, or dominions, or principalities, or powers: all things were created by him and for him.*

The reference to the thrones, dominions, principalities, and powers are to the names given various levels of angelic intermediaries, each manifesting some mystical attribute of God. Paul warns against such mystical speculations:

> Colossians 2:18. *Let no man beguile you . . .* [into] *worshipping of angels, intruding into those things which he hath not seen, vainly puffed up by his fleshly mind.*

Nevertheless, in the centuries after Paul, mystical thought invaded Christianity and hierarchies of angels were adopted in profusion, although Jesus was recognized as transcending them all. The two highest, seraphim and cherubim, come from the Old Testament, as do the two lowest, archangels and angels. The intermediate levels: thrones, dominions, virtues, powers, and principalities are, however, taken from the Gnostic theories that Paul denounces.

Laodicea

Paul seizes the opportunity to address also the church in nearby Laodicea:

> Colossians 4:16. *And when this epistle is read among you, cause that it be read also in the church of the Laodiceans . . .*

Laodicea was located about ten miles west of Colossae. The town on its site was rebuilt and improved about 250 B.C. by Antiochus II of the Seleucid Empire, who named it after his wife Laodike. It remained Seleucid till 190 B.C. when, after the defeat of Antiochus III by Rome, the region about it was awarded to Rome's ally, Pergamum.

In 133 B.C. it became Roman along with the rest of Pergamum (thereafter known as the province of Asia or, simply, Asia).

As Laodice, after its renovation, grew in prosperity, that of the nearby city Colossae declined. Hierapolis, about ten miles north of Laodicea, is also mentioned at the close of the epistle. Speaking of Epaphras, Paul says:

Colossians 4:13. . . . he hath a great zeal for you, and them that are in Laodicea, and them in Hierapolis.

Tychicus

The epistle is to be taken to Colossae by Tychicus the Asian (see page 458).

Colossians 4:7. All my state shall Tychicus declare unto you . . .

A similar statement occurs at the end of Ephesians:

Ephesians 6:21. . . . that ye also may know my affairs and how I do, Tychicus . . . shall make known to you all things . . .

It seems hard to suppose that Tychicus would make two trips to Asia Minor from Rome, if both Ephesians and Colossians were written during the Roman imprisonment. Perhaps there was only one letter, that to the Colossians, and perhaps Ephesians was an epistle written later in time by someone other than Paul in imitation of Colossians. There are certainly similarities between the two, for in Ephesians also is stressed the transcendence of Jesus:

Ephesians 1:20. . . . he [God] raised him [Jesus] from the dead, and set him at his own right hand . . .

Ephesians 1:21. Far above all principality, and power, and might, and dominion, and every name that is named, not only in this world, but also in that which is to come:

Nevertheless, if we were to maintain that there were two letters, both by Paul, we might suppose that he wrote a general letter to be taken from church to church in Asia Minor (the one we now know as Ephesians because the copy to Ephesus had happened to survive) and a more sharply focused one addressed to the Colossians specifically, because they seemed more prone to the Gnostic views than the others.

On his way to Colossae, Tychicus may have delivered copies of Ephesians to various churches, including that at Laodicea.

Thus, when Paul asks the Colossians to have the epistle to them read to the Laodiceans, he adds:

Colossians 4:16. . . . and . . . ye likewise read the epistle from Laodicea.

This may refer to the copy of Ephesians sent to Colossae from Laodicea.

Aristarchus

Paul sends greetings from those with him:

Colossians 4:10. Aristarchus my fellowprisoner saluteth you, and Marcus, sister's son to Barnabas . . .

Marcus is presumably John Mark, and if he is now with Paul, the old quarrel (see page 390) seems to have been made up.

Aristarchus, a Macedonian of Jewish background, had been with Paul in Ephesus at the time of the silversmiths' riot and had been, in fact, in considerable danger.

Acts 19:29. And the whole city was filled with confusion: and having caught Gaius and Aristarchus, men of Macedonia, Paul's companions in travel, they [the rioters] rushed with one accord into the theater.

They were not killed, however, and Aristarchus accompanied Paul to Macedonia and Greece, then back to Asia and, eventually, Jerusalem:

Acts 20:4. And there accompanied him [Paul] into Asia . . . of the Thessalonians, Aristarchus and Secundus . . .

Later, Aristarchus accompanied Paul on his eventful sea voyage to Rome:

Acts 27:2. . . . we launched, meaning to sail by the coasts of Asia; . . . Aristarchus, a Macedonian of Thessalonica, being with us.

Demas

With Paul also are Luke and Demas:

Colossians 4:14. *Luke, the beloved physician, and Demas, greet you.*

Demas is mentioned also in the accompanying Epistle to Philemon, which sends greetings from the same group:

Philemon 1:23. *There salute thee Epaphras* . . .
Philemon 1:24. *Marcus, Aristarchus, Demas, Lucas* . . .

Demas is referred to once again in a still later epistle. Apparently Demas could not, in the end, take the hardships of being a Christian and, facing the virtual certainty of cruel martyrdom, forsakes Paul—and possibly Christianity as well. Paul says sadly:

2 Timothy 4:10. *For Demas hath forsaken me, having loved this present world, and is departed unto Thessalonica* . . .

17. 1 THESSALONIANS

Thessalonica

Paul and Silas had visited Thessalonica in the course of Paul's second missionary journey but had not been well received. They had been driven out by members of the Jewish colony, indignant at what seemed to them to be heresy (see page 398). The two missionaries and their company had moved on to Berea in Macedonia, then southward to Athens and Corinth.

Nevertheless, a Christian church had been founded at Thessalonica, made up of men who were of Gentile origin chiefly, and it is these whom Paul addresses:

1 Thessalonians 1:1. *Paul, and Silvanus, and Timotheus, unto the church of the Thessalonians* . . .

The Thessalonian church is apparently vigorous and pious. Paul praises them and explains that he would like to visit them but could not at the moment. He therefore took the step of sending his tried companion, Timotheus, to them:

1 Thessalonians 3:1. *Wherefore when we could no longer forbear, we thought it good to be left at Athens alone;*
1 Thessalonians 3:2. *And sent Timotheus . . . to comfort you* . . .

Timotheus returned with good news concerning the Thessalonians, and Paul now writes to expound on some points of doctrine.

This letter must have been written during Paul's first stay in Corinth,

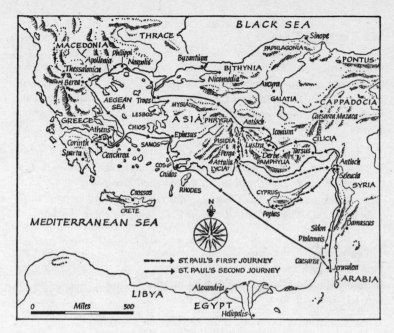

St. Paul's First and Second Journeys

after he had left Athens, for in Acts we find he was already there when Timotheus returned:

> Acts 18:1. *After these things Paul departed from Athens, and came to Corinth;*

. . . .

> Acts 18:5. *And when Silas and Timotheus were come from Macedonia, Paul . . . testified to the Jews that Jesus was Christ.*

All are together, in Corinth, and 1 Thessalonians is sent to Thessalonica in the name of all three. It follows that 1 Thessalonians was written about 50 and that it is very likely the earliest of Paul's writings to survive. There is a chance that Galatians was written as early as 47 (see page 455), but this is not considered very likely and most commentators accept 1 Thessalonians as the earliest.

The Trump of God

Apparently the Thessalonian church, mostly Gentile, is unused to the theological principles developed in Judaism by the Pharisees and is concerned over the matter of the resurrection and the final judgment. Paul reassures them and describes the second coming in dramatic terms:

> 1 Thessalonians 4:16. . . . *the Lord himself shall descend from heaven with a shout, with the voice of the archangel, and with the trump of God: and the dead in Christ shall rise first:*
> 1 Thessalonians 4:17. *Then we which are alive and remain shall be caught up together with them in the clouds, to meet the Lord in the air.*

The picture of the "voice of the archangel, and . . . the trump of God" lives with us in the common tradition of the archangel Gabriel sounding the last trumpet as the final judgment comes. Paul speaks of this last trumpet in 1 Corinthians, too:

> 1 Corinthians 15:51. . . . *we shall all be changed,*
> 1 Corinthians 15:52. *In a moment, in the twinkling of an eye, at the last trump . . .*

Nevertheless, Paul does not say it will be Gabriel blowing his horn, nor is this said anywhere in the Bible.

Paul is convinced that the time of the second coming is not to be long delayed and certainly the use of "we" in 1 Thessalonians 4:17 points up his conviction that the great day would come in his own lifetime. Nevertheless, he is careful not to specify exact times:

> 1 Thessalonians 5:1. *But of the times and the seasons, brethren, ye have no need that I write unto you.*
> 1 Thessalonians 5:2. *For yourselves know perfectly that the day of the Lord so cometh as a thief in the night.*

18. 2 THESSALONIANS

Man of Sin

The Second Epistle to the Thessalonians must have followed hard upon the first, so it too may be dated 50 and considered to have been written in Corinth.

Apparently Paul's first letter created a disturbing stir. Some of the Thessalonians rejected the possibility of the second coming, since everything seemed to be going so ill and the persecutors seemed so powerful.

Paul therefore strenuously described the day of judgment again, as a time of punishment for those who seemed so triumphant now:

2 Thessalonians 1:7. . . . *the Lord Jesus shall be revealed from heaven with his mighty angels,*

2 Thessalonians 1:8. *In flaming fire taking vengeance on them that know not God, and that obey not the gospel of our Lord Jesus Christ:*

He assures them that the great day is coming, but points out that an essential prelude to that day is the temporary triumph of evil. The very hardness of the times is, in this view, but further evidence of the imminence of the Second Coming:

2 Thessalonians 2:3. . . . *that day shall not come, except there come a falling away first, and that man of sin be revealed . . .*

2 Thessalonians 2:4. *Who opposeth and exalteth himself above all that is called God or that is worshipped . . .*

This is reminiscent of a passage in Daniel referring to the Seleucid persecutor, Antiochus IV:

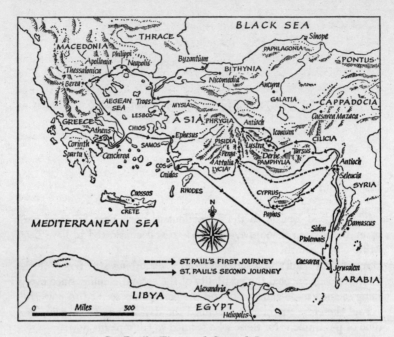

St. Paul's First and Second Journeys

Daniel 11:36. *And the king shall do according to his will; and he shall exalt himself above every god* . . .

So arises a parallel. As the success of the Maccabees came only after the dark days of Antiochus IV, so would the second coming come after the dark days of the "man of sin." Indeed, Daniel's words might be considered as referring immediately to the Maccabean era and ultimately to the day of judgment.

Paul may be echoing, here, Jewish mystical thought (which may in turn have Babylonian and Persian roots) in which there is a certain symmetry between the beginning and the end of creation. Thus, the heaven and Earth were created, to begin with, through the destruction of Tiamat in the Babylonian myth, or of Leviathan as is hinted in some Biblical verses (see page I-487). At the end of this creation, there is a second creation of a more glorious type still that comes after a second victory over the old enemy.

Ezekiel describes such a last battle between the forces of good and evil in his account of Gog of the land of Magog (see page I-594). Once Gog is destroyed, the ideal kingdom is established.

Jewish legend-makers, in the century before Jesus, gave the name Belial or Beliar (see page I-204) to this final adversary of God. This legend of Beliar may have been based not only on Antiochus IV but also on other great enemies of Jewish nationalism afterward, such as Pompey and Herod the Great.

It is to this final enemy that Paul refers when he says, in a deliberate concatenation of opposites:

2 Corinthians 6:15. *And what concord hath Christ with Belial?* . . .

In the gospels, Jesus is quoted as listing the ills that would come upon the world before the final judgment, and this includes men of evil who pretend to speak in the name of God but do not. They are false Messiahs:

Matthew 24:24. *For there shall arise false Christs* . . .

In the First Epistle of John, such false Christs are referred to as "antichrists" ("opposed to Christ").

1 John 2:18. . . . *ye have heard that antichrist shall come, even now there are many antichrists* . . .

If one speaks of "false Christs" and "antichrists" in the plural, the reference might be to evil people or evil forces generally. Paul, however, uses the singular. He speaks of "that man of sin." It is as though there is an Antichrist, a particular man or force whose business it is to oppose God, win a temporary triumph, and then be smashed into utter defeat.

It would seem quite reasonable to suppose that the single Antichrist was Satan, but this is not specifically stated to be so. The search was on, therefore, at various times in history for some individual human being who might seem to play the role of Antichrist.

Perhaps Paul had in mind Caligula who, in 41, just about a decade before the epistles to the Thessalonians were written, attempted to have himself worshipped as a god within the Temple itself.

However, Caligula had been assassinated before he could quite carry through his evil design, and, in any case, the world still stood. A dozen years or so after the epistles, Nero launched his persecution of the Christians in Rome and then many must have thought that here was

Antichrist at last. Other persecuting emperors—Domitian, Decius, Diocletian—may, in their turn, have seemed to fill the role.

Through the Middle Ages, Christians saw other Christians as antichrist and in the time of the Reformation, accusations flew thickly in both directions. Particular reformers were hailed as antichrist by Catholics; particular popes were awarded the title by Protestants.

As the world went on and the second coming was delayed, despite all these antichrists, the use of the term grew less frequent. Even men who would seem to be perfect examples of Antichrist to their enemies, as, for instance, Lenin or Hitler, were rarely (if at all) hailed with the title.

19. 1 TIMOTHY

Ephesus

Following 2 Thessalonians are three epistles attributed to Paul, which deal largely with practical advice on the management of church affairs and which are therefore often termed the "pastoral epistles."

(The word "pastor" originally meant shepherd, but has come to be used more frequently for priest, who is viewed as a shepherd of souls. The metaphoric view of humans as sheep overseen by religious leaders pictured as shepherds is common in the Bible. The most frequently quoted example is:

Psalm 23:1. *The Lord is my shepherd; I shall not want.*

The first of the pastoral epistles is written to Timotheus (Timothy, in English). It is one of a pair of such epistles and is therefore "the First Epistle to Timothy" or 1 Timothy:

1 Timothy 1:1. *Paul, an apostle of Jesus Christ* . . .
1 Timothy 1:2. *Unto Timothy, my own son in the faith* . . .

This epistle pictures a state of affairs that is rather puzzling. Paul speaks of himself as free and on his travels:

1 Timothy 1:3. . . . *I besought thee to abide still at Ephesus, when I went into Macedonia* . . .

and:

1 Timothy 3:14. *These things write I unto thee, hoping to come to thee shortly* . . .

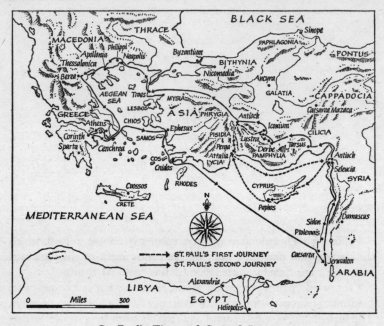

St. Paul's First and Second Journeys

It seems impossible to fit the situation in 1 Timothy into any period described in Acts and the only alternative (if Paul is indeed the writer of the epistle) is to suppose that the time referred to comes after the conclusion of Acts.

Acts ends in 64 (see page 427), the year in which Nero's persecution of the Christians in Rome took place. It would certainly seem natural to suppose that Paul would have been martyred in the course of that persecution. In the light of 1 Timothy, however, it is usually assumed that Paul was set free, presumably just before the fire at Rome that served as pretext for the persecution.

If Paul then left Rome for the east promptly, he would be out of the city when Nero seized Christians there, fed them to the lions, and made living torches out of them.

According to that view, Timothy, who had remained with Paul throughout his Roman imprisonment, would have accompanied the apostle to Ephesus and stayed there, remaining in charge of the

Ephesian church. According to later tradition, Timothy remained bishop of Ephesus for the remainder of his life, being martyred toward the end of the reign of the Roman emperor, Domitian, during another and more general persecution of Christians.

There are some who argue, however, that the pastoral epistles are not the work of Paul, but of a later writer who tried to give his views on church organization more authority by publishing them as the work of the apostle. This would make it unnecessary to make the troublesome assumption of Paul's liberation from Roman imprisonment in 64. It would also account for the fact that the style, vocabulary, and attitude of the pastoral epistles do not seem typical of Paul.

Hymenaeus

The epistle urges Timothy to deal firmly with heretics who teach false doctrine. Some have drifted away from the faith, says the writer:

1 Timothy 1:20. *Of whom is Hymenaeus and Alexander; whom I have delivered unto Satan* . . .

In other words, they have been excommunicated. Probably Hymenaeus and Alexander were Gnostics, for that particular heresy was strong in Asia Minor in the first century.

The excommunication did not serve to bring Hymenaeus back to orthodoxy, for in a Second Epistle to Timothy he is mentioned again, when false teachers are listed:

2 Timothy 2:17. . . . *their word will eat as doth a canker: of whom is Hymenaeus* . . .

Alexander, mentioned along with Hymenaeus in 1 Timothy, is mentioned again in 2 Timothy:

2 Timothy 4:14. *Alexander the coppersmith did me much evil: the Lord reward him according to his works* . . .

The bulk of 1 Timothy continues with rules for choice of bishops and deacons and with various regulations of churchly life.

20. 2 TIMOTHY

Troas

The Second Epistle to Timothy, which begins with verses almost identical with those of the First Epistle, gives additional instructions for church organization. It seems to make allusions to rather wide traveling

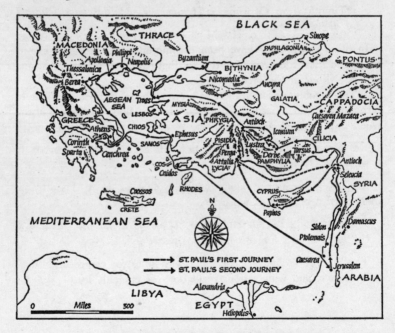

St. Paul's First and Second Journeys

after Paul's liberation from his imprisonment at Rome. He mentions Troas, for instance:

2 Timothy 4:13. *The cloke that I left at Troas with Carpus, when thou comest, bring with thee . . .*

He also mentions Miletus:

2 Timothy 4:20. *. . . Trophimus have I left at Miletum* [Miletus] *sick.*

It was during this period of freedom that Paul is assumed to have written 1 Timothy. His last missionary journey must soon have come to a close, however, for in 2 Timothy he speaks as someone who is condemned to death and is ready to die:

2 Timothy 4:6. *. . . I am now ready to be offered, and the time of my departure is at hand.*

2 Timothy 4:7. *I have fought a good fight, I have finished my course, I have kept the faith . . .*

The usual assumption is that Paul was imprisoned again and, this time, condemned and executed. The date of his death is given as 67 or 68, toward the end of Nero's reign. It follows that 2 Timothy is Paul's last epistle, if it is genuine.

21. TITUS

Crete

The third of the pastoral epistles is addressed to Titus (see page 450), who is in Crete:

> Titus 1:1. *Paul, a servant of God, and an apostle of Jesus Christ . . .*
> . . . .
> Titus 1:4. *To Titus, mine own son after the common faith . . .*
> Titus 1:5. *For this cause left I thee in Crete, that thou shouldest set in order the things that are wanting . . .*

Paul had sailed into a Cretan harbor on the occasion of his voyage to Rome (see page 424) and it is possible that Titus may have been left behind there at that time. Or Paul and Titus may have visited Crete during the supposed interval between two Roman imprisonments, and Titus may have been left behind on that occasion.

Paul warns Titus against the dangers of heresy and reminds him of the poor reputation of the men of Crete. Paul says:

> Titus 1:12. *One of themselves, even a prophet of their own, said, The Cretians are always liars, evil beasts, slow bellies.*

It is usually taken that the "prophet" being quoted is Epimenides of Knossos, concerning whom there is no hard information at all, only legend. He is supposed to have lived in the seventh century B.C. According to accounts in Roman times, he fell asleep in a cave when a boy and slept for fifty-seven years (the original Rip Van Winkle) and woke to find himself a wizard, living to an age of 150 or, according to some who are anxious to improve still further on a good story, 300.

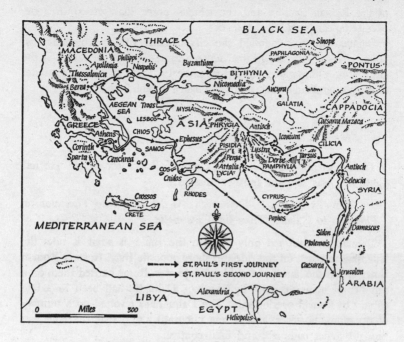

St. Paul's First and Second Journeys

Nicopolis

The Epistle to Titus seems to have been written while Paul was still at liberty for the apostle says:

Titus 3:12. . . . *be diligent to come unto me to Nicopolis: for I have determined there to winter.*

The epistle was therefore written before 2 Timothy.

The name "Nicopolis" means "City of Victory" and was a well-omened name used a number of times. The most important Nicopolis in the days of the Roman Empire was, however, one on the western coast of Greece near the promontory of Actium where Augustus (then Octavian, see page 261) had defeated Mark Antony. It was the final battle of the long Roman civil wars and made possible the establishment of the Roman Empire and the general peace that settled over the Mediterranean world for centuries.

Octavian himself founded the city on that site and named it in honor of his victory. Its greatest renown came through the fact that the great Stoic philosopher, Epictetus, came to Nicopolis about a quarter century after Paul's stay, and established a school there.

Dalmatia

Titus is mentioned again in 2 Timothy, Paul's last epistle. He left Crete and was sent on another mission:

> 2 Timothy 4:10. . . . *Demas . . . is departed unto Thessalonica; Crescens to Galatia, Titus unto Dalmatia.*

Dalmatia, mentioned only here in the Bible, is what is now the Yugoslavian coast, on the Adriatic shore opposite Italy. In early Roman times, it was the haunt of troublesome pirates. Rome battled them on a number of occasions and, by 155 B.C., Dalmatia had been forced to submit to Roman overlordship. The Dalmatians revolted on a number of occasions, however, and it was not until A.D. 9 that the land was brought under complete and final control.

22. PHILEMON

Philemon

The shortest epistle attributed to Paul, and the most personal, is one to Philemon, a native of Colossae:

Philemon 1:1. *Paul, a prisoner of Jesus Christ, and Timothy . . . unto Philemon . . .*

Philemon 1:2. *And to our beloved Apphia, and Archippus . . . and to the church in thy house . . .*

Philemon was apparently a leader in the Christian community at Colossae, for it was in his home that church meetings were held. Apphia is thought to be his wife and Archippus his son. Archippus is mentioned at the conclusion of Colossians, where Paul tells those he is addressing in that city:

Colossians 4:17. *And say to Archippus, Take heed to the ministry which thou hast received in the Lord, that thou fulfil it.*

It may have been Archippus, then, that actually led the services at Colossae, and instructed the gathering on doctrinal points.

Onesimus

Indeed, the Epistle to Philemon was written at the same time as Colossians, all are agreed, while Paul was in his first Roman imprisonment. Thus, when Paul sends the Epistle to the Colossians by the hand of Tychicus (see page 469), he sends also another person:

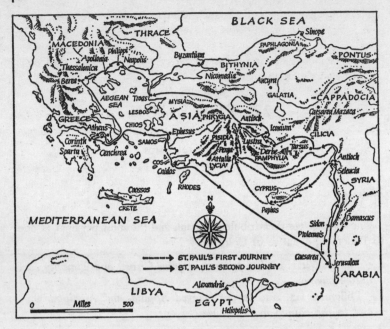

St. Paul's First and Second Journeys

Colossians 4:8. . . . *I have sent* [Tychicus] *unto you* . . .
Colossians 4:9. *With Onesimus, a faithful and beloved brother,
who is one of you* . . .

Onesimus, apparently, was a slave of Philemon. He had run away,
taking some valuables of his master with him. Somehow he reached
Rome, where he encountered Paul and was converted to Christianity.
Paul was now sending him back to his master with the Epistle to
Philemon as a personal letter of intercession. Paul says:

Philemon 1:10. *I beseech thee for my son Onesimus* . . .
Philemon 1:11. *Which in time past was to thee unprofitable* . . .

Since Onesimus means "profitable" there is a wry pun here. Paul
urges Philemon to receive Onesimus as a fellow Christian and not
as merely a returned slave to be punished. Paul even offers to be
responsible himself for any financial loss to Philemon:

Philemon 1:15. . . . *thou shouldest receive him for ever;*
Philemon 1:16. *Not now as a servant, but . . . a brother . . .*
. . . .

Philemon 1:18. *If he hath wronged thee, or oweth thee ought,*
put that on mine account;
Philemon 1:19. . . . *I will repay it . . .*

Paul recognizes Christianity as belonging to all, making no distinction of sex, race, nationality, or conditions of servitude. He says, in a famous verse:

Galatians 3:28. *There is neither Jew nor Greek, there is neither bond nor free, there is neither male nor female: for ye are all one in Christ Jesus.*

Nevertheless, while Paul urges kindness to the slave Onesimus, who is now Philemon's brother in Christianity, there is no hint anywhere in Paul that slavery might be wrong and immoral as an institution. Indeed, Paul even admonishes slaves to obey their masters, so that Christianity, however novel some of its tenets, was by no means a doctrine of social revolution:

Ephesians 6:5. *Servants, be obedient to them that are your masters according to the flesh, with fear and trembling, in singleness of your heart, as unto Christ . . .*

For that matter, nowhere else in the Bible, either in the Old Testament or the New, is slavery condemned in the abstract. Nor was slavery denounced by any ancient prophet or philosopher among the Gentiles. Slavery was so intimately entwined with the social and economic system of its time that its non-existence was unthinkable. (One wonders if it is thinkable now only because we have machines to do the work of slaves.)

All that the moral leaders of antiquity could and did do, in and out of the Bible, was to urge humanity on slaveowners. Thus, Paul recognizes Philemon's ownership of Onesimus, and sends Onesimus back into slavery. Even Onesimus' conversion to Christianity makes him no less a slave and Philemon will be within his legal rights to punish the slave. Paul can only plead with him to be kind.

23. HEBREWS

The Epistle to the Hebrews

This fairly long epistle is intricately constructed and was originally written in highly polished Greek, so that it seems to be more a carefully written sermon, cast into epistolary form. The author refers to himself on a number of occasions as speaking rather than writing:

Hebrews 6:9. *But, beloved, we are persuaded better things of you, and things that accompany salvation, though we thus speak.*

Furthermore, it does not begin as an epistle does, with the formal greetings of the writer or writers to a specifically named person or group being addressed but begins, rather, with a long well-constructed sentence that stretches over four verses:

Hebrews 1:1. *God, who at sundry times and in divers manners spake in time past unto the fathers by the prophets,*
Hebrews 1:2. *Hath in these last days spoken unto us by his Son . . .*

Who the writer might be, then, is not stated. The King James Version follows the most common tradition by ascribing the epistle to Paul, so that it is headed "The Epistle of Paul the Apostle to the Hebrews."

The most tempting evidence in favor of this is a mention at the end to Paul's other self, Timothy:

Hebrews 13:23. *Know ye that our brother Timothy is set at liberty; with whom, if he come shortly, I will see you.*

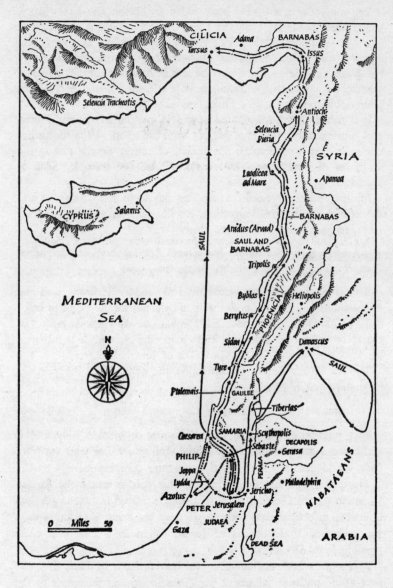

Journeys of the Apostles

Yet the verse might have been added to bolster the Paul theory, which needs bolstering badly, for there is much against it. The style is much more polished than Paul's is anywhere else. Moreover, the arguments and theology are not characteristic of Paul, and in one or two places run flatly against what he says in other epistles. The line of argument is rather that of an eloquent Jew learned in the Alexandrian philosophy of men such as Philo (see page 301).

It is usually taken for granted nowadays, particularly among Protestant commentators, that Paul did not write the epistle. Who the author might be, if it is not Paul, is not known, of course. Several among the associates of Paul have been considered; as, for example, Silas or Barnabas.

Martin Luther suggested that Apollos may have been the writer and this is a very attractive suggestion. Apollos was an associate of Paul (see page 444) and is described thus:

Acts 18:24. . . . *a certain Jew named Apollos, born at Alexandria, an eloquent man, and mighty in the scriptures* . . .

This is exactly what one would need to produce Hebrews, and one might almost say that if Apollos were not the author, he ought to be.

To whom is the epistle addressed? What does the general term "To the Hebrews" mean? Does it refer to a specific church? Is it intended for Jews everywhere? Or for Christians of Jewish background?

The one hint is that at the conclusion, the writer sends the greetings of those about him:

Hebrews 13:24. . . . *They of Italy salute you.*

This might make it seem that the writer is outside Italy and is addressing a group within Italy. Those with the writer who are from Italy would naturally send greetings to their compatriots.

Then, too, the first known use of this epistle was by a Roman Christian named Clement in 96. The epistle existed in that city before it existed anywhere else, perhaps. It may be, then, that the epistle was addressed to Christians of Jewish origin in Rome, and came possibly from Alexandria.

And when was it written? If it had been written by Paul, then the date would probably fall about 64. There are several references to the falling away of men who were previously faithful and the writer exhorts them to remain in the faith, threatening them with divine punishment if they do not:

> Hebrews 10:28. *He that despised Moses' law died without mercy under two or three witnesses:*
>
> Hebrews 10:29. *Of how much sorer punishment, suppose ye, shall he be thought worthy, who hath trodden under foot the Son of God . . .*

This might be appropriate for the time of the Neronian persecution in Rome in 64 when it took a great deal of fortitude to remain Christian, and when it was necessary for the author to reassure the faithful and promise a speedy second coming:

> Hebrews 10:35. *Cast not away therefore your confidence . . .*
>
> Hebrews 10:36. *For ye have need of patience . . .*
>
> Hebrews 10:37. *For yet a little while, and he that shall come will come, and will not tarry.*

And yet the difficulties of the Neronian persecution would fall on all Christians alike. Why, then, should the epistle exhort, according to its name, and by its whole line of argument, specifically those of Jewish background?

It is possible that the epistle was written after the destruction of the Temple in 70, when general conditions within the Christian fellowship changed radically. To the Christians of Gentile origin, this destruction would not have mattered greatly. It might even have been a source of satisfaction that the Jews who had not accepted Jesus as Messiah had thus been fittingly punished.

To the Christians of Jewish extraction, however, the end of the Temple must have been a terrible blow. Its end would have made sense to them, perhaps, only if it were followed by the establishment, at long last, of the ideal state; if, that is, the second coming had been the climax to which the Temple's destruction had been the prelude.

But the years passed after the Temple's destruction and no second coming took place. Christians of Jewish background may even have felt that the destruction of the Temple could only have been the sign of God's anger at the Christian heresy. The increasing numbers of Christians of Gentile extraction, openly hostile to Jews, might have contributed to their alienation. Conversions to Christianity must largely have ceased among the Jews, and increasing numbers of Christian Jews must have reverted to the older faith, leaving the Church virtually entirely Gentile from 100 onward.

Perhaps, then, Hebrews was written about 80, when Jewish alienation was increasingly obvious and when it seemed to the writer that Jewish defection might gravely damage the Christian cause.

Melchizedek

The bulk of Hebrews, therefore, is an eloquent attempt on the part of the writer to demonstrate, entirely through Old Testament references, that the doctrine of Jesus is superior to that of Moses, and that the old Jewish teachings can only be climaxed and properly brought to its peak in Christianity.

Thus, he endeavors to show Jesus to be the ideal high priest foreshadowed in the very first book of the Bible:

Hebrews 6:20. . . . *Jesus, made an high priest for ever after the order of Melchisedec.*

This refers to an incident that occupies three verses in the Book of Genesis. When Abram [Abraham] and his band are returning from the rescue of Lot from the hands of an invading raiding party, the patriarch passes by Salem (usually taken to be the city eventually known as Jerusalem).

Genesis 14:18. *And Melchizedek king of Salem brought forth bread and wine: and he was the priest of the most high God.*

Melchizedek was both king and priest and this was seized upon before the Exile to justify the priestly functions of the king of Judah at a time when the Temple priesthood was striking hard to reserve those functions for itself (see page I-504). Thus one of the psalms states:

Psalm 110:4. *The Lord hath sworn, and will not repent, Thou art a priest for ever after the order of Melchizedek.*

If this were a coronation psalm, the king of Judah to whom it was addressed would in this fashion be flatteringly addressed as both king and high priest "after the order of Melchizedek."

In post-Exilic times, when the kingship was gone and the priesthood retained full power, the original significance of the psalm was gone. In its place, the psalm gained Messianic significance.

Thus "Melchizedek" means "king of righteousness." And since "Salem" means "peace," Melchizedek as ruler of Salem is "the Prince of Peace" and that is a Messianic title:

Isaiah 9:6. *For unto us a child is born, unto us a son is given: . . . and his name shall be called . . . The Prince of Peace.*

Furthermore, the verses in Genesis are too brief to give the name of Melchizedek's father or his children. In post-Exilic times, there was gradually ascribed a mystic significance to this and it was taken to mean that Melchizedek had neither father nor son but existed eternally and represented an everlasting priesthood without beginning or end:

Hebrews 7:1. *For this Melchisedec, king of Salem, . . .*
Hebrews 7:2. *. . . which is, King of peace;*
Hebrews 7:3. *Without father, without mother, without descent, having neither beginning of days, nor end of life; but made like unto the Son of God; abideth a priest continually.*

Melchizedek, therefore, seems to be the representative of the Messiah, and may even have been thought by some to have actually been the Messiah, briefly visiting the Earth in order to encounter Abraham.

Abraham apparently recognized the priestly character of Melchizedek for he gave him the usual share of the spoils accorded the priesthood—a tenth (or "tithe").

Genesis 14:20. *. . . And he [Abram] gave him [Melchizedek] tithes of all.*

The writer of Hebrews comments on this by saying:

Hebrews 7:4. *Now consider how great this man [Melchizedek] was, unto whom even the patriarch Abraham gave the tenth of the spoils.*

And if Abraham himself acted the part of submission to Melchizedek, even more so must the Levites—the Jewish priesthood—who are descended from one of Abraham's descendants. If the psalmist's reference concerning "a priest for ever after the order of Melchizedek" is now applied to Jesus, it follows that Jesus' doctrine is superior to that of the Jewish priesthood by reasoning based on the Old Testament itself.

24. JAMES

JAMES

James

Seven short epistles follow Hebrews, none of which are by Paul, and none of which are addressed to specific churches. Because the problems discussed are also general, they are considered epistles addressed to Christians everywhere. They are therefore called the "general epistles" or "universal epistles." Sometimes they are called the "Catholic epistles" (because "catholic" is from the Greek "katholikos" meaning "universal").

The first of these epistles is attributed to someone named James:

James 1:1. *James, a servant of God and of the Lord Jesus Christ, to the twelve tribes which are scattered abroad . . .*

It is generally assumed that the James referred to here is James, the brother of Jesus (see page 361), who was the leader of the church in Jerusalem.

According to the Jewish historian Josephus, James was stoned to death in 62. This came at a time after the procurator Festus (see page 419) had ended his term of office and before the new procurator had arrived. The high priest, Ananus II, controlled Jerusalem during this interregnum and found himself facing the increasingly powerful party of the Zealots who, only four years later, were to instigate the disastrous rebellion against Rome.

James, as the leader of the Christians in Jerusalem, must have been abhorrent to the Zealots, not for his doctrines, but for the fact that he represented a pacifist group who urged peaceful submission to Rome. Ananus II attempted to appease the turbulent Zealots by having James

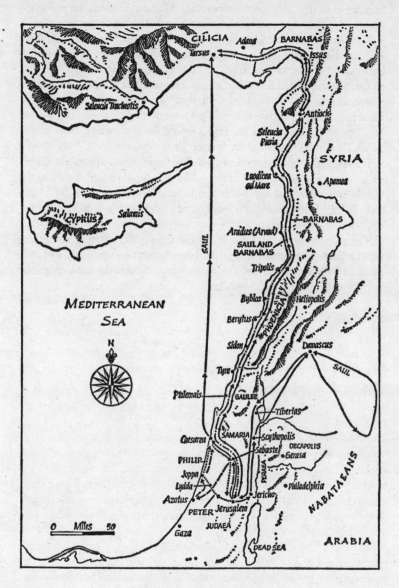

Journeys of the Apostles

executed. When the new procurator, Albinus, arrived, he naturally interpreted this as an anti-Roman move and Ananus II was deposed.

If, then, James were indeed the author of the epistle, it would have had to have been written before 62. Indeed, since the epistle is addressed "to the twelve tribes" as though the problem of Christians of Gentile origin had not yet arisen, and as the dispute over circumcision which led to the Council of Jerusalem is nowhere mentioned, it is sometimes supposed that the epistle was written before 48, the date of the Council. If that were so, James would be the earliest book in the New Testament, earlier than any of Paul's epistles.

However, the book is written in better Greek than one might expect of a relatively unlettered Galilean like James. It might be that the epistle was written about 90, in the time of the persecution by Domitian. It might then have been ascribed to James to give it greater authority.

The substance of the book is largely moralistic, advising its readers on the path of good behavior. It might almost be considered a typical piece of "wisdom literature" (see page I-507). Much the same might be said of the other general epistles.

25. 1 PETER

Sylvanus

The next epistle is one of two ascribed to Peter:

1 Peter 1:1. *Peter, an apostle of Jesus Christ, to the strangers scattered throughout Pontus, Galatia, Cappadocia, Asia, and Bithynia* . . .

Much of what this epistle contains sounds very much like Paul, and the region being addressed—Asia Minor—was one that had been proselytized by Paul's unremitting labors.

Peter was a Galilean, who was not very likely to be proficient in Greek, and if he did write this epistle he would very likely have done so through a translator. One is mentioned:

1 Peter 5:12. *By Silvanus, a faithful brother* . . . *I have written* . . .

The only Sylvanus mentioned elsewhere in the Bible, is the associate of Paul, who was joined with him, for instance, in the writing of the epistles to the Thessalonians:

1 Thessalonians 1:1. *Paul, and Silvanus, and Timotheus, unto the church of the Thessalonians* . . .

This Sylvanus is considered identical with the Silas of Acts, the associate who accompanied Paul on his second missionary journey. If Peter's Sylvanus is identical with Paul's Silas, it would follow that Peter was writing his epistle with the aid of someone well acquainted with Paul's line of thinking. Peter, throughout the New Testament, is made to appear a rather weak personality, and it is not beyond the realm of

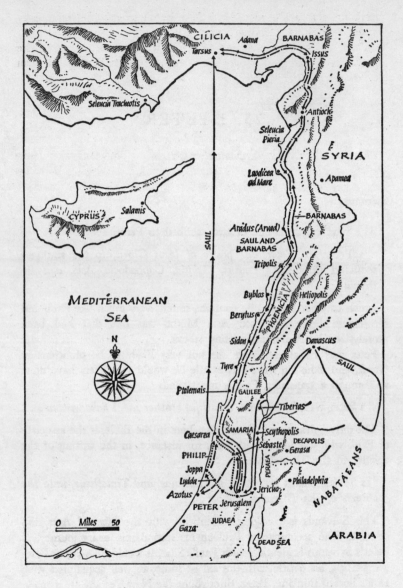

Journeys of the Apostles

possibility that in the presence of Silas he might easily be induced to express himself in a Pauline manner.

There are some who suggest that Silas was the real author of the epistle, but if that were so, why was it not ascribed to Paul, rather than to Peter?

Babylon

It might also be argued that the epistle was written long after both Peter and Paul were dead, and that it was merely ascribed to Peter to lend it authority. Thus, at the conclusion of the epistle, the writer sends greetings:

1 Peter 5:13. *The church that is at Babylon . . . saluteth you . . .*

Clearly, this cannot be taken literally. There was no church at Babylon, for, indeed, the city no longer existed. But it is an old Biblical device to use the name of a bygone persecutor in order to indicate, discreetly, a present enemy. By Babylon, therefore, is surely meant Rome.

If Peter is the author of the epistle, he is therefore writing from Rome, where he would meet Silas and make use of his services. Later legend does state firmly that Peter went to Rome, helped organize the church there, served as its first bishop, and died a martyr during the persecutions of Nero in 64. (Having received the primacy of the church from Jesus himself Peter passed on this primacy, according to Catholic doctrine, to the successive bishops of Rome that followed him and upon this is based the theory of Papal supremacy.)

If Peter wrote this epistle, then, it would have had to be written before 64. And yet the Bible says nothing directly of Peter's stay in Rome, and Paul, in the epistles written from Roman imprisonment, gives no indication of the presence of Peter there.

Furthermore, it is unlikely that the use of the term Babylon for Rome would occur before 64 or even for some time afterward. In the generation that followed the crucifixion, the chief enemy of the Christians was the Jewish priesthood and it was to Roman officials that Christians turned for protection; to procurators, governors, and even, as in Paul's case (see page 419), to the emperor himself.

The persecutions of 64 may have shaken Christian trust in Rome, but that was only the personal action of Nero, striving to please the Roman populace by putting on a show of zeal in searching for the arsonists who had presumably set the Roman fire. The persecution was confined to the city of Rome and did not last long. The Christians of the eastern provinces, where the large bulk of them were to be found, were not touched.

Then not long after the Neronic persecution, the Jewish rebellion smashed Jewish society and destroyed the Temple. After 70 the Jews of the empire were in no position to try to crush Christianity; they were in desperate danger of being wiped out themselves.

Under the Emperor Domitian, who reigned from 81 to 96, repressive measures were taken against the Jews, with whom the Christians (for the last time) were lumped together. This Domitianic persecution was empire-wide and for the first time the Christians of Asia Minor felt organized repression from the central government. The epistle, addressed to the Christians of Asia Minor, refers to such repression:

1 Peter 4:12. *Beloved, think it not strange concerning the fiery trial which is to try you . . .*

From now on, for two centuries, it is the Roman government that is Christianity's great enemy, and it is now that Rome would become "Babylon." On this basis, it might be argued that 1 Peter is not written by Peter at all, but was written by an unknown person in Domitian's time, a generation after the death of Peter.

26. 2 PETER

Simon Peter

The next epistle is also attributed to Peter:

2 Peter 1:1. *Simon Peter, a servant and an apostle of Jesus Christ, to them that have obtained like precious faith* . . .

This is backed up by a reference to Peter's past life; to his witnessing the transfiguration (see page 195).

2 Peter 1:16. *For we have not followed cunningly devised fables, when we made known unto you the power and coming of our Lord Jesus Christ, but were eyewitnesses of his majesty.*
. . . .
2 Peter 1:18. . . . *when we were with him in the holy mount.*

Nevertheless, from the style and contents, many commentators deduce that it must be of rather late origin. Its writing is related to the Epistle of Jude, which is itself late. Then, too, the epistle mentions Paul's epistles, almost as though they were already collected and considered inspired:

2 Peter 3:15. . . . *the long-suffering of our Lord is salvation; even as our beloved brother Paul* . . . *hath written unto you;*
2 Peter 3:16. . . . *in all his epistles* . . .

It is possible that 2 Peter, like 1 Peter and James, may date to the Domitianic persecution, and have been written about 90. (Indeed, the book is not mentioned prior to 200 and some commentators suggest that it may even have been written as late as 150.)

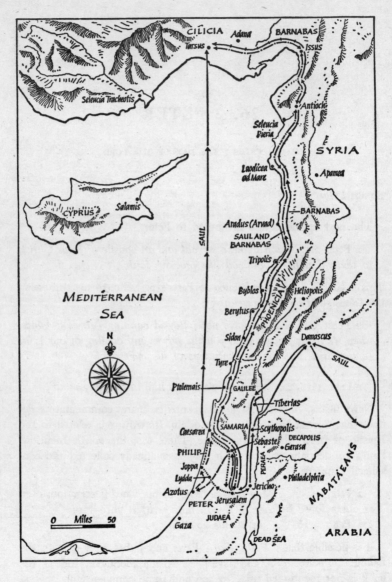

Journeys of the Apostles

The Day of the Lord

An indication of the comparative lateness of the epistle may be found in the fact that some Christians must have grown impatient while waiting for a second coming that seemed endlessly delayed. The writer of 2 Peter finds he must exercise his ingenuity to explain the stretched-out delay, after Paul's promise of imminence. He explains:

> 2 Peter 3:8. . . . *one day is with the Lord as a thousand years, and a thousand years as one day.*

> 2 Peter 3:9. *The Lord is not slack concerning his promise, as some men count slackness . . .*

The reference here is to a quotation from the psalms:

> Psalm 90:4. *For a thousand years in thy sight are but as yesterday when it is past . . .*

In other words, the writer maintains that while the second coming is imminent (since so many authoritative spokesmen have said so) that may mean imminence in God's view of time rather than man's view. And it will come:

> 2 Peter 3:10. *But the day of the Lord will come as a thief in the night . . .*

27. 1 JOHN

The Word

Three epistles follow which, like Hebrews, do not have the name of the writer in the first verse. However, the style and content are so completely reminiscent of those of the fourth gospel, that it seems certain that whoever wrote the fourth gospel wrote the epistles. Even the characteristic designation of Jesus as the "Word" appears:

1 John 1:1. *That which was from the beginning . . . of the Word of life . . .*

The three epistles are therefore ascribed to John son of Zebedee (assuming he wrote the fourth gospel). It would further seem that, like the fourth gospel, these epistles were written in Ephesus about 100. This first and longest of John's three epistles warns against antichrists (see page 477) and present an exhortation to brotherly love.

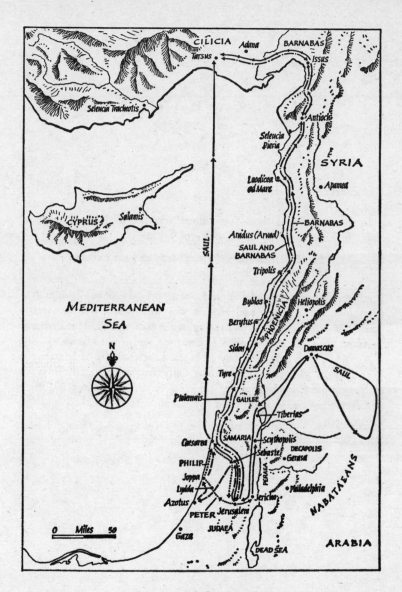

Journeys of the Apostles

28. 2 JOHN

The Elder

In the second and third (very short) epistles of John, the author refers to himself merely as an elder or priest:

2 John 1:1. *The elder unto the elect lady and her children . . .*

There have been some speculations that there was a "John the Presbyter" ("John the elder") in Ephesus who is to be distinguished from John the Apostle, and that it was the former who wrote the epistles of John and, therefore, the fourth gospel as well. This depends, however, upon the faintest possible evidence, and is not taken seriously.

As for the elect lady, this may be taken either literally or figuratively. John may be addressing a particular Christian woman, or he may be addressing the Church generally, referring to it in this allegorical manner. In either case, he again exhorts his readers to follow the command of brotherly love.

29. 3 JOHN

GAIUS

Gaius

The third epistle of John begins like the second:

3 John 1:1. *The elder unto the wellbeloved Gaius* . . .

Gaius is some otherwise unknown personage who is treated by John as an ally who will support him against the leader of another faction:

3 John 1:9. *I wrote unto the church: but Diotrephes, who loveth to have the preeminence among them, receiveth us not.*
3 John 1:10. *Wherefore, if I come, I will remember his deeds* . . .

30. JUDE

Jude

The author of this epistle, the last of the general epistles, identifies himself in the first verse:

Jude 1:1. *Jude, the servant of Jesus Christ, and brother of James, to them that are sanctified* . . .

If this is taken at face value, Jude the brother of James may be identified as another brother of Jesus. Jude is but a short form of Judas and the only pair of brothers named James and Judas in the New Testament, outside this epistle, are among the brothers of Jesus:

Matthew 13:55. *Is not this [Jesus] the carpenter's son?* . . . *and his brethren, James, and Joses, and Simon, and Judas?*

But this short epistle is very like the second chapter of 2 Peter, and like 2 Peter, it may well date from the period of Domitian. Since it is unlikely that a brother of Jesus would still be alive at that time, the epistle may be by someone called Judah, a common name, and some later editor added "brother of James" to increase its importance.

Moses

Jude, like 2 Peter, denounces certain heresies. Jude is unusual in that it contains quotes from the apocryphal literature, which it advances as authoritative. Thus, the writer compares the heretics with Satan, since

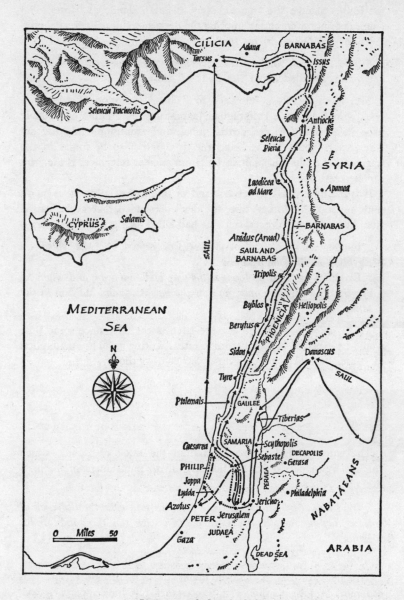

Journeys of the Apostles

the former slander the true believers as Satan slandered Moses. The writer does not even bother quoting the details of the slander, assuming it to be well known to his readers:

> Jude 1:9. . . . *Michael the archangel, when contending with the devil he disputed about the body of Moses* . . .

This is apparently a reference to "The Assumption of Moses" a book written by some Palestinian Jew during the lifetime of Jesus. It purports to tell of Moses' death, burial, and assumption into heaven. The passage about Michael and the devil is not to be found in the fragmentary copies that remain but from ancient references the matter can be eked out.

It is the devil's task to act as a sort of prosecuting attorney as men's souls are tried. In Moses' case, the devil demanded that he be barred from heaven as a murderer, since he had killed an Egyptian overseer:

> Exodus 2:11. . . . *when Moses was grown* . . . *he spied an Egyptian smiting an Hebrew* . . .
> Exodus 2:12. *And he looked this way and that way, and when he saw that there was no man, he slew the Egyptian, and hid him in the sand.*

This is another argument for the lateness of Jude, since some time would be expected to pass before so late a writing as "The Assumption of Moses" would begin to gain a cachet of authority.

Enoch

The writer of Jude also quotes from the Book of Enoch, which contains a prophecy of the forthcoming divine punishment of the heretics:

> Jude 1:14. *And Enoch also, the seventh from Adam, prophesied of these, saying, Behold, the Lord cometh with ten thousands of his saints,*
> Jude 1:15. *To execute judgment upon all* . . .

The Book of Enoch, written about 100 B.C., is not accepted as canonical by Jews, Catholics, or Protestants, but Jude apparently considered it inspired. He was even impressed by its supposed antiquity, for he stresses that Enoch is "seventh from Adam"; that is, of the seventh generation after Creation: Adam, Seth, Enos, Cainan, Mahalaleel, Jared, and Enoch.

31. 2 ESDRAS

THE PROPHET ESDRAS * URIEL * THE SODOMITISH SEA * BEHEMOTH AND
LEVIATHAN * THE MESSIAH * THE EAGLE * THE TEN TRIBES * TWO HUNDRED
AND FOUR BOOKS * EGYPT * THE CARMANIANS

The Prophet Esdras

Apocalyptic literature was popular with the Jews of the Greek and
Roman period. Its production did not cease even after the destruction
of the Temple. Indeed, the increase of misery was bound to sharpen the
Messianic longing and the dream that the world would eventually be
set right by divine intervention.

About a generation after that destruction, a Jewish apocalypse was
produced which actually found its way into some versions of the Bible.

In the usual fashion of apocalyptic writing, it was attributed to an
ancient sage—in this case Ezra, the scribe who for a period dominated
Jerusalem after the return from exile some five and a half centuries
before the apocalypse was actually written (see page I-449). Although
quite Jewish in outlook, this apocalypse interested Christians because of
its strong emphasis on Messianic prophecies.

Some unnamed Christian edited the book about 150 and added
what are now its first two chapters. A century later still, another
individual, presumably also Christian, added what are now the final
two chapters.

The mid-portion of the book was originally written in Aramaic, then
translated into Greek. The first two and last two chapters were in
Greek to begin with.

Both Aramaic and Greek versions have vanished. A Latin translation
survived, however, and was included in Catholic versions of the Bible,

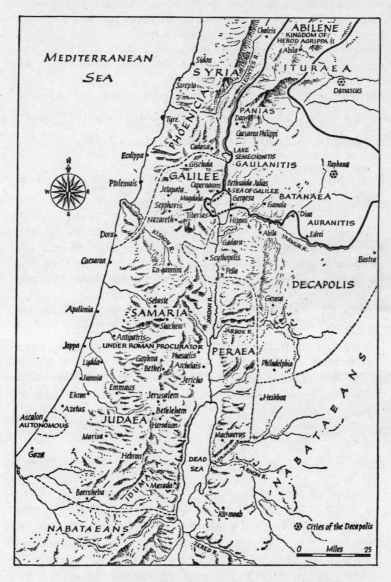

Palestine at the Time of the Jewish-Roman War

not as an integral part, but as a kind of appendix to the New Testament. It is therefore included in the Apocrypha, and the King James Version is a translation from the Latin.

Other translations, in various Oriental languages, also survive, however, and the Revised Standard Version draws on these as well as on the Latin.

The apocalypse begins by giving the name of its purported author:

> 2 Esdras 1:1. *The second book of the prophet Esdras* [Ezra] . . .

The first book is, of course, 1 Esdras (see page I-461).

Uriel

The first two chapters of the book, Christian in outlook, describe the manner in which the Jews have consistently failed to heed the prophets. It rejects circumcision, and warns the Jews that they will be forsaken and that others will be chosen in their stead. At times, phraseology very reminiscent of the gospels is chosen.

With the third chapter, however, 2 Esdras begins in its original version, and with it the first of a series of seven visions:

> 2 Esdras 3:1. *In the thirtieth year after the ruin of the city I was in Babylon, and lay troubled upon my bed* . . .
> 2 Esdras 3:2. *For I saw the desolation of Sion, and the wealth of them that dwelt at Babylon.*

On the face of it this would be the thirtieth year after Nebuchadnezzar's destruction of Jerusalem and the Temple, or 556 B.C. This, however, was a century before the true Ezra's time.

Presumably it is the author's way of referring elliptically to the fact that he was writing thirty years after the Roman destruction of Jerusalem and the Temple, or A.D. 100. Perhaps he was on a visit to the city of Rome, then at the peak and pinnacle of its worldly power and luxury, and the contrast between this and ruined Jerusalem was more than he could bear, and it set him to writing the book.

Ezra is pictured as questioning God, wanting to know whether the Babylonians (Romans) were not just as sinful as the Jews, if not more so, and why it was, then, that they should flourish while the

Jews, who at least knew God, even if they were not always perfectly virtuous, were in such misery.

An angel was sent to him to answer his question:

2 Esdras 4:1. *And the angel that was sent unto me, whose name was Uriel, gave me an answer . . .*

Uriel ("my light is God") is not to be found in the canonical Old Testament. He is an apocryphal creation, brought to life during the elaborate legends of angels and demons built up in post-Exilic times through Persian influence. Uriel was one of the seven archangels listed in the apocryphal Book of Enoch.

Because of the significance of his name, Milton, in *Paradise Lost* viewed him as the angel who was in particular charge of the sun. The Mohammedans identify Uriel with Israel, the angel in charge of music and the one who will sound the last trump on the day of judgment (the role of Gabriel in Christian legend).

The Sodomitish Sea

Uriel tells Ezra that the human mind is too limited to grasp the purposes of God but that all will become plain in the end, with the day of judgment and the coming of the ideal heavenly state. This is coming soon but only after evil approaches a climax. Then:

2 Esdras 5:4. . . . *the sun shall suddenly shine again in the night, and the moon thrice in the day:*

2 Esdras 5:5. *And blood shall drop out of wood, and the stone shall give his voice . . .*

. . . .

2 Esdras 5:7. *And the Sodomitish sea shall cast out fish . . .*

In other words, impossibilities will come to pass, heralding the end of ordered nature. The Sodomitish sea is, of course, the Dead Sea, on the shores of which Sodom had once stood (see page I-71). There are no fish in the salt-filled depths of the Dead Sea so that to find fish teeming there would be as impossible as the sun shining by night, wood bleeding, or stones crying out.

Behemoth and Leviathan

In a second vision Uriel describes more of the impossibilities that will herald the coming of the end. Then, in a third vision, Ezra describes the order of creation as given in the first chapter of Genesis. He adds additional detail, however, in line with the legends that had been added to the Biblical account in Greek times.

> 2 Esdras 6:47. *Upon the fifth day . . .*
>
> . . . .
>
> 2 Esdras 6:49. *Then didst thou ordain two living creatures, the one thou callest Enoch, and the other Leviathan;*
>
> . . . .
>
> 2 Esdras 6:51. *Unto Enoch thou gavest one part . . . wherein are a thousand hills,*
>
> 2 Esdras 6:52. *But unto Leviathan thou gavest the seventh part, namely the moist; and hast kept him to be devoured of whom thou wilt and when.*

The word "Enoch" is more properly "Behemoth" (see page I-485) and it is that which is used in the Revised Standard Version. The existence of these primordial monsters is an example of the colorful legends upon which the rabbis delighted to elaborate. They find their Biblical excuse in a single phrase in the Genesis account of the fifth day:

> Genesis 1:21. *And God created great whales . . .*

The word given here as "whales" is a translation of the Hebrew word "tannin" which is more accurately taken as signifying huge sea creatures generally. Indeed, the Revised Standard Version translates the phrase, "So God created the great sea-monsters . . ."

It is interesting that 2 Esdras refers to the sea as taking up one-seventh of the Earth's surface. The ancient geographers, unable to penetrate far out to sea, had no idea of the true extent of the ocean. Indeed, it was not until the explorations of Captain Cook in the eighteenth century that it was fully borne in on man just how extensive the ocean was; and that it occupied, not 15 percent, but 70 percent of the planetary surface.

The reference to Leviathan being kept "to be devoured of whom thou wilt and when" was in reference to the Rabbinic legend that when the Messiah came and the ideal kingdom was established, the righteous would celebrate at a great feast in which Leviathan would be eaten.

Ezra goes through this account in order to reason that all this magnificent creative endeavor was done for the sake of Israel, and yet (the complaint he makes over and over) Israel has been devastated by the triumphing heathen.

The Messiah

Uriel blames the situation on Adam's original sin in the garden of Eden, and again goes on to describe details of the end of the world. After all the signs have taken place:

2 Esdras 7:28. . . . *my son Jesus shall be revealed . . . and they that remain shall rejoice within four hundred years.*

2 Esdras 7:29. *After these years shall my son Christ die, and all men that have life.*

The word "Jesus" is found only in the Latin copy and betrays the hand of the Christian editor. In the Oriental languages, the expression is "my son the Messiah" and it is in that way that the Revised Standard Version gives it.

The Messianic kingdom, in this vision, comes not after the day of judgment, but before. It is the final act of the modern world.

The duration of four hundred years for the Messianic kingdom is found in the Latin translation. One Arabic translation gives a thousand years. Revelation, the completely Christian apocalypse, also speaks of a thousand years as the duration of the Messianic kingdom, with two resurrections, one at the beginning and one at the end of that kingdom:

Revelation 20:6. . . . *he that hath part in the first resurrection . . . shall be priests of God and of Christ, and shall reign with him a thousand years.*

It is for this reason that people speak of the "millennium" (Latin for "a thousand years") as a time of ideal bliss. Belief in this doctrine is called "chiliasm" (from a Greek word meaning "a thousand"). Those who believe that the millennium is at hand, and there have been many of these in each generation over the last two thousand years, are called "millennarians" or "chiliasts."

Then, in a fourth vision, Ezra is allowed to see the glories of a heavenly Jerusalem that would eventually succeed the destroyed Earthly one.

The Eagle

The fifth vision is a complicated one after the fashion made popular by the Book of Daniel:

> 2 Esdras 11:1. *Then saw I a dream, and behold, there came up from the sea an eagle, which had twelve feathered wings, and three heads.*

This is later interpreted by Uriel as being the fourth beast in Daniel's vision:

> 2 Esdras 12:11. *The eagle whom thou sawest . . . is the kingdom which was seen in the vision of thy brother Daniel.*
> 2 Esdras 12:12. *But it was not expounded unto him, therefore I declare it unto thee.*

The fourth kingdom is described in Daniel as follows:

> Daniel 7:7. . . . *behold a fourth beast, dreadful and terrible, and strong exceedingly; and it had great iron teeth . . . and it had ten horns.*

To the writer of Daniel, writing in the time of Antiochus IV, this beast represented the Seleucid Empire, and its ten horns were the ten Seleucid kings up to the time of writing. But now the Seleucid Empire was long since gone and it was necessary to reinterpret the beast as the Roman Empire. The twelve wings were the twelve Roman emperors up to the time 2 Esdras was written:

> 2 Esdras 12:14. *In the same shall twelve kings reign, one after another;*
> 2 Esdras 12:15. *Whereof the second . . . shall have more time than any of the twelve.*

2 Esdras 12:16. *And this do the twelve wings signify, which thou sawest.*

In order to explain this we must take Julius Caesar as the first emperor. He wasn't really, but he was often considered such in ancient times. (Thus, the Roman historian Suetonius wrote a famous and still-existing book called *The Lives of the Twelve Caesars*, about a generation after 2 Esdras was written. It dealt with the first emperors and it too begins with Julius Caesar.)

The twelve are: Julius, Augustus, Tiberius, Caligula, Claudius, Nero, Galba, Otho, Vitellius, Vespasian, Titus, and Domitian. Domitian reigned from 81 to 96 and since there are only twelve wings on the eagle, it would seem that 2 Esdras was composed late in Domitian's reign.

Augustus, the second emperor in the list, reigned forty-one years, far longer than any of the remaining eleven, so that the second did indeed "have more time than any of the twelve." In fact, Augustus' reign was to prove longer than that of any emperor ruling from Rome in the entire history of that empire.

Eventually the three heads of the eagle come into play:

2 Esdras 11:29. . . . *there awaked one of the heads . . . namely, it that was in the midst; for that was greater than the two other heads.*

. . . .

2 Esdras 11:31. *And, behold, the head . . . did eat up the two feathers under the wing that would have reigned.*

2 Esdras 11:32. *But this head . . . bare rule . . . over all those that dwell in the earth . . .*

The three heads are the three emperors of the Flavian Dynasty. The large central one is Vespasian, the two smaller ones on either side, his sons Titus and Domitian. These would be viewed by the writer of 2 Esdras with particular horror, for it was Vespasian and Titus who led the armies against the Jews when they revolted and it was Titus who took and sacked Jerusalem in 70 and destroyed the Temple.

The events referred to in the verses quoted above follow the assassination of Nero when several candidates strove for the vacated throne, with Vespasian winning out. He became emperor in 69 and ruled without dispute for ten years.

In the reign of the third head (Domitian), a new creature entered and rebuked the eagle:

> 2 Esdras 11:37. . . . *a roaring lion chased out of the wood . . . and said* [to the eagle],
>
> . . . .
>
> 2 Esdras 11:39. *Art not thou it that remainest of the four beasts . . .*
>
> . . . .
>
> 2 Esdras 12:3. . . . *and the whole body of the eagle was burnt . . .*

The lion is identified by Uriel:

> 2 Esdras 12:31. *And the lion, whom thou sawest . . . speaking to the eagle, and rebuking her . . .*
>
> 2 Esdras 12:32. *This is the anointed . . .*

In other words, the Messiah will come at the end of Domitian's reign and the Roman Empire will be destroyed while the Messianic kingdom will rise in its place.

Of course, this did not happen and, instead, Domitian's reign was followed by that of the five "good emperors" under whom, for eighty years, Rome went through its profoundest period of peace and quiet. Nevertheless, the Messianic longing among the Jews carried them through to one last set of catastrophes.

The revolt in Judea from 66 to 70 had exacerbated relations between Jews and Greeks in Egypt. Eventually, widespread riots led to considerable bloodshed on both sides with the Jews (who were in the minority) eventually getting the worst of it. The Jewish temple in Alexandria was destroyed and thousands of Jews were killed, putting an effective end to what had been the most prosperous, numerous, and intellectually productive Jewish community in the ancient world.

There remained a large colony of Jews in Cyrene to the west of Egypt proper. In 115, during the reign of Trajan, the second emperor to follow Domitian, Messianic fervor (fed by books such as 2 Esdras) led them to revolt and after two years of bitter fighting they were bloodily repressed. The teeming Jewish population of Egypt was brought virtually to an end.

Then in 132, in the reign of Trajan's successor, Hadrian, the remaining Jews of Judea revolted again. They followed the Zealot, Simon Bar-Cocheba, who proclaimed himself a Messiah. It took three years for the revolt to be suppressed and, by that time, Palestinian Jewry had been exterminated.

What Jews remained were scattered in small colonies throughout Roman Europe. They survived, but that is all. Over the course of the next eighteen centuries they were continually oppressed and often slaughtered but not until our own time did they ever again, as a people, take up arms against their enemies.

The reality, as it turned out, was quite the reverse of the visions in 2 Esdras.

The Ten Tribes

In a sixth vision, Ezra sees a man rise from the sea, battle with large numbers and defeat them with fire issuing from his mouth. This is, of course, the Messiah destroying the heathen. But then:

2 Esdras 13:12. *Afterward I saw the same man . . . call unto him another peaceable multitude.*

These are interpreted as follows:

2 Esdras 13:40. *Those are the ten tribes, which were carried away prisoners out of their own land in the time of Osea* [Hoshea] *the king, whom Salmanazer* [Shalmaneser] *the king of Assyria led away captive . . .*

The Jews were still dreaming, eight centuries after the fact, that the men of the Northern Kingdom still existed somewhere as self-aware Israelites. There remained the hope, then and for centuries afterward, that they might even make up a powerful and prosperous kingdom that would someday come to the aid of their oppressed brethren of Judah and Benjamin. They never did, of course, nor could they—for they had long since melted into the populations surrounding them.

Two Hundred and Four Books

In the seventh and final vision, Ezra is commanded to write the books of the Bible. This actually is a reference to an important historic fact. The early books of the Bible did indeed receive their present form during the Exile and immediately afterward. It was the scribes, perhaps under Ezra himself, who prepared the copies and completed the necessary editing of primitive legends, traditional law, and priestly ritual. Ezra may also have been the "Chronicler" who continued the history of Israel from Joshua's time to the rebuilding of the Temple in 1 and 2 Chronicles, Ezra, and Nehemiah (see page I-399).

One of the high points of the Book of Nehemiah is the scene in which Ezra reads the law to the assembled people and expounds upon it:

> Nehemiah 8:5. *And Ezra opened the book in the sight of all the people . . . and . . . all the people stood up:*
> . . . .
> Nehemiah 8:18. *. . . . day by day, from the first day unto the last day, he read in the book of the law of God . . .*

The remainder of the Bible, past Joshua, was added little by little, with some parts not written (let alone accepted as canonical) before 150 B.C., some three centuries after the time of Ezra. Nevertheless, the writer of 2 Esdras, looking back in time, easily idealized the situation to the point where Ezra is visualized as writing the entire Bible.

To be sure, Ezra isn't looked upon as actually composing the Bible. According to orthodox tradition, the Bible had been written by various pre-Exilic sages such as Moses and Samuel and, according to Rabbinic legends, might very well have pre-existed throughout eternity. Ezra, therefore, merely restored the Bible (according to the view in 2 Esdras) to the condition it was in before the burning of the Temple by Nebuchadnezzar.

> 2 Esdras 14.21. *For thy law is burnt, therefore no man knoweth the things that are done of thee or the works that shall begin.*

Under divine inspiration, Ezra restores the Bible, dictating the entire body of writing to five transcribers over a space of forty days:

> 2 Esdras 14:44. *In forty days they wrote two hundred and four books.*
> 2 Esdras 14:45. *. . . . the Highest spake, saying, The first that thou hast written publish openly . . .*

2 Esdras 14:46. *But keep the seventy last, that thou mayest deliver them only to such as be wise among the people . . .*

The figure "two hundred and four" given in the Latin version makes no sense. Other versions, accepted by the Revised Standard Version, give the total number of books written as ninety-four and the number to be published openly as twenty-four. This does make sense, for the twenty-four books to be published openly are the twenty-four of the Jewish canon, divided as follows:

(1) Genesis, (2) Exodus, (3) Leviticus, (4) Numbers, (5) Deuteronomy, (6) Joshua, (7) Judges, (8) 1 and 2 Samuel, (9) 1 and 2 Kings, (10) Isaiah, (11) Jeremiah, (12) Ezekiel, (13) the Twelve Minor Prophets, (14) Psalms, (15) Proverbs, (16) Job, (17) Song of Solomon, (18) Ruth, (19) Lamentations, (20) Ecclesiastes, (21) Esther, (22) Daniel, (23) Ezra and Nehemiah, (24) 1 and 2 Chronicles.

The remaining seventy books, which were hidden away from the general view, make up the Apocrypha ("hidden").

This is the actual end of 2 Esdras as originally written.

Egypt

The last two chapters, consisting of prophecies of disaster preceding the last day, seem to have been added in the third century A.D., which would make it the latest passage anywhere in the Bible or Apocrypha. God is quoted as speaking of Egypt, for instance, as follows:

2 Esdras 14:10. *Behold, my people is led as a flock to the slaughter: I will not suffer them now to dwell in the land of Egypt:*

2 Esdras 14:11. *But I will . . . smite Egypt with plagues, as before, and will destroy all the land thereof.*

This may be meant allegorically. It is the Christians who are "my people" and by Egypt is actually meant Rome. Nevertheless, the verses may have been inspired by actual events. The Jews were indeed no longer suffered to dwell in the land of Egypt for by 135, the Jews had been virtually wiped out throughout the east (see page 522).

But then in the following century, something that might have looked like retribution was visited upon Egypt and it was smitten with plagues.

In 215 the Emperor Caracalla visited Egypt and put an end to the state support of Alexandria's great Museum. It had been the city's intellectual glory for five centuries, but it was in decay now and so was Rome now that the time of the good emperors had passed.

The situation was even worse according to the tales that have been handed down to us (and which may have been exaggerated). Caracalla was offended with Alexandria for some slights its citizens put upon him. He therefore put the city to the sack, killing thousands.

Then, shortly after 260, in the reign of the Emperor Gallienus, a famine and epidemic swept Egypt. Two thirds of the population of Alexandria are supposed to have died in misery. Perhaps this was going on at the time the last two chapters of 2 Esdras were being written.

The Carmanians

Indeed, the third century saw the Roman Empire plunging into the depths of misery and anarchy. In 235 the Emperor Alexander Severus was murdered, and for fifty years afterward, emperor followed emperor, each struggling with usurpers and suffering assassination in the end, while all the realm fell apart. Christian mystics watching this have been certain that the last days were at hand.

The writer of the end of 2 Esdras describes a vision appropriate to the last days:

> 2 Esdras 15:29. . . . *the nations of the dragons of Arabia shall come out with many chariots . . .*
>
> 2 Esdras 15:30. *Also the Carmanians raging in wrath shall go forth . . .*
>
> . . . .
>
> 2 Esdras 15:43. *And they shall go stedfastly unto Babylon, and make her afraid.*

Naturally, the anarchy and confusion within the Roman Empire offered an unexampled occasion for external enemies to pounce upon her. The most powerful of Rome's enemies lay to the east. The Parthian Empire, which had caused Rome so much trouble in the time of

Herod the Great (see page 123) had declined, but in 226, while Alexander Severus was still on the Roman throne, a new dynasty, the Sassanids, had come to power in the east. The Sassanid Empire carried on warfare against Rome, as earlier the Parthians had done. And since the Sassanids came to power just as Rome was sinking into anarchy they won considerable success every once in a while.

In 240, Shapur I became the Sassanid king and he at once invaded Syria. It is very likely that his hosts from the east represented the "dragons of Arabia." If there is any doubt, the reference to the Carmanians should lay that to rest, for Carmania was a large southern province of the Sassanid Empire.

At the height of his attack, Shapur took Antioch and reached the Mediterranean. Rome painfully retrieved its position, but in 258 Shapur launched a second war against Rome and this time his successes were even greater and Rome's state of dissolution even worse. In 259 Shapur defeated a Roman army in Syria and captured the Roman emperor, Valerian. Surely this sufficed to "make her [Rome] afraid."

The enemy capture of a Roman Emperor for the first time in Rome's history and the dreadful famine in Egypt must have indeed made it seem that the last days were at hand, if the final portion of 2 Esdras was indeed being written at this time.

Shapur, in 260, even invaded Asia Minor, and 2 Esdras contains apocalyptic denunciations of that region, too:

2 Esdras 15:46. *And thou, Asia, that art partaker of the hope of Babylon* . . .

2 Esdras 15:47. *Woe be unto thee, thou wretch, because thou has made thyself like unto her* . . .

Yet neither did this vision come true. In actual fact, Rome recovered. Shapur was driven back by an Arab leader, named Odenathus. In 268 a capable emperor, Claudius II, came to the Roman throne, and began to win victories. Under his successor, Aurelian, the realm was knit together once more from the fragments into which it had fallen.

Beginning in 284, the Emperor Diocletian undertook a complete reorganization of the empire and under Constantine (who began his reign in 306) the empire turned officially Christian.

32. REVELATION

John

There are apocalyptic passages in several books of the Old Testament.
Isaiah, for instance, contains a "little apocalypse" (see page I-540) and
the latter half of Daniel is apocalyptic. However, no book of the Old
Testament is entirely apocalyptic, although one such book—2 Esdras
(see page 514)—is to be found in the Apocrypha.

During Domitian's time, however, there was written a particularly
complex and richly symbolic apocalypse. Its author was a Christian
and it was eventually accepted (despite some initial misgivings) as
canonical. It now appears as the last book of the New Testament and
is the only entirely apocalyptic book in the Bible.

Since "apocalypse" means "unveiling" or "revelation" (of matters,
that is, which would otherwise remain forever hidden because they
cannot be penetrated by the unaided reason of man) this final book
can be called either "The Apocalypse" or "The Revelation." It is
called the latter in the King James Version.

The author of Revelation names himself and makes no attempt to
place the authorship upon some ancient sage (as is generally done
in apocalyptic writing):

Revelation 1:1. *The Revelation of Jesus Christ, which God gave
unto him, to shew unto his servants things which must shortly come*

The Seven Churches of Asia Minor

to pass; and he sent and signified it by his angel unto his servant John . . .

That leaves us the question of who John might be. The most common tradition is that the fourth gospel, the three epistles of John, and Revelation are all written by the same person, and that this person is John the apostle; that is, John son of Zebedee. In the Catholic versions of the Bible, the book is accordingly entitled "The Apocalypse of St. John the Apostle."

It is true that the language of the book, while Greek, is filled with Semitic word order and idioms, and is rich in Old Testament allusion in almost every verse. One might almost consider this to prove that the author was a Palestinian Jew who thought in Hebrew or Aramaic and whose Greek had been learned late in life—as one would expect of John the Apostle.

On the other hand, the language might prove nothing one way or the other. It might very well be a self-conscious imitation of the kind of apocalyptic language used by the Palestinian Jewish writers of the previous two centuries. (We have a modern example of this sort of thing in the Book of Mormon, which was written in self-conscious imitation of the style of the King James Version of the Bible.)

Arguing against John the Apostle as writer is the enormous difference in style, vocabulary, and thought between the fourth gospel and Revelation. The two could not be by the same author and if John the apostle wrote the fourth gospel, he could not have written Revelation. Moreover if the writer of Revelation identifies himself as John and is therefore clearly not trying to conceal his identity, why does he not say openly that he is John the apostle, or John the Beloved Disciple? The fact that he does not, makes it seem that he is another John.

The King James Version seems to display caution in this respect for it does not identify John as the apostle, in the name of the book, which it calls: "The Revelation of St. John the Divine." The Revised Standard Version is even more cautious and calls it "The Revelation to John," while the Jerusalem Bible says simply, "The Book of Revelation."

Patmos

The book is undoubtedly the product of someone who, if not a native of the western coast of Asia Minor, is a resident there. The book begins in the form of a letter addressed to the churches of that region:

Revelation 1:4. *John to the seven churches which are in Asia* . . .

Asia here, as everywhere in the New Testament, refers to the western third of the peninsula of Asia Minor, the Roman "province of Asia" of which Ephesus was the capital.

John locates himself specifically near that province:

Revelation 1:9. *I John, who also am your brother, and companion in tribulation,* . . . *was in the isle that is called Patmos* . . .

Patmos is an island in the Aegean Sea, only about half the size of Manhattan Island, and about seventy miles southwest of Ephesus. Tradition has it that John was there in exile because of the danger of martyrdom if he remained in Ephesus. There seems a hint of this in the reference of John to his being a "brother and companion in tribulation" of those of Asia.

The occasion for Revelation would seem to be similar to the occasions for all apocalyptic writing. The true believers are being oppressed and the forces of evil seem to be triumphing. It becomes necessary to reassure those with fainting hearts that God is not sleeping, that all is working out according to a prearranged plan, that retribution will not be long delayed and that the final day of judgment with the subsequent establishment of the ideal kingdom will be the result of a course of events that is on the point of being initiated:

Revelation 1:3. *Blessed is he that readeth . . . the words of this prophecy . . . for the time is at hand.*

Some have suggested that the specific time of persecution that led to the writing of Revelation was that of Nero. It seems unlikely though that Revelation could be a response to Nero's persecution, short-lived as it was and confined as it was to the city of Rome. It was Domitian's much more general persecution which first visited systematic danger and misery upon the inhabitants of Asia Minor.

It is assumed then that John left Ephesus for Patmos, either in flight from persecution, or possibly carried off to prison there, in Domitian's last years; and that he returned to Ephesus after Domitian's death and the accession of the mild Nerva had put a term to the anti-Christian crisis. Since Domitian was assassinated in 96, Revelation is thought to have been written in 95.

Alpha and Omega

In his preamble, John rhapsodically describes the glory of God:

Revelation 1:7. *Behold, he cometh with clouds; and every eye shall see him, and they also which pierced him: and all kindreds of the earth shall wail because of him . . .*

Revelation 1:8. *I am Alpha and Omega, the beginning and the ending, saith the Lord, which is, and which was, and which is to come . . .*

From the very start of the book one sees how the author composes his symbols out of the very language of the apocalyptic passages of the Old Testament. He is especially fond of Daniel which, up to the time of Revelation itself, was the most successful and respected of the apocalypses, because it was canonical.

Thus, when John says, "Behold, he cometh with clouds," this is harking back to Daniel:

Daniel 7:13. . . . *behold, one like the Son of man came with the clouds of heaven* . . .

Then, when he speaks of everyone seeing him, even his enemies ("and they also which pierced him") there is a self-conscious return to the language of Zechariah:

Zechariah 12:10. . . . *they shall look upon me whom they have pierced, and they shall mourn* . . .

And in describing the Lord as eternal, the language is that of the Second Isaiah:

Isaiah 44:6. *Thus saith the Lord . . . I am the first and I am the last* . . .

John translates Isaiah's remark into the metaphoric reference to the Greek alphabet. Of the twenty-four letters of that alphabet, "alpha" is the first and "omega" the twenty-fourth and last. To say that God is "Alpha and Omega" is therefore equivalent to saying he is "first and last." In modern alphabetical allusion, John might be paraphrased as saying that God is "everything from A to Z."

The Lord's Day

The long vision of Revelation begins at a specific time:

Revelation 1:10. *I was in the Spirit on the Lord's day* . . .

There are several possible interpretations of what is meant by "the Lord's day," but the consensus is that it refers to the first day of the week, which we call Sunday. It is the Lord's day because it is the day of the week on which the resurrection took place. It was celebrated at first without prejudice to the seventh day of the week, the Sabbath, and if John is really referring to Sunday when he speaks of the Lord's day, it is the first unmistakable reference in Christian literature to Sunday as a special day.

It was not until Christianity became the official religion of the Roman Empire in the early decades of the fourth century that the

Lord's day took over the full significance of the Sabbath, and that the observance of the seventh day was dropped completely and left entirely to the Jews.

The Seven Churches

John lists the seven churches to which his apocalyptic letters are addressed, and all are in the province of Asia:

Revelation 1:10. *I . . . heard behind me a great voice . . .*
Revelation 1:11. *Saying, . . . What thou seest, write in a book, and send it unto the seven churches which are in Asia; unto Ephesus, and unto Smyrna, and unto Pergamos, and unto Thyatira, and unto Sardis, and unto Philadelphia, and unto Laodicea.*

Of these seven cities, Ephesus is the best known. It is the capital of the province, is frequently mentioned in Acts, and is the city in which the riot of the silversmiths had taken place and in which Paul had spent considerable time (see page 406).

Thyatira was the city—noted for its dye manufactures—from which came Lydia, the dye-seller whom Paul met in Philippi (see page 396). Laodicea is the city near Colossae to which reference was made in Colossians (see page 468).

The remaining four cities are not mentioned in the Bible in any book other than Revelation.

Smyrna is on the Asia Minor coast about forty miles north of Ephesus. It was an ancient town which invading Greeks took over and colonized as early as 1000 B.C., when David ruled over Israel. By 650 B.C. it was a wealthy and cultured city. But then the Lydians, who had built up a powerful kingdom in the hinterland, took the Greek-speaking Aegean coast. Because Smyrna led the resistance, Alyattes, king of Lydia, ordered the city's destruction.

According to later legend, Alexander the Great, when passing down the coast three centuries later, conceived the notion of re-establishing the city. After his death, his generals, Antigonus and Lysimachus, who temporarily dominated Asia Minor, carried through this dream and about 301 B.C. Smyrna lived again. By Roman times, it had grown almost to rival Ephesus in size and wealth.

In fact, when all the famed ancient cities of the Asia Minor coast sank into decay and ruin, Smyrna alone continued to flourish. Even after the Turks captured Asia Minor, Smyrna (now known by the Turkish name of Izmir) continued as a Greek center, right down into modern times. After World War I, Greece, which had been on the victor's side, claimed Smyrna as its own and landed an army in defeated Turkey in 1919. In the war that followed, it was Turkey that was victorious and the Greek army was driven into the sea. Izmir was sacked and virtually destroyed and its long Greek history came to an end. When it was rebuilt yet again it was as a Turkish town and it is now, with a population of nearly four hundred thousand, the third largest city in the nation.

Lying forty-five miles east of Smyrna is Sardis, the capital of the Lydian kingdom which, for a while during the sixth century B.C., included the western half of Asia Minor. In 546 B.C. Lydia came to a permanent end when it was taken by Cyrus, the Persian conqueror. Sardis was never to be the capital of an independent kingdom again, but it remained an important city for centuries. An Athenian expedition burned it in 499 B.C. and that was the occasion that gave rise to the great Persian war against Greece in the following decades. It was not until the coming of the Turks that it declined and it was finally destroyed by Timur (Tamerlane), the Mongol conqueror, in 1402.

Following the destruction of the Persian Empire by Alexander the Great, a new independent, Greek-speaking nation was founded in western Asia Minor. Its appearance as an independent nation can be traced back to 283 B.C. and its capital was the city of Pergamum, some sixty miles north of Smyrna and about fifteen miles from the coast.

At first, its rulers controlled only a small district about the city, but under the enlightened sway of its rulers that territory grew and by 230 B.C. became the kingdom of Pergamum (named for its capital) under King Attalus I.

Pergamum's great enemy was the Seleucid Empire, which was particularly threatening under its conquering king, Antiochus III (see page 45). Pergamum therefore allied itself with Rome, and when Rome won its first victories in Asia Minor, Pergamum was rewarded with large tracts of Seleucid territory.

Under Eumenes II, who reigned from 197 to 160 B.C.—that is, during the period of the Maccabean revolt—Pergamum reached the height of its prosperity and power. The city had a library second only to that of Alexandria.

Roman power in Asia Minor grew, however, and in 133 B.C., when Pergamum's king, Attalus III, lay dying, he left his kingdom to Rome in his will. He felt that only so could he keep his land from being torn apart by a struggle between various rivals for the throne. He was right and Rome took over with only minor resistance.

The city of Pergamum was no longer the capital of the area, however, for it became the Roman province of Asia and the center of affairs moved to the Greek cities of Ephesus and Smyrna. Pergamum itself began to decline in Mark Antony's time, a generation before the birth of Jesus. Mark Antony, trying to make up to Cleopatra of Egypt for the destruction of some of Alexandria's Library during the small war with Julius Caesar a dozen years before, transferred Pergamum's library to Alexandria. Pergamum still exists today, however, as the town of Bergamo (its name still recognizable) in modern Turkey.

Philadelphia is the smallest of the seven cities and is located about twenty-five miles southeast of Sardis. It was founded about 150 B.C. by Attalus II of Pergamum. He was known as Attalus Philadelphus and the city was named in his own honor. It still exists today as a small Turkish town named Alesehir, which means "red city," so called from the color of its soil.

Seven

John describes a complicated vision of the Son of man to introduce the letters he is sending to each of the seven churches, using terms borrowed chiefly from Daniel. So frequent is the use of the number seven throughout the Book of Revelation that it is usually suspected that the seven churches were chosen not because that was all there were in the province of Asia but because of the mystic qualities of the number itself.

The importance of seven in the Bible appears first in the seven days of the original week (the six days of creation plus the seventh day of rest). That is not the ultimate source, however, for it seems very likely that the first chapter of Genesis was an adaptation of Babylonian creation tales and that the seven-day week was of Babylonian (perhaps ultimately of Sumerian) origin.

The week arose from the accidental astronomical fact that there are seven visible bodies in the sky that move independently against the background of the stars. These are the Sun, the Moon, Mercury, Venus, Mars, Jupiter, and Saturn. The Babylonians found much of mystic importance in the number and motions of these bodies and founded the study of astrology, a pseudo-science that still exists in undiminished importance and influence even in our own supposedly enlightened society.

Each of the seven days of the week is presided over by a planet after which it is named. We still retain relics of that in our own Sunday, Monday (Moon-day), and Saturday (Saturn-day). The other days of the week are named, in English, for Norse deities, but in French, for instance, the planetary system is clear. Tuesday is "mardi" (Mars-day), Wednesday is "mercredi" (Mercury-day), Thursday is "jeudi" (Jove-day), and Friday is "vendredi" (Venus-day).

The seven-day week was all the more useful in that it blended closely into the lunar month, being about a quarter of that period of time. The passage of a week therefore signified a change in the phase of the moon—from new to first quarter, from first quarter to full, from full to third quarter, from third quarter to new again. Indeed, the very word "week" is from an old Teutonic word meaning "change."

The Jews borrowed the week from the Babylonians during the period of exile, and it was then that the Sabbath gained its post-Exilic significance (see page 186). It was then, also, that the number seven became of mystic importance. For the purposes of the writer of Revelation it was a fortunate coincidence that the city of Rome was widely known to have been built on seven hills.

Nicolaitans

The second and third chapters of Revelation are quite prosaic for in them John relays messages from each of seven angels to each of the seven churches in relatively straightforward language. The shortcomings of each church are blamed and their staunchness praised. The original readers for whom the messages are meant understand all the allusions, of course, but modern readers are frustrated because of the lack of background information. Thus, the church at Ephesus is praised but there are some mysterious faults:

Revelation 2:4. *Nevertheless I have somewhat against thee, because thou hast left thy first love.*

Apparently the Ephesian church in certain unspecified ways no longer shows its original enthusiasm. Still, they are praised for rejecting a sect which John views with strong disapproval:

Revelation 2:6. . . . *thou hatest the deeds of the Nicolaitanes, which I also hate.*

Who the Nicolaitans might be and what their doctrines were is not certainly known. It is to be presumed from the name that they followed the teaching of someone called Nicolas.

There is only one Nicolas mentioned in the New Testament, and he was one of the seven men appointed to be leaders of the Grecian party very early in the history of the Church (see page 344):

Acts 6:5. . . . *and they chose Stephen, . . . and Philip, . . . and Nicolas a proselyte of Antioch . . .*

A common guess in past centuries is that the Nicolaitans advocated unrestricted sexual intercourse, that is, "free love." The legend arose that Nicolas, the proselyte of Antioch, taking too literally the communist doctrines of the apostles at the very beginning (see page 341), offered to share his wife with the others. Perhaps this notion arose because Antioch, like other large Gentile cities, had the reputation of being extremely licentious, to the disapproving Jewish and Christian puritans of Roman times.

A hint in this direction is found in the letter to the church at Pergamos. It is warned:

Revelation 2:14. . . . *thou hast there them that hold the doctrine of Balaam, who taught Balac to cast a stumblingblock before the children of Israel . . .*

Revelation 2:15. . . . *also them that hold the doctrine of the Nicolaitanes, which thing I hate.*

The two heresies of Balaam and the Nicolaitans seem to be mentioned as distinct, but perhaps this is the parallelism of Hebrew poetry, where the same thing is mentioned twice in different ways. If so, what is the doctrine of Balaam?

There is a passage in the Book of Numbers that immediately follows the tale of Balaam's oracles (see page I-183) which were intended to be against Israel but which were turned in favor of Israel by God against Balaam's own will:

Numbers 25:1. *And Israel abode in Shittim, and the people began to commit whoredom with the daughters of Moab.*

It was supposed that Balaam had advised Balak, the king of Moab, to seduce the Israelites in this manner, since such seduction would bring the wrath of God down upon the sinners—to the great benefit of Moab. Thus when the Israelites later took women alive as spoils of war, Moses is quoted as angrily advocating their death and saying:

Numbers 31:16. *Behold, these caused the children of Israel, through the counsel of Balaam, to commit trespass against the Lord . . . and there was a plague . . .*

Consequently, the name of Balaam was associated with sexual license and this would tie in with Nicolaitanism as a doctrine of release from the severe sexual restrictions demanded by the Law and, for that matter, by Paul's teaching.

Another hint of this is to be found in the message to the church at Thyatira:

Revelation 2:20. *. . . I have a few things against thee, because thou sufferest that woman Jezebel, which calleth herself a prophetess, to teach and to seduce my servants to commit fornication . . .*

The Book of Life

The church at Sardis gets the negative praise that there are a few worthy among them, and for any that are worthy, the message is:

Revelation 3:5. *. . . I will not blot out his name out of the book of life . . .*

Originally, the book of life was merely a metaphoric expression signifying the list of living people. It is as though one were enrolled in a great census kept in heaven of all those alive at any time. To die would be to be blotted out of that book. Thus, Moses pleads with God for the Israelites after the incident of the calf of gold (see page

I-151) and says that he himself may as well die if the Israelites are not forgiven:

Exodus 32:32. *Yet now, if thou wilt forgive their sin—; and if not, blot me, I pray thee, out of thy book which thou hast written.*

In post-Exilic times, however, when the doctrine of the resurrection of the body and of a life hereafter was developed, the book of life came to be the list not of those alive in the world, but of those who were to be awarded a life hereafter in heaven. The Book of Daniel, in speaking of the resurrection, says:

Daniel 12:1. . . . *there shall be a time of trouble . . . and at that time thy people shall be delivered, every one that shall be found written in the book.*

Again, in the Book of Psalms, God is asked to visit punishment upon the wicked:

Psalm 69:28. *Let them be blotted out of the book of the living, and not be written with the righteous.*

Philadelphia

Philadelphia is praised:

Revelation 3:8. . . . *thou hast a little strength, and hast kept my word, and hast not denied my name.*

Philadelphia was to live up to this praise over a thousand years later. During a period of three centuries, beginning in 1071, the Turks slowly but inexorably swept over Asia Minor, eradicating Christianity and making it Moslem—a situation that exists to this day. The last city to be taken by the Turks, the last city to remain as a holdout, the one that longest did not deny the name, was Philadelphia. It fell at last in 1390 after an eight-year siege.

In 1682, William Penn was establishing a new colony on the shores of the Delaware River in the New World and was founding a city. He chose the name Philadelphia for two reasons. First, it means, literally, "love of sister (or brother)" so that a city by that name can be called the "city of brotherly love." And secondly, Penn remembered this encomium on Philadelphia in Revelation. Penn founded the city and Philadelphia is now the fourth largest city in the United States, far larger than any of the ancient Philadelphias had ever been.

Laodicea

The church at Laodicea is bitterly condemned, not for being outspokenly opposed to the doctrines favored by John, but for being neutral. John apparently prefers an honest enemy to a doubtful friend:

> Revelation 3:15. *I know thy works, that thou art neither cold nor hot: I would thou wert cold or hot.*
> Revelation 3:16. *So then because thou art lukewarm, and neither cold nor hot, I will spue thee out of my mouth.*

"Laodicean" has therefore entered the English language as a word meaning "indifferent" or "neutral."

The Lamb

The scene now switches to heaven and all the rest of the Book of Revelation is thickly mystical. John begins by describing God in the midst of the heavenly court with images drawn from Daniel and Ezekiel, and with Isaiah's seraphim (see page I-528) prominently introduced. Amid all these glories there is introduced a book sealed with seven seals. This, presumably, contains the secrets of the future, which cannot be revealed until, one by one, the seals are broken.

The hero who will reveal the contents of the book makes his appearance:

> Revelation 5:6. . . . *and, lo,* . . . *in the midst of the elders, stood a Lamb as it had been slain* . . .
> Revelation 5:7. *And he came and took the book out of the right hand of him that sat upon the throne.*

The image of the Messiah as a lamb made into a kind of greater

Passover sacrifice was introduced in the fourth gospel (see page 331). It is explicitly stated in the First Epistle of Peter:

1 Peter 1:18. . . . *ye were . . . redeemed . . .*
1 Peter 1:19. . . . *with the precious blood of Christ, as of a lamb without blemish and without spot . . .*

By the end of the first century, that metaphor had become so well known that the author of Revelation did not have to elaborate on the identity of the Lamb.

The Four Horsemen

One by one the seals of the book are broken and with each of the first four, a horse and rider appeared:

Revelation 6:1. . . . *when the Lamb opened one of the seals . . .*
Revelation 6:2. . . . *behold a white horse: and he that sat on him had a bow; and a crown . . . : and he went forth conquering . . .*
Revelation 6:3. *And when he had opened the second seal . . .*
Revelation 6:4. . . . *there went out another horse that was red: and power was given to him that sat thereon to take peace from the earth . . .*
Revelation 6:5. *And when he had opened the third seal, . . . lo a black horse; and he that sat on him had a pair of balances in his hand.*
Revelation 6:6. *And I heard a voice . . . say, A measure of wheat for a penny . . .*
Revelation 6:7. *And when he had opened the fourth seal, . . .*
Revelation 6:8. . . . *behold a pale horse: and his name that sat on him was Death . . .*

These are the "four horsemen of the apocalypse" representing the variety of evils that were to descend upon the world (specifically upon the Roman Empire, which was viewed by its populace as synonymous with "the world") to mark the beginning of its dissolution and the coming of the Messianic era.

The white horse and its rider seems to represent foreign invasion. At least the bow is the virtual symbol of the Parthian raiders, who since the time of Julius Caesar had been the terror of the east. In the days of Herod the Great, they had occupied Jerusalem, and at no time thereafter were their forces very far to the east.

The red horse and its rider also seem to signify a form of war. It may well represent the bloody disorders of civil war and insurrection.

The black horse and its rider represent famine, for the price offered for a measure of wheat ("a penny") is far higher than normal and is so high in fact that the ordinary populace could not buy enough to live.

The pale horse and its rider are named as "Death," but this is not the kind of death in general that would follow war or famine. That is taken care of by the first three horses. Rather Death represents death by disease, as when we refer to the "Black Death," for instance.

In short, the four horsemen can be most briefly described as War, Revolution, Famine, and Pestilence.

There are many who seek the meaning of the symbolism of Revelation in the events that have happened in the centuries since the book was written. To those, never did the four horsemen ride with such effect as in the days of World War I. Not only was there the bloodiest and most stupidly savage slaughter ever seen, on both western and eastern fronts, but there was a revolution in Russia that affects us even today, a famine in both Germany and Russia immediately after the war, and a world-wide influenza pandemic in 1918 that killed more people than the war did.

Never had War, Revolution, Famine, and Pestilence stalked ghastly over all the world as in the years from 1914 to 1920.

An Hundred and Forty and Four Thousand

When the fifth seal is broken, the souls of the martyrs are revealed waiting for judgment and when the sixth seal is broken, the physical universe begins to crumble. It might seem that now the climax is reached. The seventh seal ought to be broken and the great day of judgment come. However, throughout the Book of Revelation there is a strong reluctance, apparently, to let the climax come. Over and over it is delayed.

The first delay comes at this point, for after the sixth seal is broken, and before the seventh seal can be touched, there is a break:

Revelation 7:1. . . . *I saw four angels* . . .

. . . .

Revelation 7:3. *Saying, Hurt not the earth . . . till we have sealed the servants of our God in their foreheads.*

It was customary in Babylonia from the most ancient times to use seals for identification. These were small cylindrical intaglios which could be rolled upon the soft clay used by the Babylonians for a writing surface. A characteristic picture would appear, serving the place of signature on our own documents.

A slave might be similarly branded (as our cattle are out west) to show indelibly who the master was. A characteristic brand would serve the function of a seal. The picture presented here, then, is of the righteous beings marked somehow (details are not given) with a symbol (again not described) that identifies them as God's slaves to be kept safe through the final disasters.

The number of those to be saved is given specifically:

Revelation 7:4. . . . *I heard the number of them which were sealed . . . an hundred and forty and four thousand of all the tribes of the children of Israel.*

Because of the smallness of the number compared to the total population of the Earth, the notion has arisen that very few are to be saved. On the other hand, the number can't be taken literally.

The twelve tribes of Israel stand, figuratively, for all the righteous. The number 144,000 is twelve times twelve times a thousand, and we must consider the mystic significance of these numbers.

Just as seven probably derives its initial sacred character from the fact that it represents the number of planets in the heavens, so twelve probably derives its sacred character from the fact that there are twelve months in the year. From this is derived the twelve signs of the zodiac and the notion that with twelve one comes full circle. The number 144, which is twelve times twelve, is therefore completeness accentuated. It represents all the righteous (12) of all the tribes (12) and no one is left out.

As for one thousand, that was the largest number which possessed a specific name in ancient times. The Greeks used the word "myrioi" to signify ten thousand, but that is not really a name for a number. It meant "innumerable" originally, which is the sense we use it for when we speak of "a myriad objects." To multiply something by a thousand was to make it as large as one conveniently could in the language of the time. It follows that the number 144,000 does not mean specifically that number but represents an emphatic way of saying, "All the righteous! A large number of them!"

(It should be mentioned that the word "thousand" remained the largest number-word right down into late medieval times. Only then were numbers like "million" invented in Italy.)

Revelation goes on to expand on the mystical completeness of the number by emphasizing that there are to be twelve thousand from each of the twelve tribes, which are given in the following order: Judah, Reuben, Gad, Asher, Naphtali, Manasseh, Simeon, Levi, Issachar, Zebulon, Joseph, and Benjamin.

This is a strange list. Apparently the twelve sons of Jacob should have been listed, but one of the names on the list is Manasseh, the son of Joseph, and a grandson of Jacob. To make room for Manasseh, one of the sons of Jacob would have to be omitted, and the one so omitted is Dan.

This is very likely a mistake on the part of John or of some later copyist. It may be that Man was accidentally written for Dan and that a still later copyist assumed Man to be an abbreviation for Manasseh.

It is, however, difficult for some people to accept something as prosaic as a copyist's error in the Bible, so that significance is sought for even in the most trivial things. Some have suggested, for instance, that Dan was deliberately omitted because Antichrist was to spring from among those of that tribe.

The notion that the tribe of Dan was to give rise to Antichrist can come only from the passage in the Testament of Jacob (see page I-116) which goes:

Genesis 49:17. *Dan shall be a serpent by the way . . .*

It is farfetched to go from this metaphorical description of Dan as a serpent (referring perhaps to the snake as a totemistic symbol of the tribe in primitive times as the lion was for Judah and the wolf for Benjamin) to the post-Exilic identification of the serpent in the garden of Eden with Satan, and thence with Antichrist—but all this is an easy leap for mystics.

These righteous now stand before the Lamb and all their sufferings are washed away in what has become a famous phrase:

Revelation 7:14. . . . *they . . . came out of great tribulation, and have washed their robes, and made them white in the blood of the Lamb.*

Euphrates

And now at last, the seventh seal is broken and one might expect the climax of the vision to approach, but it still doesn't. Instead a new series of seven events begins in the form of seven angels, each of whom blows a trumpet in turn, with gruesome disasters following each trumpet sound. When the fifth angel blows his trumpet, hell itself opens:

Revelation 9:2. . . . *and there arose a smoke out of the pit . . .*
Revelation 9:3. *And there came out of the smoke locusts upon the earth . . .*

. . . .

Revelation 9:7. *And the shapes of the locusts were like unto horses prepared unto battle . . . and their faces were as the faces of men.*

The picture being drawn by John here is clearly inspired by the great terror of the east—the Parthian cavalry, swooping in like a cloud of locusts, dealing their deadly strokes and fading away before they could be properly opposed. The Roman general, Crassus, was defeated in this manner in eastern Syria in 53 B.C. That defeat had never been properly avenged and it was never forgotten.

The characteristic weapons of the Parthian horsemen were their bows, which they could use with great effect. Even when retreating, they could rise in their saddles and shoot, in unison, one rapid volley of arrows back at their pursuers. This "Parthian shot" was often quite effective. It is to such tactics that Revelation may be referring, when they speak of the locusts as:

Revelation 9:10. *And they had tails like unto scorpions, and there were stings in their tails . . .*

When the sixth angel sounds his trumpet, the picture of the Parthian cavalry is continued. The sixth angel is instructed:

Revelation 9:14. . . . *Loose the four angels which are bound in the great river Euphrates.*

The Euphrates was a boundary in a double sense. First it was the boundary of Israel in the great days of David and Solomon and had been the ideal boundary of Israel ever since. Second, it was the boundary of the Roman realm during most of the days of its empire. The "angels" bound in the Euphrates controlled the enemy hosts on the other side.

The army controlled by these angels of the Euphrates was made to seem unbelievably numerous—an impression made on the awed infantry when they were the object of the sudden onrush of a contingent of horsemen:

Revelation 9:16. *And the number of the army of the horsemen were two hundred thousand thousand . . .*

This is the number obtained if one makes use of the Greek "myrioi" as a synonym of innumerability, emphasizes it by repetition ("an innumerable, innumerable quantity"), and then doubles it for good measure. If "myrioi" is taken as ten thousand, it becomes two myriad myriad or two hundred thousand thousand, or two hundred million—a number equal to the entire population of the United States.

The Great City

Then before the seventh and final trumpet is sounded there is another digression and the temporary triumph of evil is described.

This temporary triumph represents the persecution of Domitian, then proceeding. The language used in describing this persecution reaches back to the Old Testament, as does everything in Revelation. The oppression of the Church by Rome is therefore cast in the terms Daniel used in describing the oppression of the Temple by the Seleucids:

Revelation 11:2. . . . *the court which is without the temple . . . is given unto the Gentiles: and the holy city shall they tread under foot forty and two months.*

This is the period of three and a half years during which the Temple was profaned in the time of Antiochus IV. This use of Temple symbolism has been advanced as evidence that the Temple was still standing at the time Revelation was written and that the book was composed, therefore, during Nero's persecution. However, Revelation uses Old Testament symbolism so consistently, that such a deduction doesn't carry conviction. John would speak of the Temple as representing the Church whether the Temple stood or not, and his readers would understand his allegory.

Two prophets are described:

> Revelation 11:3. *And I will give power unto my two witnesses* . . .
> . . . .
> Revelation 11:7. *And when they shall have finished their testimony, the beast that ascendeth out of the bottomless pit shall* . . . *kill them.*
> Revelation 11:8. *And their dead bodies shall lie in the street of the great city* . . .

This continues the allegory, indicating that the Church will be persecuted by the forces of Satan and temporarily be defeated. The particular form of the allegory may, however, be influenced by particular events. Some have suggested that the two witnesses may be Paul and Peter, the apostles martyred, according to tradition, by Nero, who could very well be described as "the beast that ascendeth out of the bottomless pit." In that case, the "great city" would, of course, be Rome.

A later copyist may have felt the great city would have to be Jerusalem and added the phrase:

> Revelation 11:8. . . . *the great city,* . . . *where also our Lord was crucified.*

The Dragon

Now the seventh trumpet is sounded, but there is still no climax. Instead, a new allegory representing the battle of good and evil is introduced and cast into terms of Babylonian mythology:

> Revelation 12:1. *And there appeared a great wonder in heaven; a woman clothed with the sun, and the moon under her feet, and upon her head a crown of twelve stars . . .*

In Babylonian mythology, this would be a sun-goddess, the twelve stars representing the signs of the zodiac through which the Sun passes each year. To John, it would represent the idealized Israel, the twelve stars representing the twelve tribes. The woman was in labor and gave birth to the Messiah:

> Revelation 12:5. *And she brought forth a man child, who was to rule all nations with a rod of iron . . .*

But there was an opponent also in heaven, and this, too, appeared in Babylonian terms:

> Revelation 12:3. *And there appeared another wonder in heaven; and behold a great red dragon, having seven heads and ten horns, and seven crowns upon his heads.*

The dragon represents chaos. It is the Babylonian Tiamat or the Hebrew Leviathan, which had to be defeated in the beginning in order to allow the ordered universe to be created, and would have to be defeated again in the end, in order to allow the created universe to come to an appropriate end. One might expect the mystic number of seven heads and seven crowns to be carried through to seven horns. The rather inappropriate number of ten horns harks back to Daniel's fourth beast, whose ten horns represents the ten Seleucid kings down to Antiochus IV (see page I-609).

The dragon also represents Satan or Antichrist. He is prepared to devour the Messiah at the instant of birth, but the Messiah has all the heavenly hosts on his side:

> Revelation 12:7. *And there was war in heaven: Michael and his angels fought against the dragon; and the dragon fought and his angels,*
> Revelation 12:8. *And prevailed not . . .*
> Revelation 12:9. *And the great dragon was cast out, that old serpent, called the Devil, and Satan . . . and his angels were cast out with him.*

This reflects the legends that grew up in post-Exilic times under Persian influence. God and Satan led opposing armies in the battle of good versus evil. Only in Revelation, however, does this Persian notion of dualism receive the canonical nod.

Milton, in his epic *Paradise Lost,* begins his description of the fall of Man at the very moment when Satan and his angels (now turned into demons) have been hurled into hell and are slowly recovering their senses after the shock of the fall.

Satan, cast to Earth, and unable to prevail against God, could nevertheless vent his spleen against those righteous men on Earth:

> Revelation 12:17. *And the dragon was wroth with the woman, and went to make war with the remnant of her seed, which keep the commandments of God, and have the testimony of Jesus Christ.*

It is that, of course, which, in the eye of the writer of Revelation, explains all the troubles of the Church.

The Beast

Satan's malevolence sharpens, out of desperation, as the end of the world approaches and he (symbolized as the dragon) passes his powers over to an Earthly entity, represented in the form of Daniel's beast— the well-known allegorical representation of the pagan empires that oppressed the righteous (see page I-609).

> Revelation 13:1. . . . *I . . . saw a beast rise up out of the sea, having seven heads and ten horns . . . and upon his heads the name of blasphemy.*
> Revelation 13:2. . . . *and the dragon gave him his power . . .*
> Revelation 13:3. *And I saw one of his heads as it were wounded to death; and his deadly wound was healed . . .*

The beast (with the usual seven heads and ten horns) is, of course, the Roman Empire, which had initially impinged upon Judean consciousness from across the Mediterranean Sea.

The statement that upon its heads are "the name of blasphemy" refers to the demand that the emperors be worshipped as gods. This emperor-worship was an official state ritual that was little more than a formality designed to bind together the citizens of the empire which were otherwise so diverse in language, custom, and religion. It was a unifying gesture equivalent to our own salute to the flag and recital of the pledge of allegiance.

It was the refusal of Christians to accede to the perfunctory emperor-worshipping ritual that made them suspect, not because of their religion but because of the suspicion that they were traitors to the state. This should not strike us as strange, for there are Christian sects these days who refuse the salute to the flag and the pledge of allegiance, claiming them to be idolatrous acts—and there also exist super-patriots who are offended at this and who take strong action against such sects when in a position to do so.

The healed wound that had killed one of the heads may refer to Nero. Actually, of the twelve Roman Emperors (counting Julius Caesar) who ruled up to the time that Revelation was written, no less than six had died by assassination or suicide: Julius Caesar, Caligula, Nero, Galba, Otho, and Vitellius. Claudius may have been poisoned and Domitian was fated to be assassinated. (Only Augustus, Tiberius, Vespasian, and Titus died undoubtedly of natural causes.)

Nevertheless it was Nero whose death would be most significant to Christians, at least up to the time of Domitian. His suicide would be marked allegorically on the beast. The fact that the Roman Empire survived and that new emperors reigned would be signified by the fact that the wound was healed.

The beast representing the Roman Empire is pictured as being worshipped by all men, but the righteous. Those who worshipped were allowed to live in peace and security; those who refused to worship (the Christians) were persecuted. Just as God sealed those righteous who belonged to him, so did the beast (the Roman Empire) seal those who indulged in emperor-worship and therefore belonged to him:

> Revelation 13:15. . . . *as many as would not worship the image of the beast should be killed.*
>
> Revelation 13:16. *And he* [the beast] *causeth all . . . to receive a mark in their right hand, or in their foreheads:*
>
> Revelation 13:17. *And that no man might buy or sell, save he that had the mark . . .*

The Number of the Beast

Even the Roman Empire is a kind of abstraction and the writer of Revelation zeroes in on a particular man, whom he is reluctant to name—perhaps because if he were to do so, he would be subject to the charge of treason and the punishment of execution. Cautiously he identifies the man in such a way that his more knowledgeable readers will know exactly whom he means and yet the law will not be able to touch him:

Revelation 13:18. *Here is wisdom. Let him that hath understanding count the number of the beast: for it is the number of a man; and his number is Six hundred threescore and six.*

To understand this we must realize that down through medieval times it was common to use letters of the alphabet to signify numbers. The Jews, Greek, and Romans all did this. We are most familiar with the Roman numerals where I=1, V=5, X=10, L=50, C=100, D=500, and M=1000. It follows that words made up of these letters would also be seen to have a kind of numerical value. If an individual were named Dill McDix, for instance, one could set each letter equal to a number, add them, and reach a total of 2212.

This is hard to do in English since only a few letters of the Latin alphabet are assigned numerical values. In the Greek and Hebrew languages, however, every letter was assigned a numerical value. Naturally, then, all words in Greek or Hebrew would have numerical meaning.

Jewish mystics in Greek and Roman times assumed that the inspired words of the Bible had significance numerically as well as literally and spent much time on the analysis of such numbers. This form of endeavor was called "gematria," a corruption of the Greek "geometria" (and our "geometry").

The "number of the beast" is an example of such gematria, the only significant example in the Bible. Commentators have considered virtually every possible candidate for the beast and the one most frequently mentioned is Nero. If his name is written in the Greek form—Neron—and if his title Caesar is added and if Neron Caesar is written in Hebrew letters, then the total numerical value is indeed 666. If the final "n" is left out, the total is 616, and some old manuscripts of Revelation have 616 rather than 666 as the number of the beast.

And yet Nero seems a poor candidate if the book were written in 95. He had been dead a quarter of a century and his death had brought no great change. Within the year Vespasian had come to the throne and he and his son Titus had given Rome a dozen years of good and humane government.

At the time Revelation was being written, however, Domitian, Vespasian's younger son, was on the throne and his persecution of the Christians was in high gear. It would be natural to refer elliptically to the living, persecuting emperor, and there is probably some way in which Domitian's name and title could be so written as to add up to 666. It may be that he bore a nickname, commonly used by Christians, with a total numerical value of 666, a number which had its own mystic significance, for it fell short of the mystic perfection of 7 three times. For that reason 666 was the acme of imperfection and a suitable number with which to represent Antichrist.

Armageddon

Against the great city ruled by the beast, and his army of men wearing his mark, are the heavenly hosts and the 144,000 righteous ones bearing the seal of God. The victory of the good is certain, for the triumphant song in heaven is:

Revelation 14:8. . . . *Babylon is fallen, is fallen, that great city . . .*

Babylon is, of course, Rome; and Rome will be destroyed. This destruction is heralded by yet a third set of seven acts of destruction. Seven vials of plagues are emptied upon the earth, one at a time, each bringing its own horrible destruction.

As the hosts of the beast are being remorselessly punished in this manner, the scene is set for the final battle between good and evil:

Revelation 16:16. *And he* [the beast] *gathered them together into a place called in the Hebrew tongue Armageddon.*

Armageddon is, more properly, "Har-Magedon" or "the Mount of Megiddo." Megiddo, a town just south of the Kishon River and fifty-five miles north of Jerusalem, was indeed the site of two important battles. The first took place in the fifteenth century B.C. when the great Egyptian pharaoh, Thutmose III, defeated a league of Canaanite cities there. This, however, was centuries before the Israelites entered Canaan, and was beyond their historic horizon.

Nearly nine centuries after Thutmose's victory, a battle was fought at Megiddo which was very much in the Jewish view and consciousness. It was between King Josiah of Judah and Pharaoh-nechoh of Egypt in 608 B.C.

> 2 Kings 23:29. . . . *Pharaoh-nechoh king of Egypt went up against the king of Assyria . . . and king Josiah went against him; and he* [Pharaoh-nechoh] *slew him* [Josiah] *at Megiddo . . .*

The death of the great reforming king made Megiddo a place that particularly symbolized calamity and disaster. The utter destruction of the hosts of evil there would balance the earlier destruction of good in the person of Josiah.

Babylon

The approach of the end is once again interrupted for still another vision. One of the angels says:

> Revelation 17:1. . . . *Come hither; I will shew unto thee . . . the great whore that sitteth upon many waters:*
>
> . . . .
>
> Revelation 17:3. *So he carried me away . . . into the wilderness: and I saw a woman sit upon a scarlet coloured beast, full of the names of blasphemy, having seven heads and ten horns.*
>
> Revelation 17:4. *And the woman was arrayed in purple and scarlet colour, and decked with gold and precious stones and pearls, . . .*
>
> Revelation 17:5. *And upon her forehead was a name written . . .* BABYLON THE GREAT . . .

Again, Babylon represents Rome in all its luxury and power. The "many waters" upon which the woman sits is taken from the Old

Testament description of the real Babylon, which was a city of canals. Thus, Jeremiah says:

> Jeremiah 51:12. . . . *the Lord . . . spake against the inhabitants of Babylon.*
> Jeremiah 51:13. *O thou that dwellest upon many waters . . .*

The author of Revelation, unable to resist the Old Testament quotation, must reinterpret it now and does so rather ineptly:

> Revelation 17:15. *And he* [the angel] *saith unto me, The waters which thou sawest, where the whore sitteth, are peoples, and multitudes, and nations, and tongues . . .*

The seven heads of the beast are finally explained in such a way as to make the real identity of "Babylon" unmistakable:

> Revelation 17:9. . . . *The seven heads are seven mountains, on which the woman sitteth.*

The interpretation goes on:

> Revelation 17:10. *And there are seven kings: five are fallen, and one is, and the other is not yet come; and when he cometh, he must continue a short space.*
> Revelation 17:11. *And the beast that was, and is not, even he is the eighth. . . .*

There seems no way of clearly working out this passage in the light of the reign of Domitian, but it can be dealt with, if it were spoken during the reign of Nero or very shortly after. Possibly the writer of Revelation is making use here of a passage of an earlier apocalypse that was indeed prepared in Nero's time, and did it without modifying its figures.

If we go back to Nero's time, we find that he is the sixth emperor (if we count Julius Caesar as the first). In that case, five emperors have "fallen" and "one is" (Nero). The seventh who "must continue a short space" would be Galba, who briefly reigned after Nero's death and was then killed by the praetorian guard, ushering in a short period of anarchy before Vespasian took over.

During this period, it was widely supposed among the common people of the empire that Nero was not really dead but had fled to safety and would return. There were several "false Neros" who tried to capitalize on this belief in that year.

It may be Nero, then, that in the view of the earlier apocalypse was the beast "that was, and is not." When he returned, he would be the eighth emperor.

But Babylon/Rome is to fall. The final battle of good and evil (presumably at Armageddon) takes place:

> Revelation 19:20. *And the beast was taken . . . and them that worshipped his image. These . . . were cast alive into a lake of fire . . .*
> Revelation 19:21. *And the remnant were slain with the sword . . .*

Gog and Magog

Now after the long series of portents, visions, disasters, and symbols, the end of history has come, and the Messianic age opens. Even that, however, is not to be truly permanent.

> Revelation 20:1. *And I saw an angel come down from heaven . . .*
> Revelation 20:2. *And he laid hold on the dragon, that old serpent, which is the Devil, and Satan, and bound him a thousand years,*
> Revelation 20:3. *. . . and after that he must be loosed a little season.*

Why should there be this thousand-year "millennium" (see page 519) to be followed by still another upheaval and an anticlimactic second battle of good and evil?

There may be a mystic symmetry here. The Earth was created in six days, followed by a seventh day of rest, according to the first chapter of Genesis. But for God a day is like a thousand years (see page 505). Perhaps, then, the Earth's duration is to parallel the week of creation with a millennium standing for each day.

First the earth will endure six millennia of labor, strife, evil, and sin, one for each of the six days of creation. Then, for the seventh day of rest, the Earth will spend one millennium under the Messiah. Only then, when the Sabbath millennium is over, can the world indeed come to an end:

Revelation 20:7. . . . *Satan shall be loosed out of his prison,*
Revelation 20:8. *And shall go out to deceive the nations . . .*
Gog and Magog, to gather them together to battle . . .

This is an echo of Ezekiel's apocalyptic vision of the last battle:

Ezekiel 38:2. *Son of man, set thy face against Gog, the land of*
Magog . . .

The forces of evil are again defeated and destroyed and now, finally,
all is over, even the Sabbath millennium, and the day of judgment is
come at last:

Revelation 20:12. *And I saw the dead, small and great, stand*
before God; . . . and the dead were judged . . .

Jerusalem

A second creation, a perfect one, now replaces the old imperfect
one:

Revelation 21:1. *And I saw a new heaven and a new earth:*
for the first heaven and the first earth were passed away; . . .
Revelation 21:2. *And I John saw the holy city, new Jerusalem,*
coming down from God . . .

The new Jerusalem is filled with the triumphant symbolism of the
number twelve both in its old and new meanings:

Revelation 21:10. . . . *the holy Jerusalem . . .*
. . . .
Revelation 21:12. . . . *had a wall great and high, and had twelve*
gates . . . and names written thereon, which are the names of the
twelve tribes of the children of Israel:
. . . .
Revelation 21:14. *And the wall of the city had twelve foundations,*
and in them the names of the twelve apostles of the Lamb.

And when the description of the city in the most glowing possible
terms is completed, the writer of the book quotes an angel to remind
the reader emphatically that all that is predicted is rapidly to come
to pass:

Revelation 22:6. . . . *These sayings are faithful and true: and the Lord God . . . sent his angel to shew . . . the things which must shortly be done.*

Revelation 22:7. *Behold, I come quickly . . .*

And with that assurance—still unfulfilled nearly two thousand years later—the New Testament ends.

DATES OF INTEREST
IN BIBLICAL HISTORY

(*Old and New Testament*)

NOTE: Many of the dates given in this table are approximate, or controversial.

B.C.

8500 First cities established in Middle East.

5000 Jericho already existing.

4004 Archbishop Ussher's date of creation.

3761 Traditional Jewish date of creation.

3600 Sumerian city-states in existence.

3100 Egypt united under single rule, 1st dynasty founded.

3000 Canaanites enter Canaan.

2700 Assyrian cities come into existence.

2570 Great Pyramid built in Egypt.

2500 Bronze Age reaches Canaan.

2264 Sargon of Agade founds Akkadian Empire.

2050 11th dynasty rules Egypt; 3rd dynasty rules Ur.

2000 Beginning of patriarchal age in Canaan (Abraham).

1971 Sesostris I rules Egypt.

1900 Babylon begins to dominate Tigris-Euphrates valley; Sumerian city-states decline.

1730 Hyksos enter Egypt.

1700 Hammurabi rules Babylon.

1650 Israelites in Egypt (Jacob, Joseph).

1570 Hyksos expelled from Egypt.

1500 Assyria becomes independent kingdom.

1490 Thutmose III rules Egypt.
1479 Thutmose III defeats Canaanites at Megiddo.
1475 Mitanni kingdom flourishing.
1450 Tyre founded by colonists from Sidon.
1400 Mycenaean Greeks at height of power.
1397 Amenhotep III rules Egypt, which is at height of its prosperity.
1390 Hittites at height of their power.
1370 Ikhnaton rules Egypt; attempts monotheistic reform; Egyptian power begins to decline; kingdoms of Moab, Ammon, and Edom established.
1290 Rameses II rules Egypt; oppression of the Israelites.
1275 Assyria conquers the Mitanni kingdom, as Assyria enters its first period of strength.
1250 Shalmaneser I rules Assyria.
1235 Tukulti-Ninurta I [Nimrod] rules Assyria.
1223 Merneptah rules Egypt; ancient world convulsed by migrations of peoples.
1211 Death of Merneptah; possibly time of Exodus (Moses).
1200 Hittite kingdom destroyed. Tarshish founded by colonists from Tyre.
1190 Rameses III rules Egypt and defeats Philistines.
1184 Trojan War.
1170 Israelites enter Canaan; Philistines settle coast (Joshua).
1150 Barak and Deborah defeat Sisera; period of judges.
1116 Tiglath-Pileser I rules Assyria.
1100 Gideon defeats Midianites; Greeks begin to settle Asia Minor coast.
1093 Death of Tiglath-Pileser I; Assyria in decline.
1080 Philistines defeat Israelites at Aphek; Shiloh destroyed.
1040 Samuel judges the tribes.
1028 Saul rules Israel.
1013 Philistines defeat Israelites at Mount Gilboa; Saul and Jonathan killed; David rules Judah.
1006 David rules united Israel-Judah.
1000 David establishes capital at Jerusalem; Aramaeans begin infiltration of Syria.
980 David's empire at peak.
973 Death of David; Solomon rules united Israel-Judah.

969   Hiram rules Tyre.
962   Completion of Temple by Solomon.
950   Rezin founds kingdom of Damascus (Syria).
933   Death of Solomon; breakup of Israel-Judah; Jeroboam I rules
        Israel; Rehoboam rules Judah.
928   Shishak of Egypt loots Jerusalem.
917   Abijam rules Judah.
915   Asa rules Judah.
912   Nadab rules Israel.
911   Baasha overthrows Nadab, seizes rule of Israel.
888   Elah rules Israel; overthrown by Zimri.
887   Omri rules Israel; founds Samaria.
883   Asshurnasirpal rules Assyria, which experiences revival.
880   Omri conquers Moab.
875   Ahab rules Israel; Jehoshaphat rules Judah; career of Elijah.
859   Shalmaneser III rules Assyria.
858   Ahab wars with Syrians.
854   Syrian-Israelite coalition holds off Assyria at Karkar.
853   Battle of Ramoth-gilead; death of Ahab; Ahaziah rules Israel.
852   Jehoram rules Israel; career of Elisha.
851   Jehoram (of Judah) rules Judah; J document in written form.
850   Mesha of Moab gains independence.
844   Ahaziah rules Judah.
843   Jehu rebels successfully and rules Israel; Athaliah usurps power
        in Judah; Hazael rules Syria and brings it to height of its
        power.
842   Jehu pays tribute to Assyria.
837   Jehoash rules Judah.
824   Death of Shalmaneser III of Assyria, which enters another period
        of decline.
816   Jehoahaz rules Israel.
814   Carthage founded by colonists from Tyre.
800   Jehoash (of Israel) rules Israel; death of Elisha.
797   Amaziah rules Judah.
785   Jeroboam II rules Israel; Israel at height of its power.
780   Azariah (Uzziah) rules Judah; Judah at height of its power.
760   Amos prophesies.
753   Rome founded.

750 Hosea prophesies; E document in written form.
745 Tiglath-Pileser III (Pul) rules Assyria; its power revives.
744 Death of Jeroboam II; gathering anarchy in Israel.
743 Tiglath-Pileser III conquers Urartu (Ararat).
740 Jotham rules Judah; Isaiah begins prophesying.
738 Pekahiah rules Israel, which is now tributary to Assyria.
737 Pekah rules Israel.
736 Ahaz rules Judah.
734 Pekah attempts to form coalition against Assyria; attacks Judah.
732 Hoshea rules Israel; Tiglath-Pileser III takes Damascus and
brings Syrian kingdom to an end.
730 Micah prophesies.
726 Shalmaneser V rules Assyria.
725 Shalmaneser V lays siege to Samaria.
722 Sargon II usurps throne of Assyria and takes Samaria; Israelites
carried off into exile; northern kingdom comes to an end.
720 Hezekiah rules Judah.
705 Sennacherib rules Assyria, makes Nineveh his capital.
703 Babylon under Merodach-baladan rebels against Assyria.
701 Sennacherib lays siege to Jerusalem.
700 Deioces founds Median kingdom.
693 Manasseh rules Judah, which is now tributary to Assyria.
681 Sennacherib assassinated; Esarhaddon rules Assyria and brings
it to the peak of its power.
671 Esarhaddon invades and controls Egypt.
668 Asshurbanipal rules Assyria; establishes library at Nineveh.
663 Asshurbanipal sacks Thebes, ancient Egyptian capital.
652 Psamtik I rules Egypt, which is now free of Assyria.
640 Asshurbanipal defeats and destroys Elam.
638 Josiah rules Judah.
631 Cyrene founded by colonists from Greece.
630 Zephaniah prophesies.
626 Jeremiah begins to prophesy.
625 Asshurbanipal dies; gathering anarchy in Assyria and Nabopolassar seizes control of Babylonia.
620 Discovery of Book of Deuteronomy in the Temple followed by
Yahvist reform in Judah; beginnings of Greek philosophy in
Miletus.

615 Nahum prophesies.

612 Nabopolassar takes Nineveh; last Assyrian holdouts at Haran.

610 Necho (Pharaoh-nechoh) rules Egypt.

608 Necho defeats Judah at Megiddo; Josiah killed and Jehoiakim rules Judah; Jeremiah delivers Temple Sermon.

605 Babylonians defeat Necho at Carchemish; Nabopolassar dies; Nebuchadnezzar rules Babylonia and crushes last Assyrian stronghold; Habakkuk prophesies.

597 Judean rebellion crushed by Nebuchadnezzar; first Babylonian Exile; Zedekiah rules Judah.

593 Ezekiel begins to prophesy in captivity; Psamtik II rules Egypt and places Jewish garrison at Elephantine; Astyages rules Media.

588 Apries (Pharaoh-hophra) rules Egypt.

587 Zedekiah rebels against Nebuchadnezzar.

586 Nebuchadnezzar takes Jerusalem and destroys the Temple; second Babylonian Exile; Davidic Dynasty comes to an end; Gedaliah assassinated; Book of Lamentations written.

585 Nebuchadnezzar lays siege to Tyre.

573 Nebuchadnezzar raises siege of Tyre.

569 Aahmes rules Egypt.

568 Nebuchadnezzar invades Egypt unsuccessfully.

562 Death of Nebuchadnezzar; Evil-merodach rules Babylonia; various documents being combined by Jewish scribes in Babylon to form the historical books of the Old Testament.

560 Amel-Marduk assassinated; Nergal-ashur-usur rules Babylonia; Croesus rules Lydia, which is at its peak of power.

556 Nabonidus rules Babylonia; his son, Belshazzar, is co-ruler.

550 Cyrus overthrows Astyages of Media; founds Persian Empire.

546 Cyrus conquers Lydia; brings Lydian kingdom to an end.

540 Second Isaiah prophesies.

538 Cyrus takes Babylon and ends Babylonian kingdom; Jews allowed to return to Judea and first group under Sheshbazzar does so.

530 Death of Cyrus; Cambyses rules Persia.

525 Cambyses invades and conquers Egypt.

521 Darius I rules Persia.

520 Haggai and Zechariah prophesy; Zerubbabel takes over leadership of Jewish returnees.

516 Second Temple dedicated.

509 Rome evicts last king; Republic founded.

500 Obadiah prophesies; Greek cities of Asia Minor revolt against Persia.

490 Persian expedition defeated at Marathon by Athens.

486 Death of Darius I; Xerxes I (Ahasuerus) rules Persia.

480 Persian expedition defeated at Salamis by united Greece; Tarshish destroyed by Carthage.

465 Xerxes I assassinated; Artaxerxes I rules Persia.

460 Malachi prophesies.

459 Ezra in Jerusalem; historical books in final form.

450 Book of Ruth written; Third Isaiah prophesies.

440 Nehemiah in Jerusalem.

437 Walls of Jerusalem completed.

407 Jewish Temple at Elephantine destroyed by Egypt.

400 Books of Chronicles, Ezra, and Nehemiah written; Joel prophesies.

300 Book of Song of Solomon and Book of Jonah written.

275 Apocalyptic portion of Book of Zechariah written.

250 Book of Ecclesiastes written; Book of Proverbs reaches final form; Septuagint in preparation in Alexandria.

180 Book of Ecclesiasticus written.

165 Book of Daniel written.

150 Book of Esther written; Book of Psalms reaches present form.

147 Parthians take Babylonia.

146 Rome annexes Macedonia; sacks Corinth.

145 Death of Alexander Balas and Ptolemy VI; Demetrius II rules Seleucid Empire. Pharisees and Sadducees begin to appear as separate parties.

143 Antiochus VI rules Seleucid Empire.

142 Death of Jonathan; his brother Simon rules over independent Judea.

141 Last Seleucid soldiers leave Jerusalem.

139 Parthians take Demetrius II prisoner.

138 Antiochus VII rules Seleucid Empire; Attalus III rules Pergamum.

134 Simon of Judea assassinated; John Hyrcanus rules Judea.

133 Antiochus VII temporarily occupies Jerusalem. Rome annexes Pergamum, makes it province of Asia.

129 John Hyrcanus conquers Moab and Samaria; destroys Samaritan temple. Antiochus VII dies in battle against Parthians; Demetrius II released and again rules Seleucid Empire.

125 Antiochus VIII rules Seleucid Empire.

104 John Hyrcanus dies; Aristobulus rules Judea and assumes title of king.

103 Alexander Jannaeus rules Judea; Maccabean kingdom at peak; Pharisees in opposition.

100 Book of Jubilees, Prayer of Manasses, Testament of Twelve Patriarchs, Book of Enoch, First Book of Maccabees written.

86 Roman army sacks Athens.

84 Roman army sacks Ephesus.

79 Alexander Jannaeus dies; civil war in Judea; John Hyrcanus II high priest.

75 Book of Wisdom of Solomon written.

67 Antipater of Idumea in virtual control of Judea; Rome annexes Crete and Cyrene.

65 Rome annexes Bithynia in Asia Minor.

64 Rome annexes last remnant of Seleucid Empire.

63 Rome (Pompey) takes Jerusalem; Maccabean kingdom comes to end.

58 Rome annexes Cyprus.

53 Roman army under Crassus defeated by Parthians at Carrhae.

48 Julius Caesar defeats Pompey and controls Rome. Psalms of Solomon written.

44 Julius Caesar assassinated.

42 Octavian and Mark Antony defeat Caesar's assassins at Philippi.

40 Parthians occupy Judea; Antigonus Mattathias high priest.

37 Herod the Great takes Jerusalem and marries Mariamne the Maccabean; Aristobulus III high priest.

35 Herod executes Aristobulus III, last of the Maccabean high priests.

30 Octavian defeats Mark Antony and Cleopatra at Actium; controls Rome.

27 Octavian assumes title of Augustus; inaugurates the Roman Empire.

25 Rome annexes Pamphilia, Pisidia, Lycaonia, and Galatia in Asia Minor.

23 Herod executes Mariamne.

20 Herod starts rebuilding the Temple; Hillel leader of the Pharisees.

7 Herod has his sons by Mariamne executed.

4 Birth of Jesus. Death of Herod the Great; Herod Archelaus rules Judea; Herod Antipas rules Galilee; Herod Philip rules Iturea.

A.D.

1 Herod Philip builds Bethsaida.

6 Herod Archelaus deposed; Judea becomes procuratorial province with capital at Caesarea and Caponius as procurator. Annas high priest.

7 Census in Judea, with consequent disorders.

10 Birth of Saul [Paul]. "Assumption of Moses" written.

14 Augustus dies; Tiberius becomes Roman Emperor; Valerius Gratus becomes Procurator of Judea and deposes Annas.

18 Joseph Caiaphas high priest; Rome annexes Cappadocia in Asia Minor.

20 Herod Antipas founds Tiberias.

26 Pontius Pilate becomes Procurator of Judea.

27 Herod Antipas marries Herodias; John the Baptist begins to preach.

29 John the Baptist imprisoned and executed; Jesus crucified.

30 The Apostles speak with tongues at Pentecost.

34 Stephen is stoned to death; Saul [Paul] persecutes the Christians; death of Herod Philip.

35 Pontius Pilate massacres Samaritans at Mount Gerizim.

36 Pontius Pilate ends term as Procurator of Judea; Marcellus procurator. Caiaphas deposed as high priest; Jonathan high priest.

37 Saul [Paul] converted to Christianity. Tiberius dies; Caligula becomes Roman Emperor; Theophilus high priest.

39 Saul [Paul] escapes from Damascus and makes first appearance in Jerusalem as Christian. Herod Antipas deposed. Caligula attempts to initiate worship of himself in the Temple.

41 Caligula assassinated; Claudius becomes Roman Emperor. All

Judea united under Herod Agrippa I; Death of Philo of Alexandria.

43   James son of Zebedee executed; Peter imprisoned. Church at Antioch flourishes; followers of Jesus first called Christians; Saul [Paul] visits Jerusalem during famine; Rome annexes Lycia in Asia Minor.

44   Death of Herod Agrippa I. Judea again procuratorial province; Cuspius Fadus procurator.

45   Saul [Paul] on first missionary voyage.

46   Tiberius Alexander becomes Procurator of Judea.

48   Council of Jerusalem; Ventidius Cumanus becomes Procurator of Judea.

49   Claudius temporarily evicts Jews from Rome; Paul on second missionary voyage.

50   Paul in Europe; writes Epistles to the Thessalonians.

52   Death of Gamaliel the Pharisee; Paul appears before Gallio, Procurator of Achaia; Antonius Felix becomes Procurator of Judea.

53   Herod Agrippa II rules Galilee; Apollos appears at Ephesus.

54   Paul on third missionary voyage. Claudius dies; Nero becomes Roman Emperor.

55   Paul writes Epistle to the Galatians; imprisoned in Caesarea.

56   Paul writes Epistles to the Corinthians.

58   Paul writes Epistle to the Romans; arrested in Jerusalem.

59   Paul tried before Felix.

61   Porcius Festus becomes Procurator of Judea. Paul preaches before Herod Agrippa II.

62   Paul imprisoned in Rome; writes Epistles to the Ephesians, Philippians, Colossians, and Philemon. Annas high priest; has James the brother of Jesus stoned to death; Lucceius Albinus becomes Procurator of Judea and deposes Annas.

63   Rome annexes Pontus in Asia Minor.

64   Great fire at Rome; Nero persecutes Christians; Peter and Paul executed. (Paul released according to one theory.) Gessius Florus becomes Procurator of Judea.

65   Paul writes First Epistle to Timothy and Epistle to Titus.

66   Jewish rebellion breaks out in Judea and in Alexandria; Vespasian and his son Titus lead Roman armies in Judea.

67 Paul writes Second Epistle to Timothy and is executed; Vespasian conquers Galilee and the historian, Josephus, is taken prisoner.

68 Nero commits suicide; Galba becomes Roman Emperor.

69 Otho and Vitellius are Roman Emperors briefly; Vespasian becomes Roman Emperor.

70 Titus takes Jerusalem, destroys Temple; Gospel of St. Mark written.

71 Vespasian and Titus celebrate joint triumph in Rome; Arch of Titus constructed.

75 Gospel of St. Matthew written.

79 Vespasian dies; Titus becomes Roman Emperor.

80 Gospel of St. Luke and Book of Acts written; Epistle to the Hebrews written.

81 Titus dies; Domitian becomes Roman Emperor.

90 Domitian initiates Christian persecution; epistles of James, Peter, John and Jude written; Jewish rabbis gather at Jamnia to establish Jewish canon.

95 Book of Revelation and Book of 2 Esdras written.

96 Domitian assassinated; Nerva becomes Roman Emperor.

98 Nerva dies; Trajan becomes Roman Emperor. Roman Empire reaches greatest extent.

100 Gospel of St. John written. Letter of Baruch, Epistle of Jeremy, and Martyrdom of Isaiah written. Death of Herod Agrippa II.

115 Jews in Cyrene revolt and are crushed.

117 Trajan dies; Hadrian becomes Roman Emperor.

132 Jews in Judea revolt.

135 Last Jewish stronghold crushed and Jewish history, as a nation, ends for eighteen centuries; Jerusalem renamed Aelia Capitolina and sanctuary to Jupiter is built on the site of the Temple.

150 First two chapters of 2 Esdras written.

226 Parthian kingdom ends. Sassanid Dynasty founds new Persian Empire.

235 Roman Emperor, Alexander Severus, assassinated. Roman Empire sinks into anarchy.

240 Shapur I rules Persia.

259 Shapur I captures Roman Emperor, Valerian, in battle.

260 Famine sweeps Egypt; last two chapters of 2 Esdras written.

268   Roman Empire, under Claudius II, begins recovery.

284   Diocletian becomes Roman Emperor; reorganizes the empire.

303   Constantine I becomes Roman Emperor; begins process of making empire Christian.

400   St. Jerome prepares Vulgate (Latin version of the Bible).

INDEX OF BIBLICAL VERSES

Volume One, The Old Testament

* Main treatment in Volume II.

INDEX OF BIBLICAL VERSES

Volume Two, the New Testament

* Main treatment in Volume I.

INDEX OF SUBJECTS

Volume One, The Old Testament

Bethshea, 229
Beth-shemesh (Dan), 250
  Ark of the Covenant and, 273
Beth-shemesh (Egypt), 113
Bethuel, 88–89
Beulah, 553–54
Bezek, 278
Bible, 441, 460, 589–90
  Apocrypha and, 426–27
  divisions of, 208–62
  translation of, 426
Big Dipper, 482
Bildad, 478–79
Bilhah, 94–95, 102
Bitter Lakes, 143
Blood, eating of, 160
Blue Nile, 111
Boaz, 264, 285, 400–1
Books, 589–90
Borsippa, 552
Branch, the, 665–66
Bread, 155–56
British-Israelites, 379
Bronze, 228
Bronze Age, 228
Bull-worship, 151–52
Bunyan, John, 493
Buz, 88–89, 483–84
Buzite, 483

Cadmus, 219
Caduceus, 176
Caesar Augustus, 319
Cain, 33
Calah, 51, 645
Caleb, 168–69
Calf, golden, 151–53
Calneh, 49
Cambyses, 442, 593, 616
Canaan, 44
  Abraham's entry into, 60–61
  early history of, 210–11
  Egypt and, 44, 131
  giants in, 72–73

Israelite conquest of, 210ff., 226–29
  name of, 218
  spies in, 168–71, 210–11
  tribes of, 75
Canaanites, 44–45
  Crete and, 201
  enslavement of, 326
  language of, 61
Cape Carmel, 346
Caphtor, 198–202
Carchemish, battle of, 393
Cardozo, Benjamin, 642
Carmel, Mount, 346
Carmelites, 346
Carnarvon, Earl of, 63
Carrhae, 60
Carter, Howard, 63
Carthage, 213–14, 332, 442
  founding of, 588–89
Cedars of Lebanon, 197
Census, during Exodus, 165–67
  under David, 318–19, 408–9
  under Romans, 319
Chaldean (magician), 600–1
Chaldean Empire, 393, 434, 602, 609–10
Chaldeans, 58, 89, 387
Charles I, 626
Chebar, 583–84
Chedorlaomer, 69–73
Chemosh, 178–79, 189, 359
Cheops, 63
Cherub, 147–49, 494
Chesed, 89
Chileab, 311
Child sacrifice, 162–63
Chilion, 263
Chittim, 201, 619
Chiun, 636–37
Christmas, 139
Chronicler, 430–32, 453
Chronicles, First Book of, 397–411
  names of, 397
  genealogies in, 399
  position in Bible of, 397

v

INDEX OF SUBJECTS

Volume Two, The New Testament

PALESTINE
in the time of
CHRIST